The MELVILLES *and the* GANSEVOORTS

Closest in Kin to

HERMAN MELVILLE

in Three Generations

(SEE PAGE 368)

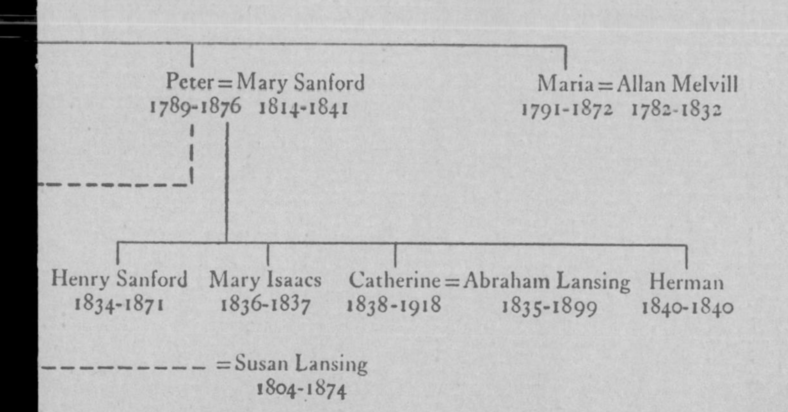

Spiritus Est Qui Vivificat

MELVILLE'S EARLY LIFE AND *REDBURN*

"Divine imaginings, like gods, come down to the groves of our Thessalies, and there, in the embrace of wild, dryad reminiscences, beget the beings that astonish the world."—*Redburn*

MELVILLE'S

ARLY LIFE AND *REDBURN*

by WILLIAM H. GILMAN

NEW YORK
NEW YORK UNIVERSITY PRESS, WASHINGTON SQUARE

LONDON
GEOFFREY CUMBERLEGE, OXFORD UNIVERSITY PRESS

1951

PRINTED IN THE UNITED STATES OF AMERICA

"At last we hoisted the stun'-sails up to the top-sail yards; and as soon as the vessel felt them she gave a sort of bound like a horse, and the breeze blowing more and more she went plunging along, shaking off the foam from her bows, like foam from a bridle-bit. Every mast and timber seemed to have a pulse in it that was beating with life and joy; and I felt a wild exulting in my own heart, and felt as if I would be glad to bound along so round the world." (*Redburn,* p. 84.)

"After running till about midnight, we *'hove-to'* near the mouth of the Mersey; and next morning, before daybreak, took the first of the flood; and with a fair wind, stood into the river; which, at its mouth, is quite an arm of the sea. Presently, in the misty twilight, we passed immense buoys, and caught sight of distant objects on shore, vague and shadowy shapes, like Ossian's ghosts."

(*Redburn,* p. 161.)

At the Mouth of the Merse

This ship is either the one on which Melville made his first voyage as a sailor or one very much like it. Its name, "St. Lawrence," is clear on the mainmast pennant, and it can be made out with a magnifying glass at both the bow and the stern. It must have been engaged on a run from some port in the United States to Liverpool, since it shows the United States flag and the background is the Mersey estuary, with Rock Lighthouse and Fort in the distance. Proportionately, the ship is the same length as the "St. Lawrence," about 120 feet. It has, on the quarter-deck, the passengers' cabin that Melville describes as small and directly forward of the wheel, and it carries, lik the "Highlander," only two ship's boa (*Redburn,* pp. 136, 377, and 383). It diffe principally from Melville's "St. Lawrence in lacking a figurehead, but Melville's shi lost its figurehead sometime after his voyag (see p. 333, n. 32), and the original paintin may have been done after this event.

It is virtually certain that the "St. Law rence" of this frontispiece was painted b the firm of Samuel Walters, Liverpool ma rine artists, who commonly pictured vesse against the Cheshire shore of the Merse with the old lighthouse and fort and often

Courtesy of the Vose Galleries, Boston, and the Peabody Museum, Salem.

ilot boat, like the one numbered 5 in the ght background, and a coastal steamer, ke the one disappearing behind the fort. Iany Walters paintings of transatlantic ailing vessels ultimately found their way the Vose Galleries in Boston, where the riginal of the frontispiece was photographed for the Peabody Museum of Salem. nfortunately, since the galleries has no ecord of the sale of this picture, further ues to its provenience are missing.

The most promising piece of evidence at could link the "St Lawrence" of the icture with Melville's ship is the flag hung at the foremast. Ships in the Atlantic trade always carried house flags or captain's flags for quick identification by mercantile observers at the port of destination. No available book of nineteenth-century identification flags prints an ensign like that in the picture, but the "B" naturally suggests Oliver P. Brown, whose long service in command of the "St. Lawrence" (from 1838 to 1852) would have entitled him to the privilege of flying his own flag. There is, therefore, every reason to believe that the picture portrays the very ship that carried Melville past the fort and the lighthouse and into the Mersey in July 1839.

To MARGARET REILLY GILMAN

Preface

THE sources for a study of Melville's early life and *Redburn* are the book itself and various collections of letters, books, and memorabilia associated with Melville and his family: the Melville Collection in the Harvard College Library, the Gansevoort-Lansing Collection in the New York Public Library, and the Shaw Collection in the Massachusetts Historical Society. These collections are denoted as M, G-L, and S, respectively.

Quotations from manuscripts have been reproduced exactly as they stand in the original; otherwise many peculiarities of character and mind would have disappeared in transcription. Because the designation of manuscript errors by *sic* would often have caused excessive interruptions to reading, it has usually been omitted. Occasionally, when no manuscript has been quoted for several pages, *sic* has been used to assure the reader that the errors are those of the original writer. All doubtful readings have been carefully checked; the reader may feel confident of a faithful reproduction, even when Melville's mother misspells his name.

This study has grown out of my doctoral dissertation accepted at Yale University in 1947. It owes much to the generous help of Miss Fanny Howe of the Public Library in Troy, New York; Miss Julie Hudson of the Princeton University Library; William H. Tripp, curator of the Old Dartmouth Historical Society in New Bedford; Lawrence W. Jenkins, director of the Peabody Museum, Salem; Westel R. Willoughby and other members of the staff of the National Archives in Washington; Captain John B. Heffernan, officer-in-charge of the Office of Naval Records and Library, Navy Department, Washington, D.C.; J. F. Smith, Esq., librarian of the City of Liverpool Public Libraries; Alexander O. Vietor, curator of the Map Collection in the Yale University Library; Miss Edna L. Jacobsen of the New

York State Library in Albany; John R. Brown of the Graduate Council of Union College, Schenectady; Frederick C. Filley, Mr. and Mrs. William Accard, Mrs. Daniel F. Nolan, H. H. Bentley, Dr. Victor H. Paltsits, Harrison Hayford, Wilson L. Heflin, and Tyrus Hillway; and the staffs of the New York Public Library, the Houghton Library at Harvard, the Harmanus Bleecker Library in Albany, the New-York Historical Society, the Massachusetts Historical Society, the Yale University Library, and the University of Rochester Library.

I wish to thank the Committee on Higher Degrees in the History of American Civilization of Harvard University, the Massachusetts Historical Society, and the New York Public Library for permission to quote from the Melville, the Shaw, and the Gansevoort-Lansing and Duyckinck Collections, respectively. I am grateful to the University of Rochester for meeting the expense of the Index and to Mrs. Rose Miglionico for preparing it. The careful editorial work of Miss Jean B. Barr and Miss Grace LeRoy of New York University Press has been indispensable. For guidance in the use of city records and legal documents, I am indebted to Michael D. Reilly and Brendan C. Reilly. Mrs. Eleanor Melville Metcalf, besides imparting family tradition and history, has generously allowed me to examine and use family papers and books. Merrell R. Davis has given me direct and indirect aid in innumerable ways. Jay Leyda has exchanged Melville discoveries with me most freely, and I have had the great benefit of examining the galley proofs of his forthcoming book, "The Melville Log." I am grateful to my colleagues Kathrine Koller and Bernard N. Schilling for invaluable criticisms of the manuscript. My debt to the patience, counsel, and abiding personal interest of Stanley T. Williams, who suggested and directed my dissertation, is a very great one indeed. The deepest of all my obligations is to my wife, Margaret R. Gilman.

WILLIAM H. GILMAN

Rochester, New York
October 1950

Table of Contents

BOOK I

Introduction

"MELVILLE is a lyric, subjective, enthusiastic genius, and all his work is autobiographical—factual or spiritual autobiography." [1] It was thus that a critic summed up, in 1932, the views of perhaps most of those who have written about Melville since his resurrection three decades ago. The known facts of Melville's life, though meager, corresponded to the events in his books. His books must therefore be his own story in his own words. Such assumptions underlie an important body of modern criticism and biography that focus upon the man in Melville at the expense of the artist. At the same time, laborious scholarship has proved that some of Melville's books are not the outright personal revelation for which they had been mistaken.[2] To date no such study has been made of the relation between Melville's early life and *Redburn,* the book which seems to picture his boyhood and youth. What is the true nature of this book? Is it the confessions and reminiscences of a writer limited to the depiction of literal truth? Or is it shaped by an artist with a fertile imagination and a vigorous creative power?

At present no adequate answers have been offered, especially in biographies. When Raymond Weaver, Melville's first modern biographer, could find relatively little about his youth among his papers, he resorted to family traditions and Melville's own books, thus establishing the custom of reading Melville biographically. In dealing with *Redburn,* he conceded that Melville's recollection of his early years “t ... iography is not invariably st ... ed nearly two full chapters of ... ssigning exact experiences, emotions, and even conversation to its author. The book was a minute amplification of Melville’s own emotions and sensations [4] when he was “a boy of seventeen.” [5] The possibility that its hero was primarily a literary creation rather than a mere projection of his creator escaped consideration.

Thus was founded the biographical fallacy that dominated studies of Melville and the interpretation of *Redburn* for nearly twenty years. John Freeman wrote that “Wellingborough Redburn is Herman Melville” [6] and the book is the story “faintly disguised” of his flight to sea in 1837.[7] With no more biographical evidence than Freeman or Weaver, Lewis Mumford rewrote the story of Melville’s youth as a kind of novel, using *Redburn* as though it were a journal and calling it “autobiography, with only the faintest disguises.” [8] Throughout the early 1930’s the biographical fallacy grew, with inevitable Freudian accretions. *Redburn* became, for example, the story of “the boy Melville, of course,” fleeing to sea at seventeen from a “cold and handsome” mother on whom he had an “overpowering fixation.” [9] Jean Simon’s biography in 1939 [10] assumed that Melville altered and exaggerated his early story in *Redburn,* and he urged prudence in judging the book as real. Then he went on to tell Melville’s history in terms of exact incidents in *Redburn* with no more justification than his predecessors for attributing some of the boy’s experiences and qualities to Melville and rejecting others. In the 1940’s Van Wyck Brooks [11] and Ellery Sedgwick [12] continued to assume that Melville and his juvenile hero were virtually identical in age and behavior. Recently Geoffrey Stone has leaned heavily on *Redburn* for Melville’s history, Newton Arvin has used it biographically for “its imaginative kind of truthfulness,” and Richard Chase, mining it for symbols of a composite figure he calls “the young man,” treats it once more as “spiritual autobiography.” [13]

Meanwhile other minds have contested the conventional concept of Melville's early life and the relation *Redburn* bears to it. In 1938 Gordon Roper found grounds for concluding that "no detail of Redburn's experience can be safely interpreted as Melville's without substantiation from some other source."[14] Willard Thorp decided that *Redburn* was not "pure autobiography"[15] and discovered specific literary sources for some of Melville's "personal" experiences.[16] F. O. Matthiessen made a real contribution to the understanding of *Redburn* by ignoring the autobiographical problem and focusing on the book solely as a work of art.[17]

Yet the *Redburn* question is still open. As long as we do not know the relation between a work based on certain experiences and the nature of the experiences themselves, we do not know what kind of book we are dealing with, nor do we know fully how to evaluate it. If a writer has merely made his own history marvelously vivid, we praise him for reproducing things seen, heard, and felt, and we feel no compunction in using his book for biography. But if we can be sure that he invented liberally and that he utilized experience for artistic purposes, we are forced to acknowledge a much higher creative power and to use the book as source material for biography only with the utmost caution.

Clearly, the proper evaluation of *Redburn* must begin with a careful study of Melville's early years. The book seems to contain much family history. Since it was not written until ten years after the chief events from which it sprang, the intervening years must also have affected it. Melville's development as an artist presumably had some bearing on it. But the major questions are: What sort of person was Melville in relation to the narrator of the book? Were they the same age? Was their personal experience the same up to and during the voyage to Liverpool which sets the framework of the action? Or were there, perhaps, significant differences?

In order to test the validity of *Redburn* as autobiography and to find better grounds for discussing its rank as art, I have written a new study of Melville's life from 1819 to 1841, using both old and unexplored sources and depending almost entirely upon objective evidence. In the few exceptions to this principle I have drawn upon some passages in *Redburn* where external facts supply a reliable check upon their accuracy. It is regrettable that there are still so few of Melville's early letters, no diary or journal, and so few letters about him. Yet the new material warrants both another biography and a revaluation of Melville's artistry in *Redburn*.[18]

Chapter I

The New York Years, 1819-1830

THE early life of Herman Melville falls as rigidly as a Greek tragedy into well-defined acts. From his birth to prosperous parents in New York City on August 1, 1819, to the winter day in 1841 when he sailed on the whaling ship "Pequod," his youth seemed molded by destiny. Four cycles of prosperity and adversity or of promise and discouragement composed Melville's first twenty-one years. His first thirteen years saw the great expectations of a happy childhood overthrown by the bankruptcy and then the death of his father. In the next five his family struggled back to prosperity only to tumble suddenly into indigence. The cycle narrowed to two years then, as Herman's well-founded hopes of a new security abruptly perished. The last act of the drama took a little more than a year to lead the weary protagonist again from confidence to desperation. The design of the gods must have seemed unmistakable: thirteen years, five years, two, one—fortune would yield to misfortune with a mathematical regularity. The hero of *Moby-Dick* was convinced that he owed his shabby role in a whaling voyage to "those stage managers the Fates" and, indeed, that his going on a whaling voyage "formed part of the grand programme of Providence that was drawn up a long time ago." [1] Ishmael's convictions of predestination may well have been born in Melville's awareness of the fate that wove into his early years a rhythmic pattern of defeat.

Like the tragic hero, his beginnings were auspicious. It

is well known that he was born in the same year as John Ruskin and Queen Victoria, James Russell Lowell and Walt Whitman. If his birth excited no public notice, it was greeted warmly in his own family. His Grandmother Gansevoort had come down from Albany for the accouchement, and an uncle and three aunts were also present. The day after Dr. Wright Post delivered Herman into the world [2] Allan Melvill wrote to his brother-in-law, Peter Gansevoort:

> With a grateful heart I hasten to inform you of the birth of another Nephew, which joyous event occurred at ½ past 11 last night—our dear Maria displayed her accustomed fortitude in the hour of peril, & is as well as circumstances & the intense heat will admit—while the little Stranger has good lungs, sleeps well & feeds kindly, he is in truth a chopping Boy.[3]

Allan Melvill was something of a ceremonialist, even in private matters. After asking his brother-in-law to "communicate the news" to friends in Albany, he folded the note with methodical care, stamped it with a seal bearing the letters "A M" in neat and delicate script, and sent it off to the mail. Then, like the industrious businessman that he was, he returned to the duties of running his small wholesale store.

A little over thirty years later, on the eve of publishing *Redburn,* his fourth novel, the "chopping Boy" imprinted a letter to his father-in-law, Chief Justice Lemuel Shaw of Massachusetts, with the same seal his father had used to complete the happy duty of proclaiming his birth.[4] Within those years, Melville's life had moved through a course of events that gave his use of the seal an appropriate symbolism. If it was one of the few physical tokens of his existence Allan Melvill was able to hand on to his son, the materials for *Redburn* were no less a legacy, however unintentional. The experience that begot the book and the reminiscences in it are inextricably linked up with the personality and the ill-starred business career of Allan Melvill. His kindness, his indulgence, and his tales of European travel gave Melville a source for Walter Redburn and for young Wellingborough's quest for a link with his father in distant Liverpool. And because Allan Melvill overworked himself and died young in futile combat against misfortune, Herman was driven before he was out of his teens into the sailor's life that later formed the framework of *Redburn.*

Fortunately, Allan Melvill could bestow other endowments on his second son. His respectable education formed part of the mold in which Herman was shaped. Born in Boston on April 7, 1782, he had grown up in an atmosphere of piety, probity, and patriotism. He had studied in both public and private schools, the West Boston Academy and Amherst Academy in Amherst, New Hampshire. In these institutions he had acquired his methodical habits, a precise calligraphy, and the custom of writing the name of God in capital letters.[5] He learned some Latin, too, and came to know Shakespeare, Cowper, and Pope, whose style and thought helped to shape his own. In his nineteenth year he set out on the travels that would assist in planting a wanderlust in his son's heart. Like other sons of good New England families, he was sent on the grand tour and passed through London, southern England, and the Lowlands on the way to Paris. Here he lived for twenty months with his older brother Thomas, a well-to-do banker, acquiring a mastery of French and making occasional excursions, on one of which he crossed the Pyrenees on horseback.[6] Back in Boston, he set up an importing business that took him frequently to Europe. The bad luck that was to mark his entire career first beset him in 1811 when the ship and cargo of which he was half owner were captured by the British.[7] But he had acquired an international reputation for trustworthiness,[8] for after touring Scotland to admire the land of his forefathers he was entrusted with dispatches from Ambassador Pinckney in England, which he carried to the American chargé d'affaires in Paris.[9] On the return trip, the ship on which he had sailed had several brushes with English commerce raiders and was finally seized and taken to Halifax.[10] A dozen such adventures marked his early travels, in which he covered over twenty-four thousand miles by land and twice as many by water.

The solid character and the reputation that Allan Melvill had formed by his twenty-ninth year are but poorly reflected in the water-color portrait done by the American artist John Rubens Smith in 1810.[11] A friendly but somewhat foppish young man leans casually in a chair, one arm thrown over the back, the other resting lightly on a convenient table. His nonchalant posture, his curling hair brushed forward over the temples, the personal seal held prominently in the fingers of his left hand, his gloves tossed at random beside his high-crowned beaver hat on the table—all delineate an easygoing man about town dedicated to attitudes of studied carelessness. Only the direct glance of his oval eyes may explain why he could be trusted with his country's official dispatches.

It has been popular to hint that Allan's youthful wanderings yielded many a pleasant and secret amour and even a natural daughter.[12] From this it follows that Melville is recording family history when the hero of *Pierre* discovers that his supposedly virtuous father had fallen into adultery with a pretty French *emigrée*. For this convenient and slanderous theory, there is no real evidence whatsoever. "[Allan] has the character of a discreet, well-informed, amiable young man," said his father,[13] whose comments on his older son Thomas are both candid and highly uncomplimentary. Allan's friendships both at home and abroad seem to have been most "discreet." His closest friends were Eben Appleton, later a merchant in Liverpool, and Lemuel Shaw of Boston, an old schoolmate at Amherst Academy and his sister Nancy's fiancé.[14] Allan's letters to Shaw are prolix and sententious, but they reveal a natural concern with right conduct and the achievement of ideals. They also sprout patches of self-conscious blank verse or wooden heroic couplets.[15] Neither prose nor verse even ventures on the risqué. But the student of Herman Melville's life will find some significance in these metrical experiments, as well as in a certain instinct for looking into the springs of human action and in candid admissions about Allan's own nature. In a moralizing and confessional mood he wrote:

. . . whatever is enforced upon us by necessity if not perfectly consonant with our feelings, stirs up the rebellious passions, & engenders discontent . . . ; as we advance from the Cradle to the Tomb our wants & wishes increase, while the power of gratifying them diminishes, we toil through life in quest of airy phantoms . . . , we frequently . . . pursue Variety throughout her sinuous course, but in the latter example we simply follow the dictate of Nature, as she has implanted the love of it in the human breast . . . you may have discovered . . . that my own disposition is highly seasoned with this ingredient . . . .[16]

Allan's son knew rebellious passions; he wrote an entire book about the quest of an "airy phantom"; his disposition was more than merely seasoned with a love of variety. Allan Melvill's early history affords no succulent evidence of moral delinquencies, but it does reveal emotional patterns that seem to have descended to Herman. And in the years Allan would not live to see, his artistic and speculative impulses, abandoned like those of most men to wither on the vine, would flourish again through the genius of his unborn son.

During one of Allan Melvill's innumerable business trips up and down the Atlantic coast and into the hinterland, he met, in Albany, New York, the woman who was to be Herman's mother. Unhappily, he confided few details to his journal, a volume he kept for the sole purpose of making capsule records of his travels. Although he first saw Albany in 1810, his visits did not become frequent till the fall and winter of 1813-1814, when he probably met Maria Gansevoort and began his courtship.[17] In August 1814 Allan briefly listed a trip to the popular resort of Ballston Spa, north of Albany, "in company with Mrs Miss & Mr P Gansevoort." During the visit he presented Miss Gansevoort with a copy of Mrs. Chapone's *Letters on the Improvement of the Mind,* inscribing it with quotations from Miss Owenson about the virtues of "prudence," "domestic qualities," and the "liberal cultivation of the mind" and adding on a flyleaf a testament of faith in Maria's guileless heart, her innocent mind, and her purity.[18] On October 4 they were married in the First Reformed Dutch Church in Albany by the Reverend John Melanchthon Bradford, the pastor and a friend of the Gansevoort family.[19] If propriety governed their wedding trip back to Boston, with Allan's sister Helen accompanying the honeymooners, the arrangement was merely conventional, and Maria said she was "much pleased with the journey." [20] Allan, with the enthusiasm that was to mark all future references to his wife, begged the mother of this "most lovely and affectionate Daughter" to allow him the freedom of addressing her as a son and to "rely upon the watchful care of him, whose chief pride and felicity is the privilege of guarding such a jewel." [21]

The jewel of which Allan Melvill was so proud was twenty-three years old, and the only daughter of General Peter Gansevoort, famous for his defense of Fort Stanwix during the Revolution and, when he died in 1812, one of the wealthiest men in the city of Albany.[22] Maria had the upbringing proper to such a background. Private tutors instructed her in sewing, painting, music, and English grammar.[23] For at least nine years she studied the pianoforte, playing on the instrument her father had brought from London and given her when she was a girl of ten.[24] Like all young ladies of her set, she went to assemblies and balls [25] and read too many "foolish and nonsensical novels," as her brother Peter said. "Though she does not possess the Beauty of a Helen," he added, "yet that she should make up, in improving her mind in useful studies." [26] Peter's estimate of Maria's beauty is substantiated by an 1820 portrait.[27] She had masses of rich dark curls and exquisitely slender arms and wrists, but a broad mouth, a large nose curving down at the tip, heavy ear lobes, and the beginnings of a double chin. Her glance is direct, but whether the steady stare, the cast of her head, and the slightly retracted corners of her mouth are the marks of pride or of diffidence is obscured by the ambiguity of the portrait. The praises her husband lavished upon her, one feels, are his response to qualities of the mind, heart, and soul rather than to features the world could applaud.

Whatever other mutual feelings united Allan Melvill and Maria Gansevoort, they seem to have been as one in their fondness for children. Gansevoort, their first, was born on December 6, 1815, and Helen Maria some two years later.[28] With two more dependents, Allan Melvill was forced to think of improving his state. For over three years he had conducted a wholesale dry-goods business, living meanwhile in the house of his mother-in-law and enjoying social connections with Governor De Witt Clinton and the best society in Albany.[29] But resolving to "re-establish [himself] on a permanent & respectable foundation,"[30] he set off for France in the spring of 1818 to secure a large stock of goods with $6,500 in capital borrowed from Major Thomas Melvill, his father.[31] He was also charged with the investigation of potential claims to a share in the £100,000 estate of the late General Robert Melvill, of Edinburgh, of whom Major Melvill had been the closest surviving kin.[32]

The journey brought Allan Melvill into the company of numerous respectable people, with whom he carefully recorded his contacts: Consul Maury and "the celebrated Mr. Roscoe" in Liverpool, "the famous Mr. Jeffrey of Edinburgh," and even Alexander, Earl of Leven and Melvill, "our legitimate Chief," Allan Melvill called him, solemnly recognizing the clan relationship.[33] In Paris Allan was received by Baron Hottinguer, his banker, and Mr. Crittenden, the ambassador, and he sat down at dinner on the Fourth of July with "fifty true Americans," whose guests included the Marquis de Lafayette and Mr. Gallatin.[34] From this voyage, his last, Allan returned with $16,000 worth of French silks, the disappointing news that General Melvill's estate had been entailed on others beyond legal recovery, and the determination to establish his business in New York, the city that he rightly believed was "destined to become the Commercial Emporium of our Country."[35]

From the long letters to Maria and his father in which Allan Melvill recorded this edifying tour, two main passions stand out: a profound veneration for his ancestors and an all-possessing love for his wife and children. As a well-read man of the world, he appreciated the historical and literary associations of the scenes through which he passed. To the lengthy guidebook information that he slavishly distilled for Maria, he added personal notes on the Scottish Highlands, which made even him an "Enthusiast," on Gads Hill, where he recollected *King Henry IV, Part 1,* and on the Hotel Dessein in Calais, "immortalized by Sterne."[36] But his chief delight arose from the sight of ancestral lands and from discovering links that bound him to aristocracy. "I cannot describe my sensations while walking on the ground where once stood the dwelling & Birth[place] of my venerated progenitor," he wrote to his father after visiting the parish of Scoonie, where his great grandfather, the Reverend Thomas Melvill, had been Presbyterian minister for several decades.[37] With an unconsciously humorous mingling of pride in his illustrious lineage, of moral earnestness, and of Yankee thrift, he added:

> Your greatgrandfather was a grandson of Sir John Melvill of Carnbee, who was knighted by James the 6th & made baron of Granton 28th July 1580, on which you may depend as a well-authenticated historical fact, confirmed by living testimony—I have also traced you back in direct lineal descent to Sir Richard de Melville, Knight in the reign of Alexander the 3d in the year 1268, & have discovered that the branch at Boston, & my great Uncle John then at Grenada, are expressly recognised in Douglas Baronage of Scotland, of which I shall purchase if possible a cheap edition, as belonging to the Melvilles of Carnbee & termed an ancient & illustrious House of the founders of which Crawford & Douglas Peerage of Scotland both say, were related to Queen Margaret consort of Malcolm Canmere & came with her from Hungary—you may also tell my good Mother, that Mrs Meason inform'd me that the Scollays of the Orkneys, from whom her husband is descended, sprang originally from the Kings of Norway, & so it appears we are of a royal line in both sides of the House—after all it is not only an amusing but a just cause of pride, to

resort back through the ages to such ancestry, & should produce a correspondent spirit of emulation in their descendants to the remotest posterity.[38]

With his pride in ancestry and his worship of respectable people and nobility went a natural admiration for European dress and manners, which he intended to emulate, though he highly resolved to shun "the extravagant vices of Europe." [39] But overbalancing his petty vanities and servility to the *haut monde* were his emotions, fears, and hopes as husband and parent. "Adieu and love me always," he wrote to Maria as his ship left Boston harbor.[40] After four weeks on the ocean, during which he once conducted the Sabbath service and reflected upon how the sea brought home man's immediate dependence upon God, his yearning for Maria and the children increased. He sent letters by four different ships from Liverpool to tell Maria he had arrived safely. His love overflowed as he wrote:

I shall not know happiness until we meet again, bear my remembrance ever in your mind, let those affections of your soft bosom be all my own, teach our tender Babes as far as their little hearts are susceptible of impressions to cherish the recollections of their absent Father, who never forgets them, & confide implicitly in the constant fidelity, unchangeable love & undivided devotion of your husband & Lover.[41]

In the romantic scenery of the Highlands he felt keenly the separation from his "only bosom friend." [42] From Paris he sent her, like Byron to Augusta, a rose he had carried with him since he picked it in Francis Jeffrey's garden in Edinburgh. Surrounded by the seductive amusements of Paris, he eschewed even the theater, devoting himself to business and to long and frequent letters to his wife. Although he always signed himself "Melvill," he never forgot to remind her that he was her "Lover," that his happiness depended on hers, and that his only purpose in being away from her was to ensure their well-being on his return.[43]

The sentiments evoked by this first absence from his wife continued to the day of his death. In his role as lover, he thought with warm passion of her physical charms and announced his devotion in every way known to the pompous prose of the day. As husband, his ambitions centered on domestic joy, with merely "rational opulence" to support it.[44] For the next fourteen years he would expend his energies in an effort, seemingly predestined to failure, to keep his family in modest affluence and to harvest the felicity that, as a practical man, he believed must certainly follow.

In November of 1818 Allan Melvill began his business career in New York with the polite newspaper announcement of his establishment as "an importer of French goods and Commission merchant" at 123 Pearl Street.[45] He was no petty shopkeeper but a wholesale merchant, selling by dozens and ells such fashionable wares as women's silk gloves, linen braids, leghorn hats, and fabrics like crepe, velvet, and tulle.[46] Before him lay the road to prosperity over which John Jacob Astor, John and Philip Hone, John Haggerty, the Depaus, and others were finding rapid transit. But competition was merciless. For a decade money was hard to get and markets fluctuated extremely. Where the Hones made fortunes in the wholesale trade, others failed by the hundreds. The difficulties facing a man with Allan Melvill's New England conscience were immense. One needed to be no less sharp and dexterous in 1818 than in 1950 to succeed in New York; but how provide even "rational opulence" for one's family and still maintain the frontiers of absolute honesty? A good name for his children to inherit, Allan Melvill said, meant more to him than mere success.[47] With such high-minded aspirations, he dealt only with gentlemen like himself whose word could be trusted, and in ten years he had built up a reputation for thorough probity, upon which he habitually congratulated himself. And yet the time would come when the chance to lay up easy treasure on earth might prove too attractive to avoid compromise with his elevated code of business ethics.

If he was a Yankee by birth and scruple, he had taken on by the time of his marriage a somewhat cosmopolitan character. He seems to have fitted well into the New York milieu, keeping special demijohns of Holland gin for his intimate friends and entertaining them over cigars and port wine. He met with fellow Scots at the convivial St. Andrew's Society and kept up his French connections through the Société Française de Bienfésance. Occasionally he took his wife to the theater, and once, while watching the comedian Matthews in *Wild Oats,* she found herself "much amused, & entertain'd, in seeing the grave and serious Mr Melvill altogether unable to control his risibility . . . ." [48] For a time he had a library, in which French titles were conspicuous—in 1805 he had brought home nearly three hundred volumes, including Rousseau, Corneille, Molière, Voltaire, and Racine [49]—and in the early years, at least, he found time for reading. But by 1823 he was forced to the embarrassing admission that he had become in spite of himself "exclusively a man of Business" and had "given up Books & everything disconnected with Trade." [50] A few years later, apparently during a depression, he was obliged to sell many of his books at auction.[51] But he still continued to bolster an opinion with an apt quotation from Shakespeare, Young, Cowper, or Pope.

Like other intelligent businessmen of the times, he interested himself in politics and followed the strict republican principles of his father. Although self-interest had seemed in his youth the "great predominating principle of human actions," [52] in mature life he roundly denounced the selfish demagogue and the spirit of party that impeded the general welfare. If he considered the people "scurvy & ungrateful Masters," [53] he still rejoiced in the French Revolution of 1830 as "a triumph of the majesty of the people over the despotism of a Tyrant." [54] Such a mingling of patrician and democratic sentiments is further curious evidence of the subtle influence extending from father to son. Herman Melville would distrust and dislike the mob. Yet he would love the common man and attack all tyrannies over the human spirit. His father could name among political friends and acquaintances such men as Daniel Webster, Martin Van Buren, Smith Thompson, who had been Monroe's Secretary of the Navy, James Stevenson, the mayor of Albany, and Governor De Witt Clinton.[55] Their names must have circulated in the Melville household and provided the young boy with a sense of important alliance with political leaders in state and nation.

Allan Melvill's code for personal conduct, for success in life, was politic and pietistic in the extreme. Notes he once made for a "talk at random," probably for delivery to a group of apprentices, warn against the use of tobacco as "Vile . . . expensive, unnatural," against drinking "more than one glass of wine," and against gambling, lies, profanity, and "immodest words." He counseled reverence for the religion of one's fathers.

> Endeavor [he urged] to secure the good will & esteem of the Ladies by uniform politeness & attention; . . . avoid Political discussion, which produces enemies, but cultivate a spirit of exalted patriotism which will lead you to adhere to the free institutions of your Country . . . ; borrow no money . . . live within your income however small, . . . for poverty & embarrassments are the scarecrow of human happiness & domestic comfort . . . .[56]

It was a commandment with him to "make no promises without deliberation but perform them religiously." With the faith of the middle class in wealth he declared that "money is the only solid substratum on which men can safely build in this world." One could compromise with the materialistic jury of public opinion, Allan Melvill thought: "Though this world respects a gilded fool more than a threadbare sage by combining honest wealth & real talent you will rise still higher in its estimate."

No Puritan could have found a better solution to the problems of keeping one's vessel of virtue pure while amassing wealth and reputation. That the author of these prudent sentiments smoked, drank, and regularly borrowed money does not necessarily make him a hypocrite. He was setting up a code for untried youth, not for mature men who presumably had learned moderation and who could not conduct business without making loans. And if he looked upon money as a just reward of piety and industry, he was only typical of his age. His precepts echo those of Polonius, Benjamin Franklin, and Lord Chesterfield, and they form an illuminating sketch of the course in practical wisdom in which Herman Melville was undoubtedly drilled.[57]

In appearance Allan Melvill was now handsome and patrician, with a certain Scotch ruggedness in nose, lips, and chin. Heavy black brows rose over his dark eyes. His thick, curly hair crowned a high forehead and was still brushed forward over his temples as in his youth, though he had developed a splendid set of sideburns.[58] In portrait and letters, he was the gentleman, tolerant, loving, and courtly. Occasionally he would indulge in heavy-handed irony or a weighty pun. The sincerity of his professions of love, honesty, and solicitude is marred by effusiveness. He would undoubtedly have thought himself modest, yet references to his own virtues escaped him with an embarrassing frequency. But his nature drew too much from the soul-searching Puritan to rest for any length of time in smug self-satisfaction. While his steady concern with his own merits must strike the reader of his letters as absurd, one cannot overlook an earnestness that must have deceived its possessor and an idealism that could only prove too lofty.

The traditional picture of Herman Melville's mother as a cold, worldly woman wrapped in the "scaly, glittering folds of pride" and rebuffing the love of her tormented son is ludicrous to anyone who has read her letters.[59] The pride of ancestry and the pride of personal appearance and the Semiramian pride of woman in which Melville encases Maria Glendinning in *Pierre* is said to have been inspired by his own mother, but if they had any place in Maria Melville's character there is no written evidence to prove it. It was not she but her husband who habitually proclaimed the fame of General Peter Gansevoort.[60] Maria Melville could joke about her own figure when pregnancy enlarged it.[61] If she was infuriated by stubbornness and self-will in others, she also acknowledged her own shortcomings with humility.[62] One side of her may have been seduced by the grandeur of affluent living, by marble houses on Broadway, and the carriages and silver services of her wealthier neighbors. She liked to watch "fashionables" promenading on Broadway and to go occasionally to "splendid parties," where two bands entertained the guests till early morning.[63] But at a deeper level she was appalled by the lack of charity and the cool malevolence of gossip in formal society. "Fashionables I am affraid have no hearts," she remarked, on finding a young couple laughing and chatting in the home of a heartbroken neighbor whose baby had died but a few days before.[64] And when a crisis in her husband's business threatened to force retreat from the fashionable world, she thought only of how to reduce expenses and shrugged off the reversal with the remark, "after all, this world has little to offer." [65]

Maria Melville was essentially a simple, domestic, and somewhat provincial woman in whom a Dutch prudence, bluntness, and reserve were softened by strong feelings of Christian charity. Her major concerns in life were her husband, her children, her aged mother, and her noble brother. In the "unfathomable & boundless ocean of domestic cares," [66] she was "an admirable hand at extricating order from confusion," a formidable house cleaner,[67] and an expert at pickling oysters in enormous batches, to be sent up the river to Albany for the approval of her mother and brother. Intellectually she came far short of her spouse. She read little.[68] Like a schoolgirl she "always disliked writing" letters [69] and when she did, the hand was crabbed, the spelling atrocious, and the thought scrambled, except when indignation or distress inspired her to simple eloquence. Although her sister-in-law, Mary Gansevoort, found her full of "cheerful and enlivening conversation" [70] and her husband declared her "powers of enchantment are proverbial," [71] Maria's letters on the whole are commonplace. However, they are a far more reliable source for her character th lodramatic mother of *Pierre* o knew her only in her old age, reliance of her son's biograph t Herman's heritage from his mother appears—her good manners, her robust physique, her honesty and forthrightness, her quick temper, her courage in the face of death and withering poverty, and her active pity for human suffering.

No family records survive of the house in which Herman was born, at 6 Pearl Street just off the Battery. It was here that he astonished his family by showing "nearly three teeth" at the age of fifteen weeks[72] and that his mother, after about a year, completely weaned him.[73] But in less than two years Allan Melvill had established his family, together with cook and nurse, farther north at 55 Cortlandt Street, a move which took the family out of a district rapidly being monopolized by business establishments. It also brought them conveniently near the landing of the Hudson River boat, which they patronized several times a year. Herman's first journey by water had followed his birth by a little over a month, when his mother took him with Gansevoort and Helen Maria on a two months' visit to her own mother in Albany.[74] Every summer thereafter he was to escape the heat and pestilential fevers of New York by excursions to Albany or to the homes of other relatives in New England. Such vacations were a boon. Allan Melvill's family was augmented in alternate years by a new baby—Augusta in 1821, Allan in 1823, Catherine in 1825, Priscilla Frances in 1827, and Thomas in 1830—and childhood sicknesses were rife. Herman endured the whooping cough when he was a little over a year old. In the winter he was down with the measles, which brought a "very bad cough, inflamed eyes & virulent eruptions."[75] By the following fall his father was able to write that "Little Herman is in fine spirits and rugged as a bear."[76] The next summer Allan Melvill, his wife, and four children, together with their nurse, traveled by packet and private carriage to Boston to visit Allan's paren[illegible] Gansevoorts in Albany, and re[illegible] December. Similar excursions [illegible] three years. Before Herman M[illegible] exposed to enough shifting scenes and interruptions of routine to condition him admirably for a life of traveling.

His earliest impressions were heavily loaded with the pleasures of life in a happy though numerous family. His father and mother lived in harmony, if not in perfect tranquillity, and they loved their children, who called them "Pa" and "Ma." Stagnation in business worried Allan Melvill periodically, and Maria's frequent ordeals of childbirth created domestic crises. "Unpleasant fainting fits" assailed her when she was carrying Catherine,[77] and the child's approaching birth brought on the nervousness which Mary Gansevoort called "that most terrible of all diseases to which she is subject."[78] Woefully, Maria admitted her condition to her brother Peter:

> My strength of mind & Body is gradually returning—I for some time had serious fears for both & it was the cause of much sorrow to me nobody can tell my sufferings when I appeared quick & ill Humour'd —Twas then I felt particularly my inability to controul myself & my great weakness.[79]

At times like these her children must have suffered, and it is likely that she could not meet all the emotional needs of her large brood. Her discipline at times could be severe. One summer Catherine and Allan were denied the vacation trips of the others for being "the most rebellious & ungovernable."[80] But Maria also felt maternal pride in the good manners and beauty of her offspring, gave them parties, rejoiced when a new house had a delightful yard where the boys could play, and longed for news of her "darling children" whenever she was away from them.[81]

Her husband was even more devoted to his boys and girls. To him it was "mere vegetation" to live without them,[82] as he frequently had to when business kept him from sharing their vacations. He never failed to give thanks for

Heaven's blessing when a new child was born. It was the welfare of his wife and children, he reiterated over and over, that animated his whole being. He did find spanking necessary, it seems. When Allan was born, Helen Maria, though only six, observed that "if Pa has many more children he will have to keep the rod in hand the whole time." [83] But perhaps Herman's remark on the occasion is equally significant: "Pa now got two ittle Boy," he said happily.[84] Allan Melvill spoke fondly of his daughters as the "young damsels" and his sons as "the youthful Heroes." [85] Habitually meticulous, punctual, and economical himself, he sought to train his boys in the best mercantile habits.[86] But even though he urged their Uncle Peter, who frequently acted *in loco parentis,* to "consider their future welfare" rather than their "present enjoyment" and not to let indulgence transcend love,[87] he indulged them himself [88] and could not find it in his heart to coerce them into pursuits that had no appeal for them. Like most fathers of the times, he carefully guarded the facts of childbirth from his children. He told them that he "purchased" new babies "from a doctor," and despite a protest from precocious Gansevoort that "he never heard of buying children except for Slaves" the story was allowed to stand.[89] Innumerable notes of sentimental delight in his boys and girls sound in Allan Melvill's letters. One may miss a deep sensitivity and a profound understanding of a child's heart and still see in Allan Melvill something more tender than a merely normal father.

Both Allan and Maria Melville were devotedly religious, and they reared their children in an atmosphere of Christian piety. However, it is notable that the religious attitudes they expressed in their letters do not reflect the severe and orthodox Calvinism usually assumed as the only kind of religion Herman Melville knew as a boy. Only four references to church attendance appear in the scores of letters written by Maria and none whatsoever in the 250 odd written by Allan. Maria's mother, with whom Herman spent his summers, was indeed a devout worshipper of the old school who went to church twice on Sundays, forbade her daughter-in-law to travel on the Sabbath, supported the church liberally, and stocked her bookcases with volumes of Dwight's and Blair's sermons, Owen on *Indwelling Sin,* bound numbers of the *National Preacher,* and Psalm Books and Bibles in both Dutch and English.[90] She was inclined to dark fore-bodings and "festering of factitious evils," as her son Peter put it.[91] In Herman Melville's family, his grandmother was the stanchest devotee of the strict religion handed down from John Calvin.

But Maria Melville's letters bespeak no such religious austerity, nor any dark concern with total depravity, the doctrine of the elect, or even the notion of sin. To her there was no wrongdoing in telling a prudential lie or in writing letters or even paying visits to fashionable acquaintances on the sacred Sabbath day.[92] In moments of joy she offered thanksgiving to God for his "spared mercy."[93] She studiously cultivated an attitude of Christian submission: "The Almighty ruler above disposes all things as he sees fit," she wrote; "Tis our duty to be resigned & patiently acquiesce in his dispensations—my most earnest prayer is that I may be enabled to do so." [94] She talked about the "troublesome, pleasant, changing world" in which she lived.[95] "The longer we live the more we are convinced of the unsettled state of all things earthly," she moralized.[96] To her, the world was mutable, religion was simple faith demanding both supernatural grace and individual will, and the ways of Providence were past finding out.

Such sentiments echo Allan Melvill's directly, and his in turn reflect those of his parents, who were Unitarians. Major Thomas Melvill was a member of the Brattle Square Church in Boston, where he listened to the Unitarian eloquence of Buckminster and Edward Everett, and he read regularly *The Christian Register,* organ for the religious liberalism of Jared Sparks, William Ellery Channing, and Henry Ware.[97] Allan Melvill seems to have shared the cheerfulness of his father's creed. His ever-present faith, founded on a rational concept of creation, lay in a benevolent, omniscient Providence "who sees the end from the beginning, & reconciles partial evil with universal good." [98] Habitually he confided himself, his family, and his fortunes to "the protection of that Almighty Friend, who orders all things aright & never forsakes those who confide in him." [99] The only alleviation for man's ills was "humble resignation to the divine will." [100] Such seeming catastrophes as death were sanctified by God for man's spiritual good; death, however lamentable, was both a proof of "the instability of human life" and a translation to the "world of endless bliss beyond the grave." [101] His simple, optimistic credo is well summed up in a grateful effusion following a successful venture in business:

> . . . may we unite with equal fervor in ascription of grateful praise, to that divine first cause, who always moulds events to subserve the purpose of mercy & wisdom, often subjects poor human nature to the severest trials, that he may better display his sovereign power, & sometimes would even seem to interpose his immediate providence, while deducing as by a miracle good from evil, & converting an absolute misfortune into a positive blessing—
>
> My humble yet ardent confidence, in the constant protection, & eventual bounty of our almighty Parent, has been strong & unwavering, this alone could have sustained me in a fearful & protracted struggle which would otherwise have overwhelmed the boldest spirit & the stoutest heart, & will I trust still enable me to meet every future emergency with composure & fortitude—I too well know that for years to come, should my life be spared, I may look forward to the periodical recurrence of doubts, perplexities & apprehensions but with the blessing of Heaven, I will yet surmount them all, & perhaps enjoy in the decline of life with my beloved Family, whose welfare is dearer than my own, the reward of honest perseverance, honorable intentions & undoubting Faith—[102]

"Forget not your Creator in the dawn of youth," wrote Allan Melvill to his nephew Guert Gansevoort, about to embark as a midshipman in the Navy; "neglect not the Bible, regard it as your polar star, its religious precepts & moral doctrines are alike pure & sublime, & equally inculcate obedience, patriotism, fortitude, & temperance."[103] The Bible was unquestionably the foundation for Herman Melville's religious education, the spiritual "polar star" of his youth. It was in the Melville family Bible that Allan studiously recorded each child's birth, the place and date of his baptism, and the name of the attending minister. Enrollment in these sacred pages must have been intended not only as unassailably accurate data but also as a parental dedication of the child to the study of the book itself and to the life of Christian virtue which it must inspire. Melville's intimate knowledge of the Scriptures and his lifelong concern with the problems of the Christian religion began with his father's reverence for the Bible.[104] It was evidently a joy to receive into his boyish heart the story of Christ's life, the wonders of the miracles, and the supreme mystery of God made man; for years later, when sailing past the island of Patmos, he would confess to "the great curse of modern travel—skepticism" and "heartily wish Niebuhr & Strauss to the dogs." "They have robbed us," he lamented, "of the bloom"[105]—the bloom of "boyhood's thoughtless faith,"[106] he must have meant, that had burgeoned in him in the dawn of youth.

He had been baptized on August 19 in his own house on Pearl Street by the Reverend James M. Mathews, pastor of the South Reformed Dutch Church on Garden Street. Although the family letters make no mention either of church or minister, the Melvilles must have attended this church until 1823, for all the children up to that year were baptized by Mr. Mathews. The christenings were an important domestic ceremony: "baptised . . . at home" reads each entry in the family Bible, and the family evidently celebrated Herman's delivery from Satan and all his works most convivially, for the day before, his grandmother had purchased four gallons of Holland gin and four of rum.[107] After 1824 Allan and Maria attended the newly built Dutch Church at the corner of Broome and Greene Streets and were friends of the pastors, Robert McLean and Dr. Jacob

Brodhead, who succeeded him. Although Allan and Maria Melville were not so devoted to their religion as to send the children to the church school instead of a lay institution,[108] we may be certain that Herman attended both church and Sunday school on Broome Street.[109]

Abram C. Dayton, who in 1830 was a boy of Herman's age and who lived nearby, has recalled the characteristic Sunday of the Reformed faith in New York in a picture with which Herman was doubtless familiar:

> The old time Knickerbocker Sabbath was in very truth a day especially set apart for worship. The laws of society so decreed, and public opinion was a stern master then; so woe betide the man, woman, or child who dared to disobey or disregard its stringent rules. From early dawn all secular affairs were religiously avoided; the family meals were but cold collations of Saturday baked meats—it was decreed that man servant and maid servant should rest.[110]
>
> No sound save the tolling of the church bell broke the awful stillness. At stated hours, three times during the day, at ten o'clock, at three o'clock, and at seven o'clock, stereotype processions of solemn men and women, accompanied by subdued, silent children even of the most tender age slowly wended their way to church, as if they were assisting at the funeral of a dear departed friend . . . . The coy maiden looked as demure as her spectacled grandmother who led her protectingly by the hand; the youth clad in best Sunday roundabout, appeared as stolid as the well-fed museum anaconda, for the boy had been crammed that morning with catechism . . . . When the bell ceased tolling and the service was about to commence, heavy iron chains were drawn tightly across the streets adjacent to the different places of worship, that no possible noise might distract the congregation from serious meditations.[111]

Dayton's account of the service in the Dutch Reformed Church is probably a reliable measure of an average youth's reactions to the "lugubrious and protracted" ritual. "The long spun out extemporary prayers doubtless were magnificent expositions of unadulterated faith to the full-grown believer, but to the youthful listener they might as well have been uttered in Sanscrit, the only intelligible portions being 'benighted heathen,' 'the lake which burns with fire and brimstone,' 'whited sepulchres,' and other kindred expressions." The dominies delivered long sermons, taking whole chapters for their texts and allowing ample space for denunciation of all whose notions of the paramount duties of men differed from theirs. At the end came the benediction, long but welcome to the youngsters, who were at last permitted to stand up instead of sitting "bolt upright, our eyes fixed upon the pulpit with no outward show of weariness." [112] All children dreaded the Sabbath, Dayton concluded, "on account of its wearisome, unnatural restraints. To them it was a silent cheerless smileless day, from the morning hour of its dawn until the little sufferers gladly sought their pillows, enlivened with the thought that six long days of sinful frolic with ball, marble, and kite must intervene before they should again be called upon to perform monastic penance." [113]

How far we may rely on Dayton's recollections in tracing Herman Melville's religious life is admittedly uncertain. We can only guess that Herman, like any boy, found the service wearisome, that he was glad when the Knickerbocker Sabbath was over, that frolic with ball, marble, and kite appealed more than sitting rigid while Mr. McLean or Dr. Brodhead thundered about benighted heathen or the lake which burns with fire and brimstone. However, we may be sure that what doctrinal notions he acquired from pulpit and catechism were tempered in daily life by his parents' liberal faith. The religious atmosphere of his home had a foundation in the Bible, but it was never darkened by the gloomy theology of Calvin. God, he learned from his father and mother, was benevolent. One must acquiesce in the infinite wisdom of Providence, who sometimes tested the merits of His children by oppression, but however much He might appear to work evil, He moved always toward eventual good. A child should pray to Him for success, for mercy, and for grace and should pour out thanks to Him for His countless favors. Above all, He was the "Almighty Friend" who never forsook the humble petitioner. It was this concept of God and His mysterious ways that must have formed in Herman's youthful consciousness. The God of the minister may have stood for Calvin's inexorable justice, but the God of his parents, with their Unitarian inclinations, was above all else merciful.

When Melville was about five years old, his father had prospered sufficiently to move uptown to Bleecker Street, then in the suburbs. The periodic epidemics of cholera in the crowded downtown areas of New York had been a constant worry to Allan Melvill. (He must have been keenly annoyed when the City Council, in the effort to reduce sources of contamination, condemned the privy back of his house on Cortlandt Street as a nuisance to be corrected.[114]) The new two-story brick house was in "the region of pure air [&] good water," its vacant lot would be "invaluable as playground for the Children," and it was both comfortable and fashionable.[115] The previous winter had brought sickness and gloom. Herman, who was usually of "plump and rosy appearance," [116] had been looking "pale, thin, and dejected." [117] The whole family was glad to have a change. Maria Melville looked forward to the large yard with grass-plot and flowers, the tea room at the end of the hall, the "Marble Mantle peices & grates for Lehigh Coal," the handsome nursery, and the pretty chambers with dormer windows in the garret, whence one had a pleasing prospect of "those elegant white Marble Houses in Bond Street." [118] Herman Melville spent the next three years in "this very court though not the west end of town," [119] playing with his brothers and sisters, "improv[ing] apace as to growing & talking," teasing his brother Gansevoort out of patience, and going regularly to school.[120]

For a year or more, he had evidently been under the tutelage of the family governess, Miss Adams, a genteel lady of mild voice and manners and a firm and systematic teacher.[121] When he was sent to school, at first he did not "appear so fond of his Books as to injure his health." [122] An attack of scarlet fever in the spring of 1826 may have curbed his capacities for scholarship and contributed to a lifelong weakness of eyesight.[123] Vacations in Albany were still part of a salutary routine; in the summer he was sent up on the Hudson River boat for a month with Grandmother Gansevoort, Uncle Peter, and his cousin Stanwix Gansevoort, Aunt Mary's son, with whom he became close friends.[124] Wrote Allan Melvill:

> . . . I now consign to your especial care & patronage, my beloved Son Herman, an honest hearted double rooted Knickerbocker, of the true Albany stamp, who I trust will do equal honour in due time to his ancestry parentage and kindred—he is very backward in speech & somewhat slow in comprehension, but you will find him as far as he understands Men & things both solid & profound, & of a docile and aimiable disposition—if agreeable, he will pass the vacation with his Grandmother and yourself, & I hope he may prove a pleasant auxiliary to the Family Circle—I depend much on your kind attention to my dear Boy who will be truly grateful for the least favour—let him avoid green Fruit & unseasonable exposure to the Sun & heat, but having taken such good care of Gansevoort last Summer I commit his Brother to the same hands with unreserved confidence . . . .[125]

Allan Melvill's genuine fondness for his son was superior to any impatience that Herman had not made much progress to this point. That he underestimated him is apparent from Herman's achievement six months later in becoming a monitor at the New York Male High School [126] and from Allan's startled revelation to Peter Gansevoort the following year:

> You will be as much surprised as myself to know that Herman proved the best Speaker in the introductory Department, at the examination of the High School, he has made rapid progress during the last 2 quarters . . . .[127]

It was in this high school, of which his father was a trustee and stockholder, that Herman received his early formal education.[128] Organized in 1824 by a group of well-to-do New Yorkers, it had quickly acquired over six hundred students. Its spacious three-story brick building, fifty feet by seventy-five, stood in Crosby Street, a walk of five short blocks for the Melville boys. Herman and Gansevoort and little Allan enjoyed educational methods here that were far ahead of their time. They found teaching that was designed primarily to appeal to their good feelings and affections. They studied a variety of subjects intended to interest each student in "some subject or other more peculiarly fitted for his own powers, dispositions, taste, or probable future pursuits." Their principal and teachers made the intelligent assumption "that what is commonly called a love of mischief in children, is in fact a love of mental occupation." Rewards were distributed not only for "improvement in learning" but for mere "good conduct." Offenses were tried by boy juries to stimulate honorable conduct, and corporal punishment was restricted to extreme cases. All exercises began with reading a chapter in the Bible, but "no catechism or instruction in the tenets of any religious denomination" was permitted.

With only one teacher for every forty students, the Lancastrian or monitorial system prevailed. The teachers taught the abler boys, who then led their fellow students in reciting whatever lessons could be got by memory. Herman's position as monitor made him "responsible for the conduct and behavior of his little class, as well as for their attention and progress." In the introductory department he gathered his class of eight into a corner of the large classroom, drilled them in "Arithmetic, the Tables, and Spelling," heard their set answers to the set questions in geography, and noted the number of correct and incorrect answers in his monitor's book. If he was a monitor of writing, he brought to his teacher every Monday a "journal of some transaction of the last week" which was expected to form "a simple and natural introduction to habits of composition." He must have been pleased to tell his father, always ready to be proud of his children, that he was a class leader, and the responsibility should have bolstered his self-confidence and spurred him to study harder. This, at least, was the expectation of the masters. And it may be that this early experience helped guide his choice of vocation a decade later when he was forced to shift for himself.

As a scholar, Herman came far short of his brother Gansevoort, who early distinguished himself in the classics and in oratory and who, according to his doting father, was "considered rather more than an ordinary genius." [129] But Herman won prizes in public speaking, too, and perhaps he took the stage in the New York High School to declaim the ringing speeches of Patrick Henry, Byron's eloquent apostrophe to the ocean, "Marco Bozzaris," or other favorite schoolboy pieces of the day.

Melville was evidently content in this first school; his earliest known letter reveals a spontaneous interest in his work:

11th of October, 1828

DEAR GRANDMOTHER,

This is the third letter that I ever wrote you so you must not think it will be very good. I now study Geography, Gramar, Arithmetic, Writing, Speaking, Spelling, and read in the Scientific class book. I enclose in this letter a drawing for my dear Grandmother. Give my love to Grandmamma, Uncle Peter, and Aunt Mary. And my Sisters and also to allan,

Your affectionate Grandson
HERMAN MELVILL.[130]

However, by his eleventh year it seems that Herman was no more fond of his books than he had been when he began school. In May 1830 his father wrote to Peter Gansevoort:

Herman I think is making more progress than formerly, & would proceed farther, if he could be induced to study more—being a most aimiable & innocent child, I cannot find it in my heart to coerce him, especially as he seems to have chosen Commerce as a favorite pursuit, whose practical activity can well dispense with much book knowledge—[131]

In the same letter Allan Melvill had written proudly of Gansevoort's position as "a distinguished scholar . . . at the head of the Class in most of the English studies." He was satisfied to let each boy develop according to his aptitudes, and it is significant, if his conjecture was accurate, that Herman was interested in commerce. He may have been the sensitive young lad whom he pictures in the first chapter of *Redburn,* exploring the world about him with excited imagination. It is clear that he was also a serious-minded boy who aspired to be a successful merchant like his father.

Melville received his education in the liberal environment of a school attended by the children of well-to-do, middle-class parents. His earliest social acquaintances were also such respectable youngsters. Twice a week, together with his brothers and sisters, he went to "small but select" dancing schools "in one of the Marble Houses in Broadway" or Broome Street, having previously prepared himself under the watchful eye of his mother in her bedroom.[132] Periodically he danced at balls and cotillions conducted by the masters. Occasionally Maria Melville mustered sufficient energy to give the children a party, for they were frequently invited to neighboring homes for entertainment and both etiquette and youthful needs demanded return parties. At the request of Gansevoort and Helen, she wrote her brother a long description of one of these happy affairs:

> . . . Thursday was named on Tuesday the invitations were written & sent Wednesday was a beautiful day warm & sunny, when I went out and purchased confectionary & Mottoes without which Gansevoort & Helen said it would be no party they had attended several in the neighborhood this winter & pretended to know a great deal about them. . . . About four oClock Mr M came home in the Broadway accommodation & delighted the Children by telling them he had agreed with the Driver, that he was to call at several of the houses near & say he would call for them a little after six, At the time appointed Doctor Broadheads two Sons came, very fine Intelligent Boys, & they gradually came to the number of 25 beyond the Childrens expectations they had invited forty & on account of the storm thought nobody would come. Mrs Barnewell came in about seven & remain'd till twelve when the party began to break up—I forgot to mention what by the Children was considered the best part of the evenings entertainment A Violin the man played admirably . . . nothing was handed round save Lemonade Port Wine . . .[133] & Cakes of various kinds the Sugar Plums, Mottoes, Blamange, preserves, Oranges & diced fruits were displayed on a supper table & really looked very

Pretty interspersed with Plates of Cake & I must say never having so many Children together before I had no idea of what was necessary for their consumption—fortunately I had provided plenty—[those] that found they could eat no more (of the Boys) emptied with a great deal of ease their plates into their Breeches pockets, all present declared they had never passed a more agreeable evening—the same was repeated to them the next day at school, & my children think their was never a more delightful party given—I feel quite happy it is over & shall ever after be cautious about promising another [134]

Maria evidently gave the children few large parties, but expended herself to the limit to make them gay and sumptuous. Gansevoort's description of another party in the neighborhood furnishes a picture of the typical amusements when the children were entertained. Boys and girls played "Pawns" or danced, sang songs, and gave recitations like "A Lady on the Field of Battle" or "O Sacred Truth," or for a spicy pastime, they played "Pillows and Keys," where boys knelt before girls or vice versa, rang the keys three times, and received for their embarrassing overtures the reward of a hurried and public kiss.[135] The Melville children shared such merriment with a large group of friends. Besides the "very fine intelligent boys" of Dr. Brodhead, minister of their church, they had neighborhood or school acquaintances in the children of James Gore King, a prominent broker, and of John Aspinwall, a wealthy merchant, with whom Allan Melvill, Maria reported, rode home daily on the Broadway horsecar.[136] For a family that began its social career in New York by living in a boarding house the first year, the Melvilles had moved well along.

By 1828, when they moved into a virtually new house at 675 Broadway, only two blocks from the old, they were ready to settle into the most comfortable kind of upper-middle-class existence. Allan, who was realizing over $5,000 a year from only one of his business ventures, "playfully" told his wife that she had at last gained her point, which had always been a house on Broadway; and Maria wrote, "My Spirits are better & I am a more agreeable companion than I have been for some time past." [137] If the house was close to Abraham Brower's livery stable and considerably north of the area where the very wealthiest and most distinguished families lived—the John Jacob Astors, the Philip Hones, the Depaus [138]—it was, as Maria boasted, "on the Fashionable side of the Street." [139] In the neighborhood lived respectable attorneys, merchants, bankers, and Knickerbocker doctors, such as David S. Jones, William Astor, James G. King, and Jeremiah Van Rensselaer.[140] The house, though narrow, had a center staircase, numerous bedrooms, some with fireplaces and marble mantelpieces, and an upstairs sitting room "with a handsome Cornish round it." [141] The deep yard behind held "a fine Garden prettily laid out with fruit trees shrubbery bulbous roots &c fine Grass plot & woodhouse," and with a vacant lot on one side there was a "delightful opening and pure air" for boyish sports.[142] The two and a half years Herman spent in these surroundings were probably the happiest of his life.

Moving into the new house had brought the bizarre experience of sleeping with his brothers and sisters in his parents' own bedroom. Painters, whitewashers, and purifiers had taken over, and as Allan reported it, "Maria, myself & our 7 bairns have passed the last two nights in the same chamber, Gansevoort & Herman on one side of our bed, & Helen Maria & Augusta on the other, all in elegant negligence on the floor—" [143] The family harmony that must have made this a comical adventure prevailed at Thanksgiving celebrations too. The day began with an offering of grateful prayers at Dr. Brodhead's church. Then came the magnificent dinner, for which Maria provided, with Dutch sumptuousness, "a famous Turkey," "a large Plum pudding," cider by the barrel, a great assortment of pies, and all the other ingredients of a family feast.[144] One of these occasions produced a near disaster. Maria wrote:

We had just commenced eating when lo & behold a cry of fire directly under our windows to which we paid no attention untill the Cook run up stairs & said the chimney was burning at a great rate, which set us all in commotion filled the rooms & Pantries with an offensive smoke & quite cooled our dinner—not so our appetites for after it was over we sat down but with less comfort finished our Meal—[145]

Maria's "nervousness" did not apparently afflict her when any real crisis had to be faced, and no one in the family was so fragile as to lose his appetite over a mere fire in the house.

Occasionally the weekly succession of school, play, and parties was varied by excursions. Allan Melvill would not allow his sons "to run abroad, or play in the street," but they could visit him, with permission, in his shop on Pine Street.[146] Not far away was the New York waterfront, where Herman and his brothers could watch a thousand ships jostling each other at the crowded piers and spilling cargoes and passengers from all over the world onto the crowded wharves along South Street. Sometimes the Melville family went on sailing trips around New York harbor, to Flushing, Staten Island, or Perth Amboy.[147] Once Herman went off alone across the Hudson to Hoboken "in high spirits" and spent the day there;[148] such expeditions may have been numerous, for Hoboken, with its pleasant walks, its numerous resorts, and its wind-swept hills above the Hudson furnished a haven for the refugees from New York's heat.

Of Herman's inner life in these jocund years in the Broadway house nothing is known directly. From his father, who wore General Peter Gansevoort's ring constantly in fond "respect to his memory"[149] and who thought of the General as "a model for the imitation of his offspring,"[150] he must have formed ideals of patriotism, honor, and courageous action and developed a comfortable sense of aristocracy. We may well suppose too that he reveled in his father's stories of his travels and that his imagination found delight in filling these out from the foreign books, etchings, and paintings in his father's library. For Allan Melvill could tell of the time when "a very severe gale" had snapped the "Main top sail, & top-gallant Sails from the Yards" of his ship or "carried away the fore topmast"; of the perilous pursuit by the British frigate "Dryad," which fired over thirty shots before the captain of Allan's ship would surrender; of the escape, in 1811, from a British cutter and a frigate, only to be captured by the illustrious "Guerrière." [151] (What a footnote to the famous victory of the "Constitution" this tale must have made!) Allan could talk too of European cities from Liverpool to Edinburgh, Paris, and Bordeaux, and especially he knew of St. Paul's, "the cloisters of Westminster Abbey," the Houses of Parliament, and Buckingham Palace. [152]

Besides the gloves, ribbons, and fine cloth Allan Melvill imported, he brought home paintings and engravings,[153] some of which must have hung in his own parlors. There were French books, like Voltaire's *Histoire de Charles XII* and a *Voyage Descriptif et Philosophique de . . . Paris,* and perhaps accounts of travel in Switzerland, or the synthesis of ancient travelers' observations which the Abbé Barthelmy had published as *Le Voyage du Jeune Anacharsis,* with plates to enthrall a young boy innocent of French.[154] There must have been guidebooks to Scotland and England and probably *The Picture of Liverpool,* to whose data on the city Allan Melvill's epistolary accounts bear unmistakable resemblance.[155] All these exotic objects supplied an infinite crisscross of highways for the imagination of a young boy to travel, unencumbered by the lessons of experience or the rigors of necessity. In such surroundings Herman could hardly have escaped dreaming of the day when he would be able to cross the stormy Atlantic and roam the storied cities of the Old World, retracing his father's footsteps and comparing the real world of streets, buildings, and men with the picture world of his father's books.

Not the least of the pleasures in Herman's early life were the visits of relatives, some of whose careers were to cast a magnetic attraction upon him in later years. His Grandmother Gansevoort came often; so did his Uncle Peter, whose special protegé he was. Uncle Herman Gansevoort and his eccentric wife came too from his farm and lumber mills at Gansevoort, near Saratoga.[156] Once his older cousin, Priscilla Melvill, who had been born in Paris, spent the whole winter with the family. Pretty, warmhearted Aunt Mary Gansevoort was a frequent guest, for long periods. More important were the visits of her sons, Guert and Peter, Herman's first cousins. Guert was commissioned a midshipman in 1823 at the age of ten and assigned to the United States Ship "Constitution." A year later, after staying with the Melvilles on Bleecker Street, he embarked on a cruise to the Mediterranean. Allan Melvill, with characteristic solicitude for members of the clan into which he had married, saw that he was properly bestowed among other "fine young gentlemen" and supplied with expensive equipment. His outfit, he wrote to Peter Gansevoort,

> will cost more than you imagine but I thought it my duty as it regarded himself, & the name he bears, to put him afloat in his country's service as a Gentleman, & with GOD's blessing I am proud to anticipate from his general deportment that he will be an honour to the family, & to the star-spangled banner he is destined to defend.[157]

Three years later Guert returned from the shores of Africa,[158] full of the strange wonders he had seen; and Herman may well have experienced at this time the kind of fantasy he describes in *Redburn:*

> As I grew older my thoughts took a larger flight, and I frequently fell into long reveries about distant voyages and travels, and thought how fine it would be to be able to talk about remote and barbarous countries; with what wonder and reverence people would regard me, if I had just returned from the coast of Africa or New Zealand . . . .[159]

The next time Herman saw the youthful midshipman he was "on his way to Brooklyn and the Pacific Ocean," as Allan Melvill described it, with a typical romantic flourish.[160]

Guert's older brother Peter had the dubious distinction of being the first, though not the last, of General Peter Gansevoort's grandchildren to go to sea as a common sailor. For three weeks before his first voyage he stayed with the

Melvilles in New York while Allan Melvill secured his sea wardrobe for him with the knowing authority that came from his own experience on the ocean. Gansevoort, "an incessant talker," plied him with questions during his stay, and Herman undoubtedly felt equal interest in the prospective sailor.[161] Two years later he became a midshipman and from his station at Brooklyn paid visits with his brother Guert to their Melville cousins.[162] Another cousin of Melville's was also a midshipman in the Navy. Thomas Wilson Melvill, Paris-born eldest son of Allan's brother Thomas, had been appointed in February 1826. He sailed in September on the U.S.S. "Brandywine," which cruised for four years in the Pacific. Whether Melville saw this hot-tempered but affectionate cousin in New York is not demonstrable.[163] But his experiences must have been circulated in the family; Allan Melvill received letters from him from distant ports like Rio de Janeiro and Callao, and we may assume that he passed on Tom's adventures to his boys.

Then too, there was Uncle John D'Wolf, husband of Allan Melvill's sister Mary, whose career as ship captain Melville would specifically mention in two of his books.[164] John D'Wolf came from a family in Bristol, Rhode Island, long engaged in the shipping business. In his early years he had sailed to Okhotsk in Russia, crossed Siberia to St. Petersburg, and journeyed back to Bristol after an absence of three and a half years. He sailed on regular trading voyages to Havana and St. Petersburg for several years thereafter, and after retirement to a farm he died in 1872.[165] There were many occasions when Herman might have seen this seafaring uncle and listened to his tales of outlandish adventure in distant countries.[166]

The many sea wanderers and far travelers in Herman's family could dazzle his young mind with their pictures of life on the ocean and of the delights of travel. His own marine experience was limited to innumerable trips up and down the Hudson on the swift steamboats of the day and to overnight voyages by packet to Providence and Bristol,

Rhode Island. In 1828 he spent the vacation with his Aunt Mary D'Wolf in Bristol.[167] Uncle John was away on one of his periodic voyages to Havana and St. Petersburg,[168] but Herman lived for three weeks in the atmosphere of a real sea captain's home and could roam about the docks or go aboard some of the many ships owned by the D'Wolf family.

In 1827 and again in 1829 Herman spent the summer in Boston with his grandparents.[169] Thomas Melvill, then in his seventy-sixth year, was still Collector of the Port of Boston, a post to which he had been appointed by Washington in 1789. He had been educated for the ministry at the College of New Jersey (now Princeton) but had later rebelled against the rigid tenets of Calvinism and placed his religious sympathies with the rising Unitarian movement.[170] For some time he was a "housewright";[171] but his service as major in Croft's regiment of Massachusetts artillery during the Revolution won him the customhouse appointment that he held till removed under the spoils system by Jackson in 1829. Known as the "last of the Mohawks" from his participation in the Boston Tea Party in 1773, he still wore, with studied indifference to convention, the cocked hat and small clothes popular in his youth.[172] His wooden house on Green Street in Boston held many a relic of the Revolution for Herman to see, the most noteworthy being the famous bottle containing tea taken from Thomas Melvill's shoes after he returned from the expedition in Boston Harbor. The sacred vial was shown to visitors by Thomas Melvill's children "with as much holy reverence as the miraculous robes of St. Bridget by the superstitious believer of the anti-Protestant faith."[173] About the living room were family portraits and various objects which Herman's Uncle Thomas had sent from Paris, including a small painting of the Madonna and child which usually stood on the piano.[174] But of all the many curiosities in the parlor, which delighted other young eyes besides his own, the one Herman was to remember most vividly was "a glass ship fully rigged, modelled after the fashion of some celebrated French vessel."[175] Years afterward he would find it a useful object around which to build Wellingborough Redburn's childish dreams of a life of travel.

As the son of Thomas Melvill's favorite son—"my sheet Anchor . . . my hope," he called Allan[176]—Herman was warmly received in his grandparents' home. His grandmother, a woman of "stately dignity and marked grace of manner,"[177] would urge him to "walk in the right Path and take Truth [and] Honesty for his Guides."[178] Any problems she would explain with the reassuring belief that "our Heavenly Father orders all for our Good and will not afflict willingly, nor Grieve the Children of Men."[179] He was also under the care of his Aunts Priscilla, Helen, and Jean. The first remembered him in her will many years later, and the last showed her continuing interest by presenting a Bible to him shortly after he returned from the South Seas.[180]

Not much can be pieced together about Herman's visits to his Boston relatives. The reports of his grandparents, dutifully relayed by his father to Peter Gansevoort, afford little substance. One reads:

> Herman returned this morn[g] in charming health & spirits after a delightful visit which was equally agreeable to his friends—my Father says "Herman has been an uncommon good Boy, & is a great favorite with us all" which commendation is fully confirmed by his Grand Mother & Aunts[181]

Herman always seems to have been "a good boy," whether at home or on visits. But it would be more interesting to know whether Major Melvill ever took Herman down to Quincy, as he took Gansevoort in 1826, to be presented to President John Quincy Adams,[182] whether Herman went regularly with his pious grandparents to the Unitarian Church in Brattle Square of which they were members, whether he ever walked across Boston Common to Kneeland Street and the house of his father's good friend, Judge Lemuel Shaw, and whether he ever spent a day or two in play with Elizabeth, the Judge's daughter, whom he would one day marry.

On Herman's return from Boston in 1827 his father wrote:

> . . . Tuesdays boat brought our beloved Gansevoort in charming spirits at the recollection of his visit to Albany, which will doubtless leave many agreeable traces on his tenacious memory & glowing fancy;—his more sedate but not less interesting Brother returned to us on Monday, & though less buoyant in mind, was equally delighted with his jaunt to Boston, where he became also a great favorite with the whole family—[183]

The letter typifies many in which both Allan and Maria Melville, despite efforts to be impartial, unconsciously favor Gansevoort. Allan thought him a genius, as we know, little suspecting the potential power in the growing susceptibilities of his second son, whose memory was as tenacious as Gansevoort's and whose "fancy" was immeasurably superior. Herman had the love and the confidence of both his parents. Maria's indignation at her brother Herman for refusing to take his young namesake to the farm at Gansevoort in the summer of 1829 (he pleaded that his wife's relatives were coming to visit) is one measure of her fondness for her son. "I am willing to bet my Ears [Herman] would feel better if he had the company of my little Son to relieve his loneliness," she wrote to her confidant, Peter.[184] "Kiss Herman for . . . us" was a typical request when Herman was away from home, and if she did not receive regular accounts of his welfare she demanded them.[185]

Nevertheless, Gansevoort was considered the brightest luminary in the circle of children. Beside him, Herman seemed "sedate." The psychological effects of running continually in second place may well have contributed to Herman's developing personality a timidity and introspection in which would accumulate the unrelieved tensions that sometimes stir individuals to creative expression. If there is no evidence in the family letters of an inchoate artistic temperament in Herman, there was at least one of the conditions which often help to energize the artist.

But the complex of circumstances that assist the formation of the artistic character is various and unpredictable. Artists have been nourished on health and on sickness, on riches and on poverty. If destiny had permitted Herman Melville to live and mature in the security of a home on Broadway, he might have grown up into a conventional businessman with perhaps a dilettante's interest in the arts. But "those stage managers the Fates," skilled in the use of ironic contrasts, were about to begin a shift of scenery, the first in the bitter drama of Herman Melville's youth.

In the summer of 1830 Allan Melvill's fortunes suddenly collapsed. Three years before, by exerting a scarcely creditable pressure on his brother-in-law, he had borrowed over ten thousand dollars to supply the capital of a firm in which he became a secret partner.[186] He would share half the profits; but in order to secure ready credit for the new firm his personal interest was concealed so that he could give the endorsement of his own probity and established reputation to the checks of his two partners. From the start, the firm was a success, and in three years Allan Melvill reaped over fifteen thousand dollars.[187] But as if in moral retribution for the dubious ethics of the arrangement, disaster fell suddenly upon him. He found himself unable to meet a particular note, and a merciless creditor refused an extension. In a few days his entire credit structure collapsed. Sometime after the firm dissolved in the spring of 1830, in accordance with the terms of the original agreement, Allan Melvill went to Albany and confessed to the Gansevoorts that he was "utterly unable to pay" what he owed Peter.[188] Catherine Gansevoort promptly added a codicil to her will charging Allan's debts to the share of Maria and her children in her estate, and Peter secured from Allan an assignment of his remaining interest in the unsettled accounts of the partnership. Though now a bankrupt, Allan attempted to form another profitable connection, but unable to raise capital he finally had to accept the management of the small Albany branch of a New York fur company.[189] Lawsuits were commenced against him, obdurate creditors served writs, and Allan was driven to considering a sale of his furniture.[190] The coincidence of these reversals with her beloved mother's severe illness made Maria's spirits "more than ever depressed," and Allan began to have fears of "permanent injury" to her health.

She is very desirous [he wrote] of removing to Albany, to enjoy once more the society of her connexions & friends & feel at home & if possible happy, which she has never been & never can be here . . . .[191]

By the middle of August Allan was forced to give up the store he had opened on Pine Street only five months before and to turn his Broadway house into an office.

Of all this confusion Herman was a reluctant witness, for plans to send him to Hadley, Massachusetts, for a visit with his Aunt Lucy had to be dropped. Though much disappointed, he bore the change "like a Philosopher," his father observed.[192] But the deprivation must have made him conscious, perhaps for the first time, of the real relation between money and freedom. The events of the next six weeks were even more bewildering for a young boy accustomed to all the pleasures and comforts of upper-class life. His father prepared to transfer the household to Albany, and though he and his brothers were "pleased with the removal" and his mother's happiness would be promoted,[193] he must have more than glimpsed the full import of his father's failure. His mother was subject to fits of "sudden depression" [194] and finally took Allan and his sisters to Grandmother Gansevoort's at the end of August. He and Gansevoort stayed on, "keeping Bachelor's Hall" with their father.[195] Soon they learned that Augusta was seriously ill in the hospital, and with their father they prayed "night and morning" for her recovery.[196] After a month of turmoil came moving day, when Maria, who had returned for this event, went off to Albany with Gansevoort and the furniture that Allan Melvill had somehow saved from his creditors. Allan planned to follow in the next passenger boat with Herman, but because of a violent storm they had to spend a comfortless night at the Cortlandt Street dock.[197] On October 9, as their boat moved quickly up the Hudson, father and son saw New York for the last time together.

The New York life, with its comfort and security, marble houses and pleasant gardens for play, happy schooldays, parties, and dancing classes, was over. And though Albany promised the pleasure of being near Grandmother Gansevoort and Uncle Peter and a score of cousins, it also held in store a grim test of the submissive faith by which Herman had been taught to live.

Chapter II

Albany, 1830-1837

WHATEVER may have been Allan Melvill's emotions as he sailed up the Hudson after the crushing defeat in New York, he thought at least that his wife and children would be happy in their new home. For himself the future still held much promise. The city of Albany in the 1830's was a flourishing center of communication and trade. The Erie Canal, completed in 1825, had made it the chief link between the grainfields, lumber mills, and fur depots of the West and North and the port of New York to the south; the Mohawk and Hudson Railroad, for which the first ground had been broken by Stephen Van Rensselaer's silver spade in July 1830, was soon to enrich the rapidly growing city. Although Yankee merchants had long before ousted the Dutch from leadership in business and politics, the latter were still prosperous and influential. Many of them were Maria Melville's relatives, and Allan Melvill would have the obvious advantages of family connection with the merchant class. His debts were staggering. Yet with typical optimism and dogged Scotch determination he took up his labors for the Denison Williams Company, furriers, reduced to what Peter Gansevoort called "a clerk's hire," [1] but hopeful, it seems, of securing capital with which to expand the company and obtain large commissions.[2]

The city in which Herman Melville was to live during the impressionable years of his adolescence was a cluster of stores, houses, gilt-domed public buildings, and churches that rose sharply from the banks of the Hudson to a plateau at the top. To the south and the north were tree-studded hills pierced regularly by pleasant creeks, or kills. Along the narrow strip of riverbank at the foot of the hill ran Market Street, its southern half crowded with small shops, its northern half dense with old and compact Dutch dwellings rapidly being converted into stores or boardinghouses. The principal thoroughfare, one hundred and twenty feet broad, was State Street, which ran west from the river up a lofty hill and connected the business area with the white-marble City Hall, the Capitol with its Ionic portico, the Albany Academy, and spacious public parks. Crossing it half way up the hill was Pearl Street, shaded by rows of trees and lined with the newer and more spacious houses. Although pigs ran in the streets and the iron rims of cart wheels created an incessant din on the rough stones, the city was generally clean and pleasant.

The people of Albany were primarily traders. Though wealth abounded, few were very rich and few very poor. If industry, thrift, and enterprise were the watchwords of the day, religion and morality were also conspicuous in public activity. Albanians supported their nineteen churches and ministers both voluntarily and liberally, and two thirds of the 30,000 inhabitants were estimated to be regular attendants at Sabbath services. Annually, 4,000 Sabbath-school children displayed their piety by a parade through the streets. Like most communities of the times, Albany was actively, even noisily, patriotic. School children, early indoctrinated with love of their country and veneration for its founders, delivered fervidly nationalistic orations at annual exercises in the academies. And in Fourth-of-July celebrations, replete with parades in which all the civic organizations took part and which concluded with church services, the entire city expressed its joy in being American and free. They climaxed their celebrations with fireworks exhibitions, balls, and banquets, at which they drank a long series of toasts to the short history of the United States.[3]

Toward the arts Albany held a variety of attitudes, from friendship to apathy, hostility, and vulgar self-consciousness. William Duffy maintained a successful theater in a "handsome building" by mingling popular drama—*The Last Nail, or the Drunkard's Doom* and *The Irishman in London*—with *King Lear, Othello, Richard III,* and *The School for Scandal.*[4] Although there were those who deplored the "bad conduct, immorality, and tavern brawls" of the "corps dramatique,"[5] the Theater had a stanch defender in the *Albany Argus* and the *Albany Microscope,* which habitually praised Duffy's noble efforts against great odds and urged the public to support the institution in order to keep it "a place of rational and intellectual amusement."[6] Periodicals fared less happily. Four literary magazines were founded in the early and middle thirties, but all shortly succumbed to indifference.[7] A Sacred Musical Society and a Philharmonic Society occasionally presented programs of Handel, Haydn, Rossini, and Beethoven;[8] a successful experiment in Italian opera was made in 1835; and minor musicians, singers, violinists, and other instrumentalists seemed to secure warm receptions on their periodic appearances on the stage of the Museum.[9] Of all the arts, painting and sculpture fared least well. Half a dozen portrait painters earned a living in Albany[10] and traveling exhibitions came frequently to Stanwix Hall or the Museum, but there seems to have been no warmth of feeling for painting generally. Like most small American cities, the place where Melville grew up apparently looked at art through puritanical and provincial glasses: when Dubufe brought his painting of Adam and Eve there in 1833, Joel Munsell, who was later to be an Albany historian, wrote in his diary:

> In the evening went to view the great moral painting, as it is called, of Adam and Eve, by Dubufe. They are certainly masterpieces, and has [*sic*] attracted thousands of women, who would have blushed to have looked upon them under any other name. . . . Saw some female acquaintances there who had a manifest disposition not to recognize any one. O modesty! What a Grundy [?] art thou![11]

The higher claims of morality over aesthetics, evident in Albany's attitude toward art, found parallels in the superior claims of intellect over sensitivity, which made lectures the most popular of public entertainments. Albanians flocked to hear discourses on law, geology, American literature, Shakespeare, moral obligations, self-instruction, and phrenology. Impelled by the same motive of learning something valuable, they maintained three libraries, for the old and well-to-do citizens, for the young men of the middle class, and for apprentices. There was also an Institute, which displayed over ten thousand specimens illustrating natural history and the useful arts. Usefulness, indeed, was perhaps the chief key to Albany life in the thirties. In official attitudes, at least, it was primarily the doctrine of utility that governed amusement, art, and education.

Nevertheless, Albany was by no means a puritanical town. It supported 415 taverns and drank, on the average, seven gallons of liquor per person every year.[12] Its judges, legislators, lawyers, and other eminent citizens foregathered regularly at the famous Eagle Tavern, whose proprietor, Leverett Cruttenden, was a Falstaffian figure with an international reputation for wit, hospitality, and thorough familiarity with the plays of Shakespeare.[13] "Albany is really very gay," wrote Mary Sanford in 1832; "there were 9 parties including the soirée last week." [14] For these *soirées,* or assembly balls, the elite of Albany society turned out every year. The dances were held at Stanwix Hall (built and owned by Peter and Herman Gansevoort) and were managed by such honorable citizens as John A. Dix and James Stevenson, the latter a close friend of Allan and Maria Melville's. For *hoi polloi* there were weekly balls conducted by Professors Graves and Whale and periodic Firemen's Balls, Apprentices' Balls, and Burgesses' Balls. Young men could entertain themselves at bowling and quoits at Castle Garden, stroll with their consorts in Academy or Capitol Park, and drop in for ice cream at the Mineral Springs, Meeks's, or Van Schoonhoven's. Other amusements included sleigh rides, excursions by river boats to nearby towns, displays of fireworks, circuses, and other traveling shows which brought a constant stream of dioramas and sideshow or vaudeville performers—Zionzcek, the Polish strong man, Mr. Wood, "whom nature in one of her wildest humours, [had] seen fit to deform in a most extraordinary manner," [15] the Siamese twins, equestrians, jugglers, and comic song artists.[16] In the Albany of 1830 old Dutch sobriety had yielded to the demand for entertainment that accompanies the accumulation of wealth and the growth toward cosmopolitanism.

Such was the city in which Herman Melville grew up. He was more than old enough now to have sharpened social sensitivities, to realize the advantages of being a grandson of General Peter Gansevoort and of belonging to the patrician class of Albany. Among his numerous relations he must have found companionship, interest, and warmth. In almost every street lived the friends and relatives—Ten Broeks, Van Schaicks, Van Vechtens, Gansevoorts—to whom his mother had been so glad to escape from the "fashionables" of New York. About two miles out in the country lived his cousins the Ten Eycks, in the elaborate mansion "Whitehall," which his Great-uncle Leonard Gansevoort had bought from the British General Bradstreet and which had been the home and headquarters of the General during the French and Indian Wars.[17] His parents, like his Uncle Peter and Aunt Mary Gansevoort, belonged to the caste that included statesmen and wealthy landowners like the Throops, the Stevensons, the Clintons, and the Van Rensselaers.[18] To be sure, the Gansevoort family, like most large clans, included one ne'er-do-well. Herman's Uncle Wessel Gansevoort, who drank heavily and had acquired a venereal disease, had been cut down from a one-fifth share in his father's estate to a niggardly allowance, to be paid only on condition that he live outside of Albany.[19] But aside from this skeleton in the family closet Herman's social background was unimpeachable, and he was undoubtedly aware of the distinction it furnished.[20]

Most certainly he passed many hours in the home of his grandmother and his Uncle Peter, where he had visited four years before. Here, in the old three-story Dutch house, were the relics of General Peter Gansevoort's glory: his diploma as a member of the Society of the Cincinnati, his silver-hilted sword, the portrait by Gilbert Stuart, the large brass drum he had captured from the British at Fort Stanwix.[21] Lafayette had called here in 1825 to pay his respects to the widow of a fellow soldier.[22] The parlors and dining room and bedrooms were a storehouse of history and of solid Dutch taste: green-baize hangings in the front room; pictures of the surrender of Cornwallis, of Washington, Jefferson, and William Pitt, and other "old oil paintings"; brass andirons with lion stands, brass tongs and poker, and an eight-day brass clock; a mahogany dining-room table and sixteen mahogany chairs; silver candlesticks, blankers and snuffers, porringers, cream pots and punch strainers; great mahogany wardrobes and bedsteads, with double mattresses and feather beds, pillows, and bolsters. The external appointments of elegance were there too—a well-cultivated flower garden, a stable, and a carriage house, where the Irish ostler Michael was overlord.[23]

Catherine Gansevoort died on December 30, 1830, and to her funeral, which her grandchildren undoubtedly witnessed, nearly four hundred friends were invited, including statesmen, merchants, physicians, ministers, and even booksellers.[24] Her son Peter lived on in the old house for three or four years. Then it was rented as a boardinghouse,[25] and much of its old Dutch furniture and silver was transferred to the Melville home.[26] In Herman's memories of his grandmother and grandfather, perpetuated also by the two silver tablespoons engraved with their names which Catherine Gansevoort ordered made for each of her grandchildren,[27] he was linked with the history of his country and its early aristocracy, and with a way of living that was comfortable, secure, and abundant.

But Catherine Gansevoort's influence on Herman's life

ended before the boy was in his teens. It was his kindly, earnest Uncle Peter who carried on the power of the old family and dispensed its accumulated wealth. In his early days he had graduated from the College of New Jersey, studied law in the office of Harmanus Bleecker, later American minister to the Netherlands, and served Governor De Witt Clinton as private secretary. At the time his sister's family needed help most, he had an affluent law practice and large property holdings and he was a state assemblyman and state senator besides, though being a Democrat in a Whig stronghold limited his power. If his business letters are models of decorum and precision, his more intimate correspondence partly veils and partly reveals a shy and affectionate nature. Albany wags made fun of his habit of bowing formally to acquaintances; his wife called him "Tibbee Tee." Without his wealth, his reputation for integrity, and his willingness to use both to aid his sister and her children, though ultimately it brought him to the verge of bankruptcy, Herman Melville's life in Albany might have been almost unrelieved misery.[28]

For outside one's circle of relatives—and perhaps inside as well—the victims of failure were not always greeted with the friendliness enjoyed by those known to possess property and bank accounts. There is evidence that Albany was outwardly pious but inwardly secular, preoccupied with making money and disposed to let the devil take the economically hindmost. We read of self-righteous convictions that the possession of virtue was inevitably rewarded by material goods and that sin was punished by poverty or death.[29] Herman Melville could not have escaped completely the cruel impact of such attitudes. How they affected him and his family is difficult to tell. But it is now clear, at least, that although his Albany years yielded harvests of tribulation and sorrow, they were also sown with hope and pleasure and the opportunity to enjoy the facilities for cultural expansion the city afforded.

For the first four months after his arrival in Albany

Allan Melvill was in desperate straits, forced to borrow steadily from his father and Peter Gansevoort, and at times in fear of prosecution for unpaid rent. But by February he was able to get along by himself.[30] He took a corner house at 338 North Market Street, five doors below the double house where Maria's mother and brother lived and conveniently near the fur store he was managing.[31] For over three years this was Herman Melville's home, and though more valuable in the eyes of the tax collectors than his grandmother's house and still respectable in its proximity to the homes of old Dutch families, it was flanked by a shop on one side and there was a temperance hotel across the corner, in unmistakable contrast to the aloof grandeur of northern Broadway. The currents of commerce, for which in his father's eyes Herman was showing a serious interest, were flowing perhaps a little too close to his immediate life for comfort.[32]

Nevertheless the comedown was, for the moment, largely geographical. His education in the best schools continued. One week after their arrival in Albany, he and Gansevoort began their studies at the Albany Academy. They still shared the company of children from the best families, as they had at the New York High School. There might be drastic economies at home, but attendance at a common public school was not among them.

The Albany Academy had been established and endowed in 1813 by such civic-minded people as Herman's grandparents to educate all except those "in a state of absolute penury." [33] Yet in 1832 common citizens complained that it "gave an education to one or two hundred young men of rich families, while the great body of the 6,000 youth of humble rank were neglected." [34] Although it catered to the wealthy, its curriculum no longer rested on the classics alone, for by 1830 it had adopted many technological studies valued for their "practical utility." These were the aims of the school according to Gideon Hawley, a trustee:

Our great aim is to make it subserve the following objects, to make study voluntary and agreeable to the pupil, to cause it to act directly on his *understanding,* and through that medium on his *memory;* to cultivate his inventive faculty, by exercises in composition and other processes requiring him to originate thought, and finally to teach him to apply the knowledge and skill thus acquired, to practical purposes most likely to occur to him in after life. All this might have been summed up by saying, that our peculiar mode of education always aims to qualify youth for the business pursuits of active life. *Practical* combined with *moral* education, is the primary law of our Institution; and to that everything else is either considered subordinate, or made to be subservient.[35]

The academy stood near the head of State Street hill in a broad park surrounded by an iron picket fence. The warm sandstone façade, ninety feet wide, the six tall pilasters, the lofty, arched windows of the exhibition hall on the second floor, the two neat wings, and the high, slender lantern—all announced a decorous and earnest spirit within.[36] The principal, T. Romeyn Beck, looked most formidable, with his crooked nose and a shock of hair like an unkempt wig, but even so students remembered him as tender as a woman in emotion, manly in character, and inspiring in the classroom. He was a distinguished scholar in medical jurisprudence, geology, and meteorology and like his colleagues, a ready wielder of the birch rod. The classics teacher, the Reverend Dr. Peter Bullions, was thorough and exact and wrote his own textbooks. Most famous of the faculty was Joseph Henry, whose invention of the electromagnet in 1829 laid the foundation for Morse's telegraph three years later. His mile-long circuit of wire, by which he proved that electric power could activate a magnet or ring a bell at a great distance, was ranged around the walls of an upper room for all the students to see.[37]

The routine of this academy was rigid, the discipline strict. The day began and ended with prayers. Students were required to study at least six hours a day. An intricate system of penalties involving loss of place in class standing, black-listing, suspension, or expulsion governed forbidden or unacceptable activities—immoral conduct, disobedience or disrespect to teachers, loud talking, leaving seats without permission, pulling or tossing of hats, even spilling ink on the floor, or "rude conduct towards each other." All class meetings were forbidden as being "unlawful combinations against the government of the Academy." The hand of the academy reached out to control its students even when they were far from its walls. All were required to attend a place of public worship on the Lord's day. And one section of the *Statutes,* a copy of which was given to every boy, reads:

> The conduct of Students, on their way home, or to the Academy, shall be decorous. Swearing, obscene language, fighting or rude conduct, shall put the offender to the foot of his classes, besides other punishment. And such offences, it is expected, will be reported, by those who wish to preserve a good standing.

One wonders just how many talebearers this system succeeded in creating. But it made some concession at least to the good in boys' nature. Teachers could exempt a class from the ordinary government provided the students pledged themselves to observe the laws. And for good conduct, for keeping one's name off the publicly posted black list, one would have the pleasure of seeing it on the merit roll and of wearing a blue ribbon at the prize examinations.[38]

To Melville the atmosphere of Albany Academy may have seemed an abrupt and hardly welcome change from the New York High School, where the curriculum was enlightened and a much more optimistic concept of the character of young boys prevailed. If he saw the birching the Principal gave fifty boys for snowballing a Helderberg farmer and the corporal punishments that were apparently an almost daily affair, he may have recalled regretfully that such treatment had been sharply restricted at his old school. The academy also went much further in the mating of religion and education. In addition to the daily prayers, religion was woven directly into the curriculum. In a prize examination in penmanship, for example, students wrote down, "A man without religion may be compared to a traveller who has lost his way in a pathless desert, having no guide to direct his steps." [39] On one occasion the students were dictated the first four sentences from Alexander's *Evidences of Christianity,* which, like Paley's *Moral Philosophy,* was studied in the later years. It would be interesting to know Melville's reaction to the curriculum and discipline of Albany Academy, to see how often his name appeared on the black list, which few could have escaped, or the merit roll, which few could have achieved, but unfortunately all records of the academy were destroyed in the fire of 1888, and one is left almost entirely to conjecture.

Some new and relevant facts, however, may be added to our knowledge of his career at the academy, which was only half as long as has been supposed. He entered on October 15, 1830, and was put into the fourth department, "in which very young boys, and others but little advanced in the rudiments of education, [were] instructed, preparatory to their admission into the next department." [40] Here he studied geography, reading and spelling, penmanship, arithmetic, English grammar, natural history, and Irving's catechisms of Grecian, Roman, English, and universal history, classical biography, and Jewish antiquities. The "reading books" were *Beauties of the Bible* and Trimmer's *Natural History.* His teacher for regular subjects was George W. Carpenter, a civil engineer who was soon to be surveyor for the city of Albany.[41] He was instructed in penmanship by Benjamin F. Foster, whose Carstairs method was praised by a board of examiners because it enabled the learner "to adopt any particular mode of writing, whether the bold and rapid style suited to the man of business, or the graceful ease and elegance of epistolary correspondence." [42] Melville's mode of writing shows mastery of neither style, as is well known, nor did he seem to learn much spelling. Although half a dozen boys in his class were eleven years old, like himself, and three were older,[43] his assignment to the lowest department substantiates his father's statement earlier in the year that he was a reluctant student. He had had at least four years of schooling in New York, probably more, and one would think that he ought to have been ready to begin the classical course at the academy, which took eight years to complete. But this was not the case. Melville studied no Latin during his first year; in the second he probably got through only the elementary grammar and reader for which the course called. Unless he took up Latin again at another school, this was all the formal education in the classics that Melville had.

Melville's education in English authors must have made literature seem like a mere appendage to the pulpit. The textbook was Murray's *English Reader,* of which Melville's copy still survives.[44] Here were gathered the most didactic selections from the prose and poetry of Dr. Johnson, Addison, Goldsmith, Cowper, Thomson, Pope, Young, and Hugh Blair, the Scottish preacher, whose sermons supplied nearly a fourth of the contents. The pious maxims of this little volume, its scorn for vice and praise for virtue, its Quaker sobriety, its benevolent humanitarianism derived from Lord Shaftesbury, and its unswerving use of poetry and prose as a vehicle for moral instruction made it as much an instrument of training in the Christian religion as in the correct style that it advocated. What effect it may have had on Melville's intellectual development is difficult to determine; perhaps there is some significance in the fact that the numerous allusions in Melville's juvenile sketches written in 1839 include no reference to any of the authors in Murray's *English Reader.* If Melville's youthful epistolary style shows the influence of the eighteenth century, his literary taste seems to have rejected the classical authors in favor of the romantics.

The educational system at the Albany Academy enabled one to learn much in brief space. It was the era when boys were ready for college at fifteen and sometimes graduated at seventeen. Melville went to school six or more hours a day, five days a week, forty-five weeks in the year. He made his daily recitations and earned his daily "numbers," on which his standing in the class was based. The system undoubtedly helped to build up the power of tenacious memory that would enable him in later years to recall with ease whatever he read or saw. Gideon Hawley spoke of the effort to appeal to the student's "inventive faculty" through exercises in composition; Melville must have written many of these and participated, like all his fellow students, in the competition for prize essays, though none of his schoolboy efforts in literature have survived. Instead, the only prize that he won seems to indicate an entirely different talent.

These prizes were distributed at semiannual examinations that the whole city was free to attend. A procession, including a band, students, faculty, trustees, judges and state officers, revolutionary soldiers, and parents, paraded from the City Hotel on Market Street up the steep State Street hill to the academy. The minister of the Dutch Church, Dr. Ludlow, opened the solemn proceedings in the great exhibition hall. Earnest students declaimed classical and patriotic selections.[45] At the end came the numerous premiums for scholarship, consisting of "books elegantly bound." [46] Among the number who marched up to the platform on August 4, 1831, was Herman Melville, to receive a "first best" in Ciphering Books.[47] This meant that for a full term he had led his class in mathematics and bookkeeping. The prize he took home was a half-leather copy of an English annual, *The Carcanet,* containing romantic poems by Byron, Moore, Scott, and others and fragments of prose from such authors as Young, Blair, Burke, Johnson, and Irving. Herman's immediate response to this public recognition of a distinctly nonliterary proficiency is not on record. Very possibly he was pleased. But at some time in his life his own prowess as a mathematician seems to have filled him with scorn. From the presentation notice pasted inside the cover, reading "Herman Melville, first best in his class in Ciphering Books," he carefully scraped the last two words. No one was to know that he had ever won a prize for such useful knowledge. The act has the mark of a youth who has turned in contempt from "practical education" to adoration of the Muses.

Of Herman's friendships during his two years at the academy little is known. He had the company of Gansevoort and later of Allan on his daily trips up the long hill. His older cousin Leonard Gansevoort was there as well as Stanwix and Hun Gansevoort, who were about Herman's age.[48] With Stanwix particularly he must have renewed the intimate friendship they had formed in 1826. Robert and Edward James, sons of an early Albany millionaire and future uncles of the novelist and the psychologist, were in the fourth department with Herman as was many a future Albany lawyer, merchant, banker, and clergyman.[49] However, he also associated with more plebeian boys, sons of butchers, carpenters, and shoemakers.[50] The activities of the students outside their lofty classrooms were limited. There were no baseball, football, or hockey teams, no program of physical exercise. Alexander W. Bradford, a friend of Herman's and Gansevoort's, later recalled internecine rivalries between "the Latins and the English" and "bitter foreign conflicts waged between the Hills and the Creeks, . . . a pugnacious tribe of barbarians who inhabited the shores of the Fox creek." [51] There were coasting in the winter and bathing in the Hudson in the summer. But the major portion of these two years was spent in learning.

Although Melville may have undertaken the classical course in his second year at the academy, it is more probable that his father, convinced of his bent for commerce, placed him in the mercantile course.[52] Gansevoort was the classical scholar, who had won prizes in ancient history and Roman antiquities (as well as in composition, penmanship, and English).[53] Herman's industry in ciphering may mean that he wanted a commercial career. On the other hand, a deeper current in him, perhaps one of which he had scarcely become conscious, may have been quietly contending against the utilitarian philosophy of his environment. Gideon Hawley boasted that American education had become

more and more practical, and *better and better* adapted to qualify youth, not for the subtile disputations of schoolmen, but for the *reali-*

ties, the *sober substantial realities* of a life of business, of *such* a life as every man desirous to act well his part in the world, must seek to live.[54]

Education, he thought, had undergone beneficial changes, "in proportion as the philosophy of Bacon, of Newton, or of Paley, is superior to that of Aristotle, or of Thomas Aquinas."[55] Thirty years later, Melville read in Madame de Staël's *Germany:* "A man, regarded in a religious light, is as much as the entire human race." Beside this he wrote: "This was an early and innate [?] conviction of mine, suggested by my revulsion from the counting-room philosophy of Paley."[56] Just when the revulsion began is not determinable. But it was undoubtedly inchoate when Melville was a schoolboy in an atmosphere that made Paley one of the gods.

At the end of his first year at the academy came a welcome interruption to his studies. In August 1831 Allan and Maria Melville went off to Boston on their usual summer vacation, taking Herman and Augusta with them. They stopped for two days in Pittsfield to visit Allan's brother Thomas, now a farmer, and years later Herman recalled this first meeting with his good uncle.

> Near this period I first saw him [he wrote]. It was in 1831, I think, at Evening, after a summer day's travel by stage from Albany. Well do I remember the meeting, upon that occasion, between him and my father. It was in the larch-shaded porch of the mansion looking off under urn-shaped roadside Elms, across meadows to South Mountain. They embraced, and with the unaffectedness and warmth of boys—such boys as Van Dyke painted.[57]

This passage, with one of the two known references to his father in Melville's writings, reveals much of the natural tenderness that Allan and Thomas seem to have felt for each other and that marked the associations of their two families.[58] Herman did not remain long at the farm; Augusta was left there, but he was taken on to Hadley to visit Aunt Lucy, now married to Justin Wright Clark, whom Maria Melville described as a "large well looking man of deep reading and observation."[59] Herman could now enjoy the vacation in Hadley that he had missed the year before through his father's bankruptcy.

The shift in fortune was deceitful and temporary. Spending the dog days by the cool Connecticut River was pleasant, and on going back to school Herman was no longer a new boy with friendships to make and strangeness to face. But the winter brought a stunning domestic tragedy. Allan Melvill was in business difficulties again by the end of the year. A trip to New York in early December for merchandise left him optimistic, but excessive overwork on his return led to nervous excitement that robbed him of his sleep. For a few days he "yielded to the wishes of his friends, and remained at home,"[60] reading the Dutch Psalm Book and Buckminster's *Sermons,* into which he wrote his reflections at the crisis of his existence.[61] He turned also to his Bible and found his troubles mirrored in the tormented Fifty-fifth Psalm, which he marked and dated January 5, 1832. "Give ear to my prayer, O God . . . The terrors of death are fallen upon me . . . ." To his premonitions he joined pleas for relief from persecution by the wicked. "Destroy, O Lord, and divide their tongues: for I have seen violence and strife in the city . . . Wickedness is in the midst thereof: deceit and guile depart not from her streets." The psalmist had been reproached by an intimate friend. Had Allan Melvill suffered likewise or been deceived in business?[62] He would then have shared the final consolation: "Bloody and deceitful men shall not live out half their days; but I will trust in thee."

Whether from worry or sickness or both, Allan Melvill shortly lost his reason. Four days after marking the psalm, his mind began to wander, and the next day he was deranged.[63] Summoned by Peter Gansevoort, Thomas Melvill hurried over from Pittsfield to find his brother "fierce, even maniacal." Doctors despaired of his recovery, and Thomas was driven to hoping against it because "in all human probability—he would live, a Maniac!"[64] For two weeks Allan lingered on in this condition. If young Pierre's presence at his father's sickbed had any foundation in life, Herman visited his father's bedroom frequently and heard his delirious maunderings.[65] One may imagine his grief and terror and that of the entire household as Allan Melvill's ravings resounded from the upper chamber. If we can have faith in Thomas Melvill's conjecture that recovery would still have left his brother insane, it must have been a merciful relief when, half an hour before midnight on Saturday, January 28, Allan died. For three days the mourners came to offer comfort. On Tuesday afternoon Maria and her children followed the hearse from their home up the steep hill to the common burying ground, in the Dutch Church section of which they watched Allan's body lowered into the grave. They might well have been thinking of the message of his last surviving letter—"my love to Maria . . . kiss the children for me . . . ." [66]

Although there is no direct evidence of the effect of Allan Melvill's death on Herman, the passages in *Redburn* that seem to reflect it are sufficiently in accord with the known facts to offer a fairly reliable guide. When Redburn sees the arch in Liverpool through which his father had passed many years before, he reflects ruefully upon

> all that must have happened to him since he paced through that arch. What trials and troubles he had encountered; how he had been shaken by many storms of adversity, and at last died a bankrupt.[67]

And Melville was very possibly speaking autobiographically when he wrote:

> But I must not think of those delightful days, before my father became a bankrupt, and died, and we removed from the city; for when I think of those days, something rises up in my throat and almost strangles me.[68]

One may be fairly sure that the death of such a loving father as Allan Melvill left the marks of enduring grief and melancholy in Herman's heart. It must also have robbed him of some of the sense of security that is important to the psychological health of a growing boy. It is certain that it changed the entire course of his existence, throwing him out into the world at a tender age to contribute to his support and substituting for the schoolboy's routine of books and classes, of jocund friendships and play, the young clerk's servitude to ledgers.[69]

In the physical sphere the loss of the head of the family was temporarily staggering. Allan Melvill died owing his father over twenty-two thousand dollars, a debt which was discharged, by his own previous insistence, from his share in his father's estate, leaving nothing for his own wife and children.[70] Another four thousand dollars owed to Peter Gansevoort had to be paid by drawing on Maria's legacy from her mother's unsettled estate.[71] Maria Melville ultimately received a fourth of her mother's large estate, of which only a small portion was absorbed by her husband's debts,[72] but for several months only Peter Gansevoort stood between the Melvilles and complete impoverishment.[73] Yet the family was resourceful and courageous. Gansevoort, who had attended to his father's business during his last illness, left school and took over the shop. Soon his mother and Uncle Peter launched him on a large scale into the wholesale and retail fur business.[74] By September he was anticipating net profits of $10,000 a year, and by February of 1833 he was preparing to meet an annual payroll of fifteen thousand dollars.[75] Within less than a year following Allan's death, the Melvilles had been restored to financial security.[76]

Very shortly after Gansevoort became a dealer in furs, Herman followed him into the business world. By the spring of 1832 he had become a clerk in the New York State Bank, of which his grandfather, the General, was a founder, and his Uncle Peter a trustee.[77] How he felt about this abrupt change in his life is not recorded; we can only speculate on what he meant by the single word "Bank" that he scrawled inside the back cover of his Murray's *Reader*. In the mahogany and oak interior of the bank building on State Street, one of the many by which the architect Philip Hooker had given Albany "its English look as against the old Dutch appearance," [78] Herman worked for two years—in the busy period that saw the expansion of railroads, canals, and a hundred business enterprises. Whatever his duties, one cannot imagine that his wages were very substantial. He was undoubtedly a mere apprentice, put to work to learn the business of banking, with the prospect of several years of patient toil before he could hope to rise in the scale. But his occupation was chosen for him with reason. One recalls his interest in commerce and his prize work in ciphering. Unlike Dickens, whose father's misfortune drove him into a miserable blacking factory, Melville's first position was probably suitable to his talents. And though he was not yet thirteen he was far from being the only boy of his background who had to exchange school for business. It was not at all unusual for youngsters of good families to begin working at an early age, and many of his own classmates left Albany Academy at thirteen or fourteen to become apprentices or clerks.[79]

Herman's first summer at the bank was punctuated by a dramatic flight to Pittsfield with the rest of the family to escape a plague of cholera. While citizens burned tar in the streets until, as Joel Munsell observed, "the city was several hours wrapt in a dense black smoke, and must have looked very much like Sodom," [80] the Melvilles piled their bedding atop a stagecoach and drove forty miles through the rain to Uncle Thomas's farm.[81] A picture of the life Herman must have led during this and other visits comes from a letter of his mother's:

> The family are very kind, the Children live on bread and milk, look brown & healthy—all have gain'd flesh, & my baby Tom is the picture of plenty & good nature, The air is delightful, we literally breathe sweets, the atmosphere is fill'd with fragrance from the new-mown hay, all around us, Gansevoort is employed in raking & turning Hay, Fishing, rowing the Ladies across, & around a large pond back of the house & in doing ample justice to the excellent Milk & delicious bread & Butter of the Farm we are happy here, but would wish to return to town as soon as would be prudent—[82]

But after only five days of these country joys, Herman returned, at his uncle's request, to Albany. There he lived through the terrible days of July and August when over eleven hundred cases of cholera developed and four hundred people died. The mayor called for a day of "prayer, fasting, and humiliation," which was observed on August 3 with all stores closed.[83] Such a response to public calamity may very well have had a deep effect upon the young bank clerk, whose later attitude toward mass misery would be, in part, a religious one.[84]

Although Herman was now in his uncle's care, his mother continued to show her customary interest and affection. Soon after his departure from Pittsfield she expressed the hope that Herman was "made to occupy his time when out of the Bank in reading, & writing to me." [85] Apparently he fulfilled her expectations, for on August 7 she wrote:

> My best love to Herman His last letter was much praise'd, for its superiority over the first, the hand writing particularly, he must practice often, & daily.[86]

The next day she added to a letter of her daughter Helen's to Uncle Peter: "My best love to Herman, who I hope is a good Boy & endeavours to make himself useful by writing &c." [87] She meant copying papers in Peter Gansevoort's law office, not literary endeavor, and her concern for her son's behavior is clearly an offshoot of her principle, stated in the same letter, that "a Boy without employment is a troublesome intruder, & ready to be tempted." Indeed, Maria Melville's entire attitude toward her son was a mingling of love with the hope that he would prove himself both good and "useful." Her interests and sentiments are noteworthy in a woman who has been popularly imagined as austerely proud and niggardly in affection. One can hardly imagine a more normal mother. And any suspicion of insensitivity to budding genius must be modified by the fact that at this time Herman seems to have displayed no artistic talents. One wonders, for example, why Herman should have to be *made* to occupy his spare time in reading. Was he still averse to books as he had been in his schooldays in New York? Or was the required reading not to his liking? One cannot know. But it is not apparent that up to this point Herman had any such passion for learning as had induced his brother Gansevoort to read Rollins' *Ancient History* and similar works before he was eleven.[88]

For two years after the cholera scare Herman lived the uneventful life of a bank clerk, walking daily from the house where his father had died to the stately bank building two streets distant. Sometimes the bank sent him out of town on business; once he rode on the new railroad over to Schenectady with his fellow clerk Frederick Leake and had to put up over night at Davis' Tavern. There Gansevoort, to his great surprise, accidentally ran into him "in the barroom,"[89] where Herman was perhaps celebrating his temporary release from watchful eyes at home with a glass of ale or wine. Or the boy may have felt that since he was expected to live in a man's world he had a right to indulge in its pleasures. At any rate he must have matured considerably if the bank was willing to entrust him with its affairs outside the city.

The only other interruption to Herman's work in the bank was a week's vacation on Uncle Thomas's farm in August 1833.[90] Meanwhile, Gansevoort's fur business, though sometimes shaky, was prospering, and in the spring of 1834 the family moved into a new house at Number Three Clinton Square, a small and recently created park adjacent to the North Dutch Church.[91] At about the same time, Peter Gansevoort, who had made a distinguished marriage to Mary Sanford, daughter of the Chancellor of New York, brought his bride to live in Number One Clinton Square, two doors from his sister. The Melvilles were now back in surroundings as elegant as those they had left in New York. Daily they climbed the flight of brownstone steps to an entrance flanked by staid Ionic columns, luxuriated in the two high-ceilinged parlors with tall windows and black marble fireplaces, and retired at night to comfortable bedrooms on the third floor and in the garret. Below stairs was a full basement where Maria's "woman" did the cooking.[92] At the back of the yard was a stable where Gansevoort kept the two horses he could now afford, one to haul the store wagon, the other for business trips and pleasure riding.[93] Gansevoort's success meant also, for his sisters, the opportunity to continue their education in Albany's best private school. Augusta, Catherine, and Priscilla Frances could now attend the select Albany Female Academy.[94] In the general prosperity the dark pall cast over the family by the death of Allan Melvill must have lightened considerably.

Why Herman should have exchanged these surroundings for the rigors of life on a farm is a puzzle. Yet it is certain that he had given up clerking in the bank by the late spring of 1834, and it is almost certain that he spent most of this year working with his Uncle Thomas in Pittsfield.[95] His reason for leaving the bank has been assigned by guesswork to weakness in mathematics, restlessness, and plain failure. One has just as much right to conjecture that a combination of festering grief and cumulative shock at the death of his father together with long hours on a high stool in a back room recording bills and loans had injured his health. In any case he was to enjoy in the long months in Pittsfield the company of a man whose rich experiences would fill out the inevitable tedium of a farm hand's life.

This was his Uncle Thomas, a banker and gentleman reduced to farming, of whom Herman was very fond despite or perhaps because of his many misfortunes. He had made much money in Paris by 1800, had entertained lavishly, known Lafayette and James Monroe and Joel Barlow, and been acting American consul.[96] His marriage in 1802 to Marie des Douleurs Fleury united him to one of the first bankers of Paris, M. Recamier, an uncle who had adopted her.[97] But "fortune and his own too sanguine temper were his undoing," Melville wrote later, continuing:

I remember his telling me that upon one occasion, after prosperously closing in London some considerable affair, he held in his hands, before a cheery coal fire, the proceeds—negotiable bills, and for so large a sum, that he said to himself—holding them at arm's length, "This much is sure—here it is—the future is uncertain. Break it off, then, and get thee back to Boston Common." But a false friend—Hope by name (not one of the noted Amsterdam House) advised to the contrary.[98]

After losing his fortune Thomas Melvill returned to America in 1811, became commissary at Pittsfield with the rank of major during the War of 1812, and afterwards settled down in "Broadhall" to farm. The mansion, with its "ample hall and staircase, carved woodwork, and solid oaken timbers . . . remind[ing] one of the massive gundeck beams of a line-of-battle ship," [99] overlooked the broad acres from which he eked out no more than a bare living for his numerous family. His mottled career included a rejected appointment to the United States Senate, a term in the state legislature, and several terms in jail for debt.[100] Indeed, life on his uncle's farm may have been healthful, but it must also have taught Herman the woes of poverty. Although the Major answered his young nephew's pleas for stories with intimate pictures of Versailles and "those martial displays and spectacles of state which he had witnessed in Paris in the time of the first Napoleon," [101] he was forced at times to wear the same set of underwear all winter,[102] and not one of his many letters about the farm reveals anything but hard times, with frequent sickness and sometimes death. Imprudent but lovable and penitent for the indiscretions that had reduced him, Uncle Thomas embraced the Episcopal creed,[103] put his faith and confidence in God, and endeavored "to submit without murmuring . . . [to] an over-ruling Providence." [104]

With this mild-mannered and kindly gentleman with the "faded brocade of old French breeding," whose contrast with his rural surroundings was touched by pathos, Herman often shared the chores of the farm.

. . . I frequently raked with him in the hay-field [he says]. At the end of the swath, he would at times pause in the sun, and taking out his smooth-worn box of satinwood, gracefully help himself to a pinch of snuff, partly leaning on the slanted rake, and making some little remark—quite naturally, and yet with a look which—as I now recall it—presents him in the shadowy aspect of a courtier of Louis XVI, reduced as a refugee, to humble employment in a region far from the gilded Versailles.[105]

Herman used to watch his "plainly clad but courtly uncle" exchange pinches of snuff with Edward A. Norton, a widely traveled man of fortune, in the barroom of Pittsfield's principal tavern while they bandied reminiscences of the Continent. He concludes his recollections on an affectionate note:

By the late October fire, on the great hearth of the capacious kitchen of the old farm-mansion, I remember seeing the Major frequently sit just before early bed-time, gazing into the embers, his face plainly expressing to a sympathetic observer that his heart—thawed to the core under the influence of the genial flame—carried him far away over the ocean to the gay Boulevards.

Suddenly, under the accumulation of reminiscences, his eye would glisten, and become humid. With a start he would check himself in his reverie, and give an ultimate sigh; as much as to say, "Ah, well!" and end with an aromatic pinch of snuff. It was the French graft upon the New England stock which produced this autumnal apple; perhaps the mellower for the frost.

. . . But enough. He survives in my memory, a cherished inmate—kindly and urbane—one to whom, for the manifestations of his heart, I owe unalloyed gratitude . . . .[106]

Besides his uncle, Herman found companionship among his many cousins. Three of them—Thomas, Priscilla, and Henry—seem to have derived intense passions from their French and Spanish mother.[107] The others were the Yankee sons and daughters of Thomas Melvill's second wife Mary, who endured with astonishing fortitude the birth of nine children and the hardships of farm life and later the frontier.[108] But it was Thomas, the eldest, whose life may have borne most heavily upon that of his younger cousin.

In the New York days Herman had undoubtedly heard of Thomas's part in the cruise of the U.S.S. "Vincennes." He had been to Tahiti and Hawaii, and at the Marquesas Islands he had visited the Typee Valley where Herman was to spend a month in captivity only eight years later.[109] If Tom's adventures in the remote Pacific islands aroused dreams of exotic lands in Herman, his subsequent career may very well have contributed a precedent for a very different sort of life from that of the romantic officer of the United States Navy. For in 1834 Tom had been forced to resign his commission after neglecting three times to take a prescribed examination.[110] It seems that in his disgrace he refused to return to his father and took to drinking.[111] Whatever the causes, he used desperate remedies. On June 7, 1835, he shipped on the Fairhaven whaler "Columbus" for the Indian and Pacific Oceans, and for the next ten years, until his death on the whaler "Oregon" in 1844, he served on one whaling ship after another, spending only a few months ashore between voyages.[112] Whether Herman Melville ever saw him between trips is impossible to prove. But he must have known what Tom was doing. The two branches of the Melvill family were very close, as the multiplicity of visits to Pittsfield and Maria's expeditions to Lenox when Uncle Thomas was in jail readily indicate. One cannot calculate the effects on Herman of having a cousin who had embarked on the adventurous business of whaling. It may be imagined, however, that his adolescent imagination surrounded cousin Tom with a romantic aura that would help determine his own course a few years thereafter.

Of Melville's other cousins in Pittsfield and of his relations with them, few records survive. One wonders how he responded to cousin Henry, who was "not of *sane mind,*" [113] although he appears to have been harmless. More interesting, for her possible contribution to the character of Isabel in *Pierre,* was Priscilla Melvill. A letter of hers, warm with memories of the pleasures the Melvill cousins had enjoyed together, reveals a romantic and passionate nature from which Melville may have borrowed the incandescent ardor of Pierre's fateful half sister. Writing to Augusta Melville shortly after the marriages of Herman and Allan, she begs forgiveness for neglecting to answer her warmly welcomed letter.

> Will you not cast the broad mantle of charity [she begs] over this piece of seeming neglect—and take me to your heart again, as on certain freezing mornings that are within the memory of both of us—when I was wont to be encircle'd in those graceful arms of yours, tighten'd by the chords of affection (& something else—that I will not name even on paper) untill I could fancy myself clasped in the cold embrace which we poor mortals think of with dread—perhaps you are shocked and besides, must think it strange that I feel a desire, to revive sensations that cause a shudder through the shrinking frame—But my pen is running wild tonight—& I must not allow it to be so unmanageable.[114]

Like Isabel, Priscilla's mother had been French and had died when she was young and her father was an American gentleman. It is very probable that Melville drew some lineaments of his most baffling character from memories of this dynamic cousin.[115]

Melville's Pittsfield experience brought him a simple and healthful existence, an acquaintance with earthy country life as opposed to the urban niceties of New York and Albany, and an introduction to manual labor that would prepare him for dipping his hand into the tar pot as a sailor. The travels of his uncle and his cousin added further range and variety to the large if vicarious experience he had already gleaned from his father and his Gansevoort cousins. And life on the farm, where the daily fare was largely bread, butter, and milk, where there was never enough money for the needs of living, not to mention taxes and debts, and where his beloved uncle had only his "Sunday cloathes" to work in,[116] must have constituted an apprenticeship to the poverty that was, in a short time, to affect his own family.

But as in his own home, the spirit of Christian submission was dominant. Thomas Melvill once wrote to his father:

> I do not complain, at my situation, as it respects myself, individually it is just and right—it is the just recompense of past follies, and imprudence—But that my poor family should consequently suffer for them—Ah, there's the rub! . . . and it would be insupportable, were it not that I have at length learnt to put my confidence & trust where alone it ought ever to have been.[117]

A strongly moral tone, an acceptance of evil as just punishment for one's sins, were thus part of the atmosphere in Uncle Thomas's household. Herman was also exposed to the tenets of the Episcopal Church, of which his uncle was a vestryman [118] and which would have added something to his own religious inheritance of mingled Calvinism and Unitarianism. One wonders too whether Melville received any impress of Catholicism, for Thomas Melvill's French wife had been a Catholic and on her deathbed had expressed the wish that her daughter Priscilla be raised in her own faith.[119] We have, of course, no outside index to Herman's religious life during these months with his uncle. But he must at least have become aware that other creeds besides his own could attract good and pious people, and the fact that his own relatives belonged to them ought to have contributed a foundation for a spirit of religious tolerance.

Melville's sojourn in rustic Pittsfield seems to have ended early in 1835. Possibly tiring of his farm labors, he returned to Albany and went to work for Gansevoort, whose business, despite a fire in the factory he had built the previous year, was again flourishing.[120] For nearly two years Herman worked in the narrow three-story brick shop down on South Market Street where a hundred shopkeepers vied for business, where young "counter-jumpers" gathered in doorways to stare impudently and dart facetious remarks at the ladies passing by, and where one sometimes found "an enormous quantity of dead rats" piled before a neighbor's store.[121] Here where Herman's father had lost the battle against doom, Gansevoort, who was not yet twenty-one, was winning success as a man of business, known and accredited in New York as well as in Albany. Gansevoort bought the stock, kept the accounts, and engineered, with the help of his mother and uncle, the bank loans, which sometimes amounted to as much as $20,000. It is clear from the inventories, the money invested, and the turnover that the store was by no means a Pyncheon cent shop but a substantial enterprise which might well have produced a modest fortune. Although the main business was wholesale, Gansevoort also catered to everyday shoppers, sometimes bringing in his own fine lady friends to examine a cape or fur hat.[122] Herman's experience was useful in helping with the books, but he waited on customers too.[123] In the summer he sold plain cloth caps and "Brush Hats of the finest quality" and in the winter Morocco and Circassian caps, buffalo robes, and raccoon sleigh robes.[124] His wages were possibly five dollars a week, enough at least to provide a little independence.[125] Many times, while Gansevoort was touring the surrounding country or going as far away as Baltimore to sell furs or collect debts, Herman must have been in charge of the shop. He was now enmeshed in a family business, and there is every reason to suppose that with its continued success he might have become a partner with Gansevoort and lived out his days as an obscure Albany merchant.

He still felt the need of education, however, and about the time he went in with Gansevoort he entered the Albany Classical School,[126] an institution which had just opened an "elegant building" across Clinton Square from the Melville house.[127] Here Herman found himself under the instruction of Charles E. West, a young chemistry and natural history scholar who had formerly tutored the sons of De Witt Clinton and Governor Marcy and who had founded the school.[128] Its stated aims were "to secure the two great ends of education; the cultivation of the intellect and the formation of character under the influence of the Christian religion." [129] Charles West had recently become an ardent Presbyterian, and the principal, Samuel Center, was a clergyman.[130] As at the Albany Academy religion and education were again joined in Melville's schooling. But the Classical School paid shrewd attention to reality, for besides offering the classical and English courses Center and West assured their patrons that they furnished every facility to prepare young men for business careers.[131] Melville's interests, however, seem to have undergone a change now that he had come to know through firsthand experience what commerce was like. Years later Charles E. West remembered him as a favorite pupil, not distinguished in mathematics, but very much so in the writing of "themes" or "compositions," and fond of doing it, while the great majority of pupils dreaded it as a task, and would shirk it if they could.[132]

One may imagine that experience in the mercantile world, the world for which his father had considered him most apt, had now begun to generate currents of resistance which he discharged through his youthful pen.

Perhaps too he was finding stimulus in his own uncharted reading. At some time between leaving the academy and writing his first essays, in 1839, he had read widely, if not deeply, in poetry, ancient history, and art. Where did he get the books in which to build up the facility of reference that sparkles in these *juvenilia?* In describing Pierre's cultured development, Melville says: "Not in vain had he spent long summer afternoons in the deep recesses of his father's fastidiously picked and decorous library."[133] In the conventional interpretation of *Pierre* as transparent autobiography, this casual sentence has been accepted as proof that Melville did all his early reading from his father's books. Yet a considerable number of those books had been disposed of sometime in the 1820's, and one wonders how many actually survived Allan Melvill's financial troubles and his loss of active interest in reading. There must have been some other field for Herman's literary excursions.

He may have drawn books from the Athenaeum, like Gansevoort, or the Albany Library, of which Uncle Peter was a member.[134] Such novels as T. S. Surr's *Jacqueline of Holland,* Lockhart's *Reginald Dalton,* Thomas Colley Grattan's *Winter in London,* and *Thaddeus of Warsaw* were always about the house as well as more serious works like Watts's *The Improvement of the Mind.*[135] Since Gansevoort took the trouble to write out careful criticisms of whatever he read, the discussion of current reading was doubtless a habit in the household. It was probably at this time that Herman began to read Byron, who was one of Gansevoort's favorites, and Scott, whose *Tales of a Grandfather* Gansevoort owned in eight volumes.[136] The novels of Cooper were also popular in the family circle. Peter Gansevoort was a personal friend of Cooper's and his library contained *The Red Rover*.[137] Gansevoort read *The Prairie* in 1834 and greatly admired the characters of Paul Rover and Ishmael Bush. And years later Herman said that Cooper's works were "among the earliest he could remember" and that in his boyhood they produced "a vivid and awakening power" on his mind.[138] Specifically, he remembered reading and enjoying *The Red Rover* in these "uncritical days" of his youth.[139]

But whatever opportunities to read may have been offered by Peter Gansevoort's personal collection and his membership in the Albany Library, Herman shortly had the chance to draw directly from another library, whose books were chosen particularly for their appeal to a younger generation. On January 29, 1835, Herman became a member of the Albany Young Men's Association, and until the spring of 1837 he enjoyed its privileges.[140] This association was open to young men from sixteen to thirty-five, "without distinction of pursuits, profession, or calling." [141] It had a debate hall and comfortable reading rooms in a pleasant brick building on North Market Street not far from Gansevoort Melville's fur store. Here the members could sit and read the latest newspaper or magazine, browse in the library, or chat about the all-engaging subject of politics. Perhaps Herman owed his election when only fifteen to the influence of Gansevoort, who had become an active debater in the group, and who was later elected to the Executive Committee.[142]

But the library offered a wide range of riches to explore, for it was "the peculiar aim of the Association to cherish . . . a taste for literary pursuits." [143] Here were a thousand picked volumes containing most of the standard British and American poets, novelists, and essayists, numerous books reflecting interest in "the sciences and their application to the useful arts," [144] scores of volumes on morals, ethics, and religion, strongly liberal in their point of view, and many books of travels, history, biography, and statecraft.[145] The works of Byron and Moore, and the *Arabian Nights,* upon which Melville drew in his first writings, were here in great quantity; here he could have found Shakespeare and Sheridan, Coleridge and Chesterfield, and other authors whom he was later to use for decoration; it was here that he undoubtedly read Peter Porcupine and Junius, whose style he admired, and learned something about the work of Locke and Newton. His interests were also serious enough to induce him to read the *Edinburgh Review,* to which he refers familiarly in a letter in 1837.[146] The catalogue of this library forms the basis for Melville's first known reading list.

The association had other intellectual resources besides its bookstacks. The club encouraged members to write essays upon subjects of their own choice, the best of which were read publicly. Perhaps Melville took advantage of this opportunity to slip occasional fugitive sketches into the box set up for the purpose. In all probability he attended some of the very popular lectures that were a regular part of the association's goal of "mutual improvement." He must have joined the large audiences at the debates, especially those in which Gansevoort took part, on such subjects as whether the poor laws ought to be abolished and whether genius is innate. The regular debating group of the association withered, however, in 1836 and died completely the next year, and Herman, who was now old enough to command attention in public contests, joined first the Ciceronian Debating Society and when that failed, the Philo Logos Society. Apparently he plunged into the activities of the organization with passionate vigor, for he soon found that he had acquired an unenviable reputation and at least one enemy. Taking advantage of the debased standards of contemporary journalism, a correspondent who signed himself "R." complained of Herman's conduct to the public at large through the columns of the *Albany Microscope* on April 15. All associations, he wrote, were bothered by "pestiferous animals of a two-legged kind; who have crept in unawares, and scattered the seeds of dissolution in the once fair and flourishing institutions . . . . Such an animal is the P***o L***s Society cursed with. He is there known by the title of Ciceronian Baboon; and his personal appearance fully establishes the correctness of the title. He is also known as *dignitatus* melvum . . . ." R's venomous letter went on to outline the success the society had enjoyed in achieving its purpose of "improvement in composition, elocution and debate . . . until the bohun upus melvum was transplanted into its fertile soil, from the Ciceronian Debating Society, of which he was the principle [*sic*] destroyer." The main charge against Melville was that like a "wary pettifogger" he had "no fixed principles but can hear as the wind blows without gripings of conscience. This he considers a masterly display of his political powers." It was R's hope that in thus exposing this "two-faced gentleman" he was warning Albany associations not to accept his ilk, and if they had already done so he hoped they would get rid of him speedily.

The attack was mean in spirit and pretty clearly the work of a jealous rival for leadership. Herman did not answer. There was little for him to say, for his assailant was skulking behind a lone initial, and even if Herman had known who he was, there was no issue on which to contest him. But it will be apparent that the vindictive and cowardly attack in no way deterred Herman from enthusiastic work in the Philo Logos Society. The Albany press carried no reports of its debates, but Herman must certainly have done his share in making them spirited.

In the Philo Logos Society, as in the Young Men's Association, Herman was thrown into the company of lawyers, teachers, businessmen, and painters, who took an active interest in art, letters, and public affairs. The atmosphere no doubt stimulated his inner drives toward intellectual expansion. There were also other activities, which may be inferred from various hints. In the summer, Herman went swimming in the Hudson: for years later, when he was in the Pacific, he recalled "the noble stream upon whose banks [he] was born; in whose waters [he] had a hundred times bathed." [147] There is evidence that he went to William Duffy's Theater, which his Uncle Peter occasionally patronized. If the experience Melville records in his story "The Fiddler" is autobiographical, he attended with great delight at least one performance by the actor and violinist Joseph Burke, an astonishing English prodigy, who at the age of fifteen had taken both England and America by storm.[148] Doubtless he went, like his brothers and sisters, to traveling menagerie shows, lectures, or cotillions.[149] And Herman probably took part in patriotic displays, like the parade of the Albany Young Men's Association on July 4, 1836. The group marched from its rooms in Knickerbocker Hall to the Second Presbyterian Church, where songs, prayers, and odes were offered and where "the Declaration of Independence was read, and well read," by Gansevoort Melville.[150]

There was also much pleasant family intercourse during these years. Maria Melville, whose husband once said she loved her brother Peter more than himself or her children,[151] may have found it difficult to yield first place in his affections to her new sister-in-law, but she declared to Peter that she loved her "for her own self independent of her lord," [152] and Mary Sanford Gansevoort's son Henry preferred to play with Maria's children instead of at his own house.[153] It is difficult to believe that dinner parties at Peter Gansevoort's, where Clintons, Van Rensselaers, and Van Burens were entertained,[154] did not sometimes include his sister and some of her children. To this generous uncle, on whom the family still depended, Herman had undoubtedly transferred some of the affection he had for his own father. He would have called at Number One Clinton Square frequently. Herman's other uncle, for whom he was named, occasionally came down from the north to stay for a long visit with his sister and nephews and nieces, and perhaps Herman shared Gansevoort's feeling that Uncle Herman was "a very pleasant man in a family," more than any other he knew.[155]

Herman's other Aunt Mary, whom Maria thought of as the "guardian Angel" of her children when she was away,[156] was also living in Albany, with her sons Stanwix, Leonard, and Guert, and the Melvilles joined them in jovial family gatherings[157] or exchanged popular novels.[158] Guert had returned to Albany in 1831 from a three-year cruise on the U.S.S. "St. Louis," which had taken him to the west coast of South America and Mexico.[159] From another cousin, Midshipman Hun Gansevoort, Herman may also have received accounts of remote lands.[160] And at "Whitehall," where his Ten Eyck cousins lived, Herman could assimilate, on occasional visits, the stream of colonial and national history that surrounded the spacious old mansion and the air of comfortable Dutch wealth gleaming from every piece of silver and brocaded hanging.[161]

To his numerous brothers and sisters Herman seems to have been close, though much of the evidence comes from later years. They were bound by mutual obligations and common suffering. But it fell upon the two older boys, Gansevoort and Herman, to provide for the needs of all the others, and they tried to maintain their mother and sisters and smaller brothers in the way of life that Allan Melvill had wanted them to have. Thus Helen was sent to the exclusive boarding school in Lenox, Massachusetts, of Mrs. Sedgwick, the sister-in-law of the novelist.[162] Helen's lameness was a concern to all the family, and everybody was pleased when, in her seventeenth year, an operation finally enabled her to walk without limping.[163] Her esteem for Herman prompted her to hope for letters from him when they were separated.[164] Like Gansevoort, she had read romantic Oriental literature and was wont "to sigh after the spicy gales and aromatic breezes of eastern climes."[165] If Herman was too young at that time to share a passion for the exotic East with his older sister, he ultimately acquired it, as his writings a few years later prove. His fondness for Helen endured into manhood, when he presented her with a copy of his *Battle Pieces* inscribed "Mrs H M Griggs from her affectionate brother H. M."[166]

Herman's sister Augusta appears to have had the deepest literary sensitivities among the girls in the family. Maria Melville would sometimes read to her daughters such fictionalized sermons as *Justina, or The Will,*[167] but it was Augusta who responded most actively. Early in her youth she began to collect and memorize all the poems of Vaughan, Herbert, and Crashaw she could lay hands on.[168] By fifteen she was writing compositions on such figures as Luther, Grotius, and John Howard, the English prison reformer.[169] She was perfervidly religious, thrilling to Sabbath-school hymns, and viewing death and salvation as a happy release from life's heaped sorrows.[170] Her letters limn a woman of supercharged emotions, full of gusto, impulsive, affectionate, and anxious for the affection of others. During the Albany years she formed a friendship with the family of the patroon, Stephen Van Rensselaer, which probably begot mutual visits between the Melvilles and the wealthiest family in the city.[171] Her brothers she worshiped, with the intensity of a sister at first and then of a lifelong spinster. She "idolized" Gansevoort; her "very heart strings were entwined about him." [172] And Herman was her "noble-souled brother" whose admirers automatically won a place in her heart.[173]

Allan Melville, Jr., was the "most rebellious" of the family, a constant anxiety to his mother and a thorn in the tender flesh of his Uncle Peter. He was four years younger than Herman and still a schoolboy in Albany Academy while Herman was sharing the responsibilities for the family maintenance. The bonds between them would later appear, however, in Herman's dedication of *Mardi,* his third novel, to Allan. Toward Catherine, Priscilla Frances, and Tom the baby, Herman appears to have had the warm affections of a much older brother. A later letter to Catherine is full of gentle flattery and tender nonsense,[174] and the passage in *Redburn* in which the hero recalls the "happy, careless, innocent look" upon his "little brother's face, when he was sleeping an infant in the cradle" [175] doubtless reflects Herman's kindly feelings. Tom would become his favorite brother, with interests in the sea that would bring them closer together than the business and professional careers which Gansevoort and Allan would follow.

But for the present, Herman, in his sixteenth and seventeenth years, was walking shoulder to shoulder with Gansevoort, and their mutual responsibilities would have reduced the gap of four years between them. With a majestic figure, "some might say colossal," and large black eyes and "the glance of a Webster," [176] Gansevoort was earnest, methodical, and conscientious, if somewhat egotistical and humorless. Under pressure, he could, like his mother, become cross and scold those about him.[177] He had turned an intellect well-trained in the classics to profit in business despite natural inclinations toward oratory, politics, and law. Catapulted into the position of head of the family, he matured quickly, and he doubtless guided or sought to guide his brother. Gansevoort was fond of Herman and solicitous for his welfare,[178] though it is difficult to believe that his stolidity could have encouraged the closest sympathy. It is certain, from the disparate paths they took, that their temperaments contrasted sharply, Gansevoort being cool, deliberate, and persistent, Herman ardent and mercurial.

Among the other links that bound Herman to his family was their religious life. The great bell of the North Dutch Church was constantly booming in his ears from the steeple a few yards from his house. His mother had joined this church by profession of faith shortly after her husband's death, and Helen and Augusta followed her into that communion.[179] Membership records list neither Herman nor his brothers, but Herman went to Sunday services with his family, probably taking his place in the gallery with the other "Sunday scholars"—an unruly lot, it seems, for we hear the complaint that "Playing with penknives, and pins, kicking & jostling each other [was] of common occurrence." [180] There is no doubt that he attended the Sabbath school regularly, for his mother considered its religious instruction indispensable to a boy's early training.[181] When he was older, it seems, he could make his own decisions about churchgoing, as did the hard-working Gansevoort, who drily confided to his journal that he stayed home from church on the theory that Sunday was a day of rest.[182]

Herman's minister at first was the Reverend Dr. John Ludlow, a large man of "muscular frame and hard features," with an eye "clear and almost stern," and a voice that "thundered through the largest edifice, commanding the most distant hearer, and often overpowering those who sat nearer to the pulpit." If he was gentle and considerate as a spiritual counselor, his theology was ponderous and resembled that "of the most evangelical Reformers." [183] John Ludlow must have had a special care for the Melvilles, for Maria's mother had depended upon him for years and had given freely to his church and it is clear that Maria conversed with him often after her husband's death.[184] When he left the pastorate in 1834, he was replaced by Thomas E. Vermilye, whom the young Melville might well have found more to his taste. While his preaching was evangelical, it resulted in no "sensational effects" and was marked by "grace of manner and beauty of style." Besides, he had strong literary tastes, "a peculiarly genial spirit," and a cordiality that included not only the devotees of other faiths but those of no church at all.[185] No trace of Herman's reactions to these ministers of the Gospel remains in his works or letters, but the thundering vociferousness of the one and the genteel moderation of the other must have had their share in fixing his attitude toward the church.

It was doubtless during his Albany years that he was required to build upon the foundation of earlier studies the elaborate structure of the Reformed creed contained in the official catechism. The simple concepts of God and of one's relation to him that were suitable for childhood had to be enlarged by those studied definitions which would fortify the visions of faith with the certainties of reason. The growing youth must learn why he believed what he believed. In his catechism Herman learned that man, though created good, was miserable and depraved because of the fall of Adam and Eve, that he was unable to do any good of himself, that God would punish both disobedience and corruption, that man could escape this punishment only through the mediation of Christ and the possession of true faith that his sins were forgiven him. Good works were required of him; he must love his neighbor, defend his good character, and "promote his advantage" wherever possible. He must relieve the needy, speak the truth uprightly, and yield himself to the Lord all the days of his life. Two majestic means to the knowledge of God existed: the created universe, "a most elegant book, wherein all creatures, great and small, are as so many characters leading us to contemplate the invisible things of God," and "the holy and divine Scriptures," in which God revealed His own sacred will. This will was omnipotent. Those who professed the faith in the Dutch Reformed Church devoutly affirmed that "not a hair of our head . . . nor a sparrow can fall to the ground without the will of our Father." They rejected "all that was repugnant to this, concerning the free will of man, since man is but a slave to sin." God's direction of affairs extended into every corner of the universe, and into all the events of human life: "herbs and grass, rain and drought, fruitful and barren years, meat and drink, health and sickness, riches and poverty, yea, and all things come not by chance, but by his fatherly hand." Yet it was also true that God would provide for all the needs of soul and body, and we may picture Herman Melville, in the midst of the tribulations of his adolescence, declaring that God "will make whatever evils He sends upon me, in this valley of tears, turn out to my advantage." [180]

To Herman's training in the catechism of the Reformed Church may be traced many of his mature attitudes. His pervasive humanitarianism reflects early indoctrination in the eleventh commandment. His perception of symbolic meanings in nature is linked to the interpretation of nature as a book allegorizing the invisible spiritual world. But the catechism also established a concept of the operations of the universe that the course of his own life must inevitably force him, like Job, to question. The church wisely attempted to instill in the individual an unshakable faith, enabling him to endure all things and be patient in adversity and grateful for prosperity. Herman had to test this faith against the tormented death of his father and the abrupt shifts in his own fortune. In these events he had to perceive a pattern designed by God for his ultimate advantage. The unconditional affirmations of divine omnipotence must also have raised the questions of evil and of freedom of the will, in which he would exhaust himself during his maturity.

It is dubious, however, if these spiritual perplexities, from which some of his most profound writing emerged, would have settled upon him had he been allowed to go on living peacefully at Number Three Clinton Square, enjoying his family and friends, and watching his income grow with the profits from the fur and hat business. The store was prospering in the spring of 1836, for Gansevoort had to advertise for "Twenty Hat Trimmers" and "Two boys as apprentices to the Hatting Business." [187] This was the peak of prosperity, and therefore the appropriate time for the reversal. Sometime during the summer, perhaps as a result of the *Specie Circular* and the contraction of credit on all sides, a crisis developed in the little brick store. Maria Melville came to the rescue with mortgages and sales of her property by which she raised $6,000.[188] But by November Gansevoort's employees were begging for overdue wages, the rents of house and store were unpaid, and he was having difficulty meeting small bills.[189] Herman and Gansevoort were not so straitened that they could not pay their dues at the Young Men's Association in January 1837. However, the battle to maintain themselves and their family in a decent way of life had turned against them. In a few years they had valiantly overcome the disastrous effects of Allan Melvill's death. In the inscrutable wisdom of God, another ordeal of suffering was about to begin.

Chapter III

Pittsfield and Lansingburgh, 1837-1839

ON APRIL 15, 1837, Gansevoort went into bankruptcy, just as his father had done seven years before.[1] Within a few weeks his mother was driven to the same helpless expedient.[2] These financial humiliations marked the end of the short-lived era of prosperity, and for many years afterward the Melville family felt the relentless horrors of lawsuits, mortgage foreclosures, enforced sales of their personal possessions, unpaid debts, and poverty. For Herman, the following two years became a period of mounting crisis. Every effort to chip out a better foothold failed; it was even difficult to hold on at all. Meanwhile, he was developing psychologically, intellectually, and socially from nonage to the beginnings of manhood through events that would bring him to the first decisive moment in his career.

Herman knew immediately about his family's collapse. On April 28 he went to the New York State Bank where he had served two years as a clerk and watched his mother sign a bond for her enormous debt.[3] He was undoubtedly aware of the extent to which Gansevoort had gone down, with obligations of over thirty-three thousand dollars and assets of only seventeen thousand dollars.[4] He may even have known the sordid embarrassment of people forced to sacrifice their family silverware to importunate creditors.[5] His brother and his mother did their best to make honorable settlements. Both of them stipulated that from their assets the small debts owed to Albany tradesmen and to friends for borrowed money be paid first. In June Gansevoort went to New York to collect what he could from debtors in order to repay his own creditors as far as possible.[6] He spent much of the summer there in tedious efforts to wind up his broken business with credit, and from the wreck he salvaged enough to maintain the family in Albany. On July 20 he was able to send a hundred dollars to Frederick Yates, his landlord, "being in full for the rent of Ma's house until the 1st prox—," and in September he secured another hundred dollars.[7] But the family was in severe distress. On August 17 Maria Melville paid a bill of $6.44 on her brother's account and immediately wrote to him, "I shall be obliged to you for the small amount if convenient to day." [8] The honorable thing had been done, and the Melville family bore the ensuing sufferings. Since Allan was not learning anything at the Albany Academy, he was put to work as a clerk in his Uncle Peter's law office.[9] When the fall came, Herman met his responsibilities by going to Pittsfield and becoming a country schoolteacher.

One imagines that the name of Thomas Melvill had been helpful in securing Herman entrée in a profession which may have had more appeal than commerce to his aroused intellectual interests. In the spring of 1837 Thomas, as a member of the Pittsfield School Committee, had deplored "the lamentable state" of the common schools and found them behind the age in topics of study and modes of teaching and deficient in competent teachers.[10] Perhaps Herman was introduced as part of a hoped-for reform. For his personal experience in a country school we have his own story, as he wrote it to Peter Gansevoort.

Pittsfield Dec 31st 1837 [11]

My Dear Uncle

At my departure from Albany last fall with Robert [12] you expressed a desire that I should write you when my school should have gone into operation,—but, when in a few weeks I again returned, you did not repeat your request; still, however, I considered my promise binding—& it is with pleasure that I now proceed to redeem it.

I should have taken up my pen at an earlier day had not the variety & importance of the duties incident to my vocation been so numerous and pressing, that they absorbed a large portion of my time.

But now, having become somewhat acquainted with the routine of buisness,—having established a systim in my mode of instruction,—and being familiar with the charactars & dispositions of my schollars: in short, having brought my school under a proper organization—a few intervals of time are afforded me, which I improve by occasional writting & reading

My scholars are about thirty in number, of all ages, sises, ranks, charaters, & education; some of them who have attained the ages of eighteen can not do a sum in addition, while others have travelled through the Arithmatic: but with so great swiftness that they can not recognise objects in the road on a second journey: & are about as ignorant of them as though they had never passed that way before.

My school is situated in a remote & secluded part of the town about five miles from the village, and the house at which I am now boarding is a mile and a half from any other tenement whatever—being located on the summit of as savage and lonely a mountain as ever I ascended. The scenery however is most splendid & unusual, embracing an extent of country in the form of an Ampitheatre sweeping around for many miles & encircling a portion of your state in its compass.

The man with whom I am now domicilated is a perfect embodiment of the traits of Yankee character,—being shrewd bold & independant, carrying himself with a genuine republican swagger, as hospitable as "mine host" himself,[13] perfectly free in the expression of his sentiments, and would as soon call you a fool or a scoundrel, if he thought so—as, button up his waistcoat.—He has reard a family of nine boys and three girls, 5 of whom are my pupils—and they all burrow together in the woods—like so many foxes.

The books you presented me (and for which I am very gratefull) I have found of eminent usefulness, particularly John O Taylors "Dristict School"—an admirable production by the by, which if generally read is calculated to exert a powerful influence and one of the most salutary & beneficial charactar.—

I have given his work a diligent and attentive perusal: and am studying it, to the same advantage,—which a scholar traveling in a country—peruses its hystory,—being surrounded by the scenes it describes.

I think he has treated his theme in a masterly manner, and displays that thourough knowledge of his subject—which is only to be obtained by Experience.

Had he been perfectly familiar with the circumstances of this school,—the difficultys under which it labours, and in short with every thing pertaining to it,—he could not have sketched it in a more graphic manner, than he has, in his description of the style in which schools of this species are genneraly conducted.

Intimatly am I acquainted with the prevalence of those evils which he alledges to exist in Common-Schools.

Orators may declaim concerning the universally-diffused blessings of education in our Country, and Essayests may exhaust their magasine of adjec[tives] in extolling our systim of Common School instruction,—but when reduced to practise, the high and sanguine hopes excited by its imposing appearance in theory—are a little dashed.—

Mr Taylor has freely pointed out its defects, and has not been deterred from reproving them, by any feelings of delicasy.—If he had, he would have proved a traitor to the great cause, in which he is engaged.—But I have almost usurped the province of the Edinburgh Reveiw—so as I am approaching the confines of my sheet I will subscribe myself

Your affectionate nephew
HERMAN MELVILLE

My love to Aunt Mary
& a kiss to Henry—
Remember me to Uncle Herman HM

The unconscious self-portraiture in this letter is most valuable. Here are a youthful openness and idealism and the anxiety to fulfill even minor promises. But shadows are here, too, and some of the perceptions that come with maturity. At eighteen Melville was quick to note the divergence between appearance and reality, between the school described by superpatriotic orators and those in which real country children got a meaningless whirl through the curriculum. He penetrated to the core of his host's Yankee character and noted with the air of an aristocratic Whig his "genuine republican swagger." His pupils he organized with his father's methodical firmness. Burrowing humbly in the woods atop a "mountain" [14] was a chilly contrast to the civilized comforts of Number Three Clinton Square, but Melville uttered no complaint.

His literary style had developed a spontaneous earthiness that breaks through the formalities of eighteenth-century rhetoric. His feelings about the scenery are in tune with Gothic romanticism, recalling both Irving and Poe, and his description is stilted and generalized, but he can also write a compact character sketch with homely details and apt similes. Melville reveals an ironic but genial humor, a typical family affection, some evidence of care in phrasing,[15] and a sensible self-criticism (he declines to rival the *Edinburgh Review* in ex-cathedra pronouncements). That magazine, which he had undoubtedly read in the Albany Young Men's Association, had helped to form his style and contributed, it would seem, to his thought, for the allusion suggests intimacy. His private literary apprenticeship, begun two years before at the Albany Classical School, was going forward in his spare time, which he improved by "occasional writting & reading." Although the tone of this phrase does not suggest a dedicated spirit, Melville may have understated his literary endeavors out of modesty. He would have found some retreat from schoolroom cares and an isolated existence a necessity, and writing was a major form of release.

It is regrettable that Melville failed to give further indications of his reading. His reference to the scholar reading the history of the country through which he is traveling suggests that he himself had been reading travel literature and perhaps filling his mind with visions of adventure in places quite remote from Washington Mountain in Pittsfield. He had presumably been sucking wisdom from the *Self-Teacher* Uncle Peter gave him when he visited Albany in November.[16]

However, J. Orville Taylor's *District School* was a direct influence on his thought at this time.[17] This popular book was a frank and thorough statement of the defects in the common-school system and of the ideals of American education. Assuming the fundamental goodness of man, Taylor demands studies and techniques reflecting a benevolent rationalism, of which, nevertheless, the moral teachings of a theistic Christianity are to be the foundation. The superstitions that control the lives of the ignorant (and he considers most people ignorant) are to yield to enlightened instruction in the practical arts and an intelligent religious belief guided by the Scriptures. Teachers, says Taylor, governing by "goodness and affection," will serve "the very end and object of all government . . . to make men govern themselves." "If we would be *patriotic* citizens," he points out, "we must be *well-informed, religious men.*" It is the duty of a teacher, he maintains, to mingle religious instruction with regular education and to urge on his pupils the religious notions held by the community in general, for example, that "there is a God," that "we are all responsible to him for our conduct," that the soul is immortal, that "we have a revelation from heaven," that men must be personally attached to a Supreme Being, and that penitence for sin and forgiveness through a Saviour are necessary for a life of piety.[18]

What Melville accepted and what he discarded from Taylor cannot be determined. His specific endorsements dwell more on Taylor's revelation of defects in the school system than upon his philosophy of education. However, considering the powerful influence of religion in his own education, both at home and at the Albany Academy and the Classical School, there is no reason to think that he rejected Taylor's recommendations. He must have shared also in Taylor's idealistic concepts, for he held American education to be a "great cause." The realities were disillusioning, but Melville seems to have retained a strong sense of things as they should be in contrast to things as he found them.

Since Melville considered Taylor "perfectly familiar" with the difficulties and evils he himself had to face, we may picture his situation with some accuracy. The small school building (now moved down the road and turned into a dwelling house [19]) had a location which Taylor deplored, "close by the road's side, where the passing of travellers and the rattling of carriages divert and distract the mind." [20] In the typical school that Taylor described, the room was cramped, poorly ventilated, and heavy with smoke and impure air, making the teacher's position thoroughly unhealthy and the scholars drowsy and stupid. The seats were so high that students could not reach the floor with their feet and so crowded that the movement of one student disturbed the entire bench. The few, small windows were often covered with hats, and the weak illumination made "the whole appearance dismal and painful in the extreme." Parents frequently governed their children so poorly at home that a teacher found it most difficult to control them at school. Wages were low—about eleven dollars a month, or as much as an illiterate farm laborer could expect and only half as much as a mechanic commanded. The general prevalence of meager pay made "the teacher's profession low and disreputable" and made teachers "dislike their business and anxious for some other occupation." [21]

Such was the kind of school in which Melville taught. Such were the conditions under which he lived for several months. That his existence was not only arduous and unprofitable but also a failure is the implication of existing evidence. J. E. A. Smith, the Pittsfield historian who knew Melville in later life, left this picture of him:

> He was for one term teacher of the common school in the "Sykes district," under Washington mountain, of which he had some racy memories—one of them a rebellion in which some of the bigger boys undertook to "lick" him—with what results those who remember his physique and character can well imagine.[22]

But in another version of this rebellion an anonymous gossiper of 1852 asserted that Melville was driven "out of school by two naughty boys." [23] That the revolt actually occurred is most probable. Smith's word "memories" intimates that he had heard the story from Melville himself. Pittsfield school children could be extremely intractable: when Charles E. West had been teaching in the town ten years before, he had had to procure "two tough whips" before he could bring his rough charges under control.[24] Melville's technique would appear to have been different. Years later, in reading the account of Shelley's teachers, he underlined the words "kindness was regarded as sentimentalism." [25] If he was thinking of his own career, it would seem that he treated his class with the gentleness in which he had been bred and got revolt in exchange. There is also reason to believe that he found the teaching exasperating, for he noted in his 1849 journal that Rousseau as a schoolmaster "could have killed his scholars sometimes" and that Johnson's life as an usher was "intolerable." [26] It is likely that Melville marked these trivia because they referred directly to his own experience. Thus the Pittsfield school work may very well have added to his disillusion a personal humiliation and a bleak sense of failure.

It would have been only natural for Herman to escape his backward charges by an occasional visit to "Broadhall." Uncle Thomas had given up the hopeless struggle against debt some months before and gone out to settle in Galena, Illinois.[27] His son Robert and Robert's wife, Susan, who were now working the farm, may have welcomed Herman to the scene of his earlier vacations. But one term of schoolteaching seems to have been quite enough for him. By January Herman was back in Albany. Finding the Philo Logos Society moribund, he set about reviving it (with the assistance of Uncle Peter, who seems to have lent a room and furniture in Stanwix Hall). On February 9 Herman was elected president,[28] and immediately he found himself embroiled in a controversy that makes up one of the most amusing and illuminating chapters in his early life. Its history, we must warn ourselves, comes only from Herman and his antagonist, and neither was in the least impartial. It is framed in false rhetoric, self-righteousness, and unilateral claims to monopoly of the truth. In lame imitations of Swift, Junius, Churchill, and Peter Porcupine, Melville and Charles Van Loon fought out their quarrel with what each of them clearly believed to be *saeva indignatio.* They were the same age, and both had entered and left the Albany Academy at about the same time, Van Loon to become a druggist's apprentice, though he was now studying to be a Baptist minister.[29] The warriors were equally matched.

The arena was the *Albany Microscope,* devoted, according to its account, to "Popular Tales, History, Legends and Adventures, Anecdotes, Poetry, Satire, Humour, Sporting, and the Drama." It did fulfill its purpose, but well before 1838 more than half of its four weekly pages were given over to gossip, scandal, and letters from pseudonymous correspondents attacking the folly, crime, and vice of specific individuals in Albany. No modern paper could survive the reckless assault on private lives that was the *Microscope's* principal function, but the modern definitions of libel and slander had not then been established. So Melville and Van Loon were free to kick, gouge, and stamp on each other while Albany's respectable citizens and young men about town looked on.

The fracas began when a certain "Sandle Wood" challenged Melville's announcement in the *Albany Evening Journal* that he had been unanimously chosen to head the Philo Logos Society at a meeting in the society's rooms in Stanwix Hall. According to "Sandle Wood," the society owned no rooms anywhere, it had sunk into oblivion a few weeks before, and the election was a "farce" and a "hoax."[30] Melville's reply, in the next issue of the *Microscope,* began with a series of noble flourishes about the class of "narrow-minded and jealous" individuals to be found in every community, "moral outlaws" who attempted to plunge "wooden daggers in the side of public virtue." Then he attacked. "In the *van* of these notable worthies stands pre-eminent, that silly and brainless *loon* who composed the article in your last week's paper . . . ." The charges, said Melville, were "infamous fabrications, . . . as destitute of a single fact as is the author of parts." Anyone who wished could call "at No. 9 Gallery, Stanwix Hall, next Friday evening at 7 o'clock" and see the Philo Logos Society in full operation with its officers doing their duty. He signed himself "Philologian" and settled back to see if his pun would work.

Clumsy as it was, it flushed Herman's real enemy into the open. Though denying he was "Sandle Wood," Van Loon came rushing to the attack, snarling "coward slanderer" and "black hypocrisy." His opponent, he said, was well-known in the Philo Logos Society as the *"Ciceronian baboon,"* and since Van Loon could think of no retaliatory play upon Herman's name, he assailed him directly as "Hermanus Melvillian" and called him "a moral Ethiopian" without conscience or principles but possessed of a "brazen cheek" and a "black and bloodless heart." So offensive was he to the society that it had once declared officially that " 'the conduct of Hermanus Melvillian was disgraceful to himself, discreditable to the society, and insulting to the chair.' " After stabbing the society to death, Van Loon charged, Melville had resurrected it by getting himself elected president at an unconstitutional election, and when Van Loon exposed his "base treachery" in an open meeting Melville had replied in "abominable falsehoods." Having lashed this "rascal naked through the world," Van Loon was now done with him.

Herman's rejoinder, running to some twenty-five hundred words, filled a front-page column in each of the following issues of the *Microscope*. The first installment, after an inflated apology to the editor, was largely an essay on the character and literary achievements of *"Mr. 'Sandle Wood' alias 'Ex-President' alias C*****s V*n L**n."* Herman deplored the rashness and passion of Van Loon's abusive letter, which the author's "otherwise respectable understanding" must certainly have disapproved. The attack upon him, he said, was unchristian and steeped in hatred, and it showed how hollow were Van Loon's "religious professions of meekness, forbearance, and love." Herman had always thought that "the fish-women of Paris and the Thames" were masters of this form of literature, but he doubted if Billingsgate itself, or Peter Porcupine, or papers which the common hangman had burned could match Van Loon's "loafer eloquence." The fact that Van Loon was preparing for the ministry gave Herman the opportunity for some stinging sarcasm, for after professing indifference to his "hatred, hostility, and revenge," he added

> May these truly Christian attitudes cling around the sacred lawn with which you are hereafter to be invested, and your angelic nature be a fit illustration of the peaceful spirit of the gospel you profess.

In his second installment, Herman got down to the facts. He had joined the Philo Logos Society because several members asked him to. The motion of censure cited by Van Loon had actually been rejected viva voce. Sometime after this, Herman had gone away, leaving the society in good condition, but when he returned it was half-dead. With several others he tried to revive it, while President Van Loon kept aloof. As for the disputed election, it was perfectly constitutional, but at a subsequent meeting Van Loon, in envy and wrath, provoked an uproar whereupon "a large and triumphant majority" vindicated Herman's conduct as president, ratified his election, and sharply censured Van Loon. In revenge, said Herman, the former president had written the malicious "Sandle Wood" letter, and when he was exposed had turned loose a torrent of abuse. With this, Herman would have ended the controversy, though he could not resist a Parthian postscript: "Your incoherent ravings may be continued if you choose; they remind me of the croakings of a Vulture when disappointed of its prey."

It was now Van Loon's turn, and his counter was also divided between two issues of the *Microscope*. Nettled by Herman's charge that he lacked Christian principles, he asserted that if those principles required him to sacrifice the right of free discussion or to allow hypocrisy to go unreproved he would disavow them. But they did not, and hence, he said, with calculated malice,

> If . . . (for we are fallible mortals) in denouncing you as a "moral Ethiopian . . . ," I have done violence to the spirit of the gospel, most cordially do I recall the objectionable language, and in the meek and charitable spirit of Peter the Apostle, honestly and conscientiously pronounce you Herman Melville, a "child of the devil, full of all subtility and all mischief."

Then he produced his rebuttals. Herman had avowed that when he left Albany the Philo Logos Society was "apparently healthy and prosperous." But while away he had written a letter, from which Van Loon quoted, asking him if the society was "on the rapid decline I left it in." Furthermore, Van Loon had a certificate from Lotus Niles, former secretary of the society, certifying "that a resolution was adopted in the Philo Logos Society pronouncing the conduct of H. Melville 'disgraceful to himself, discreditable to the society, and insulting to the chair,' and that, the resolution stands in full force at this date." Thus Herman was a liar on two counts. Van Loon then gave his version of the meeting in which, according to Herman, the society censured him. Herman had been unable to explain why he had called an election meeting on an unauthorized night; the "triumphant majority" which censured Van Loon was a "bare majority of one." After calling upon Melville to repent his crimes and "cordially" forgiving him, Van Loon was through—though he again denied being "Sandle Wood" and invited the editor of the *Microscope* to publish the fact if it was true.

It is doubtful if the controversy would have gone any further anyway, but it had gone far enough to attract the interest of a peacemaker, whose plea for an end to the warfare appeared on the same page as Van Loon's final assault. "Americus," who called himself "a friend to Messrs. Van Loon and Melville," paid tribute to the "attainments and character" of both gentlemen and their labors in building up the Philo Logos Society, reminded them of "the intimacy of their former acquaintance," and suggested a private meeting to patch up the friendship instead of this "wrangling altercation" in the public press. The next week, Van Loon wrote that he would "cordially meet Mr. Melville on terms of friendship, when he shall have brought forth 'fruits for repentance.' " It is hard to believe that Herman was able to bring himself to make peace with such a Pharisee, but at least he dropped the public controversy completely. It would seem that he had guessed wrong about "Sandle Wood," since the *Microscope* printed no identification of that person with Van Loon, but he probably had other motives than this for withdrawing from a battle of which the public was obviously tired. The chief advantage he reaped from the affair was the opportunity to capitalize on it by appealing, in a letter to the *Microscope,* for more support of debating. The merits of practice in debate, he wrote, were clear from the testimony of Burke, Clay, and Franklin, the latter of whom "attributed the early development of his natural resources to the same mind-stirring, soul-animating cause." Herman was clearly fired with enthusiasm for the discipline of oratory and argument. It was unfortunate that it should have seduced him into a sordid and embarrassing quarrel. But whatever the facts of the case, he came off better as far as dignity and restraint were concerned.

The somewhat murky light we have on this whole episode reveals the outlines of a very buoyant and ambitious young man, stormy and reckless and seeking fulfillment in leadership. However reticent and amiable Herman may have been as a boy, it is clear that by now irrepressible thoughts and feelings were thrusting out at every sally port. He was no longer a pale and docile foil to Gansevoort. Notable is his impatience with professed devotees of Christianity who speak without charity and act without love. Herman's own abandonment of rigidly Christian behavior may be charged to the intensity of youth and to infatuation with rhetoric, but his obvious loathing of Van Loon's smugness belongs to his permanent horror of hypocrisy. His prose, with its meager and pretentious allusions, bears the pathetic marks of a talent that has been denied a sufficient education. His reading of the late eighteenth-century political satirists seduced him into fumbling imitations of their burlesque, invective, and limitless exaggeration. Yet he had developed some power in polemics, and his mature writing would reflect both the passion and the satirical frame of mind that Junius and Peter Porcupine had already helped to mold. He was also an enthusiast for the bombastic rhetoric that young America loved. And just as Whitman's early training in oratory affected the sweeping periods and the sustained apostrophes of *Leaves of Grass,* so Melville's apprenticeship in the forensic manners of Webster, Clay, and others helped to organize the rhythms of *Typee* and *Mardi* and *Moby-Dick.*

Not the least interesting element in Melville's relations with the *Albany Microscope* is its possible effect on him. That he read it there can be no question. Even if neither he nor Gansevoort was a subscriber, the Young Men's Association received the weekly issues, and the paper was well calculated to pique the curiosity of Albany's junior citizens. In contrast to the stiff propriety of the *Evening Journal* and the *Argus,* it was lively and bold, even reckless or ribald.[31] It printed weekly notes on the circus and vaudeville and long accounts of the numerous balls. Its dramatic criticism dealt not only with the professional theater but also with amateur organizations, and it kept its readers informed, like Louella Parsons, of all the activities of their favorite actors and actresses. At its serious level, when it commented on the work of the legislature or pleaded for help for the poor in Albany after the Panic of 1837, it was often sensational but always frank and unequivocal about unpleasant matters. It scrutinized the daily life of Albany from steeple, back window, and keyhole, fattening on gossip and scandal, but also exposing real vice with a ruthless hand.

No young man could have read the *Albany Microscope* without acquiring a realistic concept of ordinary human behavior, nor could he have missed a substantial education in all that is vicious, criminal, and depraved. Herman lived in an upright section of town, next door to a church, and he moved in the most proper circles, but he knew that within a few minutes' walk of Gansevoort's store were streets where every kind of vice was practiced, and he knew that even some of Albany's respectable citizens, members, perhaps, of the state legislature, indulged in them. The *Microscope* informed him that gambling dens operated openly, that it had a list of young men routed by fire from "a house of notoriety in Division Street" and forced nude into the street "from the chaste embraces of their paramours,"[32] that the city was spotted with assignation houses, that it would expose certain gentlemen carrying on affairs with other men's wives, that "bold and daring blackguards . . . made it a continual practice both before and after nightfall, of visiting a common and public brothel . . . in Pine Street," whence one was forced to hear "the drunken carousals of the visitors, the indecent expressions of the inmates, and the continual quarrelling of the *pimp* who keeps it, and his *mistress*."[33] Such reports were expanded in the fictional sketches tracing the miserable careers of young men who gave themselves up to dissipation—and naturally the paper carried regular advertisements for Levison's Hunter's Red Drop, a professed cure for "the venereal." The *Microscope's* war against vice reached its culmination in the infamous Pine Street murder case, which was written up in lurid detail in two of the issues in which Herman's letters to Van Loon were printed. Thus Herman heard the wretched story of young Robert Shepherd, who, after carousing at Stanwix Hall and the Mansion House, hurried over to a brothel on Pine Street with two friends. Denied entrance, they raised such a tumult that Thomas Rector, the proprietor, struck Shepherd a mighty blow on the head with the door bar with the result that he died the next day. "Our city," exclaimed the *Microscope* in horror,

is filled with *houses of prostitution* and *gambling halls*—and our preachers, who are the legitimate guardians of the public morals, are as silent as the grave! Our youths grow up amidst the wickedness and abominations of our city; our watch-house, jail, and police [station] are daily filled with young men, many of high-bred notions and of pretended respectability, and our public monitors raise neither a voice or a pen![34]

The *Microscope* continued to publicize the case right up to Rector's trial for murder, of which it printed the entire record, including the testimony of several prostitutes and their companions at the time of the murder.

No one would expect any direct reflection of this kind of knowledge in Melville's early life or even in his works. It does not come easily to the surface, and gauging its effects is nearly impossible. But it is undeniable that as a youth Melville did not live intellectually in a state of paradisaic innocence and that he had had some kind of education in the realities of sexual immorality. It has often been forgotten that Melville grew up before what we call Victorianism, with all its connotations of fastidiousness, prudery, and suppression, ascended the throne. The Albany of his adolescence talked quite openly about dirt, poverty, and monstrous evils in the pages of the *Microscope,* and Herman could not help listening.

All during the Philo Logos controversy, affairs in Melville's home had been steadily deteriorating. As early as February Maria Melville was forced to consider moving from Clinton Square although she had no idea where she would go.[35] Gansevoort's efforts to provide for his family finally collapsed. Then he fell ill and became an outright burden.[36] Peter Gansevoort, who had underwritten all his nephew's and his sister's debts, was unable to support the family in an expensive house, however much he worshiped Maria's "most lovely, interesting & promising family of young children."[37] The inevitable end came about the first of May, when the Melvilles left Albany and settled in Lansingburgh, ten miles to the north, where they could live much more economically.[38]

The new home of Herman's debt-ridden family was a

village of some three thousand inhabitants lying along the Hudson just below the point where the Mohawk, after flowing over the beautiful falls of Cohoes, joins the larger river.[39] The town thought well of itself, it seems; a laudatory if not grammatically pure editorial in one of its two newspapers thus pictured its beauties at the very time Herman Melville first saw it:

Our village is no longer the "old brown town," for the footsteps of the carpenter has been planted upon our dwellings, and the hand of the painter has been there; they have wrested from old father Time what he was just crumbling to dust . . . . The *Lighters* of years gone by have decayed and are forgotten, and well they may be, for freight boats, and sloops of the largest class are now not strangers at our wharfs, and the "heave oh" of the boatmen is not a song to be frightened at.[40] Coequal with the improvements in the externals of our village has been the increase of business and the accumulation of wealth. Liberal also, perhaps to a fault, are our citizens when any proposed public good is on the tapis, and this liberality is the more truly commendable as what is given is not capital invested in prospect of certain returns, but freely contributed to benefit [the] community.

In conclusion we state, that the healthful situation of the place, the beauties of the adjacent scenery, the morality and strictly business character of the people, added to the sociality and intelligence of their every day intercourse—the freedom from sectarian interference in religious matters, and for other reasons too numerous to mention, the village of Lansingburgh is becoming the resort of many who prefer the quiet life of a country village to the noise and unhealthful atmosphere of a thronged city.[41]

Lansingburgh was evidently as Philistine in spirit as a thousand other American towns of the day. Melville found himself living in a small community that placed heavy premiums on wealth, material progress, and "a strictly business character." Although there was "some good society, . . . considerable sociability, and but little formality," there was little to "please a young gay person." [42] And Lansingburgh had few resources of the kind that Albany offered—no theater or museum, no musical society except a church choral group, and only small public libraries.[43] Two young men's clubs held weekly meetings, read essays, and conducted debates, but Melville could not have paid the membership dues. In all probability, he endured the pangs of exclusion from the normal social pursuits of his contemporaries, which only a year before had been readily available for him. As for economic opportunity, Lansingburgh had little to offer. It boasted a few manufactures and a considerable trade in grain and lumber, but its location well beyond the navigable depth for steamboats had already doomed it to gradual decline as a river port.[44]

However, Melville and his family were not completely isolated from people of their own blood and background. Melville's Aunt Mary Gansevoort and his cousins Guert and Leonard and Catherine Gansevoort Curtis now lived across the river at Waterford, and there were frequent visits back and forth. Uncle Peter came up from Albany, and Aunt Priscilla Melvill made a visit from Boston in August 1838.[45] Maria Melville's cousin, Maria Peebles, lived only two blocks away,[46] and though she and her husband were prosperous landowners and held superior rank in the village, they were friendly to their impoverished cousins and assisted them periodically with small loans.[47]

The Melvilles found a house on River Street at the corner of North, "very pleasantly situated on the bank of the Hudson."[48] Next door was the house of Colonel William Knickerbacker, director of the Bank of Lansingburgh, a "worthy deacon of the Presbyterian Church," and one of the wealthiest citizens in the town.[49] On the other side was the former residence of Horatio Gates Spafford, a lawyer and philanthropist, and in the same block were the commodious houses of Colonel Esek Hawkins and his son.[50] The new home of the Melvilles, with a brick façade but unpainted wooden sidings, contrasted sharply with the elegance of Clinton Square. Yet it had both comforts and refinements: a garden, a wide, pillared porch, ample living space in its dozen rooms, a large Dutch oven, white marble fireplaces ornately carved, and bay windows on the front from which one might look out to the river. With even a modest income, Maria and her family might have lived peacefully here on River Street in quiet Lansingburgh. But there was no money whatever, and in a short time Maria discovered that the Knickerbackers, who bought the house in 1839, were "an inquisitive little family, with very contracted minds, and the most unpleasant of all beings to be indebted to." [51]

In spite of her financial helplessness, Maria promptly promised her new landlord half a year's rent in advance if he would put up blinds on the front of the house immediately. Then she asked her brother Peter for one hundred dollars to pay the rent and buy wood and provisions.[52] He responded with his usual generosity, despite his own enormous debts. However, he could not forego, as lawyer and brother, a gentle chiding for her folly in offering to pay rent in advance. He told her that it would give her many creditors the impression that she was living handsomely in Lansingburgh, and those who were not already foreclosing mortgages on her Albany property would annoy her with a sale of her furniture.[53] The money disappeared very rapidly, and by August Maria had asked for and received another hundred dollars.[54]

Like everyone else, Herman was undoubtedly sharing in the family distress. Nothing is known of his activities in June and July, but on August 1 he set out for Pittsfield again.[55] His departure from home on his birthday has gloomy implications. Possibly he left in order to maintain himself on his uncle's farm and reduce the strain on his mother's threadbare purse. He may have remained there until the fall, at which time his Aunt Mary Melvill and most of his cousins left "Broadhall" for the seven weeks' journey out to Galena to join Uncle Thomas.[56]

Conditions were still straitened when he returned to Lansingburgh. By the end of October his mother had "to borrow money to pay for Coal and some winter stores." [57] Fortunately Peter held a balance in her favor from a judgment against an insurance company, and for once she was spared the embarrassment of begging. But Gansevoort, her chief support, was still an invalid. He "remains about the same," wrote his mother, "but his Symptoms are more favorable, he is less irratable and capable of self command." [58] The tensions in the household must have been extreme during Gansevoort's illness, and he was not to regain his health until the following spring.

It was clear that some new measure had to be taken if the Melville family was to make any pretense to independence. Gansevoort was idle, Allan was barely earning his keep in Albany, and Herman's teaching in Pittsfield had apparently brought neither the wish to continue nor any cash return. In this crisis Herman struck out boldly into a new field. On November 12 he began the study of surveying and engineering at Lansingburgh Academy.[59]

This school, like the Albany Academy, had been founded by townspeople ambitious for their children to receive a good practical education in an atmosphere of moral edification so as to assure integrity in character and success in business. Its two-story building, which stood on North Street near the Melville house, had just been refurbished in the spring of 1838, and the school, recovering from the doldrums of the previous years, had reopened under the charge of the Reverend Ebenezer D. Maltbie, a Congregationalist minister.[60] Since there were only two instructors at the academy at this time—the other being Harriet White, head of the female department—Melville must have come under the direct instruction and influence of this pious and popular clergyman.[61] If he mingled moral exhortation with his teaching, he would only have been following the well-established precepts of his dual calling as minister and educator. Melville's reactions to the church and Christianity in 1839 and even later may owe something to the character and example of the Reverend Ebenezer Maltbie.

To teach the subjects offered at the academy, Mr. Maltbie must have been a busy and versatile scholar. The curriculum included Latin, Greek, and Hebrew, mathematics, surveying and engineering, natural philosophy, astronomy, intellectual philosophy, logic, rhetoric, and bookkeeping.[62] Emphasis fell on practical education, for of the eighty-one students only nineteen took the classical course, or the higher branches of the English course.[63] But a milieu concerned largely with preparation for material success was favorable to Melville's present goal. He too was learning a profession that would make him a useful member of society. It is significant that he himself must have chosen to study surveying and engineering. Perhaps he was revealing an influence that had lain dormant since he was a pupil of George W. Carpenter, the civil engineer who had been his instructor at the Albany Academy. In any event, in an era of almost unlimited development of railroads and canals, a career as an engineer offered wide opportunity and substantial economic rewards for ambitious neophytes.

The course Melville pursued was thorough. In mathematics he and his fellow students had to make "constant use of the blackboard, and to give full explanations of the principles" on which they based their answers.[64] Melville learned his logarithms, plane trigonometry, and the use of rod, chain, and theodolite either from Jeremiah Day's *The Mathematical Principles of Navigation and Surveying* or Charles Davies' *Elements of Surveying,* both of which were in use in the academy at the time.[65] The school also boasted of a "valuable Library and Apparatus, illustrative of the science of Natural Philosophy, Chemistry and Astronomy." [66] Here Melville may have extended the scientific knowledge that was the main object of his studies and laid the foundation for his mature interest in natural science.

What Melville was doing outside of Lansingburgh Academy is mostly uncertain. Occasionally, at his mother's urging, he would write a note to Allan. One of these, which both mocks the pompous epistolary style and fulfills his duty with matchless brevity, has a playfulness that contrasts sharply with his immediate state:

Nov 10th 1838

ALLAN MELVILLE

Sir

I am with the profoundest regards

Your obdt Servt

HERMAN MELVILLE[67]

From his postscript it also appears that he went down to Albany from time to time to see his brother and old friends like Eli Fly, a fellow clerk of Allan's in Peter Gansevoort's office.[68] It seems to have been during this year that he fell in love with Mary Eleanor Parmelee, a granddaughter of Cornelius Lansing, the founder of Lansingburgh. Together they went for walks along the sparkling Hudson, and when Herman was able somehow or other to acquire a volume of Tennyson's early poems, he gave it to her, and they would sit on the grass in the quiet afternoons and read to each other. But it was mostly a one-sided romance. Herman had distinguished grandparents, but they were of little immediate help to a suitor who was still a student, with no work, no income, and only vague prospects. Besides, Mary Parmelee was in love with Peletiah Bliss, whose father had a substantial bookstore which he would later inherit.[69]

There are no other records of Melville in these years. In their absence it has been supposed that since Wellingborough Redburn belonged to the Juvenile Total Abstinence Association in his village Melville must have done the same, but the assumption is questionable. At nineteen, Melville was somewhat old for membership in a "juvenile" association. Newspaper references indicate only one temperance society in the village, which met in the Methodist Church. There is nothing in Melville's own creed or that of his family to associate him with Methodism. Both wine and spirits were staple commodities in the household of his grandmother, his father, and his uncle. It is true that Allan Melvill had urged young men not to "drink more than one glass of wine" on any occasion. On the other hand, the enthusiasm for convivial pleasures that bursts out in one of the sketches Melville wrote in the spring of 1839 is ill-suited to an earnest devotee of temperance. "Pour down whole floods of sparkling champagne, my dear M—, until your brain grows giddy with emotion," he urges, and a few paragraphs further on he writes enviously of the exemplary Mussulman, "gloriously drunk through all the ages of eternity."[70] These sentiments are incompatible with those of Wellingborough Redburn when he laments the first breaking of his temperance pledge. However, they are reasonable expressions of *joie de vivre* and romantic excess in a healthy youth of nineteen. Redburn's reminiscences are unreliable clues to Melville's temperance affiliations in Lansingburgh.

His religious feelings during these critical years of adolescence must also remain a matter of speculation. Redburn recollected walking by the village graveyard "every Sunday . . . after church in the afternoon." When he left home, he took with him his Sunday boots, then almost new, which he "used to keep looking at . . . during church." On his first Sunday at sea, he is startled that there is no church to go to as there was at home.[71] Although the details are artistically contrived, they point to a regular habit of church attendance and a pious observation of the Sabbath by Melville in Lansingburgh. There is, however, no record of Melville's membership in any church in the village. His sister Catherine belonged to the Presbyterian Church, which she joined in 1843.[72] However, there is absolutely no way of knowing whether Melville went to church regularly, as Redburn did in his village, and there is at least some evidence that Herman's soul was fermenting with rebellion against the religious environment he had always known.

In the midst of his many frustrations, Melville must have found a sustaining hope in his studies. He would have been borne along during the winter of poverty and illness in the family by the expectation of work and an income. By the spring of 1839 he was ready to make his own way in the world in an occupation of his own choosing. A draft of a letter by his Uncle Peter tells the story:

Albany 4 April 1839

Mr. Bouck

Herman Melville, a young man of talent & good education is desirous to obtain a situation in the Engineer Department of the Canals —. The inclosed Certificate of Mr Maltbee[73] the Principal of an Academy in which Mr Melville has endeavored to prepare himself for the business of surveying & engineering & the enclosed letter from Mr Maltbee to John B. Jarvis Esqr[74] shew the proficiency he has made in these studies—He however submits his application, without any pretension & solicits any situation, however humble it may be. He indeed would prefer a subordinate station, as he wishes to advance only by his own merit—He is the young man I introduced to you last evening—As he is my nephew & possesses the ambition to make himself useful in a business which he desires to make his profession, I feel extremely anxious that he should receive employment—. Your kind interference in his behalf, will be considered a personal favor to

Your sincere friend

P. G.[75]

The events behind this letter may be reconstructed with reasonable accuracy. When Melville had finished his course, Mr. Maltbie personally interested himself and wrote a letter of recommendation to John B. Jervis. As the engineer who had planned the enlargement of the Erie Canal in 1835 and as the chief engineer of the Chenango Canal, Mr. Jervis was an influential figure in the canal system of New York.[76] The most cordial relations existed between him and William C. Bouck, at this time one of the acting canal commissioners of the state.[77] Herman Melville evidently brought Mr. Maltbie's letter to his uncle and asked for his assistance in finding a job. Moving with his usual diplomacy, Peter Gansevoort introduced Herman to Mr. Bouck and, when Bouck's reaction proved favorable, made the direct appeal for him.

His letter tells us much about Melville's talents, ambitions, and personality in his twentieth year. His early interest in mathematics, which presumably waned during his studies at the Albany Classical School, had revived and carried him through what must have been a difficult, concentrated course. As late as 1839 he wanted to make engineering, not letters, his life work. In character, he was forthright and self-reliant. Despite his poverty he was unwilling to utilize his uncle's influence and his family name any more than was necessary to secure a toehold in business. He asked no special concessions from his future employers. With humble spirit he would start at the bottom, American fashion, and expect to rise solely on his merits. An aristocratic pride and an almost defiant spirit of independence burned in Melville's heart as he stood on the threshold of manhood, hoping for the chance to prove himself but begging special favors from no one.

The canal position was, for Melville, an urgent need not only to absorb restless energy and provide a cash income but also to maintain a healthy psychological equilibrium. A young man nearing the age of twenty who has earnestly prepared "to make himself useful" requires assurance from the world that he is worth a day's pay. But Fortune, who likes, perhaps, to be wooed by a less adamant spirit than Melville's, declined his proud overture. The hoped-for situation did not materialize.[78] Melville's preparation for a career in engineering came to naught, and he had to turn to another field for the self-fulfillment and the revenue he needed so badly.

His mother's circumstances at this time were worse than they had been even in the fall. By April she had acquired debts of nearly fifty dollars "in borrow'd money & Bills." [79] But in all her poverty she still kept a servant whose wages amounted to one half of the rent Maria had such difficulty in paying.[80] One would imagine that she and her older daughters could have carried on the household without assistance. Helen was now twenty-two, Augusta eighteen. The younger children, Kate, fourteen, Priscilla Frances, twelve, and Tom, nine, were well beyond the age when a nurse or maid is virtually indispensable to a mother's health.

But Maria evidently had to retain, in her impoverishment, at least one of the marks of her former affluence. Her breeding demanded a certain way of life, though she had no means whatsoever to sustain it.

In the dual emergency created by failure to secure the canal position and his mother's indebtedness, Melville called upon the only other talent he had, and submitted his first known compositions to the *Democratic Press and Lansingburgh Advertiser*. On April 20, the paper printed the following notice:

To Correspondents. The communication of "L. A. V." is received. An interview with the writer is requested.

Evidently the interview was satisfactory, for within a few weeks two "Fragments from a Writing Desk" appeared in the paper over Melville's pseudonym, L. A. V.[81] Although the sketches are scarcely immortal literature, the mere fact that they were published was an achievement for Melville. Both the *Democratic Press* and its Whig opponent, the *Lansingburgh Gazette,* regularly devoted their front pages to belles-lettres, but a novice had to compete with the most popular authors of the day, Irving, Hawthorne, Whittier, Holmes, Bryant, William Leggett, and the prolific Mrs. Sigourney.[82] Any work by these writers could be reprinted without the expense of royalty payments. Melville's sketches also had the competition of many a lowly aspirant to Parnassus who, by writing sentimentally of the death of a baby or of virtue triumphant, could win an audience that worshiped mawkish melancholy, piety, and a false refinement.[83] Other types of writing that seemed to have been popular in Lansingburgh as elsewhere were the humorous tale in Yankee dialect, the western, the political or patriotic story or poem, and the love poem weakly imitating Lord Byron. The qualities in Melville's work that probably appealed to William J. Lamb, the editor of the paper, were spontaneity, local reference, and the popular confessional style, all of which distinguished it from most of the stereotyped articles served up in the weekly literary diet. However, if Melville hoped to be a successful author whose financial rewards would rescue his family from poverty, he was disappointed. No further sketches by L. A. V. appeared in the village press, and Melville's career as a writer had to wait another seven years, until he could draw on real experience.[84]

The "Fragments from a Writing Desk" are distinctly amateurish compositions, but they reveal even more about Melville than his uncle's letter to William Bouck. They offer clues about his personality, outline his intellectual life, and foreshadow his later literary techniques. The first is a confessional letter addressed by a callow protegé to his older and sophisticated mentor, M—, a scholarly Bohemian who reads black-letter volumes, carouses with champagne, and possesses all the graces of a man of the world.[85] From a similar self-realization, the writer has been held back by a "hang-dog modesty, my *mauvaise honte,* as my Lord Chesterfield would style it"; but by a masterly assertion of self-confidence he decides that he has all the virtues necessary to be a citizen of the *beau monde*—physical beauty, wit, intelligence, elegance in dress, "and every polite accomplishment." Equipped with these, he lords it over the sheepish village beaux and enthralls all the ladies with his cosmopolitan polish. He praises the bucolic beauty of the girls, so superior in its "unborrowed charms" to the artificial adornments of their sisters in the city from which the writer has come. Fully half the letter describes three of these exquisite damsels. The two final paragraphs apologize for the length of this "catalogue of the Graces" and conclude in a flight of elaborate rhetoric.

The first section of this strange effusion owes a heavy debt to Lord Chesterfield that suggests much about Melville as a young man. His introduction to the arbiter of English and American manners undoubtedly came through the *Principles of Politeness and of Knowing the World,* which his father had owned, which had shaped Allan Melvill's code, and which he clearly considered an admirable guide for young men.[86] Here was gathered together the essence of Lord Chesterfield's worldly wisdom, conveniently digested under such headings as "Modesty," "Genteel Carriage," "Elegance of Expression," "Knowledge of the World," "Dignity of Manners," and "Rules of Conversation." But since the little volume does not contain the phrase *mauvaise honte* to which Melville refers, he had evidently read further in Chesterfield, perhaps in the edition of the *Letters* owned by the Albany Young Men's Association.[87] Judging by the derivative ideas in the "Fragment," Melville modeled the wit, dress, and manners of his hero after Chesterfieldian rules.

When Melville made his hero guilty of *mauvaise honte,* he was thinking of Chesterfield's repeated use of this phrase to describe the awkward bashfulness of socially inexperienced young men, which made them ashamed of going into company and confused when they got there.

> As for the *mauvaise honte,* [wrote Chesterfield to his son] I hope you are above it. Your figure is like other people's; I suppose you will take care that your dress shall be so too. . . . What then should you be ashamed of? And why not go into a mixed company with as much ease, and as little concern, as you go into your own room? [88]

As if carrying these precepts into practice, the narrator in Melville's sketch concludes that his figure has "every manly grace," and he dresses "in a style which would extort admiration from a Brummel." [89] In society, unlike the sheepish village boys, he walks boldly up to the ladies, delivers gracious compliments, exchanges repartee, and in a burst of supreme confidence, kisses "round the whole circle." [90] Chesterfield had pointedly contrasted "the awkward country fellow" and the gentleman in their manner of coming into a room. The one is disconcerted, does not know what to do with his hands, stammers when spoken to; the other enters the room "with gracefulness and modest assurance, addresses even persons he does not know, in an easy and natural manner, and without the least embarrassment." [91]

Melville's hero goes well beyond Chesterfield's formula. He escorts all the ladies into the banquet, leaving the poor victims of *mauvaise honte* to enter "stumbling, blushing, stammering, and alone." [92]

Melville also molds the walking habits of his hero according to Chesterfield's admonitions. To Chesterfield, walking fast in the streets was a mark of vulgarity, implying the hurry of business. It might "appear well in a mechanic or tradesman, but suits ill with the character of a gentleman, or man of fashion." [93] Similarly Melville's hero walks the Broadway of his village "with a certain air," scornful of "the little sneaking vermin who dodge along the street as though they were so many footmen or errand-boys," while he maintains a "slow and magisterial gait" that he can "at pleasure vary to an easy, abandoned sort of carriage, or to the more engaging, alert, and lively walk . . . ." [94]

It is presumptuous to assume an identity between Melville and his paper hero, who abandons all modesty in the effort to overcome his native bashfulness and who worships an artificial standard of conduct, dress, and manners. Still, Melville must have had a lurking respect for the notions with which he invests his character. Otherwise it is difficult to explain his choice of subject and to account for a treatment that is sympathetic rather than satirical. Some manifestations of Melville's own dreams, at least, are discernible in this brash and comical young "distingué," as he calls himself. Since Melville's father learned his manners at the school of Lord Chesterfield, it is reasonable to believe that Melville himself had some admiration for the same code and that he projected this into his first composition.

The second part of the "Fragment" also reveals something about Melville. The sketches of the three most charming girls in the village are drawn with a romantic idealism and a youthful voluptuousness that suggests a fervent disciple of Thomas Moore. Melville describes the figure, the face, the nature of each with reckless enthusiasm, and with allusions to the chastity of Diana, the nobility of Cleopatra and of Scott's Rebecca, the beauty of Venus, and the compassion of Coleridge's Genevieve. It is the second, however, who inspires the longest and most abandoned praise, and after a long description of her Circassian coloring, the "dark, rich orbs" of her eyes which "blaze into your very soul the fires of day," and the "melting tenderness" which heals all wounds, Melville concludes:

> If the devout and exemplary Mussulman, who dying fast in the faith of his Prophet, anticipates reclining on beds of roses, gloriously drunk through all the ages of eternity, is to be waited on by Houris such as these: waft me, ye gentle gales, beyond this lower world, and
> "Lap me in soft Lydian airs!" [95]

The debt to literary sources in this "Fragment" is large, but some of its tone and color come most certainly from Melville's inner feelings. Perhaps he had Mary Parmelee in mind when he wrote so warmly the detailed portrait of the second village beauty. The passions evoked are stereotyped and far from dangerous, but they may merely veil deeper sensations that Melville's lost letters to Mary would expose.

No melancholy darkens this lace-edged portrait. Only the blind idealizations of a young romantic heart quiver in its tremulous rhetoric. It is a surprise, then, to encounter the flamboyant skepticism of the second "Fragment." [96] The narrator of this bizarre adventure sallies forth into a moonlit April evening for a walk along the river. When he flings himself down and falls into sentimental reverie, a cloaked figure drops a note at his feet, inviting him to follow the bearer to an assignation. Accepting the challenge, he pursues the mysterious female for nearly an hour, trying vainly to catch up with her. At last he arrives at a secluded country villa where in answer to his guide's low call, a large basket is lowered and they are both drawn to an upper window. Two brawny arms lift the somewhat fearful narrator into a large room, whence his guide conducts him through a low door that opens to the touch into a brightly lit and gorgeously decorated apartment. Here he finds a woman of matchless beauty, reclining on an ottoman and holding in one hand a lute. Her melancholy expression quickly lights up when he approaches her, sinks on one knee, and promptly declares his boundless passion. Several minutes pass while he becomes more ardent in praise and more eager for acknowledgment. But the woman, for all the burning fire in her eyes, remains silent. "Speak!" he cries. "Tell me, thou cruel! . . . . Am I loved,—even wildly, madly as I love?"

She was silent; gracious God! what horrible apprehension crossed my soul?—Frantic with the thought, I held her from me, and looking in her face, I met the same impassioned gaze; her lips moved—my senses ached with the intensity with which I listened,—all was still,—they uttered no sound; I flung her from me, even though she clung to my vesture, and with a wild cry of agony I burst from the apartment!—She was dumb! Great God, she was dumb! DUMB AND DEAF!

Despite the atrocious anticlimax here, the mosaic of Melville's psychological state revealed in the light of his bizarre imagination is fascinating. Even more than in "Fragment Number One," he translates into fantastic experience his inner urges toward sensuous enjoyment. He writes with youthful exuberance and self-conscious bravado. His hero, like the gentleman lover of the first "Fragment," is modeled on Lord Chesterfield and Lord Byron. He wears a beaver hat and a cloak, carries a cane, and swears like the "jolly cavaliers"; though he half believes the age of chivalry is dead, he accepts a romantic challenge like a true courtier. Despite a very ungentlemanly show of trepidation as the mysterious adventure unfolds and a temporary embarrassment at the dazzling Oriental beauty of the lady in the apartment, he soon recovers his "good-breeding" and matching her passionate gaze with his own, achieves a speedy conquest. However, this dashing hero is somewhat less self-confident than the narrator of the first "Fragment." Melville lightens his portrait with humor at the expense of the hero's self-esteem, and by weaving threads of mock seriousness into the pattern, prepares for the Byronic disillusionment of the ending. The exaggerated acceptance of woman in the first "Fragment" is more than tempered by the exaggerated rejection in the second. Melville's exposure of his hero to an abrupt reversal of his rosy anticipations reveals a significant early attraction toward ironic themes and situations.

Besides the clues to Melville's personality, these sketches supply a skeleton index to his intellectual development up to the end of his twentieth year. Into them he poured the distillations of his youthful reading. Foreshadowing the sense of plenitude that reaches its summit in *Mardi* and *Moby-Dick,* he crowds his pages with allusions to literature, art, and mythology. He refers directly to Burton's *Anatomy of Melancholy* and quotes lines or phrases from Chesterfield and Burke, from Campbell's "The Pleasures of Hope," from *Hamlet, Childe Harold's Pilgrimage,* "L'Allegro," Coleridge's "To Genevieve," *The Rivals, Romeo and Juliet,* and three unidentified poems.[97] Knowingly, he cites Minotti's spectacular sword work in Byron's "The Siege of Corinth,"[98] Rebecca's fiery defiance of Bois-Guilbert in Scott's *Ivanhoe,* the visions of loveliness in the latter portion of *Childe Harold's Pilgrimage,* "the royal mistress of Antony," and "the offerings laid upon the sacrificial altars of the Hebrews." From Eastern literature he culls recollections of the *Arabian Nights,* Circassians and houris, the Mussulman and the Prophet. To the profusion of literary reference he adds a sumptuous display of allusion to mythology and art. Apollo, Cupid, Venus, Diana, Prometheus, the three Graces, and "the sylvan god" mingle with the Phidian Jupiter and the Venus de' Medici, the Doric, Ionic, and Corinthian orders, pictures of Jupiter and Semele, and of Psyche before the tribunal of Venus, and fables of Greece and Rome illustrated in damask tapestries.

The wealth of allusions in these humble compositions signifies that Melville's imagination had early been aroused by his wanderings in the realms of gold. It is not to be wondered at, however, that in his excessive love of display, he combines common with remote references, that he is inaccurate, and that he does not scruple to invent sources to suit his needs. His reading had been wide but not deep, and his mind, lacking the discipline imposed by a careful study of the classics, felt no more obligation to exactness than to restraint.

Several slips reveal Melville's lack of precision. He changes "touch" to "kiss" in quoting Romeo's lines,

> Oh that I were a glove upon that hand,
> That I might touch that cheek.

He refers to the "counterfeit presentiments" instead of "presentments" in *Hamlet.* He turns Burke's "The age of chivalry is gone" into the more pedestrian "The days of chivalry are over." He equips Minotti, the hero of "The Siege of Corinth," with a two-handed sword which Byron does not mention. He refers to the last part of Canto II of *Childe Harold's Pilgrimage* in such a way as to make it sound like a full gallery of beautiful women, though only three or four of the twenty-five stanzas bear him out. Finally, his references to mythology and ancient painting are a better tribute to his imagination than to his knowledge. Of the picture of Psyche before the tribunal of Venus and the "several magnificent pictures illustrative of the loves of Jupiter and Semele" no records exist.

Thus Melville's allusions in his first compositions are often unscholarly, generalized, and inventive. As he matured in authorship he grew more exact and particular. But he never lost the artistic habit of allowing his imagination free play with the materials that stimulated it and of representing truth without being harnessed to fact.

In his first published work Melville utilized his reading freely to decorate his story and provide parallels for his ideas. He was also swayed by easily recognizable social and literary currents. Besides the indebtedness to Lord Chesterfield for the standards and attitudes of the gentleman in society, he leaned heavily upon literary Orientalism, and especially Thomas Moore and Lord Byron. Both had much to do in shaping a romantic attitude toward the world around him.

In the second "Fragment" Melville describes the lady's apartment as "beautiful and enchanting as any described in the *Arabian Nights.*" Innumerable editions of this collection of romantic legends had appeared by 1839, and Melville had evidently read at least one of them.[99] While his first publication makes mention of Circassians, the Prophet, and the devout Mussulman waited on by beautiful houris through all eternity, it is the second that bears indubitably the stamp of the Persian romances. The fundamental situation follows the pattern of at least four *Arabian Nights* stories.[100] The messenger of a beautiful lady invites a stranger to a clandestine rendezvous in her home, with the expectation of unmeasured delight. The stranger accepts the summons and follows his guide to the appointed place. He falls in love with the lady and either fulfills his desires or meets sharp disappointment, sometimes in the form of a scurvy trick. The lady of the piece is always beautiful beyond anything the adventurer has ever seen before. Her nature is sensual, her dress splendid and voluptuous, and the apartment that forms her background is a rich mélange of perfumes, jewels, gold, porphyry, and embroideries.

The curious ending of the second "Fragment" may have been suggested to Melville by "The Story of Beder, Prince of Persia, and Giahure, Princess of Samandal." [101] In this, the Prince falls violently in love with a beautiful slave girl and utters passionate sentiments similar to those of the hero in the "Fragment," but receiving no response to his protestations, he begins to think that she may be dumb. Her silence persists for a year, but he continues to show earnest love for her. When she finally speaks, it is to inform the Prince that she has purposely held her tongue in order to test his love. Melville may well have seen in this situation the possibilities of a surprise ending and altered it to make the girl's dumbness real instead of pretended.

If it is clear that Melville had visions of the *Arabian Nights* in mind when he wrote the second "Fragment," it is equally evident that his Orientalism had been nourished by the nineteenth-century romantic poets, whose exploitation of Eastern legend and history had established a literary tradition twenty years before Melville began to write. Thus he employs certain props in his stories common to the Oriental tales of Moore and Byron as well as to the *Arabian Nights*. Andalusians, Circassians, and beautiful women sitting on ottomans and playing on lutes are conventional fixtures in *Lalla Rookh, Childe Harold's Pilgrimage,* "The Giaour," "The Bride of Abydos," and *Don Juan.*[102] In the second "Fragment" the lady's ardent, burning, and steadfast look recalls that of Zelica in *Lalla Rookh:*

> And then her look! oh! where's the heart so wise
> Could unbewilder'd meet those matchless eyes? [103]

The hero's passionate glance in return, which forces the lady to drop her head, suggests the warrior Hefed before his beloved Hinda:

> How shall she dare to lift her head
> Or meet those eyes, whose scorching glare
> Not Yeman's boldest sons can bear? [104]

Melville may have been thinking of the description of the lovely Nourmahal in *Lalla Rookh* when he created the second lady in the first "Fragment." His reference to "the liveliest visions of the Fairy Land" may have derived from these lines:

> But where is she now . . . .
> When all around her is so bright
> So like the visions of a trance,
> That one might think, who came by chance,
> Into the vale this happy night,
> He saw the City of Delight
> In fairy-land, whose streets and towers
> Are made of gems and lights and flowers! [105]

In other ways for which no close parallel can be shown, he seems influenced by the amatory and sensuous poetry of Thomas Moore. The ardor of his feelings and the voluptuousness of his imagination must owe a good deal to the poet for whose works there was a steady rage in America during the 1820's and 1830's.

The influence of Byron on Melville, evident in these first sketches, is probably more extensive than has been supposed. He drew on his knowledge of Byron for direct and indirect allusions, as has been pointed out. There are further parallels. His phrase, "the mind which beams from every feature of the face" recalls Byron's "the mind, the Music breathing from her face."[106] Melville's hesitation in describing the second lady, while not uncommon in literature generally, is like Byron's hesitation as he begins to describe Zuleika in "The Bride of Abydos" and Gulbeyaz in *Don Juan.*[107] When the hero enters the apartment in the second "Fragment," he finds it "redolent of the most delicious perfumes." "The Bride of Abydos" snatches

> . . . the urn wherein was mixed
> The Persian Atar-gul's perfume
> And sprinkled all its odours o'er
> The pictured roof and marble floor.[108]

Finally, Melville employs the same literary allusion that Byron had used in a story similar in many details to the second "Fragment." In Canto V of *Don Juan* the captured hero is brought through long galleries to a gigantic portal, and thence into a room resplendent with jewels and gold. At a distance lies a beautiful lady, the Sultana, and Juan approaches and kneels before her. As Juan feels his resolute purity begin to weaken, Byron says:

> As through his palms Bob Acres' valour oozed
> So Juan's virtue ebb'd, I know not how.[109]

In the "Fragment" the hero, on the way to the rendezvous, becomes unnerved at the suspicious adventure, and Melville says that he "felt with Bob Acres in *The Rivals* that 'my valour was certainly going.'" Melville was obviously familiar with the line from his own reading in Sheridan, but considering his numerous direct references to Byron and the echoes, it is probably not mere coincidence that Melville hits upon the same allusion.

It is lamentable that no other writings survive from Melville's early period to study for Byronic influences. But Melville's first compositions owe much to Byron, not only in direct and indirect references, but also in the extravagant expression, in the disposition to project one's self or one's dreams into one's literary creations, as Byron did in *Childe Harold,* and in the sting of disillusion with which the second "Fragment" ends.

In the final analysis Melville's first writings tell us a good deal about their enthusiastic but untutored author. In his twentieth year, despite the dismal days on which he had fallen, he could write with good humor and spontaneity, welling up out of an undeniable urge to self-expression. His attitude toward life is lusty and bumptious. The suggestions of romantic revolt against his refined and thoroughly proper background are strong. If his enthusiasms are somewhat youthful, they still evidence zest for the life of experience as well as for art and literature, both classical and modern. He could indulge in the wildest of romantic effusions, as in the first "Fragment" and much of the second. However, he could also subdue them with humor, ridicule, and disenchantment.

His literary style has the faults common to beginners—verbal and imaginative extravagance, self-consciousness, undue length. Yet in many ways his first works anticipate the style of his best period. He learned very early to fill out his story with a wealth of allusion, literary, historical, and artistic. The second "Fragment" begins with an exclamation as do *Typee* and *Mardi;* its abruptness is repeated in *Redburn, White-Jacket,* and *Moby-Dick.*[110] The suspense secured by deliberately delaying the ending and the dramatic climax itself are repeated in *Typee* and *Mardi* and worked out in Wagnerian form in *Moby-Dick*. Of profound significance is the fact that the "Fragment" tells the story of a frustrated quest. The pattern of this adolescent experiment with the marvelous is the essential pattern of *Mardi, Moby-Dick,* and *Pierre*. Here Melville's hero pursues the trivial end of sensuous perfection. At the very end he is suddenly disappointed. In the works of Melville's greatest period his characters wander over the entire globe and the infinite world of the mind in the pursuit of ultimate beauty, or of power over nature and evil, or of truth and justice. All of them—Taji, Ahab, and Pierre—are the losers in their quests. The ending of the second "Fragment" shows that as early as his twentieth year Melville's mind had formulated, however crudely, the concept that pursuit of the ideal is foredoomed to disillusion and defeat.

In painful contrast to the romantic and socially superior young man of Melville's imagination in the two "Fragments" was their unfortunate author, whose actual existence at the time his articles were published was approaching the climax of its futile course. The events leading up to the denouement may be detailed very briefly. Melville, as we have seen, had offered his sketches to the press on April 20, at a time when his mother had gone further into debt than ever before. The first was printed on May 4 and the second on May 18. Whether Herman received the encouragement of pay for his work is not known, but from a letter of his mother's to Peter Gansevoort it is clear that he was forced to seek some other means of subsistence besides authorship. The letter also provides a clear picture of the desperation that had settled upon the family.

May 23d [1839]

MY DEAR BROTHER—

When I left Albany a month since I brought with me fifty Dollars from each of my Brothers you & Hermen

You will remember my telling you I owed for borrow'd money & Bills forty Eight Dolls. my Rent fell due on the first of May which was $31.25—leaving me $20.75—I have been under the painful necessity of again borrowing from Mrs Peebles besides something owing the Shoemaker. Can you send me a remittance this week. I think some plan must be resolve'd upon, or something decided about my support untill my Sons can do for me, & relieve my mind from an insupportable weight of uncertainty—

Hermen has gone out for a few days on foot to see what he can find to do—

Gansevoort feels well enough to go about, & will leave for new York in a few days.

My love to Mary—& the Children—

Your
only
Sister
MARIA.[111]

If Maria Melville's state of mind was insupportable, Herman's must have been equally so. One can easily picture the wounds to his pride, the frustration, and the despair that must have accumulated as he traveled back and forth on foot seeking employment. In his mind he was harboring dreams of Chesterfieldian and Oriental elegance; in reality he was marching from one to another of Lansingburgh's huddle of shops and factories and the farms of the surrounding country looking for any kind of job. But it was no use. "Herman has returned from his expedition, without success," wrote Gansevoort on the twenty-fourth of May.[112] Furthermore, there was no immediate help to be expected from his uncle. Peter Gansevoort habitually noted on his sister's appeals for money that he had sent the sum requested within a day or two; but Maria's letter above bears the ominous annotation, "1839. May 23 Letter from Maria G. Melville." In Albany a falling out was developing between Uncle Peter and his nephew. As Allan saw it, Peter wanted to "rid himself of all further expenses & responsibility" for his sister's son. Within a few days, he picked a quarrel, provoked Allan to disrespectful language, and rejecting his lukewarm apology, told him to get out.[113] For Herman, as for the rest of the family, the only hope lay in Gansevoort's recovery and his approaching return to New York.

What can be said of Herman Melville's character at the time that he faced the crisis of his youth? The question is of special importance because of the relation between the author of *Redburn* and its juvenile protagonist. The years in the bank and in Gansevoort's store must have taught Herman a good deal of the ways of the world, trained him in prudence, and worn off the edges of his youthful illusions. The exposés of naked vice he had read in the *Albany Microscope* were also part of his informal education. The year on his uncle's farm and the plunge of his own family into poverty brought a further education in the means of meeting reality and fostered the spirit of self-reliance that distinguished Melville at the time when he sought work on the canal system. He had also learned to make accurate judgments and to recognize the gap between the ideal and the real. A fairly mature perspicacity directs his observations on the American school system and his satirical and disillusioned treatment of romance in the second "Fragment." If the "Fragments" suggest indulgence in adolescent dreams of grandeur and of mastery in love, they also indicate a ripening sexual interest. It may be that Melville was more highly developed intellectually than he was socially. His reading during the later years of his youth had been more extensive than his education in society, from which he had been cut off, to a considerable extent, by his brother's failure in business. Nevertheless, all the evidence from his early years, whether direct or implied, indicates that at nineteen he was as mature as the average young man of his age. The protections afforded by his earlier upbringing, with its security, its genteel mode of life, and its tendency to preserve the youthful outlook formed in the home, had been stripped away. Now, within two months of his twentieth birthday, Melville was prepared for the tests of manhood the immediate future was to bring.

Chapter IV

The Sea and the Land, 1839-1841

MARIA MELVILLE hated to write letters, but when the welfare of her family was concerned she did not hesitate. Thanks to one of these notes we can now compose the probable story of Herman's actions in the crucial last week of May 1839. He could choose between waiting at home for something to turn up and making a bold and novel venture. His spirits were too restless to accept a passive role. Gansevoort was ready to leave for the busiest port in the country. Herman had not seen New York since he was eleven, but he remembered the multitude of ships that left every day for ports in England, France, and South America. Gansevoort knew businessmen in New York who might speak a word for him with a shipowner or master. He therefore asked his brother to hunt up a job for him. In a few days Gansevoort left, taking along Allan, whom Uncle Peter had discharged, and Herman waited eagerly for news of Gansevoort's success. Maria's letter tells the rest of the story:

1st June 1839

MY DEAR GANST—

Your letter of yesterday was receiv'd & preparations forthwith commenc'd Herman is happy but I think at heart he is rather agitatated, I can hardly believe it & cannot realize the truth of his going both my boys gone in one week.

How uncertain & changeing are all things here below—but no more of this or you will stop reading. I have put up all I had for Herman that I thought would be useful, endeavour to procure for him every thing within the range of his means that will make him comfortable. write me where his Vessel is bound, and the probable time of his Sailing. Helen went over to Waterford yesterday with Catherine & Leoneard & has not yet come back She will feel bad to have him go without his seeing her—send Allan up at once—I was rejoiced to hear of your safe arrival without injury—

My respects to Mrs. B— & Husband accept my best love my dear Son from your Mother

MARIA

Augusta & all join in affectionate love & remembrance to you—[1]

Herman's departure from home occurred with unexpected suddenness. Although Gansevoort did not mention the destination or sailing time of Herman's "Vessel," he had probably learned that it was to sail early the following week and had written home immediately urging Herman to hurry to New York.[2] Someone picked up his letter at the post office on Friday,[3] undoubtedly in the afternoon, for had it been in the morning Helen would still have been at home and she would have been able to bid Herman good-by. Herman's mother promptly began to get his clothes in order and do the necessary washing and mending, and when she had finished she wrote the letter for Herman to carry to Gansevoort.[4] One can only guess how long her preparations required; but it could hardly have been before Saturday afternoon that Herman left Lansingburgh, journeyed four miles to Troy, boarded the connecting boat to Albany, and took one of the Hudson River steamboats to New York.[5] His departure came too swiftly to prepare for the emotional impact of breaking away from the family circle.

Herman's going was a blow to his mother, but she met it with what her husband would have called characteristic fortitude. "How uncertain and changeing are all things here below," she exclaims philosophically. Her religion had taught her to present an attitude of acceptance to all the vicissitudes of fortune, and she was well furnished with the pious phrases necessary to preserve equilibrium. To Gansevoort her moralizing was merely tiresome, and Herman was now old enough to share Gansevoort's impatience—as old as Gansevoort had been when he flippantly disposed of the duty of attending church. "No more of this or you will stop reading," says Maria, in humble acknowledgment of the difference between herself and the younger generation. The phrase is a helpful clue to divergences in religious attitudes. Maria tried to bear her many crosses with Christian submission. Her sons, frustrated by sickness, unemployment, debt, and nagging poverty, were evidently much less capable of seeing in all this the hand of a benevolent Providence testing human merit by oppression and moving, as Allan Melvill had seen it, through evil toward good. For Herman, "boyhood's thoughtless faith" had probably given way to adolescent doubt.[6] For the rest of his life he would keep deserting his early religious credo, just as it had kept failing him. But for all its inadequacies and its terrible exactions, he would never be able to throw it off completely.

His whole psychological mood at the time of his departure was confused. His mother saw that he was happy, as he must have been at the prospect of travel and adventure in place of the empty life at home. He was about to share in the experiences he had heard of from his father's tales of half a dozen voyages across the Atlantic and from the narratives of his Gansevoort cousins. What taste for the sea he had acquired through these means had perhaps been extended by his reading of Cooper and Byron. Thus there was much to anticipate when Gansevoort's letter arrived. On the other hand, Herman was also "agitated at heart." The excitement of facing the unknown and forebodings about the hardships of a sailor's life must have stirred him. He would be leaving his family and going entirely upon his own. Because he was conscientious and knew his mother's urgent need of money, he must have realized the potential loss to the family welfare. And despite the fact that he was finally going to travel, it was not as a patrician merchant like his father but as a common sailor.

Yet there was really no choice. Had Melville been able to order his own future, he would not have elected to go to sea. He had wanted to be an engineer and surveyor, with reasonable security. He might have kept at writing and perpetuated the strains of Thomas Moore and Lord Byron in periodical literature. He would have taken any job as a stopgap, but when all his efforts produced neither help for his mother nor opportunity for himself, he set out on the highway of escape his brother had opened for him. Hard times, the goad of thousands of other victims of the Panic of 1837, was the chief agent of destiny that drove Melville in rebellious flight to the ocean.[7]

If Melville was perturbed in spirit, he must still have been to some extent prepared for the life ahead of him. From his cousins Guert and Peter Gansevoort he had picked up an acquaintance with nautical routine. And though he apparently never attempted to follow them into the service of his country as an officer,[8] in his venture to Liverpool in the merchant marine he was paying their brother Leonard the compliment of imitation. The histories of Melville and this particular cousin, running in such parallel lines, must have brought them into close sympathy, and the older boy had undoubtedly passed on the fruits of his experience to the younger.

Like Herman Melville, Leonard Gansevoort belonged to a large family and had suffered the loss of his father when he was a boy.[9] He had attended Albany Academy when Herman was there. For a period, his family, like the Melvilles, had enjoyed a certain prosperity and had then fallen on evil times.[10] When he was nineteen, Leonard had gone to sea, not as a naval officer like his brothers, but as a whaler.[11] In November 1837 he had shipped as a sailor on the packet ship "England" of New York, journeyed to Liverpool, spent a few weeks there, and returned on the same ship at the end of January 1838.[12] From his home in nearby Waterford he and his brother Guert, by then a lieutenant in the Navy,[13] had visited Melville's house in

Lansingburgh in June 1838.[14] He was there again on the day before Herman left home[15] and while he was eagerly waiting for Gansevoort to find a ship. Unquestionably there had been frequent intercourse between the two cousins, from which Herman would have learned about the work of a sailor, the conditions in the forecastle, the clothes and equipment one would need, and Leonard's impressions of Liverpool. With a practical schooling from Leonard to counterbalance his own accumulation of romantic notions of the sea, Herman should have been mentally prepared for the realities as well as the novelties of the days ahead.

The moment of Herman's departure from the little house on North Street was hardly a joyful occasion, for either himself or his family. Gansevoort had left only a few days before; Maria Melville could hardly believe that Herman was going too. "Both my boys gone in one week!" she exclaimed, veiling her sensitivities in a commonplace. Gansevoort, at least, would be in New York studying law, but Herman was going to be a sailor, and Maria Melville thought that a sailor's occupation was fit only for those who had neither talents, nor inclination for study, nor ambition to excel.[16] She had no snobbish pride that would be immeasurably wounded by Herman's inglorious plunge into the society of common seamen, but she must have felt disappointment that the world had offered him no better opportunity.

In addition, she had to send Herman off with somewhat scanty equipment. After two years of impoverishment, a young man in his late teens is not likely to have an extensive wardrobe. But Maria supplied him with everything she had that she thought would be useful, and one can safely assume that this included at least one change of clothes, extra linen and socks, food for the journey, and enough money to get him safely to New York. Thus equipped, he left home and sailed down the Hudson that he had traveled so often in the days before his father's untimely death. In New York he made his way through the rain two miles uptown, very his old homes on Cortlandt Street and goal was the house of Alexander W. teteenth Street, where his brothers were staying.[18] Bradford, the son of the minister who had married Herman's parents, was one of Gansevoort's intimate friends and had known Herman from his youth.[19] After a brilliant career at Union College he had married and come to New York, where he was now moving toward prominence not only in his profession of law but also in scholarship, politics, and literature.[20] For the next three days he was host to Herman and his two brothers.

From figures that Gansevoort jotted down on the letter his mother had written, it is possible to conclude that Herman had some intention of going to sea as a whaleman.[21] If so, he was reasoned out of his folly. Instead, he secured his berth as a "boy" with Captain Oliver P. Brown aboard the "St. Lawrence," bound for Liverpool, and learned that the ship was scheduled to sail on Tuesday, June 4.[22] He signed the required shipping articles at one of the many offices in New York.[23] With the help of Gansevoort, whom Maria had instructed to "procure for him every thing within the range of his means that [would] make him comfortable," Herman purchased articles for a sea wardrobe. Perhaps he read on Monday the advertisement for his ship:

> Passage for Liverpool
> First Packet—To-morrow
>
> The splendid fast sailing packet ship ST. LAWRENCE, Captain O. P. Brown, will positively sail as above. A few more cabin and steerage passengers can yet be very handsomely accommodated at low rates, if immediate applications be made on board, at Pier 14 East River . . . .[24]

On Tuesday, presumably, he left the Bradford house, went down to Pier 14 at the foot of Jones Lane, and passing by the tangle of masts and spars and bowsprits pushed out over South Street, reported for duty on the "St. Lawrence."[25] It would be strange indeed if Gansevoort or Allan or both did not come to the pier to bid him good-by. However, because of the rain and the onshore east wind, both of which had persisted for three days,[26] the sailing of the "St. Lawrence" was postponed, and Herman's adventure began in anti-climax.

Thus it was on Wednesday, June 5, that his nautical career began. Although the dismal rain and cold continued, the wind shifted to the northwest, and refusing to wait like the packet ship "Rochester" and a fleet of outward-bound vessels for perfect conditions, Captain Brown took the "St. Lawrence" down the harbor, probably moving off on the flood tide about half past two in the afternoon.[27] By the standards of the regular packets, with which she was trying to compete, the "St. Lawrence" was not a particularly large ship, only 119 feet 6 inches long, 25 feet 6 inches wide, and 12 feet 9 inches deep, with a displacement of 356 58/95 tons.[28] The "Rochester," for example, was twice as large, as was the packet ship "England," on which Leonard Gansevoort had sailed.[29] However, as Melville says in *Redburn,* the "St. Lawrence" was not a packet, leaving New York on fixed days on a schedule, but apparently a "regular trader," traveling between the same ports and sailing only when her cargo and passenger list were sufficiently full.[30] Melville describes her easygoing career when he makes Redburn say:

> . . . I had no reason to regret that the *Highlander* [as he calls the "St. Lawrence"] was not a liner; for aboard of those liners, from all I could gather from those who had sailed in them, the crew have terrible hard work, owing to their carrying such a press of sail, in order to make as rapid passages as possible, and sustain the ship's reputation for speed.[31]

The "St. Lawrence" had no particular nautical distinction. She did have a figurehead, a fact which Melville remembered when he supplied Redburn's ship with a carved figure of a Scottish Highlander "in full fig." [32] Otherwise she was a conventional three-masted, square-rigged ship with two decks that had been built at Duxbury, Massachusetts, six years before and was therefore relatively new. In 1838 she had been added to the large fleet that enabled Howland and Aspinwall, her owners, to do the biggest business of any New York shipping firm at the time.[33]

By a species of irony it is the coldly official crew list of the "St. Lawrence" that furnishes the earliest physical description of Herman Melville. With his twentieth birthday two months away, he was nearly five feet nine inches tall with a light complexion and brown hair.[34] Even more ally, the name of the only member of the ship's com- destined to achieve a pedestal in history was mis- y entered as Norman instead of Herman.[35] Melville's mates seem to have been a representative group of ican sailors, with two foreigners for contrast. Beyond tails of the crew list, no information about the men gave him his first real education in a sailor's life has to light so that there is little basis for believing what lle says about them in *Redburn*. But half a dozen have els at least in the pages of that romance. Joseph M. [illegible], Jr., was the first officer, and if Melville, like Redburn, was assigned to the first mate's watch, it was this experienced sailor from New York who routed him out at watch call, ordered him into the rigging, and handled his landlubber's ignorance with whatever patience or impatience he possessed. The second mate, who as in all ships stood halfway between the crew and the officers, with some of the responsibilities of both, was a Yankee, Nathan or Nathaniel Heard of Massachusetts, and if *Redburn* is to be credited, he declined the honor of having Melville in his watch. It was a District of Columbia Negro, Moses Walker, Jr., who concocted the slumgullion and ship's coffee that Melville had to eat for his four months on the "St. Lawrence." Among the ordinary crew members, James Johnson, a twenty-year-old sailor born in Ireland was perhaps the "remarkably robust and good-humored young man from Belfast in Ireland" who turns up in *Redburn,* though he may have been Jack Blunt, who was also an "Irishman born." Peter Brown, a native and citizen of Greenland, unquestionably accounts for the "Greenlander" in *Redburn.*

And the name of Rober rn in New York and was thir Red-burn's Jackson, the most who was also "a native of New York City" and might have been "thirty or perhaps fifty years" old.[36] Finally, Melville's captain, Oliver P. Brown, was probably a native of Stockholm, Sweden, who had been naturalized some fifteen or twenty years before, a background which may have prompted Melville to call him Captain Riga and give him a Russian origin.[37]

Redburn is so much a blend of fact and fiction that it would be dangerous to picture Melville's life with his shipmates on the "St. Lawrence" in any other than general terms. One may safely assume that some of them came aboard drunk and "tapered off" with jugs of Jamaica rum for a few days, that they were at times sociable and kind and at other times unapproachable, surly, and abusive, that they swore liberally and salted their discourse with obscenities, and that most of them were experienced sailors who held all greenhorn landlubbers in contempt but were glad to teach a newcomer a sailor's skills if he was courageous, unassuming, and willing to learn.[38] Except for Jackson, they do not appear even in Melville's unflattering account to have been as bad as many merchant crews were a century ago.[39] In *Redburn* Melville says nothing about thievery, fist fights, degeneration, or mutiny, things so naturally interesting that he would have been certain to include them if they had occurred. Nor was their condition under Captain Brown particularly grievous, if the contemporary rate of desertion is a reliable yardstick. Only three of them, less than 20 per cent, left the ship at Liverpool whereas of four ships that sailed from New York within two weeks of the "St. Lawrence" the percentages of desertion were 45, 48, 62, and 70.[40]

As a greenhorn sailor, Melville's lot on the "St. Lawrence" was arduous. To be sure, he was not a mere youngster, like Redburn, isolated by a gap of years from almost everyone in the forecastle. Laurence Crawford was nineteen, exactly his own age, the Irishman was twenty, and five of the others were twenty-four or under. However, their advantages in experience offset their equality in years. Since Melville had no previous education as a sailor, he shipped as a "boy," at insignificant wages.[41] In the American merchant marine at this time a boy's pay ranged from three to eight dollars a month, though sometimes, being considered an apprentice, he received nothing.[42] In *The Seaman's Friend* Richard Henry Dana, Jr., has described the duties of "boys":

> If decks are to be cleared up or swept, rigging to be coiled up, a man is to be helped in his job, or any duty to be done aloft or about decks which does not require the strength or skill of a seaman, a boy is always expected to start first and do it, though not called upon by name.[43]

Melville's other duties were to stand watches, slush down the masts, hold the log reel, and loose and furl the light sails (a "boy" was allowed to steer only during a calm).[44] His experienced shipmates would have taught him the names and uses of all the ropes and how to reef and furl the royal sails and make the common hitches, bends, and knots.[45] Yet in the weeks needed to master the mere names of things aboard ship, Melville must have felt constantly the annoyance of being inferior and inept. And since it was a boy's duty to clean up the pigpen and the chicken coops which passenger vessels carried, he undoubtedly had the humiliating chore that Redburn found such a disillusioning introduction to the life of a sailor.

Presumably Melville learned quickly, undaunted by the coarse burgoo eaten out of wooden tubs, the plain wooden bunk in the dark forecastle, the rough and often dangerous work of hoisting and trimming sails, the frequent drenchings, and the humble position. Having toiled for nearly a year as a farm hand, he knew the strains of manual labor and perhaps the dignity as well. His wish to take a subordinate place when he applied for work on the canal system indicates that he would have accepted his lot on the "St.

Lawrence" manfully, without false pride or smug assumptions of superiority. In breeding, education, tastes, and manners he was different from his crew mates, as Richard Henry Dana was on the "Pilgrim," and he undoubtedly experienced the force of that instinctive hostility the majority feel toward the elite. In these circumstances, did he behave like the supercilious dandy of the first "Fragment," aping Lord Chesterfield and lording it over his boorish associates? Was he in actuality like the callow, snobbish, and conceited Redburn, who condescended to the sailors on the "Highlander" and even made a foolish attempt to meet the captain on equal social terms? Did he boast of an ancestry reaching back to English knights and Norwegian kings? Or did he share Dana's native wisdom and take care to be a shipmate and not to put on the gentleman?

Perhaps the best answer to these questions lies in Melville's own assertions in *Mardi:*

> Now, at sea, and in the fellowship of sailors, all men appear as they are. No school like a ship for studying human nature. The contact of one man with another is too near and constant to favor deceit. You wear your character as loosely as your flowing trowsers. Vain all endeavours to assume qualities not yours; or to conceal those you possess. Incognitos, however desirable, are out of the question. And thus aboard of all ships in which I have sailed, I have invariably been known by a sort of drawing-room title. Not—let me hurry to say—that I put hand in tar bucket with a squeamish air, or ascended the rigging with a Chesterfieldian mince. No, no, I was never better than my vocation; and mine have been many. . . . And never did shipmate of mine upbraid me with a genteel disinclination to duty, though it carried me to truck of mainmast, or jib-boom-end, in the most wolfish blast that ever howled.
>
> Whence, then, this annoying appellation? for annoying it most certainly was. It was because of something in me that could not be hidden; stealing out in an occasional polysyllable; an otherwise incomprehensible deliberation in dining; remote, unguarded allusions to Belles-Lettres affairs; and other trifles superfluous to mention.[46]

This candid confession gives the best clues to Melville's situation aboard the "St. Lawrence" that anyone can find at

ith what we have learned about his
rly years. He had known comforts,
eel atmosphere, had read widely, and
authorship. It was impossible for him to disguise his social and intellectual character. But he had also been disciplined against arrogance by a liberal education in hardship. It is incredible that he behaved on the "St. Lawrence" like the noxious snob in the first "Fragment" or the presumptuous juvenile in *Redburn*. Melville, we may well believe, was never better than his vocation.

Since no details of the voyage of the "St. Lawrence" are available, we must omit the Atlantic crossing and take up Melville's story in Liverpool.[47] On the second of July, after a passage of twenty-seven days, the "St. Lawrence" worked her way up the Mersey River and into Prince's Dock.[48] For six weeks she remained there, discharging her 920 bales of cotton and taking on her cargo of iron bars, copper, earthenware, tin plates, wire, blankets, and hemp.[49] It was not Melville's duty to help with these operations, which were handled by dockmen and porters. Ships' crews in Liverpool were kept busy at painting, scraping, and caulking the seams,[50] but they were given generous time off. Melville had, for the first time, the opportunity to explore a foreign city, one with which he had a few associations through his father's two brief visits thirty years before. Whatever his cousin Leonard Gansevoort may have told him about dirty, sprawling Liverpool, it was probably a disappointment to Melville to learn for himself that as far as the pleasures of sight-seeing were concerned he might just as well have stayed in New York.

In 1839 Liverpool was a wealthy, enterprising city and the second port in England, partially because of its profits from the infamous slave trade but more especially because it was the terminus of a network of inland waterways that made it the natural outlet for the manufactures of the Midlands and the North. In its rapid growth, it had achieved singularly little civic beauty, and what there was lay most of the time under a thick pall of black smoke or enveloped in the constant rain.[51] Its principal attraction, for both traders and tourists, was the chain of intercommunicating docks, built of solid masonry, that stretched for over two miles along the east bank of the Mersey. Beyond these, there was little to see. As an English visitor described it:

It is here among the docks, on the river, or along the opposite shore, that all the poetry of Liverpool is to be found: for the town itself is singularly deficient in old and romantic associations. . . . It is to the great towns of Europe what America is to the great nations of Europe.[52]

For the American traveler, Liverpool was merely a port of entry, a convenient point at which to recover from the Atlantic crossing in preparation for journeys to the Lake country, or Scotland, or the Cathedral towns. Isaiah Townsend, who had once bought caps from Herman Melville in Albany, found Liverpool a "stupid bartering place" in 1840. In other countries, he wrote, one is taken first to the cathedral; in Liverpool your hosts take you first to the Market Hall, "considered by its good burgesses of all their public buildings *facile princeps*."[53] Three men who were to know Melville only a few years later and to be among his enthusiastic critics shared Townsend's opinion. Bayard Taylor spent a single day in the city; Thurlow Weed, a politician and editor in Melville's own city of Albany, found little to interest the ordinary tourist; and N. P. Willis gave Liverpool a passing glance, found it very much like New York, and moved on. So did Edward E. Salisbury, later to be professor of linguistics at Yale, who when crossing the Mersey in 1836 "was struck with the resemblance of the opposite shore to that of Brooklyn, N. Y., and when on the other side [was] forcibly reminded, by the appearance of Liverpool, of the city of N. Y."[54]

Thus when Melville first saw Liverpool, like Redburn he undoubtedly found the dingy warehouses along the Mersey "very deficient in the elements of the marvellous" and bearing "a most unexpected resemblance to the warehouses along South Street in New York." [55] His composite impression after he had had time to explore the city was assuredly that of Redburn:

It was the humiliating fact . . . that upon the whole, and barring the poverty and beggary, Liverpool, away from the docks, was very much such a place as New York. There were the same sort of streets pretty much; the same rows of houses with stone steps; the same kind of sidewalks and curbs; and the same elbowing, heartless-looking crowd as ever.[56]

To the "poverty and beggary" of Liverpool Melville devotes several pages of impassioned social protest in *Redburn.* That the conditions he describes actually existed is corroborated from numerous sources. Margaret Fuller observed with sympathy and dismay "the squalid and shameless beggars" of the town.[57] In 1844 an observer found the extremes of poverty and wealth in Liverpool "hardly credible," with ordinarily industrious people forced to pawn clothes for bread and live in crowded cellars and often reduced to beggary or crime.[58] More than one third of the population was confined to close courts or cellars, where six to thirty people huddled into tiny sties of two or three rooms. The overflow from filthy ashpits and privies in the courts seeped into the wretched hovels of the poor or oozed its stinking way to the street. With the polluted atmosphere and the appalling concentration of human beings in damp and windowless rooms, typhus fever and consumption raged perpetually; Liverpool, with an average age at death of seventeen years, was the most unhealthful town in all England.[59] The overcrowding and consequent misery were the worst in that very part of the city which spawned the sailor's boardinghouses, gin palaces, and brothels alluded to in *Redburn.*[60] It was this area, too, that probably supported most of Liverpool's 2,900 prostitutes.[61]

Even if Melville was not completely unprepared for this overwhelming panorama of vice, poverty, and woe, he must have been deeply shocked at the contrast between America and England. In America at the time, he says, such a thing as a native pauper was virtually unknown.[62] One can easily attribute some of his later humanitarianism to the effects on him of Liverpool's miserable slums. The occasions were there for the attacks on Western civilization which he made later, not only in *Mardi* and *Redburn* but as early as *Typee*. The grotesque contrasts of opulence and destitution in Liverpool must have seemed the utter reverse of the Christian ideal. Melville's own poverty had undoubtedly germinated the seeds of religious questioning. The wretched scenes he witnessed in Liverpool in 1839 nourished it toward the powerful fruition Melville reached in his intellectual maturity: ". . . Why create the germs that sin and suffer, but to perish?" asks Babbalanja, in *Mardi*. It is the focal question in the book, "the last mystery which underlieth all the rest. . . . that mystery Oro [God] guards; and none but him may know." [63] The share of Liverpool in prompting the question was perhaps immeasurable.

It was Melville's pennilessness, of course, that limited him to the observation of one side of Liverpool life. He was entitled to only a few dollars' advance on his meager wages.[64] Liverpool had facilities for the pleasures he had once known in Albany, but all of them, the Athenaeum and Lyceum Reading Rooms, the Royal Institution, with its display of paintings which Margaret Fuller admired, and even the Zoological Gardens, demanded admission fees or were open to strangers only if properly introduced by one of the proprietors. Two of Liverpool's three theaters were closed in the summer, and the third was no more available for Melville than the handsome Baths near St. George's Dock or any of Liverpool's other elegant institutions maintained for the edification of the well-to-do.[65] His sight-seeing was restricted to the docks, which evidently fascinated him,[66] to the few public buildings like the Exchange and the Customs House, to the glittering shop windows on fashionable Lord Street, and to the endless streets teeming with indigent people. It is no wonder that a week after his arrival he wrote his mother that he would gladly exchange all the sights of Liverpool to see one little corner of home.[67]

In Liverpool Melville was a young man of good education and cultured tastes deprived of the means and the social station to indulge his natural interests. His plight contrasts sharply with the situation of another young man of similar background who, only seven years later, was to become Melville's sponsor in the literary and social circles of New York. In November 1838 Evert A. Duyckinck, son of an affluent publisher, had sailed for Europe to make the grand tour like a hundred other scions of moneyed American families. Traveling in style, Duyckinck moved in leisurely fashion from Paris to Rouen, from Brussels to London, taking in the riches of Europe's cathedrals, galleries, theaters, and landscapes and recording them urbanely in his diaries.[68] About three weeks after the "St. Lawrence" deposited Melville the sailor in Liverpool for six weeks of seamy existence, Evert Duyckinck arrived there on his way to York and the North. Melville took his meals at a sailors' boardinghouse and slept in the forecastle;[69] Duyckinck stopped at the popular Adelphi Hotel, "where one may live very well," as he noted. Feeling none of the uneasiness of the poorly dressed sailor, Duyckinck looked in at the Exchange Reading Room, listened to Harriet Martineau's father preach in the Unitarian Chapel, and observed with pleasure the beautiful paintings in the Grecian Chapel of the Church for the Blind. There is no record that Melville encountered anybody in Liverpool of his own country and station; Duyckinck had the good luck to meet a friend, Dr. Moore, just as that gentleman was getting off the packet "Shakespeare" from New York. It was, wrote Duyckinck, "an incident worth a great deal in a strange land."

It is possible that Fate, which had brought these two young men to the same city at the same time, but in such different circumstances, may have thrust them into even closer contact. In reporting on his churchgoing Redburn talks of the many clergymen who addressed sailor audiences wherever they could find them.

Whenever, in my Sunday strolls, [he says] I caught sight of one of these congregations, I always made a point of joining it; and would find myself surrounded by a motley crowd of seamen from all quarters of the globe, and women, and lumpers, and dock labourers of all sorts.[70]

Melville had undoubtedly seen and joined such gatherings; so had Evert Duyckinck. On Sunday, July 28, he noted: "Met today two street preachers, one on the steps of the exchange, with two elderly persons on each side—his audience chiefly of sailors, talking well . . . ." Since Melville went frequently to the Exchange to view the statue of Nelson in the courtyard, it is far from impossible that he was there on the Sunday Duyckinck heard the street preacher; so the "audience chiefly of sailors" whom Duyckinck observed so cursorily might very well have contained the man for whose works he would later become the principal American eulogist and whose personal friendship he would enjoy for over three decades.

Melville's description of the preachers who went into the streets to seek out their sailor audiences is one of the few incidents in the Liverpool section of *Redburn* that receives any kind of confirmation from a separate source. Of greater significance is an experience for which the witness is Melville himself. On Redburn's first stroll through Liverpool, he goes up Chapel Street and through an old archway into the quadrangle of the Merchant's Exchange, in the center of which he finds a statue in bronze representing Lord Nelson. He describes the figure of Victory dropping a wreath on the dying admiral's brow, while Death, represented as a skeleton, gropes under his robe for his heart. The figures of four swarthy captives around the base, supposed to represent Nelson's major victories, remind Redburn of slaves in the market place.

How this group of statuary affected me, [he concludes] may be inferred from the fact, that I never went through Chapel Street without going through the little arch to look at it again. And there, night or day, I was sure to find Lord Nelson still falling back; Victory's wreath still hovering over his sword-point; and Death grim and grasping as ever; while the four bronze captives still lamented their captivity.[71]

That Melville had actually paid visits to this statue is evidenced by an entry in the journal he kept in 1856, when he found himself in Liverpool again, after seventeen years. "After dinner," he wrote, "went to Exchange. Looked at Nelson's statue, with peculiar emotion, mindful of 20 years ago."[72] The exact nature of his "peculiar emotion" may only be guessed at. It is safe to say that he was thinking back to the days when, as a friendless and obscure sailor in a foreign city, the monument to Nelson was one of the few objects of pleasure he encountered in his lonely wanderings.

Of Melville's further experiences in Liverpool, a few are identifiable with Redburn's and others may be safely assumed as true. When Redburn, on one of his Sunday strolls, came across the Moorish arch forming the entrance to the noted Liverpool and Manchester Railway, he was surprised by the feeling that he had seen the unusual sight before. The mystery did not clear until several months later when in looking over an old copy of the *Penny Magazine* at home, he saw a picture of the very place and remembered that he had seen the print years before. It seems certain that this reminiscence was Melville's, for the print of the Moorish arch had appeared in the *Penny Magazine* in 1833.[73]

On the same Sunday, Redburn joined a crowd of mechanics, artisans, and soldiers in St. George's Square, "near the base of George the Fourth's equestrian statue," to hear the harangue of a pale and worn young man whose inflammatory speech revealed him as a Chartist.[74] Again, Melville is reflecting his own experience; the Liverpool *Mercury* for July 5, 1839, reported that just such a stripling, about eighteen years of age, was giving outdoor lectures on Sundays about Chartism. Melville's comment, assuming it to be his immediate reaction, is interesting for its mingling of human sympathy and political conservatism. He went away thinking the young man "must be some despairing elder son, supporting by hard toil his mother and sisters; for of such many political desperadoes are made." [75] Despite his own penniless state and the shocking destitution in Liverpool, his political sympathies had not apparently been aroused to the point where he would abandon the thinking of his own class.[76]

Melville's picture in *Redburn* of the shameless stratagems of professional beggars, while convincing enough in itself, is borne out by such stories as the newspaper account of the mendicant woman who was found to be collecting over a pound a day with borrowed twins.[77] He also speaks of a sailor who had murdered a woman of the town, an incident which he calls typical of "the events which take place in the lowest and most abandoned neighborhoods frequented by sailors in Liverpool." In the three weeks from July 12 to August 2, the Liverpool *Mercury* reported four stabbings in Liverpool, all by sailors. Its columns in the summer of 1839 contain innumerable stories from the police court of the depredations of prostitutes, who within a few weeks plundered as much as ten thousand dollars from the hordes of drunkards, in the open streets as well as in houses.[78] There is no doubt that Melville observed the sordid parade of vice and crime he describes in *Redburn*. Did he feel somewhat righteously about the miscreants that "with sulphur and brimstone they ought to be burned out of their arches like vermin"? Very probably. He knew that such reprobates flourished even in Albany, but perhaps he was not yet old or wise enough to hate the sin and love the sinner.

Only these experiences are verifiable, but we may also feel sure that Melville, like Redburn, went to church regularly in Liverpool. Wherever he wandered in future years, even in the South Seas, he tried to be at service on Sundays, and when he returned to Europe ten years later he attended church on six of the seven Sundays of his sojourn, sometimes going twice in one day.[79] In Liverpool he could choose from among forty-two churches, including the Floating Chapel. At the latter, where he went at least once, it seems,[80] he may have seen the Reverend Doctor William Scoresby, former master of a Greenland whaler, whom Melville was to cite in *Moby-Dick* as "the best existing authority" on the Greenland whale.[81] In the other churches he had his only opportunity to see Liverpool from the inside and to mingle on terms approaching equality with people like himself. What spiritual nourishment he secured and what comfort and exhortations to good, what points of doctrine he heard expounded and how he accepted them, are indeterminable. However, he must often have felt a pang of loneliness when the congregation broke up and walked away to their comfortable homes.

These excursions could have brought only an accumulation of disappointment and the urgent wish to see something of the real England. In this respect, he was most certainly like Redburn. "I often thought," says the latter, "of London's being only seven or eight hours' travel by railroad from where I was; and that *there,* surely, must be a world of wonders waiting my eyes." Such a dream would have been most natural for Melville. At different times his father had spent over six weeks in London. Melville was assuredly reminiscing when he makes Redburn recall his father's story of "going up into the ball of St. Paul's in London." In Liverpool we may be sure that Melville looked regretfully at the few dollars he had received from Captain Brown and sought to multiply them into the cost of train fares, a hotel room, and perhaps a ticket to the Theatre Royal, where his father had once seen *The Beaux' Stratagem.*[82] But it is doubtful, despite Redburn's trip to London, that Melville reached the city in 1839. Instead, he probably had to wait ten years before he could emulate his cosmopolitan father. Ironically, when he was finally able to see the Lord Mayor's show and St. Paul's, the first struck him as "a most bloated pomp" and the second left him feeling "homesick and sentimentally unhappy." [83]

The American traveler could see Liverpool in three days or less, according to a contemporary guidebook.[84] At the end of only one week there, Melville had been homesick and bored. Liverpool could offer only the same tiresome round of strange faces, strange streets, and strange buildings. It was the threshold of England, but beyond it Melville was unable to go. His mind turned to America and home, and the "St. Lawrence" must have looked ultimately like the vehicle of a new escape.

At first he thought that the ship might not return to New York but go to Charleston or some port in New England.[85] But on the nineteenth of July the *Liverpool Mercury* carried an announcement which Melville doubtless greeted as the best possible present for his twentieth birthday:

> To Sail on the 1st August
> FOR NEW YORK
> The fine first-class American Ship
> ST. LAWRENCE
> O. P. Brown, Master;
>
> Burthen 500 tons: [86] coppered and copper-fastened, and is a very desirable conveyance for goods and passengers.—For terms of which, apply to Captain Brown, on board, Prince's Dock . . . .

A few days later Melville saw the ship begin to load her cargo.[87] As in New York, however, there were delays, and though the ship was later advertised to clear on August 2 and sail on August 3,[88] it was not until the thirteenth that she actually got off. Melville's description of the scene is authentic:

> Owing to a strong breeze, which had been blowing up the river for four days past, holding wind-bound in the various docks a multitude of ships for all parts of the world; there was now under weigh, a vast fleet of merchantmen, all steering broad out to sea. The white sails glistened in the clear morning air like a great Eastern encampment of sultans; and from many a forecastle, came the deep mellow old song *Ho-o-he-yo, cheerily men!* as the crews catted their anchors.[89]

Melville was homeward bound, and one can but believe that he saw with little regret the "dingy warehouses along the Mersey" dropping out of sight.

Melville's return to America was, as far as can be ascertained, an uneventful voyage. Some of the vessels leaving Liverpool were swarming with hundreds of immigrants whose lives in the overcrowded steerages would present a pageant of human misery before the long crossing was finished. The "St. Lawrence," however desirable a conveyance she may have been in the opinion of her agents, carried little human freight.[90] The journey took half again as long as the eastward crossing because of prevailing head winds, and since the routine on shipboard was no longer a novelty, the seven weeks' passage must have brought many periods of ennui and impatience for the sight of American soil. Did Melville find a companion of similar background to share the long days and nights as Redburn did in Harry Bolton? One cannot be sure. However, there were new faces in the crew, one of whom may have been Harry's prototype. Of the fourteen Americans and two foreigners who sailed the ship to Liverpool, three, McLain, Williams, and Thompson, had deserted her.[91] Jackson and Brown had also left the ship long enough to be struck from the crew list but had rejoined it before the day of sailing.[92] The places of the deserters had been taken by Thomas Moore, Antono Ton, and Henry Gill.[93] Only the correspondence between "Henry" Gill and "Harry" Bolton offers any clue to the autobiographical truth of the intense friendship recorded in *Redburn.*

By Sunday, September 29, forty-seven days after leaving Liverpool, the "St. Lawrence" was off Sandy Hook, where transatlantic vessels took on their pilots.[94] The ship was becalmed most of the day, providing Melville with an experience upon which he would draw in *Mardi* as well as in *Redburn.*[95] The next day the ship evidently passed quarantine without detention [96] and traveled up through the Narrows. This was the scene, as Melville represented it:

Now rose the city from out the bay, and one by one, her spires pierced the blue; while thick and more thick, ships, brigs, schooners, and sailboats, thronged around. We saw the Hartz Forest of masts and black rigging stretching along the East River; and northward, up the stately old Hudson, covered with white sloop-sails like fleets of swans, we caught a fair glimpse of the purple Palisades.

Oh! he who has never been afar, let him go once from home, to know what home is. For as you draw nigh to your old native river, he seems to pour through you with all his tides, and in your enthusiasm, you swear to build altars like milestones, along both his sacred banks.[97]

Although Melville was undeniably glad to get back to New York, the ship did not dock until the next day: there were the official inspections of the cargo and the crew to undergo. It was on Tuesday, October 1, that the "St. Lawrence" came finally to her pier, and Melville's first voyage was over.[98]

The trip had undoubtedly disillusioned him. From a decent and pious environment, where certain civilities were demanded, Melville had plunged into the crude milieu of the forecastle with its inevitable drunkenness, profanity, and ribaldry and its unfeeling directness in personal relationships.[99] The experience would have brought perpetual shock to any young man who had been bred to a sensitive reserve. Melville must have suffered during his four months on the "St. Lawrence" from the sense of belonging to a different world, of speaking a different language, of thinking different thoughts. In Liverpool the spectacle of poverty had thrust upon him a widened knowledge of disease in the social body and of man's capacity for evil. There also, since he was without money, the sensations of the outcast would have multiplied. He had felt few of the satisfactions of people like Evert Duyckinck. On the other hand he had at least crossed the ocean, learned something about a foreign country, and quieted his wanderlust for the time being. He could feel some of the assurance that comes from direct experience with the rawest kind of life, for he had lived daily with coarse men and done a man's work. His disappointments were keen, but his courageous venture had at least worked tough fibers into the fabric of his being.

Still, the Liverpool trip evidently left Melville with no desire for a career in the merchant service. Such an ambition was common to many thousands of young Americans, both rich and poor, in an era when ships and profits were rapidly increasing. Even the sons of wealthy merchants often went to sea without losing caste, for with sufficient determination they could rise quickly. Nathaniel Silsbee, who had captained an East Indian trader at the age of twenty-one, had ultimately become a senator from Massachusetts; William Sturges, who shipped at seventeen and rose to captain two years later, ended as head of a firm that controlled much of the China trade.[100] Most of the masters of the New York packet ships, precursors of the modern transatlantic liner, came up through the service, from boy to seaman, first mate, and captain.[101] And as is well known, Melville's younger brother Thomas, who went to sea at sixteen, secured in a few years the command of the "Meteor," a clipper ship trading with the Orient.[102]

But if Melville had any such aspirations, his next step would have been to find work on another ship or even on the "St. Lawrence," where his previous experience would entitle him to the rank of ordinary seaman.[103] He might in a few years have become mate and then captain of one of the hundreds of merchant ships in New York. But Melville did not go back to the merchant service. Instead, he returned to his mother's home in Lansingburgh and attempted once more to find a satisfactory niche in the life that had offered so little before. What he found there was disheartening enough to have driven him back to sea.

Mortgages were foreclosing on his mother's real estate; worse still, she had just learned that Abel Whipple, a creditor, feeling "he had been played with long enough," was determined to go through with a sheriff's sale of her furniture.[104] The fear Peter Gansevoort had expressed over a year before had now been realized. Herman had to face the painful notoriety of having family possessions advertised at auction in the papers; there may even have been notices tacked up in the courthouse or on the doorpost of the house on North Street. Unless the furniture was bought in by a relative or friend, as frequently happened, Herman may have found his own home despoiled of comforts and more barren than the forecastle of the "St. Lawrence."

His family's poverty had changed only for the worse. Very soon after his return he went down to Albany with an urgent request for funds from Uncle Peter, who could give him only a meager fifty dollars.[105] But it was a futile stopgap. A month later Maria Melville, in the most desperate and poignant appeal she had yet made, wrote of her "struggle with absolute want," the frantic routine of paying off her debts with borrowed money only to be poor again in a few days, the dishonesty continually forced upon her because she had to impose on the good faith of the butcher and baker with little prospect of paying them back. "This is not right," she protested, and if her brothers were going to let things go on this way, her "sense of honesty" commanded her to break up the family and find harbor for the children with whoever would take them. Peter had told her that the times were hard; her answer had the obstinate logic of the poor the world over:

> If I could postpone my wants untill the times become easy, I would do it with all my heart—but you are not to learn, but must know—that Shelter, food, & fuel, cannot be postponed—neither Shoes or the wearing of them to those in the habit of wearing them . . . .[106]

Maria's appeal produced only twenty dollars, which Peter Gansevoort had already borrowed to pay some of his own bills,[107] though later in the winter her brother Herman was able to send more.[108] Meanwhile her son had had a little luck. About the first of December Herman began teaching school again, in Greenbush, a hamlet thirteen miles southeast of Lansingburgh, where a handful of houses clustered around a few stores and the Dutch Church.[109] The name of his school is uncertain. Perhaps it was one of the several district schools; more probably it was the Greenbush and Schodack Academy. He seemed to be much interested in his work and alive to the responsibility of educating the sixty students in the school.[110] For a country schoolteacher, he had been promised a good salary, and though the cost of board and clothing was going to eat up the whole of his first quarter's income, he planned to turn over $150.00 to $200.00 a year to his mother.[111]

His prospects gave his mother much cheer while he himself was still capable of flippant humor. A few days after seeing his brother Allan, now clerking for Ten Broek and French at five dollars a month in Albany,[112] he wrote to him:

MY DEAR SERGEANT

How is you? Am you very well? How has you been?—As to myself I haint been as well as husual. I has had a very cruel cold this darnation long time, & I has had and does now have a werry bad want of appetisement.—I seed Mrs Peebles tother day and she did say to me to not to fail to tell you that she am well

No more at present
from your friend
TAWNEY[113]

He seems to have been mimicking both Negroes and the Cockneys he had listened to aboard the "St. Lawrence" as well as the tireless banalities of social converse. He was boarding in Greenbush, where he could see his good friend Eli Fly, who lived there and who sometimes walked with him to Lansingburgh for a week end.[114] At Christmas Maria Melville urged Herman to invite Eli home for the holiday so that he could repay some of the older boy's kindnesses while she herself made "every preparation" in her power to entertain her sons in the traditional way.[115] With only driblets of money coming in at uncertain intervals, it was her fortitude that kept the family together and maintained a home for Herman to come to.

It must have been during this year that Herman was attracted to Harriet Fly, Eli's sister, and either loaned or gave to her the little volume of verse and prose he had received as a prize at the Albany Academy eight years before. The various autographs, markings, and brief marginal comments in the book create a fascinating puzzle of identification and chronology that defies all but the most general interpretations. Harriet Fly inscribed her name on various pages, once writing romantically on a side margin, "Harriet, Fly, Fly, Fly away." Another hand, which looks like Herman's, added "Harriet" beside "Fly," one of the poems. Most cryptic and pregnant of all Harriet's markings is the line, "I wonder who we are to have 10 June 1840 l— H—." "Love, Harriet" is a safe guess, of course, but "who we are to have" and at what? A party? A wedding? Some vital secret in Melville's life seems to be locked up in these tantalizing words.

His own share in the inscriptions presents difficulties too. In view of Gansevoort's long illness and consequent irritability, Herman probably approved by the marginal "yes" someone's observation that "sickness breaks down the pride of manhood." A similar "yes" appears beside a publisher's blurb that the volume was "the only kind of book really enjoyable in the open air." It is possible that Herman copied these lush verses into the book:

> Come tell me, says Rosa, as kissing, and kissed
> One day, she reclined on my breast.
> Come tell me the number, repeat me the list,
> Of the maids you have loved and caressed.

This uninhibited quatrain also seems to be in Melville's handwriting:

> Give me my Love that billing kiss
> You taught me one delicious night
> When growing epicures in bliss
> We tried inventions of delight.

Either Herman or someone else who had access to the book wrote "beautiful, pretty, splendid, odorifierous" over "To a Kiss," which begins

> Humid seal of soft affections
>   Tenderest pledge of future bliss
> Dearest tie of young connexions,
>   Love's first snow-drop, Virgin kiss!

Markings beside other saccharine lines, which pay tribute to the rich rewards of a woman's love or note how the lover in solitude can recapture all the physical and spiritual sensations of mutual passion, may also be Melville's. Considering his bent for the Oriental, he probably wrote the words "I Salam" after a poem entitled "To a Lady Who Complained That the Rose Which She Had Put in Water Was Fallen to Pieces." It is nearly certain that he copied inside the back cover the three stanzas of Air XVI in *The Beggar's Opera*.[116] When he wrote:

> And I would love you all the day,
> Every night would kiss and play,
> If with me you'd fondly stray
> Over the hills and far away.

could he have meant a direct message for Harriet? At least it has the marks of a romantic gesture.[117]

Whatever markings or copied verses in this book are Herman Melville's, it is certain that he had read it often. The wisdom of the Age of Reason has some space, but excerpts from Byron, Moore, Scott, and Young dominate its pages. They must have had a large share in shaping Melville's moods and his ideal of romance and love. They could also provide escape from the gradual realization that once more his hopes for stability were groundless. The trustees of his school let four months go by without paying him.[118] Gansevoort wrote occasional letters and sent newspapers from New York to cheer him up and protest against the irresponsible conduct of his superiors,[119] but though Herman wrote faithfully to his mother,[120] he was in no mood to answer his brother. His board bills were mounting daily and he found it harder every week to postpone a settlement. Apparently he received some small compensation, for he was able to give his mother three dollars in May,[121] but by that time he knew that chance had tricked him again. He had to tell his mother that his school was scheduled to close toward the end of the month for lack of funds.[122] She was then more than $200.00 in debt, and the news wore her down to a numb hopelessness and drove her to consider taking up some kind of work with her daughters.[123]

For a week or two after the Greenbush school closed, Herman filled in at the tiny, one-room district school in Brunswick, a two-mile walk from home.[124] But he had already formed a plan to escape from the heartbreaking defeats of life at home. "He thinks of going far west, as nothing offers for him here," wrote his mother, crying out in her anguish: "Oh that the Lord may strengthen me to bear my troubles . . . ." [125] For the second time within a year she bowed to economic fact and threw no barrier across Herman's path. Sometime after the fifth of June, Herman left home again, this time not for the sea but for the frontier, where his Uncle Thomas and some of his cousins had settled three years before.[126] It is surely no coincidence that Eli Fly planned to go west at the same time.[127] Unlike his independent venture into the merchant marine, Herman most certainly had a good friend on his western trip to share the fortunes of the open road.

Very likely he received enough of his back salary when his school closed to keep him fed and in shoes on the journey to Galena, in the northwest corner of Illinois. His motive in going there is obvious. Galena was still small, but the business growing up around its rich lead mines was attracting many merchants, lawyers, doctors, and mechanics who had fled from the unemployment and overcrowded professions in the East.[128] And Herman's Uncle Thomas was both secretary of the Chamber of Commerce in the town and one of the managers of its Colonization Society.[129] Also, he had been appointed two years before to consider the expediency of introducing the common-school system into Galena.[130] Whether Herman intended to continue teaching or to go back into business, Thomas Melvill seemed like an influential patron. The venture was most promising.

In reality, there was anything but a pot of gold at the end of the long rainbow arching out to the prairies of Illinois. Melville must have been discouraged at the reunion with his uncle's family, for they were far worse off than they had ever been in Pittsfield. Thomas Melvill was indeed, as Herman was to write many years later, "a marked contrast to his environment." [131] The former major, diplomat, and banker was wearing threadbare clothing and living in a humble little house. The climate was unhealthful, and his family was constantly plagued with fever. Most of his fellow townsmen were German and Irish immigrants whose instinctive attachment to the Democratic party not only provoked the anger of the conservative Easterner but prevented his election to political office.[132] Very possibly Herman found that being the nephew of Thomas Melvill was no asset. Whatever the reason, his fortunes seem to have prospered no more than his Micawber-like uncle's. Scores of Yankees found jobs and homes in Galena, but to Herman it was only another Lansingburgh.[133]

Lacking contemporary records of the effect of the West on Melville in his twenty-first year, we must turn to allusions in his books for clues to his impressions and even to the course of his travels. In telling the story of Steelkit, the former bargeman on the Erie Canal, Ishmael refers to himself as "once a vagabond on his own canal" and the recipient of "good turns from one of these Canallers." [134] If this is, as it seems, an authentic reminiscence, Herman must have worked his way out to Galena along the most obvious route, the Erie Canal and the Great Lakes.[135] Specific references to the things he may have observed are scattered throughout Melville's works. In the journal he kept in 1856 he noted that the Tiber was as "primeval" as the Ohio and the Po as yellow as the Mississippi.[136] In *White-Jacket* he is "reminded of a scene once witnessed in a pioneer village on the western bank of the Mississippi" when a giant Indian marched down the street with a crowd of human hands painted in red upon his blanket.[137] In *Redburn* he pictures the hero as telling English listeners about "Illinois, and the river Ohio, and the fine farms in the Genesee country, where, in harvest time, the laborers went into the wheat fields a thousand strong." [138] Once, in his letters, he refers figuratively to the lead in Galena, an allusion that would seem to have been suggested by his own acquaintance with the town.[139] And to the end of his life he remembered the fields of waving maize and the stacks of golden grain in Illinois, for he employed them as a symbol in a late poem, "Trophies of Peace—Illinois in 1840." [140]

At least three effects of Melville's western journey may be stated with some degree of assurance. To his growing consciousness, the hegira added a store of experience upon which he would later draw for democratic and humanitarian thought. In *Redburn,* for example, he extended a welcome to Irish and German immigrants based upon his direct knowledge of the advantages the fertile lands of Ohio and the prairies of Wisconsin would offer to them.[141] Secondly, his journey gave him an insight into the true progressive character of his country so that he would later write, "the Western spirit is, or will yet be (for no other is, or can be), the true American one." [142] Finally, it seems certain that his knowledge of the Mississippi provided the framework of *The Confidence Man* (1857). His description of the details of a Mississippi river boat is full and accurate, and it is highly probable that he had traveled on the river between St. Louis and Cairo, Illinois, which he describes with apparent familiarity.[143] In most of his novels Melville built his story around a personal experience or a scene with which he was familiar. In *The Confidence Man* he undoubtedly returned to the only period of his travels he had not yet exploited in his books.

Sometime in the fall Herman returned to Lansingburgh, very possibly by way of the Ohio River, Kentucky, and Virginia.[144] Lingering at home only long enough to tell his family about his travels and run up a bill of seven dollars, which he left unpaid,[145] he set off again on the endless hunt for a job, this time going down to New York, where he could have Gansevoort's help. Eli Fly was still with him, and while combing the streets for employment they managed to live for $2.50 a week, not counting dinners, which they ate through Gansevoort's generosity at Sweeny's on Fulton Street. Herman had allowed his hair to grow long and his whiskers to flourish during the summer of vagabondage, but he now paid a visit to a barber and began to look "more like a Christian than usual." [146] Fly finally managed to find work; Herman had no luck whatsoever. Gansevoort worried about him more and more. Still a student at law, he could not support Herman indefinitely; besides, Gansevoort's health was failing again, and only a sea voyage, he thought, would refresh him. For Herman, "those stage managers the Fates" were now forcing another drastic move, about the last one left for an American boy in the forties with absolutely no hope of employment.

No one can tell exactly how and by whom a decision was reached, but it seems certain from family letters that others besides Herman had a share in it. All we know is that about a week before Christmas Gansevoort wrote home that "Hermans destination would be decided" on Christmas Day [147] and that Gansevoort was in Boston shortly after the holiday. Whether he and Herman went home first, as seems most likely, to settle Herman's destiny in a family conclave or whether they went directly to Boston remains uncertain, but at least the evidence supports a rather different picture of Herman's departure from that in the opening pages of *Moby-Dick,* where the young Ishmael has no brother to depend on or family concerned about his future.

The best guess is that Herman, thoroughly weary of his sterile life on land, hit upon the sea again as the only escape and that the experience of Leonard Gansevoort and Thomas W. Melvill strongly influenced his planning. Leonard had completed a whaling cruise of nearly two years in 1837, and Tom was now a veteran with service in three New Bedford whalers over a period of six years. In the dignified Melville and Gansevoort families, they had set a precedent their younger cousin could find both reassuring and challenging. Besides, Melville had undoubtedly read some of the vast literature of whaling[148] and knew that despite the hardships a whaling voyage could carry one to remote corners of the earth, to exotic and perhaps barbarous countries. He had also read *Two Years Before the Mast* with "strange, congenial feelings" while he was waiting fruitlessly for a job to turn up on land.[149] A long voyage like Dana's, but on a whaler, would solve many problems for him. At the worst, he could count on food, clothes, and shelter, earned by his own labor.[150]

Did he remember how valuable it had been for Dana to have friends who knew the owners of the ship, and did he look for an intermediary with his own prospective employers? It is not unlikely. Gansevoort's chief object in going to Boston was to get a loan from Lemuel Shaw for a cruise to restore his health. He also saw his numerous aunts.[151] It is reasonable to suppose that Herman had also appealed to Shaw and that Shaw helped him through one of his many friends in New Bedford.[152] Thus Herman might have gone over to Boston after the farewells at home, made a final visit with Shaw, and called on his aunts with Gansevoort to say good-by. And since Gansevoort left Boston on New Year's Day and since he seems to have known the character of Herman's shipmates before they sailed,[153] it would seem that Herman had his company on the railroad to New Bedford and even on the dock across the river in Fairhaven, where the brand-new whaler "Acushnet," Captain Pease, was laying in last-minute supplies for her maiden voyage. Melville took his gear aboard and waited for the final moment. On Sunday, January 3, the ship slipped her moorings and dropped down the river toward the bay and the wide ocean beyond, and he was free again of the land of no promise.

Had Melville now been able to survey his youth with the wisdom of age, he might well have said with Edmund in *King Lear,* "The wheel is come full circle; I am here." The backward glance took in roads traveled from seaport to river port to a village a thousand miles inland and quickly retraced as if by predestination to salt water. He had followed them through the comforts and assurances of the good life where mutability was synonymous with improvement, through days of sudden, inexplicable disaster and death, through glistening hopes and over their heaped ruins to other hopes, and through desert lands where the visions of success were only mirages. The successive stages of the journey were shorter and shorter but as he grew older and more demanding, seemed less to be borne. The long ordeal came to an end only at the shore of the ocean, where limitless expanses of water smiled ambiguously upon the arid land.[154]

BOOK II

Chapter V

Melville as an Artist

BETWEEN the close of Melville's early life and his return to its most dramatic event for the subject matter of his fourth book, nearly a decade elapsed. Yet in one way or another the experience of all these years affected *Redburn.* His life at sea, his return to civilization and his intellectual awakening, his immediate personal life, and particularly his growth as an artist all had a share in making the book what it is. A detailed account of the decade lies outside the present purpose, but it is germane to recall in brief what happened during the years of action and the years of thought that followed them.[1]

Melville's experience between 1841 and 1844 completed the maturation in knowledge of men and the world begun on the "St. Lawrence" and in Liverpool. He shared four different forecastles with mixed crews of American whites and Negroes, with Englishmen, Scotsmen, and Australians, and with natives of the South Seas. He lived with coarse, mean-spirited wretches who cursed, gambled, got drunk, committed sodomy, wasted away with syphilis, deserted, and mutinied, and with others who lived as decently on ship as on shore, read books and recited poetry, stood by a comrade, resisted all tyranny, and said their prayers. Melville came to know men in their noble roles as well as in their ignominy. He took orders from captains he thought inhuman, or incompetent and cowardly, or pompous with authority and determined to bend all other wills to their own. He learned at firsthand the perilous complexities of whale-hunting, its carelessness about human life, its frenetic zeal for gain, and he collected an oral anthology of sea lore and myth. He looked in at a score of strange harbors, from Rio de Janeiro to the barren, ill-named Encantadas, and visions of nature that neither Wordsworth nor Emerson ever knew swarmed upon him among the ice floes and tempests off Tierra del Fuego and in the trackless Pacific.

These years of growth included a full repast of adventure: desertion from the "Acushnet" at Nukahiva in the Marquesas, a month among the naked, voluptuous savages of the Typee Valley, six months on an Australian whaler, a part in a comic-opera mutiny and several weeks in the public stocks in Tahiti, a period of foot-loose vagabondage around the islands, another brief term on a whaler, and then Hawaii. The old appeal of a settled life returned momentarily; after a job as a pin boy in a bowling alley,[2] Melville signed an indenture as clerk to a respectable merchant. But without even starting to work he joined the Navy, undoubtedly to get passage home, and for fifteen months he studied life in his country's service. Through all this Melville was growing with each new venture, so that when he walked ashore from the "United States" on October 3, 1844, he was well emancipated from the servitude of youth to illusion. The spectacle of a white Protestant civilization intruding in the South Seas to destroy through its own corruption the people it pretended to be saving, the knowledge of political chicanery and imperialistic force by which the islands had been brought to heel, the familiarity with man's inhumanity to man in every corner of the globe—all this had made a thinking man of him. Although his reaction fell far short of social revolution or atheism, he knew now that these evils were the concrete realities of the world. He never fully denied the credo in which he was raised, but he was now in a position to assess its direct bearing on every aspect of life. A perfect integrity impelled him to do so, and he soon discovered the necessary powers to articulate his judgments.

The life of physical experience was over; the life of intellectual experience was about to begin as Melville set a restless and increasingly powerful imagination and an earnest moral sense to work upon the raw materials stored in his memory. To the student of Melville's books, the most significant ring in his expansion is the circle of artistic power, which despite conflicting waves widens steadily as Melville moves toward his climactic work in *Moby-Dick*. At first, as was natural, he exploited his sensational adventures. According to tradition, his friends, excited by his tales, urged him to put them into print. Within a year after his return to his mother's house in Lansingburgh, he had completed the writing of *Typee*. His brother Gansevoort, now a successful lawyer, had served the Democratic party faithfully by his oratory in the campaign of 1844 and had been rewarded with an appointment as secretary to the legation at St. James. He took the manuscript with him to England and secured its publication by John Murray in February and April 1846. In April it appeared in America under the imprint of Wiley and Putnam. *Typee* was an instantaneous success, the first book about the South Seas to treat its subject artistically rather than with the careful detachment of the official explorer or the drabness of the travel chronicle, with its undiscriminating record of places visited and things seen. Melville, like Byron, woke up one day to find himself famous.[3]

Typee purports to be the personal recollections of the author-hero from the time his ship approaches the Marquesas Islands to his dramatic escape from the Typee Valley sometime later. Actually it consists of a few true adventures, a mass of ethnological information largely derived from previous travelers and delightfully colored by Melville's fancy, some Rousseauan defense of unspoiled primitive life, and a hair-raising but fictional story.[4] Melville expands his four weeks in the Typee Valley to four months.

To give his narrative suspense, he underlines his constant fear of being eaten by his supposedly cannibal hosts. At the climax, he discovers the half-eaten remains of a fresh human corpse, and horror-struck at the fate which he believes in store for himself, he makes a final successful effort to escape. This last melodramatic episode provides a fitting finale to a narrative in which excitement is a major artistic goal, but it is undoubtedly as much an invention as the discovery of the corpse. For by Melville's private admission this horrifying revelation is a fiction. According to his wife he stated that whatever may have been his fears, he never found evidence that the Typees were actually man-eaters.[5]

Thus in his very first book Melville wrote as an artist. He borrowed freely from others and invariably improved upon his sources. He exploited his actual experiences to the limit and then went beyond them to develop the dramatic possibilities of the situation in which he had found himself. Furthermore, with the contempt of the artist for mere literality, he insisted that *Typee* reflected his "anxious desire to speak the unvarnished truth." [6] When the veracity of the book was assailed in the New York *Courier and Enquirer,* he concocted an article in defense and sent it to his friend, Alexander W. Bradford, who was to use his personal influence in New York literary circles to get it published in the very journal that had made the attack. Melville intended the article to offset any effects the "malicious notice" might have "on the success of the book as a genuine narrative," and he wished it published "as if written by one who had read the book and beleived it . . . ." [7] Although the article never appeared in print, it offers testimony to Melville's very liberal view of what constitutes the truth.

If Melville was the artist in *Typee* he was also the social and religious critic. He had gone to the Typee Valley as the product of an advanced and prosperous civilization which nevertheless had not made him or a multitude of others happy or even physically comfortable. As he reconstructed his life there, he recalled that the Typees, despite their supposedly inferior civilization, were happy, well fed, and inwardly disciplined to an exceptional concord. Without the benefits of Western culture, they escaped poverty, sickness, and internal strife. They were ignorant of the restraints and inspiration of Christianity, yet they seemed to be free of sinful taint, at least in their dealings with one another; theft, murder, even hatred, seemed unknown, but honesty and kindness were native. If it was true that their religion of taboos was superstitious and tyrannical and that their ideal economic state was due to nature's bounty and a static population, life in the valley was still an eloquent commentary on the failure of white civilization with all its science and discipline to achieve anything comparable. Thus Melville could sum up his social criticism by saying that the islands ought to reverse the flow of education and send half a dozen missionaries to teach Western man how to live.

Soon after the publication of *Typee,* Melville went to work on a sequel. *Omoo,* published in April 1847, took up his story where *Typee* had left off and carried it through the mutiny at Tahiti, the subsequent vagabonding around the Society Islands, and the author's re-embarkation on a whaler. Although *Omoo* advanced his reputation, it was not as imaginative as *Typee.* Melville wrote of his ramblings colorfully and humorously and indulged a talent for skillful depiction of character. Jermin, Captain Guy, Benbow, the savage Maori, Zeke and Yank, the two potato farmers on Imeeo, and especially Dr. Long Ghost he visualized as human beings. *Omoo* is a spicily picaresque narrative, crowded with robust frolics and escapades of sailors, rascals, and beachcombers. As in *Typee,* Melville adorned his story with charming scenic description. He also kept up his fire of social criticism, developing further the defects of civilization and the failure of the self-chosen representatives of Christ to live by Christian principles and to extend the benefits of Christianity to pagan peoples.[8] However, he did not apparently elaborate as much on fact as he had done in *Typee,* perhaps because his adventures needed little touching up to make interesting reading.

By the end of July 1847 Melville had begun *Mardi.*[9] Apparently it was to be another volume of South Sea narrative, for the first thirty-eight chapters continue in the adventurous vein of *Typee* and *Omoo.* But between the commencement and the conclusion of the book occurred a series of events in Melville's personal life that strongly influenced his artistic growth and fundamentally altered the nature of *Mardi.* Melville married, settled in New York, and secured access to the whole intellectual and cultural world of the metropolis. The results were apparent in the last three quarters of *Mardi,* in the financial tensions surrounding the writing of *Redburn* and *White-Jacket,* and in Melville's attitude toward the products of his pen.

How long Melville had known and courted Elizabeth Shaw, the daughter of his father's best friend, is problematical. While he had been at sea, however, his sisters had paid visits to the Shaws in Boston (Helen remained one entire winter), and Elizabeth had been Helen's guest in Lansingburgh.[10] Melville had dedicated *Typee* to Lemuel Shaw in the fall of 1845 and had visited him early in 1846.[11] On a pleasant day in August 1847,[12] in the forenoon of which he had picked, significantly, one of the few four-leaf clovers he ever found in his life,[13] Herman was married to Elizabeth Shaw in the New South Church in Boston.[14] Meanwhile, Allan Melville was carrying forward his plans for marriage, and after that event, on September 22, the two brothers combined their families and adding their mother and sisters, lived in New York at 103 Fourth Avenue.[15] The arrangement seems to have been harmonious, and there is no external evidence that Melville's marriage was anything but satisfying. Until 1850 he lived in these surroundings, and it was here that he wrote most of his next three books.

However, he had taken on the responsibilities of a family without a regular income to support it. Officially, he was "Herman Melville, Gentleman." [16] Six months before his marriage, an attempt to secure an appointment in the Treasury Department at Washington had failed,[17] leaving him dependent upon the sales of his books. For a new writer, working in a period when only a few were able to count on a living from authorship, Melville fared rather well.[18] The income from his writings was more than sufficient for ordinary expenses. Besides, his generous father-in-law had loaned him $2,000 to invest in the New York house.[19] Thus, though he was never free from financial pressure, he was able to enjoy, during his most prolific period, the plays, the music, the memberships in libraries, and the social intercourse that New York offered in abundance.

During these years in New York, Melville's intellectual horizon broadened immeasurably. Through Evert A. Duyckinck, he was introduced to William Cullen Bryant, Bayard Taylor, N. P. Willis, Charles Fenno Hoffman, and probably Irving and Poe and to many others of the New York literary set. He went to Duyckinck's Saturday evening parties, where the Knights of the Round Table gathered regularly for discourse over a bowl of punch.[20] He attended plays and concerts and the opera, took a lively interest in art, and contributed sketches and reviews to Duyckinck's *Literary World* and to the humorous *Yankee Doodle*. From the New-York Society and from Duyckinck, who owned a library of over seventeen thousand volumes, he borrowed books by the dozen, reading Thomas Browne, Plato, Rabelais, Milton, Hartley's *Observations on Man,* Bayle's *Philosophical Dictionary,* Fuller's *The Holy and Profane State,* Macpherson's *Fingal,* the classics in translation, and innumerable other works.[21]

The results appear in *Mardi,* where Melville sought to amalgamate his personal observation with his reading and reflection to form a work of vast human significance. Also, he tried to treat all his material, rather than portions of it, in an artistic manner. Abandoning his original intention of writing another exciting romance, he set out to compose an allegory of man and the world. After a few chapters of straightforward adventure, he pictures the hero Taji as rescuing the beautiful maiden Yillah from a priest and his three sons who were taking her to be sacrificed. Shortly after Taji lands on Odo, Yillah disappears. Desperate at the loss of the incarnation of all beauty, Taji proposes to search for her. He is joined by Media, the king of all the islands in the archipelago of Mardi, Babbalanja, a philosopher, Yoomy, a poet, and Mohi, a historian. They visit the islands of the kingdom, which have only allegorical meaning: Dominora is England, Vivenza the United States, Maramma, the land of dogmatic and ritualistic Christianity, Serenia the country of ideal Christianity. Into the theme of the romantic quest Melville weaves rich satirical commentary on contemporary events and national characteristics: the French Revolution of 1848, the Chartist movement and English imperialism, the gold rush, the Mexican War. The five seekers conduct interminable dialogues, discussing war, the nature of literary reputations, the problems of fate and free will, and the apparent dualism of matter and spirit, good and evil. It is soon apparent that their pursuit of Yillah is the pursuit of ultimate beauty and truth. All except Taji find the goal of their quest in Serenia, the land of simplicity, charity, and unshakable faith in the wisdom of Oro (God). Taji alone is unsatisfied with the compromise. At the end of the book he leaves to pursue the lost Yillah out into the infinity of the open sea.

Mardi shows that for Melville the need for a complete evaluation of man's religion, his politics, and his social being had asserted itself. He posed the baffling problem of good and evil in the universe and stated the inner needs of man for a perfect and permanent beauty and for a final answer to the question, "What is Truth?" In page after page, his adoption of a poetical prose that scans with precision reveals a desire to achieve a rhythmical expression of beauty. His description of scenery is permeated with a passionate and transcending imaginativeness superior to anything in *Typee* or *Omoo*. If Melville, as Matthiessen has said, had known how to bring together "the immediate with the abstract, the concrete event with the thought rising from it," *Mardi* would probably have been what he intended it, an artistic achievement of the first magnitude.[22] If it fell short of his hopes, it nevertheless marked a tremendous development in Melville as a creative artist.

The completion of *Mardi* at the end of January 1849 gave Melville a temporary respite from his literary labors. On the thirtieth he went to Boston to be with his wife when their son Malcolm was born.[23] After that event, on February 16, he passed nearly a month in the home of his father-in-law on Mount Vernon Street, where he lounged on the sofa and read Shakespeare carefully for the first time. Occasionally he enjoyed social evenings with Richard Henry Dana, who found him "incomparable in dramatic story-telling." [24] He heard lectures by Emerson—"the Plato who talks through his nose," he called him [25]—and attended Fanny Kemble Butler's readings of *Macbeth* and *Othello*. Of her he wrote to Duyckinck with unwonted indelicacy:

> She's so unfemininely masculine that had she not, on unimpeachable authority, borne children, I should be curious to learn the result of a surgical examination of her person in private.[26]

His letters during this period, full of a boisterous good fellowship, are charged with the spirit of criticism and discovery and the intellectual insurgence that resounded in chapter upon chapter of *Mardi*. "I love all men that *dive*," he wrote, ". . . the whole corps of intellectual thought-divers that have been diving & coming up again with blood-shot eyes since the world began." [27] And of Shakespeare, whom he found "full of sermons-on-the-mount, & gentle, aye, almost as Jesus," [28] he said:

> I would to God Shakespeare had lived later, & promenaded in Broadway. Not that I might have had the pleasure of leaving my card for him at the Astor, or made merry with him over a bowl of the fine Duyckinck punch; but that the muzzle which all men wore on their souls in the Elizabethan day, might not have intercepted Shakespeare from articulation. Now I hold it a verity, that even Shakespeare, was not a frank man to the uttermost. And, indeed, who

in this intolerant universe is, or can be? But the Declaration of Independence makes a difference.[29]

The problem of finding and telling the ultimate truth, which was to concern Melville through the writing of *Moby-Dick* and *Pierre,* was thus heavy on his mind, even in these weeks of relaxation. And though he said that his mood had changed since writing *Mardi,*[30] it is clear that the inner compulsions toward further intellectual exploration and perhaps to more books like *Mardi* were asserting themselves strongly. "Would that a man could do something & then say—It is finished," he wrote, "not that one thing only, but all others—that he has reached his uttermost, & can never exceed it." [31] And he planned, on his return to New York, to steep himself in Bayle's *Dictionary,* Plato's *Phaedo,* and Sir Thomas Browne.[32]

We do not really know that Melville's pen was inactive in Boston, but he makes no mention of writing there, and it is reasonable to suppose that he would await the reception of one book before starting another. Hence it was apparently after his return to New York on April 11 [33] that he began *Redburn,* an entirely different book from the kind he wished to write. But Melville had a newborn son, and before long he seems to have felt that the royalties on *Mardi* were not going to discharge his ever-present bills. On April 23 he observed to his father-in-law that *Mardi* had been "cut into by the London Atheneum, and also burnt by the common hangman in the Boston Post."

However [he added] the London Examiner & Literary Gazette; & other papers this side of the water have done differently. These attacks are matters of course, and are essential to the building up of any permanent reputation—if such should ever prove to be mine . . . . Time, which is the solver of all riddles, will solve Mardi! [34]

Though the reception of *Mardi* was generally unfavorable, it had received significant praise.[35] Evert Duyckinck had acclaimed it in the *Literary World,* and there was much reason for Melville to feel some encouragement, had he been content to accept anything less than complete understanding of his difficult allegory and unanimous applause.[36] There is nothing to support one critical affirmation that he was so irritated by the reception of *Mardi* as to conceive his next book in a mood of bitter recrimination against the world for all the defeats he had suffered at its hands.[37] The contrary seems to be true. "I have already received assurances that 'Mardi,' in its higher purposes, has not been written in vain," he wrote Richard Bentley on June 5.[38]

Nevertheless *Redburn* was written under pressure.

> When a poor devil writes with duns all round him, & looking over the back of his chair—& perching on his pen & diving in his inkstand . . . what can you expect of that poor devil? What but a beggarly "Redburn!" [39]

Thus Melville described its composition to Duyckinck, and he told Dana that he had written *Redburn* (and *White-Jacket*) "almost entirely for 'lucre'—by the job, as a woodsawyer saws wood . . . ." [40] He must have driven himself at top speed to get it done. On June 5, when he offered it for sale to Richard Bentley, he could say:

> In size the book will be perhaps a fraction smaller than "Typee"; will be printed here by the Harpers, & ready for them two or three months hence, or before. I value the English Copyright at one hundred & fifty pounds, and think it would be wise to put it forth in a manner, admitting of a popular circulation.[41]

One may conclude that *Redburn* was more than half finished at this time. Though Melville actually "enlarged it somewhat to the size of 'Omoo,' " [42] he completed it by July 2. On that day Harper made an agreement to "publish a certain manuscript entitled 'My First Voyage etc.' " [43] Melville's brother Allan negotiated the contract, which called for the immediate payment of $300.00 on account of half profits. Since the book was "going through the press" by July 20,[44] it must have been off Melville's hands completely within a few weeks.[45] He dedicated it, fittingly, to his younger brother Thomas, who was now serving in the merchant marine on a China trader.

For the kind of book which Melville was writing, the literary milieu offered certain hazards. Books about the sea had been popular from the time of Scott's *The Pirate* (1822) and Cooper's *The Spy* (1823). With his series of fourteen nautical novels, including the autobiographical *Afloat and Ashore* (1844) and *Miles Wallingford* (1844), Cooper led a large school of marine novelists on this side of the Atlantic. His followers included Joseph Holt Ingraham, "Harry Danforth" [C. J. Peterson], Edward Z. C. Judson, M. M. Ballou, and many others, most of whose works, especially Judson's, were on the level of dime novels.[46] A similar wave of sea stories flooded the periodicals and annuals.[47] Melville's particular genre was the nautical reminiscence, a type which had existed as early as Nathaniel Ames's *A Mariner's Sketches* (1830) and *Nautical Reminiscences* (1832) and which achieved its classic form in Richard Henry Dana's *Two Years Before the Mast* (1840). Both Dana and Ames were Harvard undergraduates who had, as gentlemen's sons in the merchant marine, turned their personal histories into marketable wares. Their success was virtually predestined in a nation that was rising rapidly in commercial enterprise and was deeply interested in high adventure and remote lands. The hallmarks of Dana's narrative were a simple veracity in the relation of unusual experiences and a wish to promote the welfare of seamen. Although there had been similar books before Dana, the great spate of them after 1840 reveals the principal source.[48] Former sailors, of all degrees of intelligence, rushed to press with their memoirs until the market was overloaded.

Another type of literature Melville had to bear in mind when he wrote *Redburn* was the travel narrative, written usually by a person of good education, either as the incidental offshoot of his rambles in Europe or like the works of N. P. Willis and Bayard Taylor as specific undertakings in journalism.[49] Such reports had been flooding the country for years with firsthand accounts of the Atlantic crossing, the sight of English soil, the castles, cathedrals, and museums of England, and the royal family and conspicuous aristocrats, like Prince Esterhazy, Lady Blessington, and Count D'Orsay.[50]

By 1849 the reading public was thoroughly steeped in the literature of travel and nautical reminiscence in its many forms. An author about to add to it could scarcely expect large circulation without some innovation or embellishment. The less artistic met the situation by loading their pages with shipwrecks, fights, floggings, and encounters with Spanish privateers and Malayan pirates. Many of the incidents must have been true, but the critics, who probably reflected the taste of the more intelligent public, were becoming calloused to the tale of thrilling adventure and to the loquacious memoir of the honest-hearted tar.[51]

The book market in England, where Melville must also look for royalties, was also overloaded with nautical literature, though the quality seems to have been higher than in America. For fifteen years Captain Marryat had been exploiting his own career as a midshipman in half a dozen novels mingling high adventure with humor and realism. Of lesser power were the nautical romancers Captain Chamier and Michael Scott, and the log writers like William Butterworth and George Cupples.[52]

Melville was well acquainted with the literature of travel and the sea, and he knew that originality was a prerequisite for success.[53] Yet his voyage to Liverpool did not in itself offer rich material since he could not rely on such exotic sights and people as he had painted in *Typee, Omoo,* and *Mardi. Redburn* would have to depend upon a fresh approach to a familiar story. To write a chapter of autobiography re-creating his own experiences at the age of twenty would have been merely to fall into line behind Dana and his imitators, who had virtually exhausted the possibilities of stories of young gentlemen of that age on their first voyage as sailors. Besides, Melville had tasted the wines of freedom which reward the artistic manipulation of experience. He could use the literal truth to good purpose, but he had the creative mind's contempt for it.

His intentions in writing *Redburn* need not rest upon hypothesis; they can be clarified from documentary evidence in his own hand. To Richard Bentley he wrote:

> I have now in preparation a thing of a widely different cast from "Mardi":—A plain, straightforward, amusing narrative of personal experience—the son of a gentleman on his first voyage to sea as a sailor—no metaphysics, no conic-sections, nothing but cakes & ale. I have shifted my ground from the South Seas to a different quarter of the globe—nearer home—and what I write I have almost wholly picked up by my own observations under comical circumstances.[54]

If these words are given careful examination, both by themselves and in the light of all relevant evidence, they point to the fact that Melville did not intend *Redburn* to be received as autobiography. The prefaces of *Typee, Omoo,* and *White-Jacket* all claim their contents to be the true relations of the author's adventures. *Redburn* has no Preface at all, and its title and subtitle assign the experiences to a fictional character. Melville's statement to Bentley is as much of a Preface to *Redburn* as exists. He was writing the personal experiences of a son of a gentleman, with amusement as a central purpose. Despite the fact that he himself was the son of a gentleman and had made a first voyage as a sailor, he does not maintain that the book would narrate his own history. Rather it would seem that he intended to describe a character independent of himself but similar in background and adventures. The mood of "cakes and ale" and the "comical circumstances" contrast strongly with the conditions of Melville's own voyage ten years before. Furthermore, a clear admission of invention appears in the last sentence; most of what Melville wrote was drawn from observation but not all of it. The remainder was presumably to be filled out by his ready imagination.

It remains to be seen how large was the fraction produced by Melville's imagination and just how accurate was his statement that he had gathered the materials "almost wholly" from observation. Meanwhile we have to consider a further confession of fictional content in *Redburn*, imbedded in Melville's comment on a review of the book. During his excursion to England in 1849 he noted in his journal on November 6 that he had attended Julien's Promenade Concert at Drury Lane. He added:

At Julien's also saw Blackwood's long story about a short book. Its' very comical—seemed so, at least, as I had to hury on it—in treating the thing as real. But the wonder is that the old Tory should waste so many pages upon a thing, which I, the author, know to be trash, & wrote it to buy some tobacco with.[55]

The "long story" was the review of *Redburn* in *Blackwood's Edinburgh Magazine* in November,[56] which begins by stating that in *Redburn* Melville had done his best to dissipate any doubts that he had "really served before the mast." The critic, disclaiming any intention of investigating the true relation between *Redburn* and Melville's life, agrees to "accept Mr. Melville . . . for what he professes to be." He summarizes the story in fourteen pages, taking exception wherever he believes Melville has departed from strict reality. For example, he rejects not only the romantic excursion to the London gambling house but also the story of the woman who, with her three children, starved to death under a Liverpool sidewalk.

Mr. Melville [writes the reviewer] is at liberty to introduce fictitious adventure into what professes to be a narrative of real events; . . . but here he is perverting truth, and leading into error the simple persons who put their faith in him.[57]

On the whole, Melville's hurried reading of the review would have conveyed the idea that to the critic *Redburn* was essentially "a narrative of real events" in the life of the author. For Melville's comment that the review was "comical . . . in treating the thing as real," the only logical explanation is that *Redburn* was not a true history of his own experiences on the Liverpool trip. It was amusing to him that anyone should have mistaken it for factual autobiography.[58]

To the implications of the Bentley letter, this hitherto neglected note from Melville's diary adds further confirmation of artistic invention in *Redburn.* Together they offer grounds for an explanation of the fact that the manuscript was originally called "My First Voyage." Melville apparently conceived the boy Redburn as telling about his experience in the first person. For such a narrative, "My First Voyage" seemed an obvious title. It is with these three words that both the first and the last chapters end. Had it been retained, however, it would have led to an awkward ambiguity. In advertisements and on the title page, the reader would have seen *"My First Voyage,* by Herman Melville," but on the first page he would have begun to read about Wellingborough Redburn's first voyage. As "My First Voyage" was not meant to indicate that the book contained Melville's autobiography, the title had to be changed for the sake of clarity.

It could of course be contended that Melville wrote *Redburn* as his own "confessions and reminiscences" with no such character as Wellingborough Redburn, and that he then revised it, but the possibility seems remote. Harper accepted the manuscript on July 2, and eighteen days later it was going through the press. For the revisions required before the book went to the publisher's, Melville would have had little time. Afterwards he was busy with the composition of *White-Jacket,* to which he must have given steady attention in order to complete its 170,000 words in two and a half months.[59] It is most unlikely that Melville made any other change in *Redburn* than altering the title to prevent misinterpretation of its content.

A final suggestion about Melville's intention in writing *Redburn* may be gleaned from some remarks he made in reviewing Browne's *Etchings of a Whaling Cruise* in 1847.

> Of late years [he wrote] there have been revealed so many plain, matter-of-fact details connected with nautical life, that, at the present day, the poetry of salt water is very much on the wane.[60]

While praising Browne for doing for the whaleman's existence what Dana had done for the merchant sailor's, Melville also wrote that "Browne's narrative tends still further to impair the charm with which poetry and fiction have invested the sea." Melville, it seems, had an ambivalent attitude toward the literature of the sea as represented in Dana and Browne. Realism had its value in toning down the romantic treatment of the ocean; nevertheless, the realistic writer lost a certain "charm" that poetry and fiction had supplied. In the nautical chapters of *Typee, Omoo,* and *Mardi,* which deal with life on various whalers, Melville treated realistic material with romantic freedom, as a comparison between these books and Browne's narrative readily reveals. Thus, both in critical theory and in practice, Melville was a romantic realist. With this approach to his material, it is only logical to suppose that he shaped out the idea of *Redburn* along romantic lines and that he felt at perfect liberty to tell his story with as much imagination as seemed suitable.

The best clue to Melville's artistic method in *Redburn,* imbedded significantly in the book itself, is his statement that

> Divine imaginings, like gods, come down to the groves of our Thessalies, and there, in the embrace of wild, dryad reminiscences, beget the beings that astonish the world.[61]

In the linking of reminiscences with the mythological image of the dryads and with the quality of wildness, Melville confesses indirectly but clearly that his mind modified and distorted even recollected facts. *Redburn* is the love child of wavering memory and preternatural imagination.

Chapter VI

Art and Autobiography

IF THE exposition of Melville's intentions in writing *Redburn* and his own awareness of the artistic process working in him casts light on the book, a detailed study of his method ought to make its nature even more clear. For the framework of fact he selected liberally from the events of his youth and of the voyage to Liverpool late in his twentieth year. His homes on Bleecker Street and Broadway become Redburn's "in old Greenwich Street." Allan Melvill, like Walter Redburn, was an importer of French goods and a veteran of many trips across the Atlantic. In Melville's home were most certainly the English and French books, the old European guidebooks, and the portfolios of French prints that delighted Redburn. Into the boy's domestic recollections Melville worked even such minute details as those of his own mother's formidable house cleanings.[1] Both the author and his fictional creation had declaimed speeches on the stage of the high school. Both enjoyed happiness, comfort, and great expectations as the sons of well-to-do gentlemen. Both suffered spiritually and physically as a result of the bankruptcies and early deaths of their fathers.

Despite these parallels, Melville romanticized freely in working up the materials of his youth. For example, Redburn recollects an old uncle, a sea captain, who had traveled with Captain Langsdorff and used to tell stories of sailing to Archangel and crossing Siberia in a dog sled. Redburn saw him only once, for he was killed in the White Sea a few years afterwards. Although the reminiscence refers to Herman's uncle, Captain John D'Wolf, whose career is more or less truthfully represented, he did not die in the White Sea but was alive when Melville was writing *Redburn,* and for twenty-three years afterwards. His fictitious death adds the charm of sadness to the young boy's recollections.

A more noteworthy example of romantic *rifacimento* is the story of the little glass ship, modeled after a famous French frigate, that stood on a table in the sitting room of the Redburn home. It was the principal influence in converting Redburn's dreams of being a "great voyager" into the "definite purpose of seeking [his] fortune on the sea." Thirty years before, Walter Redburn had brought "La Reine" home from Hamburg as a present to Senator Wellingborough, Redburn's great-uncle, "who had died a member of Congress in the days of the old Constitution" and from whom Redburn received his name. On the Senator's death the gift had been returned to its donor.[2] In real life, however, this ship was most probably the one that rested in the parlor of Thomas Melvill, Herman's grandfather. Allan Melvill may have presented it to his parent; he certainly did not present it to Herman's great-uncle, Leonard Gansevoort, "in the days of the old Constitution," that is, between 1781 and 1789. Besides, though Leonard Gansevoort had been a member of Congress from 1787 to 1788, he did not die until 1810; Allan Melvill is not known to have met any of the Gansevoort family until 1813; and Herman was not named after his great-uncle but after his mother's brother, Herman Gansevoort. The embellishments in this anecdote are obvious. The idea of having a superbly real glass ship crystallize a boy's dreams of travel into a firm purpose is ingenious, but Melville's own history was somewhat different.

Such alterations, however, provide only the external coloring, not the inner artistic design of the story. In reading *Redburn,* we quickly perceive a highly significant discrepancy between the life of the hero and that of his author. As we know, Melville's father went bankrupt in 1830, moved to Albany, began a financial recovery, but died from overwork two years later. The Melville family, after a period of crisis, enjoyed over four years of relative prosperity before Gansevoort's failure forced them in 1838 to move to Lansingburgh. It was still another year before Herman went to sea. In Redburn's story, however, his father becomes bankrupt and dies in New York. Thereupon his mother moves "to a pleasant village on the Hudson River," and the period of this move is "some time previous" to Redburn's taking to the sea.[3] Redburn's calamities fall upon him in fairly rapid sequence and at a tender age. He has barely made the transition from childhood into youth, from riches to rags, before he is thrust out by hard times to earn his living as a sailor.

The central fact in Melville's artistry is that he conceives Redburn as a young boy. All the physical trials and the emotional anguish are intensified in poignancy because they happen to a wide-eyed adolescent. "I was then but a boy," says Redburn on the very first page. His age, we judge, is about fifteen, for he is eight years younger than his brother, who is evidently in his early twenties. Later, Redburn describes himself as "young and small" and "quite young and raw," and he speaks of his "boy's bulk" and his small backbone.[4] He is a pathetic character, pious, tender, and courageous but woefully untried and full of boyish illusions. He has never had to work before he enters a sailor's life. He has little knowledge of what physical equipment to take with him, knows nothing about sea usages, and is uninformed about the city to which he is bound. But at every turn he feels the shock of physical distress, embarrassment, and disillusion. The chief appeal of the story of Wellingborough Redburn is founded on the youthful hero's complete inexperience and immaturity.

The picture of Melville in June 1839 testifies to his skill in conceiving Redburn's character. He was nearly twenty years old, less than four years younger than his brother Gansevoort. In contrast to Redburn's pathetically small stature, Melville was taller than all but two of the other men on the "St. Lawrence." He had worked nearly a year on his uncle's farm. For years he had heard from his cousins about the life of a sailor; Leonard Gansevoort had made the very same voyage as a sailor on a merchant vessel that Herman was preparing for, and he knew how dull Liverpool was. Undoubtedly Herman faced hardship and disappointment, but he was much better prepared through experience and maturity to endure them than was Redburn. However, if he had represented his own mature reactions, he would have sacrificed much emotional appeal. The public for which Melville wrote was familiar, through Dana's *Two Years Before the Mast,* with the experiences of a twenty-year-old son of a gentleman. To avoid the perils of imitation, into which several others had fallen, Melville developed a younger character and looked at the harsh realities of the world largely through his eyes. He sought to create the greater drama implicit in the struggles of a completely inexperienced boy against an environment that nearly overwhelms him. It was thus that he attempted to solve the problem posed by contemporary literary conditions.[5]

As Melville fashioned the story of the poor, embittered, outcast Redburn, he introduced scores of artistic embellishments on his own experience and many a scene that originated only in his imagination. It is undoubtedly true that his own motives for going to sea are reflected in Redburn's. As the latter explains it:

> Sad disappointments in several plans which I had sketched for my future life; the necessity of doing something for myself, united to a naturally roving disposition, had now conspired within me, to send me to sea as a sailor.[6]

Here are the unmistakable echoes of Melville's failure to find work in his chosen career of surveying and engineering and perhaps of a defeated ambition to write.

In other respects, however, Melville's story differs quite

widely from Redburn's. He left home suddenly, and though he was "agitated," he was also "happy," to quote his mother. Almost certainly, he departed at some prosaic hour in the afternoon. And he was able to look forward to the company and help of his older brother Gansevoort in New York. On the other hand, Redburn had been preparing for his trip for months. There was ample time for his mother to knit him a pair of mittens. His departure occurs at the romantic hour of dawn, and it is completely melancholy. After breaking away from his weeping mother and sisters, he runs as fast as he can to the corner where his brother is waiting. The older boy accompanies him part way to the steamboat, filling him with "sage advice above his age" and making him promise to take care of himself.

> We walked on in silence till I saw that his strength was giving out—he was in ill health then,—and with a mute grasp of the hand, and a loud thump at the heart, we parted.
>
> It was early on a raw, cold, damp morning toward the end of spring, and the world was before me; stretching away along a muddy road, lined with comfortable houses, whose inmates were taking their sunrise naps, heedless of the wayfarer passing. The cold drops of drizzle trickled down my leather cap, and mingled with a few hot tears on my cheeks.
>
> I had the whole road to myself, for no one was yet stirring, and I walked on, with a slouching, dogged gait. The gray shooting-jacket was on my back, and from the end of my brother's rifle hung a small bundle of my clothes. My fingers worked moodily at the stock and trigger, and I thought that this indeed was the way to begin life, with a gun in your hand! [7]

This is indeed a lugubrious scene. The mute but moving farewell, the lonely road, the pathetic little bundle of clothes at the end of the rifle, the indifference of the world's comfortable householders, the rain and the teardrops, the extravagant self-pity and youthful bitterness—it is a sentimental and woeful picture. But there was no elder brother to make Herman's departure quite so painful, and the other objective evidence argues most potently that the scene is literary contrivance rather than personal history.

The proportion of literal truth and fiction in the next episode is more difficult to determine. On leaving home Redburn wears a miserable pair of old trousers with a large patch sewed on by his mother. The evening before, his brother has given him an old shooting jacket, to save the expense of another, and his fowling piece, to be sold for cash. He carries no food for the trip and only a dollar for money. On board the boat for New York he finds that the fare has suddenly been raised to two dollars, "owing to the other boats not running." After forcing the captain's gruff agent to accept his dollar, he gets angry at the comfortable passengers who have witnessed his excruciating embarrassment and observed his shabby clothes and points his gun directly at one of them. Having cowed the entire group, he leaves the cabin to spend the rest of the trip on deck.

It is barely possible that this incident had its source in Melville's own trip on the Hudson boat in 1839. Transportation was controlled by monopolies, but an "antimonopoly" boat had appeared on the river on May 29, when it made its first run from New York to Albany, advertising a fare of one dollar.[8] Within a day or two she was removed for alterations and did not resume running until June 5, so that Melville could not have traveled on her.[9] Since the other antimonopoly boat did not run on Saturday, when Melville must have made his trip,[10] it may well have been that the combined monopoly lines unexpectedly raised their fares. Thus Herman may have had to pay more than he had planned.

On the other hand such sudden shifts in rates were commonplace at the time,[11] and the Melvilles could hardly have been ignorant of the practice. It is scarcely credible that Herman's mother sent him off without food for the eleven- or twelve-hour journey. Gansevoort could not have given him the shooting jacket and the fowling piece the night before. The incident as described is melodramatic and unreal. Under any normal circumstances, a young boy who menaced people with a gun would hardly have been allowed to go scot-free by passengers and crew. And the New York and Albany newspapers, which carefully reported all untoward events on the river steamers, would hardly have missed an opportunity to air such a scandal.[12] The truth of all or even most of the circumstances in the episode is open to grave question.

So is the following scene, the interview on the "Highlander" between Redburn, his brother's friend Mr. Jones, and Captain Riga, which smacks much more of deliberate humor than of fact. The witty Captain smiles, and jokes, and pats young Redburn on the head while he blandly mocks his ancestry, punctures foolish Mr. Jones's well-intentioned pretense that Redburn is being sent to sea by rich relations, and withholds Redburn's advance in the best-humored manner imaginable and for reasons all admit are unimpeachable. If Melville drew any of these details from an actual interview with Captain Brown, we may be sure that he amply embellished them. Perhaps he was recalling from J. Ross Browne's *Etchings of a Whaling Cruise* a somewhat similar episode, which in his review of the book he had called "irresistibly comic." [13] If it was Alexander W. Bradford who helped Melville find a berth on the "St. Lawrence," it is hard to believe that with his intellect and practical training as a lawyer he could have been a silly young fop like Mr. Jones. And what ship captain would pat anyone on the head who was five feet eight and a half inches tall? [14]

For the story of Redburn's stay in New York, Melville deftly altered his own experience to emphasize the loneliness and helplessness of the young boy forced to shift for himself on the most slender means. Redburn receives a welcome dinner and kind treatment at the home of Mr. Jones, but to buy a few articles for his voyage, such as a knife, a red-flannel shirt, a belt, and some stationery, he pawns his brother's fowling piece for $2.50. He spends part of his time writing to this brother a letter full of misanthropic thoughts. After three nights at Mr. Jones's, Redburn goes to the "Highlander" alone, finds that the expected sailing has been delayed because of the rain, spends the night in the forecastle, and goes hungry till the next day for want of a single penny. Once at sea, he finds himself without tin pot, pan, spoon, dungarees, practical shoes, or bedding, equipment which he has had neither the means nor the foresight to provide. His consequent suffering makes a distressing picture of improvidence.

In creating this somewhat harrowing sequence, Melville conveniently omitted the facts that Allan and Gansevoort were staying at Alexander W. Bradford's and that Gansevoort had been instructed by their mother to help him obtain everything within his means that would make him comfortable. Unlike Redburn, Melville was not cut off from his family and thrown on his own resources. He probably had help and companionship in buying his equipment. It would have been unnatural for his brothers not to have accompanied him to the "St. Lawrence," and that he slept in the forecastle and went hungry for a full day is doubtful. One suspects also that, through Leonard Gansevoort, Melville was far more familiar than Redburn with a sailor's needs; from his mother's reference to "his means," it would seem that he was better able to provide for himself. However, adherence to all the literal facts in creating the story of Redburn's trials would have turned upon it the light of common day. Melville preferred to deepen the picture with all the somber hues at his command.

On the basis of Redburn's juvenile character and of certain debts to sea lore and literary tradition, we can safely assign a large number of other incidents to Melville's invention. In preparation for his career Redburn cuts off his hair because he thinks that every little bit will help in making him "a light hand to run aloft." Finding it difficult to follow the mate's orders to push some shavings into the long boat at a certain place, he chooses a more convenient spot and when the mate berates him, he insists, boylike, that his own place is better and demands to know *why* the mate has chosen another. His worst error is an ill-fated attempt to pay a social call on the captain in his cabin. Such humorous incidents, playing on the ignorance and conceit of young boys at sea for the first time, were commonplace in forecastle tradition, and they were the stock in trade of a generation of nautical writers. Their subject was the greenhorn sailor, who belongs as much to folklore as Mike Fink or Paul Bunyan. In one standard situation the young greenhorn would refuse to obey an officer until he had secured his rubbers. Thus a cartoon in David Claypoole Johnston's *Scraps* (Boston, 1840) captioned "A Lesson in Seamanship" has the following dialogue:

"Well now capting it's tew bad to send me up this rope lather in sich weather as this."

"You must obey orders *whether* or no."

"Well if I must go won't you be so good as to step down stairs for my rumbrella and ingee-rubber shoes?" [15]

Melville builds the situation into a much more comic vignette:

. . . The water began to splash about all over the decks, and I began to think I should surely get my feet wet, and catch my death of cold. So I went to the chief mate, and told him I thought I would just step below, till this miserable wetting was over; for I did not have any waterproof boots, and an aunt of mine had died of consumption. But he only roared out for me to get a broom and go to scrubbing, or he would prove a worse consumption to me than ever got hold of my poor aunt. So I scrubbed away fore and aft, till my back was almost broke, for the brooms had uncommon short handles, and we were told to scrub hard.[16]

Several such episodes dot the callow mariner's first days on board ship. Many are suspiciously like those in Captain Marryat's *Peter Simple,* published fifteen years before. By the time of *Redburn* Peter Simple had become a byword for the greenhorn sailor, and many reviewers promptly saw the resemblance.[17] Thus one of Peter's difficulties arises from his ignorance of slang and nautical terms. On his second day afloat, a veteran midshipman says to him:

"So, Master Simple, old Trotter and his faggot of a wife have got hold of you—have they?"

I replied, that I did not know the meaning of faggot, but that I considered Mrs. Trotter a very charming woman. At which he burst into a loud laugh.[18]

Similarly, when Redburn first boards the "Highlander," the mate asks him, "Have you got your traps aboard?"

I told him I didn't know there were any rats in the ship, and hadn't brought any "trap."

At this he laughed out with a great guffaw, and said there must be hayseed in my hair.[19]

Peter Simple has an aristocratic grandfather whose name and position he constantly invokes; Redburn is always referring to his great-uncle the senator or to his father, the wealthy merchant. When Peter thinks he is insulted by a foretopman, he declares:

"I am an officer and a gentleman. Do you know who my grandfather is?"

. . . "Who is he! why he's the *Lord knows who.*"

"No," replied I, "that's not his name; he is Lord Privilege." (I was very much surprised that he knew that my grandfather was a lord.)[20]

In a similar passage, Redburn's ancestry is mocked. A sailor calls him "Jimmy Dux [he says], though that was not my real name, and he must have known it; and also the 'son of a farmer,' though as I have previously related, my father was a great merchant and French importer in Broad Street."[21] Redburn and Peter have much the same kind of difficulty with nautical terminology. When stirrups are mentioned, Peter looks around but can see no horses, and he thinks that the surgeon, not the boatswain, must be the proper gentleman to "bleed all the buoys."[22] In a much less broad vein of humor, Redburn is constantly getting into the bad graces of the mate for using land terms for sea objects, saying pails instead of buckets, pegs instead of plugs.

Thus it is forecastle tradition and the work of literary predecessors rather than personal experience that account for many of Redburn's perplexities.[23] But Melville was capable of higher powers of creation, as he shows in a scene in which a sailor who had come aboard drunk rushes suddenly up from the forecastle, throws himself overboard, and drowns, all to the immense horror of Redburn, which, with his subsequent abuse from the sailors for seeming cowardly, is traced out in meticulous detail.[24] The incident reads like the truest of confessions; Melville seems to be saying with indisputable conviction that "this is what happened to me; this was *my* sorrow and *my* terror." In sober reality, however, there could have been no such occurrence aboard the "St. Lawrence." The ship's papers reveal that all the men who composed the crew in New York arrived safely in Liverpool.[25] Thus, although the story of the suicide, with its sequence of fright and suffering, is vivid, impassioned, and convincing, it is not autobiography but an admirably dramatic piece of fiction.

With only scraps of objective evidence upon which to rely, few judgments of Melville's art in depicting the crew of the "Highlander" can be made. He used real people, like the Greenlander, the Irishman, and Jackson, the mates, the cook, and the steward, but where fact leaves off and invention begins is impossible to say. We do know that Melville described Max, the Dutchman, as having red hair and red whiskers, a distinction held by none of the real sailors. The point would be too trivial to mention except that Melville's modification of fact in this instance, like his clear invention of the suicide and the consequent actions of the crew, suggests that he manufactured the traits of his sailors whenever his models lacked qualities sufficiently exploitable in literature.

A paucity of sources also makes it impossible to study in any detail Melville's artistry in utilizing the materials the outward-bound voyage of the "St. Lawrence" afforded him. He adhered to fact, as we know, in representing the "St. Lawrence" as a "regular trader" and in certain details of time and place such as the fact that the ship left New York late in the spring, that she spent about a month in the crossing, that she arrived in Liverpool early in July, and that she was berthed in Prince's Dock, the haven for most of the American trading vessels on the Liverpool run. These matters indicate that Melville made no changes in his own story where there was nothing to gain by them and where something might be lost. *Redburn* owes much of its power to a realistic account of life at sea. Both critics and public admired this quality more than any other, and Melville's craft had always included a certain accuracy about basic nautical matters, designed to secure credibility not only for his fanciful elaborations but for the straightforward realism as well. Indeed, if Melville had not been deterred by the fastidiousness of his audience, many of his scenes would have been more realistic than they are.[26]

The chapters describing Redburn's existence in Liverpool, which seem for the most part to be a truthful description of that city, rely for their appeal on the same vivid realism that flavors the nautical chapters. The sailor's boarding-house, the crowds of men, women, and children milling around in the open streets at night, the long lines of beggars outside Prince's Dock, each with his peculiar stratagem to attract charity, the wretched family who starve to death—these and many other scenes have the ring of direct reporting. Although some of them may have been inspired by newspaper or other accounts, known conditions in Liverpool in 1839 substantiate Melville's lurid depiction of poverty and woe. From the effect of the city on other travelers, we can safely feel that Melville shared some of Redburn's disillusion. We also know that he drew upon his personal experience in such incidents as hearing the Chartist orator, encountering the entrance to the tunnel of the Liverpool and Manchester Railway, and visiting Lord Nelson's monument in the courtyard of the Exchange. The truth of these few reminiscences suggests that many of the others are real and that much of Melville's art in the middle portion of the book consists of heightened journalism.

Nevertheless, the hand of the imaginative artist is still

busy. Redburn's crowning disillusion occurs when he finds that Riddough's Hotel, where his father had stayed thirty years before, has been torn down. The precious old guidebook to Liverpool he had venerated as infallible because his father had used it turns out to be valueless, and Redburn, utterly stunned, sits down on a shop step to draw the moral from his experience. Like the suicide incident, this illuminating discovery—it is the climactic event in *Redburn*—sounds unassailably authentic. It has been generally accepted as the straightforward record of an event that defeated his fond hopes and completely robbed him of his cherished sentimentalizings.[27] But such a view is only another unwitting tribute to Melville's powers of imagination.

The first clues to Melville's inventiveness come to light when we compare the account of Walter Redburn's visit to Liverpool with the information furnished by Allan Melvill in his diaries and letters. The fictional father had written in the old guidebook which his son later used, "Walter Redburn, Riddough's Royal Hotel, Liverpool, March 20th, 1808." Among the memorandums he made on various flyleaves were expenses for a "Dinner at the Star and Garter" and a "trip to Preston (distance 31 m.)." He also jotted down notes—"Dine with Mr. Roscoe on Monday," "Call on Sampson & Wilt, Friday" [28]—which indicate that he remained at least six days since March 20, 1808, fell upon a Sunday. On the other hand, we learn from Allan Melvill's carefully kept travel journal that on March 20, 1811, after a coach trip from Carlisle, he "reached the Liverpool Arms at ½ p 2 A. M." and that he left for Manchester on the twenty-third. On May 13, 1818, at the end of a twenty-one-day voyage from Boston, he "left the Ship in a Boat, landed at 8 AM & took lodgings at the Liverpool Arms," and on the fifteenth he took a coach for the North. These were his only visits to Liverpool. Neither one occurred in 1808 nor lasted more than three days, and Allan Melvill stayed at the Liverpool Arms, not at Riddough's Hotel.[29] His journal reveals no separate trip to Preston (it is true that he passed through the town on the way to Carlisle in 1818). He may have dined at the Star and Garter, for that was a well-known Liverpool hotel, like Riddough's and the Liverpool Arms.[30] However, he did not meet William Roscoe until 1818, and even then he did not apparently dine with the great banker and poet.[31]

It is evident from this comparison that Melville must have had some exact information about his father's trips to Liverpool. He dates Walter Redburn's stay at Riddough's Hotel March 20, 1808, the very month and day of his father's first visit, if a different year. It is unthinkable that this is a mere coincidence. The senior Redburn's memorandum that he was to dine with William Roscoe indicates that Melville was aware of his father's association with the poet. The guidebook that Walter Redburn and his son used was an actual volume, *The Picture of Liverpool* (Liverpool, 1808), though Melville dates it 1803, and he made use of it in composing *Redburn*.[32] It seems undeniable that he possessed the very copy owned by his father, which probably contained memorandums and dates in Allan Melvill's hand. If Melville had access to the journal, as he undoubtedly did, he would have found there also the mention of the Liverpool Arms and the date "March 20." [33]

These details have important implications. If Melville took his father's guidebook to Liverpool, he would presumably have found written in it the correct name of the hotel where Allan Melvill stayed, which was not Riddough's, but the Liverpool Arms. Its location, halfway down Castle Street, was supplied in the text and on the accompanying map,[34] and it was still standing in 1839, under the name of the Queen's Arms.[35] However, the old name was well within the memory of living individuals, and since the hotel had been famous in its day, being the Liverpool Corporation House and the headquarters of the Canning party, there should have been little trouble in identifying it.[36] Thus it is more than likely that if Melville actually attempted to find the very hotel where his father had "slept and dined, smoked his cigar, opened his letters, and read the papers,"[37] his efforts were successful. On the other hand, if he did not have the guidebook with the dotted lines showing Allan Melvill's course, then his story of Redburn's disappointed search must have been fabricated ten years later. Without knowledge of where his father stayed or what he did, Melville could not have attempted to follow his career, and he most certainly could not have suffered Redburn's crushing disenchantment. Hence, Melville's narrative is either a modification or even a reversal of the facts or a complete invention, depending on the information he possessed in 1839 about his father's trips to Liverpool.

In any event, it is indisputable that Melville did not find that his father's hotel had been leveled to the ground as Redburn did. Was the incident purely imaginary? Or did Melville find a hint in the guidebook from which he drew so many other details of Liverpool? In this volume the description of Riddough's Hotel as an elegant hostelry with every accommodation for the elite traveler invests it with a certain hopeful grandeur.[38] Its location at the foot of Lord Street is mentioned for the convenience of the reader. However, if Melville went with his guidebook in hand to compare the real hotel with the one described, he would have found that it had been converted into shops.[39] The transmutation from splendid hostelry to lowly mercantile establishments could easily have supplied him with a hint for the example of worldly mutability that he developed later in *Redburn*.

After Redburn has assimilated the shock of finding his father's hotel razed to the ground, he makes one more attempt to vindicate his faith in the treasured guidebook. A passage concerning "The Old Dock" impels him to walk to the place where he may see the astonishing sight of "so great a number of ships afloat in the very heart of the town."[40] When he arrives at the designated spot, he finds neither dock nor ships, and a policeman explains that the place had been filled in years before to make room for the

Customs House. At this unforeseen announcement, Redburn breaks into another sardonic outburst on the uselessness of "old morocco," and his disillusion is virtually complete. It is, however, almost certainly a literary disillusion and not Melville's own reminiscence. Redburn had studied the guide-book carefully on the passage to Liverpool; he had "perused one by one the elaborate descriptions of public edifices" and mastered all details in the accompanying engravings.[41] Had Melville done the same he would have found, in the middle of the description of the Exchange buildings, the information that because the Old Dock interfered with pedestrian traffic and many people fell into it and drowned, the Corporation of Liverpool was about to fill it up and lay it open for a market place.[42] Thus he could scarcely have shared Redburn's utter surprise at finding that the project had been carried out. Melville's use of the guidebook in *Redburn*, including the hotel incident, shows that here again, instead of reproducing his own experience, he is employing his familiar technique of adaptation and invention for dramatic ends.

The first half of *Redburn* concludes with the climactic failure to find Riddough's Hotel. The second half, with its long descriptions of the docks, its straightforward narratives of poverty and crime, and its pious editorial comment, is not so artistically wrought as the first. Nevertheless, Melville continues in his role of literary magician, transforming the cold facts of guidebook information into decorative anecdotes, fashioning illusions of a mighty reality from little glimpses of life, and producing living experiences from the insubstantial air of his imagination.

To enlarge on Redburn's disillusion with England, Melville pictures him as frightened away from a peaceful field by a sign reading "Man Traps and Spring Guns" even though such treacherous devices had been forbidden by law twelve years before Melville saw Liverpool.[43] From the very guidebook he employed so skillfully in shaping a momentous disillusion for Redburn, he culls the substance of several "personal" observations. According to Redburn, a policeman tells him the history of the Old Dock, already referred to. From the lips of the shipkeeper of the "Highlander" he hears a tale about a one-hundred-year-old ship that entered King's Dock when it was first opened. Drunkards used to fall asleep on the tombstones of St. Nicholas' Church down near the docks, says Redburn, and one day, finding a rum-soaked figure stretched out there, he moved his arm and found underneath the ironic inscription, "Here Lyeth Ye Body of Tobias Drinker." [44] Despite the convincing tone of these anecdotes, Melville cribbed them from *The Picture of Liverpool,* adding enough embellishment to lift them from the prosaic level of their original form.[45] It is characteristic of his bold plunder of sources that these stories are introduced soon after his refusal to quote from the book. Were he to do so, he says, he would be charged "with swelling out [his] volume by plagiarising from a guidebook—the most vulgar and ignominious of thefts." [46] It was not the first time that Melville had practiced a harmless fraud upon his readers. But as if in confession of his methods, he wrote elsewhere in *Redburn* that "spun-yarn" is made on shipyard from "odds and ends of old rigging called 'junk,' the yarns of which are picked to pieces, and then twisted into new combinations, something as most books are manufactured." [47]

One suspects a similar literary source for at least part of the chapter on the "Irrawaddy," a fascinating ship from distant India. The story of the ship is told to Redburn by one of the English-speaking lascar sailors, but the encyclopedic detail and the native Indian words are strongly suggestive of indebtedness to some marine dictionary. In the absence of evidence, however, it is unfruitful to devote space to speculation on minor matters. For there remains a major question about Melville's artistic method in *Redburn,* the question of the authenticity of the London trip, and of the scenes in Aladdin's Palace, the opulent gambling house where Redburn spends an adventurous night with Harry Bolton, a young aristocrat who has gambled away one inheritance and is about to gamble once more in order to avoid the alternative of seeking his fortune in America.

The episode has interested both literary critics and biographers for a century. The reviewer of *Redburn* in *Blackwood's Edinburgh Magazine* discarded it as being "in the very stalest style of minor-theatre melodrama" and asserted that the gambling den "existed nowhere (at least in London) but in our sailor-author's imagination." [48] Raymond Weaver, while admitting the incident might be founded on fact, thought that the account of the adventure sounded "hollow and false" and that, "in this part of the narrative, Melville [was] making brave and unconvincing concessions to romance." [49] Later he changed his mind and came to accept the London trip,[50] a point of view in which he has the company of Lewis Mumford, who thinks "the very vagueness and mysteriousness smells of reality." [51] John Freeman credits the story on the theory that the magnificence of the gaming house had so impressed Melville that he included it in *Redburn,* just as he had already drawn upon it for the luxurious details of the lady's apartment in the second "Fragment from a Writing Desk." [52] Finally, Willard Thorp believes the visit to the gambling den is imaginary, though he cites the biography of Melville in the Duyckincks' *Cyclopaedia of American Literature* as confirmation of the London journey.[53]

The problem is clearly one of both art and biography. Some of the existing opinions may be disposed of without difficulty. The Duyckinck biography does not really confirm the London journey, for that detail was evidently borrowed from *Men of the Time,* an earlier biographical dictionary, and the latter may have taken it from *Redburn.*[54] Mumford cites as proof of his contention the fact that "Melville treated Israel Potter to a similar experience on his first visit to Paris, although there is no foundation in Israel's story for his being confined to his room until the time comes for departure." [55] However, Israel Potter's adventure seems to have no bearing whatsoever on Redburn's. Israel carries secret dispatches from American agents in England to Benjamin Franklin, who confines him to an adjoining room for security, whereas Redburn merely remains in a vacant apartment in Aladdin's Palace while Harry goes off to gamble away his remaining funds. More proof than this is certainly demanded if we are to believe that Redburn's experience was Melville's. John Freeman's evidence, now that we know that the Liverpool voyage occurred after the writing of the second "Fragment" rather than before loses all value; in fact, the resemblance between the description in the second "Fragment" and in *Redburn* supports a theory quite the reverse of Freeman's.

A cogent argument for the imaginary character of the London gambling house lies in the extravagant description Melville furnishes. Was he depicting an interior that he had seen? Or was he relying on details derived from a literary source? A comparison between the lady's apartment in the second "Fragment" and the rooms in the gambling house in *Redburn* suggests an answer. In the first we find chandeliers hung by silver rods from the ceiling giving a "soft and tempered light" and a "dreamy beauty" to the scene.[56] In the second, the "vivid glare" from the gas lights is "softened by pale, cream-colored, porcelain spheres, shedding over the place a serene, silver flood." [57] Tripods representing "the Graces bearing aloft vases" adorn the apartment; [58] in the gaming house "three marble Graces" hold a candelabrum over the stair landing.[59] The guide in the "Fragment" conducts the narrator "through a long corridor" to a door that "open[s] to the touch"; [60] similarly, Harry Bolton leads Redburn "up the long winding slope of [the] . . . stairs" straight to a door that, "on magical hinges, [springs] softly open to his touch." [61] In the gorgeous rooms which the narrator and Redburn enter are further remarkable resemblances, best revealed by a parallel arrangement:

"Fragment No. 2"	*Redburn*
Disposed around the room, were luxurious couches, covered with the finest damask, on which were . . . executed after the Italian fashion the early fables of Greece and Rome.	Long lounges lay carelessly disposed, whose fine damask was interwoven, like the Gobelin tapestry, with pictorial tales of tilt and tourney.
Attached to the walls by cords composed of alternate threads of crimson silk and gold, were several magnificent pictures illustrative of the loves of Jupiter and Semele, Psyche before the tribunal of Venus, and a variety of other scenes, ...[62]	The walls, covered with a sort of tartan-French paper, variegated with bars of velvet, were hung round with mythological oil-paintings, suspended by tasseled cords of twisted silver and blue. They were such pictures as the high-priests, for a bribe, showed to Alexander in the innermost shrine of the white temple in the Libyan oasis: . . . such pictures as Martial and Suetonius mention as being found in the private cabinet of the Emperor Tiberius: . . . such pictures as you might have beheld in an arched recess, leading from the left hand of the secret side gallery of the temple of Aphrodite in Corinth.[63]

Besides these striking parallels in physical details and in phrasing, there are others in tonal quality. Oriental atmosphere dominates both scenes. In the "Fragment" the room is "as beautiful and enchanting as any described in the Arabian Nights," and it is "filled up in a style of Eastern splendor," including the familiar ottoman.[64] In *Redburn* the gambling house is named Aladdin's Palace. It has "Moorish-looking tables," "oriental ottomans," "Turkey rugs," and "Persian carpeting," and the waiters make salaams.[65] At some point in both narratives the hero is seized by a sense of dread and a desire to be safe in familiar surroundings, and each is self-conscious amidst the opulence in which he unexpectedly finds himself. However, the hero in the earlier sketch masters all his misgivings whereas Redburn is nearly overwhelmed by them. Although the gambling-house scene is much longer and richer in detail than the early sketch, the resemblances are substantial indications of a nonfactual source.

The extravagance, the apparent inspiration from literary sources, and the melodrama of this incongruous passage greatly diminish its authenticity. Furthermore, if we assume for the moment that Melville was telling things as they happened to him, a glaring disparity appears. Unless his memory was defective, Melville's schedule of action in *Redburn* shows that he could not have made the trip to London and still returned to America on the "St. Lawrence." Redburn makes the acquaintance of Harry Bolton on the day following a Sunday stroll in the country when he had been in England "four weeks or more." [66] Since the "St. Lawrence" arrived in Liverpool on Tuesday, July 2, the date of the encounter would have been Monday, August 5, or thereafter. Harry becomes Redburn's companion in his "afternoon strolls and Sunday excursions," on one of which they meet Lord Lovely, an old friend of Harry's.[67] About a week after this meeting, Harry invites Redburn to go to London with him. This event, then, would have fallen approximately on August 12. They spend one night at a public house in Liverpool, take the train to London the next day, pass that night in the gambling house, and return the following evening to learn that the "Highlander" had been advertised that morning to sail in two days. By the calendar, it would have been August 14. In the next two days the crew of the "Highlander" build enough bunks to accommodate the five hundred emigrants she has taken aboard, and on the morning following the completion of their task, the ship sails. Her departure, according to the implications of Melville's account, would have occurred on August 17. However, the date of the departure of the "St. Lawrence" was August 13. Furthermore, whereas Redburn does not hear of her announced sailing date until three days beforehand, Melville must have known for weeks that departure was imminent. As early as July 9 he had heard a rumor that the "St. Lawrence" might go to Charleston.[68] The "St. Lawrence" had been advertised on July 19 to sail as early as August 1. On August 2 it was announced that she would sail the following day. On August 6 the captain had filled the places of the three deserters with three other seamen, an action that was usually taken just before sailing.[69] Melville had not left the ship before this time, for his name appears on the crew list as of that date. Unlike the names of the known deserters, it is not marked "Run," a notation that would have been justified if he absented himself from the ship either before or after August 6 for a full forty-eight hours as Redburn did. If he had deserted between August 6 and 13, he would also have risked the loss of his wages and equipment,[70] and he would have had to find a berth on another ship for transportation back to New York.

Thus the truth of the flight to London is substantially challenged. Some other hints, if not conclusive in themselves, throw additional doubt on the story. For one thing, Melville gives no indication in his 1849 journal of having been in London before, though when he visited Liverpool seventeen years after his first voyage he returned to one of the scenes of his wanderings.[71] Again, for a boy who notices a thousand sordid details of Liverpool life and who is prepared to exult in the real England with its picturesque abbeys and minsters, its historic landmarks, and its broad, green fields, Redburn shows surprisingly little response to the sights along the railroad to London. He passes off the journey in half a hundred words, mentioning villages, meadows, parks, arching viaducts, and tunnels in a very general manner. Yet the only route by which he could have gone ran through Coventry and Rugby; from the railroad station at Harrow one could glimpse an outline of the school; the grounds and ruins of Berkhampstead Castle, residence of the kings of England from the time of Henry III, were adjacent to the railroad.[72] No one would be so foolish as to insist that Melville would have exclaimed over these scenes in *Redburn* if he had observed them personally, but their absence still broadens the base of disbelief for the whole fantastic episode.

In his account of the return trip of the "Highlander" Melville recovers speedily from the artistic lag of the central section of *Redburn.* In the very first chapter following the departure from Prince's Dock he writes a scene of thrilling realism. Just before the ship sailed, a one-eyed crimp had carried aboard an apparently drunken sailor whose sallow face indicated Portuguese nationality and whose name was "down on the ship's papers as Miguel Saveda." That night the crew notice a horrible smell in the forecastle, which they attribute to the presence of a dead rat, but the real source is Miguel, whom Jackson finds dead in his bunk, where the crimp had placed him:

> Upon this the men rushed toward the bunk, Max with the light, which he held to the man's face.
>
> "No, he's not dead," he cried, as the yellow flame wavered for a moment at the seaman's motionless mouth. But hardly had the words escaped, when, to the silent horror of all, two threads of greenish fire, like a forked tongue, darted out between the lips; and in a moment, the cadaverous face was crawled over by a swarm of worm-like flames.[73]

Max drops the lamp, and the corpse, covered with "spires and sparkles of flame," burns on with a faint crackling noise. Melville describes the open, fixed eyes, the mouth wearing "an aspect of grim defiance," and even the way that the tattooed letters of the man's name burn white so that "you might read the flaming name in the flickering ground of blue." [74]

In a few minutes, the men pitch the body into the ocean, where it falls "among the phosphorescent sparkles of the damp night sea, leaving a coruscating wake" as it sinks.[75] Redburn is left speculating on the horrible revelation that the man had been dead for some time before the crimp brought him aboard to secure his month's advance.

This incident is as terrifying as any that Melville ever wrote, and its multitude of precise details gives it the authority of an eye-witness account. "This event thrilled me through and through with an unspeakable horror," says Redburn, and we feel that the sentiments spring from Melville's somber memories. Yet, like the suicide with which the voyage began, this bizarre accident did not occur on the "St. Lawrence." Of the three men who were shipped in Liverpool, none was named Saveda, and all crossed safely to New York, where their presence on board was attested by a customs official.[76] Perhaps Melville had read somewhere about a case of animal combustion. Whatever his source, the scene is a masterpiece of nautical realism, terse, graphic, and horrible. And because Melville carefully controls the element of horror, he rises well above the sensationalist school of nautical writers. While avoiding a cultivated morbidity, he rivals Poe's artistry in depicting the grotesque.

Melville sustains this quality of dramatic realism in his account of the Irish immigrants who compose most of the "Highlander's" cargo. Nearly six of the fifteen chapters he devotes to the homeward journey describe the ingenuousness, improvidence, and misery of these hapless refugees. So ignorant are they of geography that they think Cape Clear, at the exit of the Irish Channel, is America. They bring food for a two or three weeks' passage, and when it is gone, "scores" of them wander the decks, plundering the chicken coop, waylaying the steward, and robbing the bread barge. Of those who do have enough food, many "scores" get no chance to do their cooking, for the ship has only one galley and in the constant fighting for places, many lose out. Worst of all, this swarming mob—there are about five hundred of them, according to Melville[77]—is shut up for nearly a week in the dark, unventilated steerage, filthy with human offal, and the breeding place of a pestilential fever that infects over thirty-six passengers, thirty of whom die. During the panic, the crew, including Redburn, are ordered into the steerage to throw down a barricade foolishly erected by the healthy around the bunks of the sick to prevent spread of the disease. This is Melville's supposed reporting of the scene:

> The sight that greeted us, upon entering, was wretched indeed. It was like entering a crowded jail. From the rows of rude bunks, hundreds of meager, begrimed faces were turned upon us; while seated upon the chests, were scores of unshaven men, smoking tea leaves, and creating a suffocating vapor. But this vapor was better than the native air of the place, which from almost unbelievable causes, was fetid in the extreme. In every corner, the females were huddled together, weeping and lamenting; children were asking bread from their mothers, who had none to give; and old men, seated upon the floor, were leaning back against the heads of the water-casks, with closed eyes and fetching their breath with a gasp.[78]

At the mate's orders, the crew attempt to knock down the barricade.

> But hardly had we touched the chests composing it, when a crowd of pale-faced, infuriated men rushed up; and with terrific howls, swore they would slay us, if we did not desist.
>
> "Haul it down!" roared the mate.
>
> But the sailors fell back, murmuring something about merchant seamen having no pensions in case of being maimed, and they had not shipped to fight fifty to one. . . . we were obliged to depart, without achieving our object.[79]

This scene and all the others describing the poor immigrants gave Melville "most bitter occasion to reflect on the criminal nature of the universe," according to one of his romantic biographers.[80] But such facts as are now available reveal an entirely different character in Melville's narrative. For example, his description of the ignorance of the passengers who mistake Cape Clear for America, though possibly true reporting, may have been an elaboration of a hint in Nathaniel Ames's *A Mariner's Sketches* (1830), especially since the anecdote immediately following bears an unmistakable resemblance to one in the passage from Ames.[81] Melville describes an old Irishman who stands in the bows for hours as if expecting to see New York any minute (it is two thousand miles away).

> The only thing [he writes] that ever diverted this poor old man from his earnest search for land was the occasional appearance of porpoises under the bows; when he would cry out at the top of his voice: "Look, look, ye divils! look at the great pigs of the s'a!" [82]

In Ames's account of his trip from Ireland with one Irish family aboard, the story reads:

> While on the passage a large school of porpoises played around the ship; the oldest boy ran to the after hatchway and called to his sister, "Jasus, Molly, come up stairs and see the wild *bastes* of the *sa!*" [83]

Considering that Melville borrowed one of the most exciting scenes in *White-Jacket* from Ames's book,[84] his reliance on Ames for this snatch of humorous monologue seems credible. Melville refined the profane naturalism but retained the earthiness and enlarged it a trifle to suit his own needs.

This literary pilfering, however, is trivial in comparison with the large-scale appropriation which, unless Melville relied entirely upon his imagination, he must have committed to gather the details of immigrant life on the "Highlander." He was probably struck by newspaper or magazine accounts of immigrant ships, which in 1849 were bringing to America hundreds of thousands of refugees from the Irish famine under exactly the same conditions he described.[85] In fact, he virtually acknowledges his source: "the only account you obtain of such events is generally contained in a newspaper paragraph, under the shipping head." [86] In any event, it is evident that the stirring scenes in *Redburn* are fictional, for the "St. Lawrence" did not carry four or five hundred starved and miserable immigrants to New York, nor even the "scores" who wandered hungry about the decks and drove out the craven crew. In the steerage of the "St. Lawrence" there were only thirty-two passengers, none of whom died on the voyage.[87] Melville's multiplication of this handful into the vast herd of living and suffering and dying people on the "Highlander" is an excellent achievement in the art of visualization.

The discovery of the passenger list of the "St. Lawrence" supplies further clues to Melville's inventiveness. The "Highlander" carried a young Italian emigrant named Carlo whose physical beauty, charming conversation, and ability to produce a wide repertory on his hand organ inspire an entire chapter of intimate feelings, yet nobody named Carlo, nor any Italian for that matter, appears on the official list.[88] Another chapter narrates the adventures of two sets of triplet boys named O'Brien and O'Regan, though none of the thirteen children on the "St. Lawrence" were even twins. Melville also invented some thirteen beings to inhabit the cabin in addition to the two men actually there on the "St. Lawrence," "Mr. L. A. Kettle" and "Mr. Andrew Coats."[89] Either may have provided some suggestions for the "abominable-looking old fellow, with cold, fat, jelly-like eyes,"[90] the only one of the fifteen cabin passengers to be described at any length, but the "two or three buckish-looking young fellows" who talk about "going on to Washington to see Niagara Falls" are creatures of fiction as are the several ladies and the American lady who dies on the voyage. But the absence of real-life models was no deterrent to Melville, who describes with great contempt the cowardice and hysterical prayers of these apparently real travelers when threatened by the plague and even "reports" a dialogue in which one of the young blades ridicules the speedy recovery of his friends' courage after the danger is past.

In one more event that marks the homeward course of the "Highlander" Melville displays his capacity for dramatic description. He tells the story with photographic accuracy:

[Jackson's] hat and shoes were off; and he rode the yard-arm end, leaning backward to the gale, and pulling at the earing-rope, like a bridle. At all times, this is a moment of frantic exertion with sailors, whose spirits seem then to partake of the commotion of the elements, as they hang in the gale between heaven and earth; and *then* it is, too, that they are the most profane.

"Haul out to windward!" coughed Jackson, with a blasphemous cry, and he threw himself back with a violent strain upon the bridle in his hand. But the wild words were hardly out of his mouth, when his hands dropped to his side, and the bellying sail was spattered with a torrent of blood from his lungs.

As the man next him stretched out his arm to save, Jackson fell headlong from the yard, and with a long seethe, plunged like a diver into the sea.

It was when the ship had rolled to windward, which, with the long projection of the yard-arm over the side, made him strike far out upon the water. His fall was seen by the whole upward-gazing crowd on deck, some of whom were spotted with the blood that trickled from the sail, while they raised a spontaneous cry, so shrill and wild, that a blind man might have known something deadly had happened.[91]

For all its pictorial realness, which includes even the blood-spattered faces of the spectators, this awesome scene is purely fictional. Robert Jackson was still aboard the "St. Lawrence" when she ended her voyage in New York, nor did Melville transfer to him the fate of some other shipmate, for all the members of the original crew who had not deserted in Liverpool returned alive.[92] The death of Jackson instead of being inspired reporting is one of the many artistic tours de force with which the pages of *Redburn* are liberally strewn.

With this incident, Melville returns, as far as is known, to a largely factual narration of the ship's progress, past quarantine and up the Narrows into the lower harbor. He remembered that the "St. Lawrence" had passed in sight of the battleship "North Carolina," which had come to anchor in New York late in June 1839, and made Captain Riga point it out to the cabin passengers.[93] But what else in the few remaining pages of *Redburn* is refurbished truth or impassioned romanticizing, it is difficult to tell. Presumably the bitter scene in which the Captain refused Redburn his wages because he ran away to London was not something Melville had to face. Besides the evidence against the London escapade, a defect in the logic of Redburn's story suggests that Melville really received his pay. Redburn leaves the "Highlander" quite penniless, but his creator neglects to explain how the boy got money to pay his fare on the steamboat he boards for the journey home. Perhaps Melville departed from the "St. Lawrence" with his earnings, but when he came to write his book he determined to expose the battered hero to one final defeat. From a literary point of view, at least, the painful blighting of Redburn's last expectation has the value of consistency.[94]

Although the sources in the oral traditions of the forecastle may be beyond recovery, it is undeniably possible to extend the study of the literal truth in *Redburn*. The pages of magazines, newspapers, and obscure books, perhaps dime novels, may well contain the original stories on which many incidents in *Redburn* are based. It would be interesting to see these sources arranged in parallel form as a means of examining Melville's habits of composition more precisely.[95] But the background of enough of the book is now known to reveal Melville's highly artistic techniques. The author of *Redburn* was a great illusionist, a master of literary legerdermain. It has been fashionable for some time to consider his book autobiography with elements of romance. It is more nearly correct to call it romance with elements of autobiography.

The question of spiritual truth in *Redburn* is far more difficult to deal with. It can be easily contended that despite all the discrepancies research can expose between Melville and Redburn, the book is a romance only on the surface, that its real meaning as autobiography lies deep below, where all but the obdurate will quickly find the tragic story of Melville's own youth. *Redburn,* to quote the biographer who founded the modern autobiographical interpretation, is Melville's attempt to revenge himself "upon his early disillusion by an inverted idealism,—by building for himself 'not castles, but dungeons in Spain.'" It is a book of "malicious self-satire, and its obverse gesture, obtrusive self-pity." [96] And the most studied exponent of biography through psychological revelations presumably included *Redburn* when he said that Melville's early work is the "biography of his self-image." [97]

In the absence of an early diary or letters or such evidence as the autobiography that Dickens incorporated into *David Copperfield,* it is difficult to give more than guarded and tentative acceptance to such assessments of *Redburn,* regardless of brilliance or confident appeals to mental science. It seems undeniable that Melville's own poverty and disappointments account in large measure for those features in Redburn's story. But to insist that Redburn's emotions were Melville's neglects the fact that Melville was older and more experienced than Redburn and that many of the fictional hero's passionate outbursts arose from incidents which did not occur. The bitterness in the book adumbrates the bitterness and misanthropy to be found in *Pierre* and *The Confidence Man,* but to sift out the exact proportions of Melville's and Redburn's personal discontent would be an arduous task indeed. At any rate, to argue that Melville's own experience dictated his book is to make the much more dangerous and essentially antiliterary assumption that writing is merely the product of physiological determinism and to deny that the artist has freedom to choose effects for dramatic purposes. The real concern of the critic is the validity of these created effects just as the real concern of the biographer is the validity of the evidence that Melville was truthfully representing his youth in *Redburn.* Without a great deal more evidence by which the book may be tested, it seems the legitimate source only for the most general impressions of Melville's spiritual history.

Chapter VII

The Little Nursery Tale

NOW that we know a good deal about the differences in fact between *Redburn* and Melville's early life we can approach the book critically with much less danger of mistaking contrived effects for self-revelation and much more chance of estimating its value and significance properly. For a work which its author sneered at as "a little nursery tale" [1] and as "trash, [written] to buy some tobacco with," [2] it contains surprising riches, and it tells us much about Melville's strength and weakness in literary technique and about his social and religious thinking in 1849. In looking at these and other facets of the book we shall want also to bear in mind the neglected question of relation to similar elements in Melville's other books so that we may perceive the place of *Redburn* in his artistic development.

Architecturally, the book looks eminently simple. Melville seems merely to have followed the lines laid out by his voyage to Liverpool in 1839. The first five chapters introduce the hero and take him to sea. Twenty-two chapters describe the crew, the ship, and the events of the crossing, nineteen narrate Redburn's adventures in Liverpool and London, fifteen detail the homeward passage. The last chapter, half of it epilogue, knots up the one loose thread with the final tragedy of Harry Bolton.

However, on internal examination much more studied arrangement of materials comes to light. Within the simple framework supplied by his first voyage, Melville contrives effects suggesting an artistic awareness of the value of variety, contrast, and climax. Each main division of the book concludes with a scene of major disillusion or disappointment in the hero's expectations; the outward voyage with the failure to find his father's hotel, the Liverpool chapters with the failure to see the beauties of London, the homeward passage with the failure to receive his wages. In the intervals between these climaxes, Melville periodically spices his narrative with dramatic incidents. A scene of high emotional tension occurs in chapter ii, the suicide in chapter x, a near shipwreck in xix, the death of a starving family in xxxvii, the combustion of the corpse in xlviii, and Jackson's death in lix. In the first section of *Redburn,* Melville deftly interweaves passages of narrative with description and exposition and contrasts his tonal effects skillfully, balancing bitter or tragic scenes with humorous ones. Immediately following the chapter in which Redburn endures the most humiliating effects of poverty comes the humorous interview with Captain Riga. Directly after the wretched boy is abused by his crew mates for showing fright at the drunkard's suicide, we read the comic description of his efforts to escape washing the deck. Melville's power weakens somewhat in the Liverpool chapters, despite many scenes of stirring realism and his faculty for making locality vivid, as he had done in *Typee* and *Omoo,* by personalizing impressions instead of merely reporting facts. In the third section, however, where he has people to write about, he recovers himself, mingling bare horror with robust humor and warm human sentiment with trenchant satire.

The chief clue to Melville's arrangement of materials in *Redburn* is a developing sense of drama. He had not yet learned the trick of choosing events with a predetermined effect and working steadily toward climaxes. Although like Defoe he continually throws in anticipatory remarks, the London visit is the only point for which he makes much preparation, and even here the technique is unsophisticated. But in the juxtaposition of varied elements, in the rising movement of several individual chapters, and in the elementary use of climax in the principal sections of the book, Melville reveals some concept of dramatic structure. In this respect, *Redburn,* more than any of his other early books, anticipates the art of *Moby-Dick,* where Melville's dramatic sense reaches its fullest expression.

Despite these merits in construction, *Redburn* has several minor flaws and a major one that is disastrous. Melville makes a number of slips. After referring to one of the sailors as "an old bachelor," he later describes him as married. Redburn hopes that Harry Bolton will succeed in getting hired as a sailor on the "Highlander," but not until Harry has been accepted does he warn him of the harsh treatment he will receive and recommend that he go as a passenger. After Redburn has left the ship without a penny, Melville neglects to explain where he secures the money to pay his passage on the river boat which brings him home. Such defects, arising no doubt from hasty composition, occasionally impair the verisimilitude that is one of the chief properties of *Redburn.*

In addition, Melville shows various weaknesses of a writer who has not completely matured. He includes too much in his story, he attempts scenes for which he has no talent, and he abandons consistency in tone to indulge a taste for fantasy. The chapter about the two passengers on the outward journey could well have been omitted, as could some of the description of Liverpool, especially chapter xl, an omnium-gatherum of sights along the docks.[3] The episode of the London gambling house is tawdry and melodramatic, designed perhaps to cater to a public that enjoyed scandalous scenes of high life as long as vice was righteously denounced.[4] Chapter xlix, with its rhapsody on music, clashes sharply with the plain manner that dominates the book.

The ruinous defect is a disrupting shift in the angle of vision.[5] Melville sets out to picture the world through the eyes of a young boy and to convey the rude impact of experience upon his romantic and tender consciousness. He holds to this point of view with great success for almost all of the first half of the book. After the guidebook incident, however, his technique fails. Despite occasional sounding of Redburn's reactions, much of the description of Liverpool is unenlivened by the intensity of a boy's feelings that give strength and relevance to earlier commonplace incidents. The lapse is followed by a persistent decline into the editorial manner. Melville continually employs Redburn's experiences as points of departure for adult comment upon poverty, immigration laws, music, the duty of the clergy in the church militant, America as the promised land, and other topics. If the comment is eloquent, if it frequently resembles Swift's savage indignation, it is artistically defective. It robs the book as a whole of the sequent development and consistency necessary in a well-sculptured work of art.

In reviewing his literary career to Hawthorne in 1851 Melville wrote:

> What I feel most moved to write, that is banned,—it will not pay. Yet, altogether write the *other* way I cannot. So the product is a final hash, and all my books are botches.[6]

One suspects that as far as *Redburn* is concerned, "what I feel most moved to write" meant the impassioned strictures on the evils of contemporary life as Melville saw it in 1849. Conversely, "the other way" of writing probably meant the depiction of the young boy's experiences. If this is so (and it seems most reasonable), it explains why *Redburn* is a "botch." Unable to hold himself down to the adolescent point of view for the entire book, Melville continually tried to indulge what he took to be his higher instincts by inserting social and moral criticism. Artistically, however, he misjudged his true power. He would have written a much better book had he held to the development of Redburn's character under stress. But when, in his irrepressible urge to arouse the conscience of his times, he submerged the story of his lovable young hero, he did great damage to the structure of his narrative. He also made a tacit confession that he had not yet achieved the full control of material which the mature artist commands.

But it would be unjust to ignore Melville's achievement in portraying Redburn merely because the boy's character shifts. For when we consider only the youthful Redburn it is difficult to think of another boy in nineteenth century American literature who comes to life quite as vividly. Tom Sawyer or Huckleberry Finn may always be better known, but neither is as sensitive a person as Redburn, and neither is exposed with the same psychological penetration or the same sense of the tragedy of adolescence. Taking full advantage of the first-person confessional manner, Melville explores with an almost cruel frankness the romantic expectations and the anguish of a poverty-stricken and disenchanted youth at every level of joy and wonder and suffering. The film of Redburn's consciousness is an ultrafine medium that fixes every experience with a heightened, even a morbid, intensity. It detects with relentless honesty the good and the bad, within himself as well as outside. Because of his almost inexhaustible awareness, Redburn is a many-sided character, who easily transcends the conventions governing his type. He is egotistic and extroverted, haughty and submissive, foolish and shrewd, blindly prejudiced and mercifully tolerant. He is capable of both anger and laughter. He pities others almost as much as he does himself, and he has a strong sense both of human folly and human dignity. Melville is guilty of sentimentalism, exaggeration, and inconsistency in his portrait, but its best lines and colors depict a boy who might have rivaled Pip or David Copperfield had Melville known how to make him the hero of a novel instead of a mere romance.

Melville's artistry in delineating a boy's impulses, sorrows, dreams, and unsophisticated mental processes takes immediate hold in the idyllic first chapter on Redburn's boyhood. He perceives quite clearly the way a vigorously imaginative youth extends or transforms the objects that arouse him until they have a direct reference in his own senses. The child Redburn hears his father's tales of the cathedrals and churches and long narrow streets of Europe, and at the end of his meditations he wonders whether the children across the ocean are allowed by their papas to wear boots, which Redburn prefers to shoes because they are more manly. The waves in a painting of a fishing boat seem "toasted brown," and by childish synesthesia, Redburn thinks that a piece of the picture might taste good. With Redburn on board an actual ship and out on the actual ocean, Melville's power of recording impressions rises to match the boy's expansion in sensibility. Going out of the Narrows seems to Redburn "like going out into the broad highway, where not a soul is to be seen." The utter loneliness and desolation outside, where the only view is that of the sky and the water meeting, make it incredible that there could be any land or people beyond the horizon. To him, the thought "of steering right out among those waves, and leaving the bright land behind, and the dark night coming on, too, seemed wild and foolhardy." [7] Melville precisely crystallizes the panic that settles upon an inexperienced soul when his instincts for the things in which he feels secure erupt in sudden conflict against the untried reality. A few pages farther on Melville recognizes how a healthy young mind quickly throws off its fears under the rush of impressions, for once recovered from seasickness, Redburn immediately looks around him and observes "how grand and majestic, how solitary and boundless, and beautiful and blue" the sea is. Melville's description harmonizes perfectly the thing seen and the mood and nature of the observer:

As I looked at it so mild and sunny, I could not help calling to mind my little brother's face, when he was sleeping an infant in the cradle. It had just such a happy, careless, innocent look; and every happy little wave seemed gambolling about like a thoughtless little kid in a pasture; and seemed to look up in your face as it passed, as if it wanted to be patted and caressed. They seemed all live things with hearts in them, that could feel; and I almost felt grieved, as we sailed in among them, scattering them under our broad bows in sun-flakes, and riding over them like a great elephant among lambs.[8]

Here Melville has found superb images reflecting love of innocence and fear for its preservation to capture Redburn's hypersensitive feelings.

Even more impressive and more significant in his development is his insight into psychological processes. With a relentlessness that anticipates the merciless probing into Pierre's motives, Melville strips Redburn down to his naked soul, exposing the sufferings he endures through his own pride and self-consciousness as well as through the world's cruelty. The river-boat scene is a most bitter account of a boy's emotional ordeal. Feeling "that desperation and recklessness of poverty which only a pauper knows"[9] and morbidly conscious of the mighty patch sewed on his trousers by his mother, he squirms under the suspicious glances of his well-dressed fellow passengers and works himself into a rage at the mere thought that they would turn him out of the cabin if he so much as addressed them like a fellow human being. When Redburn discovers that he cannot pay the fare, he finds himself under the brutal spotlight of impersonal stares, and unable to endure the humiliation, he impetuously menaces the nearest gazer with his fowling piece. Afterwards he is heartily ashamed of his "demoniac feelings." If the incident is less a representation of real life than the literary projection of a small boy's revenge fantasy, it nevertheless dramatizes the torture of poverty. Redburn's intense, if irrational, feelings boil feverishly to the surface: his righteous insistence on his own worth as the son of a gentleman, his resentment at being poor, his hatred for those who remind him, even unwittingly, that he has lost his birthright, the boyish passion that blinds him to the inconsistency of wanting to join a group of people he has just called cheerless, stony-eyed, and heartless, and his hatred of himself for venting his passions.

In several other scenes Melville maps with equal accuracy the various anguishes of spirit a boy can suffer, but it is in the episode of the drunken sailor's suicide the first night at sea that his psychological power burns most intensely. Redburn is terrified, and when he finds that he is to occupy the very bunk just vacated by the dead man his horror is uncontrollable. The sailors taunt him with cowardice, but since they have seemed frightened themselves, Redburn is outraged at their hypocrisy.

And they did not say I was cowardly [he reports] because they perceived it in me, but because they merely supposed I must be, judging, no doubt, from their own secret thoughts about themselves; for I felt sure that the suicide frightened them very badly.[10]

Melville presents here an intricate sequence of internal and external conflict in which Redburn's honesty about himself and his vivid intuition of the ruthless fraud by which the others would assert their prestige ironically sharpens his suffering instead of relieving it. And Melville was capable of carrying the episode to a fearful climax of adolescent tragedy. When Redburn impetuously shouts back that the sailors are cowards too, they all abuse him worse than before, and Jackson threatens to pitch him overboard if he ever stumbles against him in the rigging.

At first, [says Redburn] all this nearly stunned me, it was so unforeseen; and then I could not believe that they meant what they said, or that they could be so cruel and black-hearted. But how could I help seeing that the men who could thus talk to a poor, friendless boy, on the very first night of his voyage to sea, must be capable of almost any enormity. I loathed, detested, and hated them with all that was left of my bursting heart and soul, and I thought myself the most forlorn and miserable wretch that ever breathed. May I never be a man, thought I, if to be a boy is to be such a wretch. And I wailed and wept, and my heart cracked within me, but all the time I defied them through my teeth, and dared them to do their worst.

At last they ceased talking and fell fast asleep, leaving me awake, seated on a chest with my face bent over my knees between my hands. And there I sat, till at length the dull beating against the ship's bows, and the silence around me, soothed me down, and I fell asleep as I sat.[11]

The trustfulness, the self-pity, the tender sensibilities, the defiant courage, and the frankness of innocent youth come marvelously alive in this passage, and the final picture of Redburn, hunched over a sea chest in the darkness of the forecastle and symbolizing utter defeat and sorrow, compels a sympathy in full proportion to Melville's intent.

If Melville saw clearly the tragic drama of adolescence, he saw its comic possibilities too and made Redburn the fumbling actor in a number of scenes that exploit his vanity, false humility, and naïveté. In part he was original; in part he was, as we know, merely following oral and literary tradition. But whether imitating or not, Melville is ingenious, and he traces psychological sequences with a care and perception lacking in his predecessors. Two scenes stand out in particular as examples of both nautical humor and character portrayal that strikes well below the surface. The first night out of port Redburn's self-deceiving piety traps him into patronizing a sailor, with embarrassing results. The discovery that one of his crew mates knows nothing of religion or books inspires Redburn both to a condescending pity and to a complacent gratitude for his own good fortune. His solicitude is painful:

> Thinking [he says] that my superiority to him in a moral way might sit uneasily upon this sailor, I thought it would soften the matter down by giving him a chance to show his own superiority to me, in a minor thing; for I was far from being vain and conceited.[12]

But his immediate behavior is vain indeed. He asks the sailor whether the bell that is rung at regular intervals over the forecastle where the watch was sleeping "would not tend to disturb them and beget unpleasant dreams." Then he adds:

> . . . I was particular to address him in a civil and condescending way, so as to show him very plainly that I did not deem myself one whit better than he was, that is, taking all things together, and not going into particulars.[13]

Redburn gets his moral punishment abruptly, for the sailor to whom he feels so superior laughs in his face and calls him a greenhorn, and the other sailors join in the mockery until, says Redburn,

> if I had not felt so terribly angry, I should certainly have felt very much like a fool. But my being so angry prevented me from feeling foolish, which is very lucky for people in a passion.[14]

Even in mortification Melville makes Redburn analyze what is happening to him.

In the other scene, Redburn, with his snobbishness unarrested, makes up his mind to pay a social call on the captain, flattering himself that he shares with him the inestimable advantage of being a gentleman. Washing the stains of the chicken coop from his shooting jacket, he marches arrogantly to the quarter-deck only to be turned back by the astonished mate. But the next day he presumes to address respectful observations on the weather to Captain Riga and solicit his good health, and when the captain, apoplectic at the breach of etiquette, hurls his cap at him, Redburn industriously retrieves it and hands it to him with a bow. The mate hurries him forward, demanding to know if he is mad; "but I assured him," says Redburn, with uncompromising righteousness, that "I was in my right mind, and knew perfectly well that I had been treated in the most rude and ungentlemanly manner by both him and Captain Riga."[15] Since Redburn does not really suffer anything but a puncture in his inflated ego, the scene is pure comedy, untainted by the bitterness that flavors other servings of Melville's "cakes and ale."

Yet it is not the comedy of inexperience that makes the characterization of Redburn significant. It is the tragedy of learning the hopeless gap between the supposed and the real, the tragedy of innocence, idealism, and brotherhood exposed to a world of evil and cynicism and self-interest. Melville had voiced some of this in *Typee,* more in *Mardi,* and the conflict between appearance and reality was to dominate *Moby-Dick, Pierre, The Confidence Man,* and *Billy Budd*. In *Redburn,* Melville simply catches it from the level of a young boy's eyes. In his acute awareness of the meaning of things that happen both to himself and to others, Redburn is only the youngest member of Melville's family of tragic heroes or tragic victims, whose patriarch is Captain Ahab. He has the strain of innocence, as Matthiessen saw, that links him with Billy Budd, and he has, besides his false pride, a true sense of human dignity and of the inviolability of human beings that impels him, like White-Jacket, to wince at seeing a rope laid on a fellow sailor, and like Billy Budd, to resist by instinct any tyranny over the soul. Like Taji and Ishmael, he is another of the "isolatoes" whose social and spiritual predicaments became more and more the subject of American works, from *Walden* and *Huckleberry Finn* to "Gerontion," "Prufrock," and *Look Homeward, Angel.* Although Redburn does not realize it, it is the failure of the American dream that produces the sense of being an outcast with which he leaves home. The emotional brutality of the sailors leaves him "a kind of Ishmael" on the ship. And his isolation in Liverpool and the monstrous poverty of the place furnish glimpses of the growing conflict in the nineteenth century between man and the modern city. In his love of historical tradition, Redburn is the civilized Westerner who seeks to assimilate and be assimilated by his own culture. But in Liverpool Redburn finds a commercial and relatively new metropolis, blind to the past and interested only in profit, inhuman in itself and dehumanizing its swarming populace. It allows widows and children to starve, and except for its churches it thrusts Redburn out of doors. In Redburn's awareness of the way a large city crushes both body and spirit in man, Melville makes one of the earliest statements of the cleavage between the individual and his environment in the modern world.

Both on the streets of Liverpool and in the hold of the "Highlander" Redburn lives as the embodiment of moral innocence and physical health and beauty. Nowhere does his nature stand out more clearly than when he shares the picture with the sailor Jackson, apostle of wickedness and the most memorable secondary character in the book. This bald, yellow-skinned, wicked-looking man, with a broken nose and a horrible squinting eye that darts and gleams like a snake, boasts of service in the infamous slave trade and of every kind of dissipation and vice, which have left their grim traces, as Melville early points out, so that Jackson faces "the prospect of soon dying like a dog, in consequence of his sins." [16] Physically the weakest man in the crew, he tyrannizes the others, and for occult reasons which Redburn can never understand, they not only submit but even wait on him like servants. An atheist who jeers savagely at the religious beliefs of the other sailors, he is also a misanthrope who in his malevolence "would like to see the whole ship swallowed down in the Norway maelstrom . . . ." [17] He is given to violent attacks of coughing, to which Melville continually subjects him just at the peak of some verbal triumph or outrageous harangue. Within the framework of the story the coughing constantly reveals the sickness gnawing at Jackson's vitals and prepares for the sudden end, and as a moral device it acts as the only force able to contest Jackson's diabolical supremacy. Melville treats him moralistically to the very end, taking particular pains to anticipate his everlasting doom. As the "Highlander" nears America, Jackson's coughing increases and he treats the crew more outrageously than ever before. "The prospect of the speedy and unshunnable death now before him seemed to exasperate his misanthropic soul into madness," says Melville, "and as if he had indeed sold it to Satan, he seemed determined to die with a curse between his teeth." [18] Jackson dies exactly according to promise. Just as Shakespeare delays the death of Claudius until Hamlet catches him with his sins heavy on his soul, so Melville arranges Jackson's demise at a point where his frightful profanity and his unregenerate mood will ensure his everlasting perdition.

But though Jackson's career is, with significant variations, almost completely evil, his malevolence does not beget dramatic action. He is simply a kind of character who fascinated Melville, the first in a line stretching through Bland in

White-Jacket to Claggart in *Billy Budd,* written some forty years later, and including Captain Ahab.[19] But whereas in his last book Melville could make the contrast between wickedness and innocence active and organic in Claggart and Billy Budd—indeed, he learned to do this as early as 1855, in "Benito Cereno"—in 1849 he could not. Redburn shudders transfixed as he views the ocean of malice glistening in Jackson's snakelike eye, he fears him and suffers from his hatred, but the conflict between the two engenders no complex crisis. In Jackson, Melville showed that he could create character but could not involve it in important moral action.

Melville's technique in delineating the other dramatis personae in *Redburn* is only a further demonstration of the portrait painter's skill that he showed in *Typee* and *Omoo.* We do not know their thoughts as we do Redburn's. Few of them have any mobility. Melville depicts Captain Riga as bland and well-bred ashore but rough and coarse at sea and touches up the picture with a humor that recalls both Dickens' satires of hypocrites and Smollett's coarseness. He vents on him the same distaste for the pompous authority of the quarter-deck that marks *White-Jacket,* yet he keeps his bias from distorting the portrait into caricature so that the Captain remains a most lifelike figure. Harry Bolton, with follies and extravagances too absurd for belief, comes off less well. Melville's sense of balance deserts him when he has Harry dress up in false whiskers and mustache to deceive his friends. He is badly melodramatic in inventing Harry's conduct in the gaming house, where Harry sees a bell rope as an invitation to suicide and nails his empty purse to a table with a terrific stab of his dirk. What sympathy Melville evokes for the impulsive, frank, and generous fellow yields to impatience as he puts him through more of the greenhorn-sailor routine at sea, especially when Harry deliberately wears his brocaded morning gown because he is to serve the morning watch. Whether or not Melville ever knew a prototype for Harry in real life, his depiction is little more than amateurish.

We are conscious of better craftsmanship when Melville holds himself within the limits of Redburn's adolescent sensibility. The Greenland sailor, for example, appears to us through Redburn's youthful eyes. The boy is incredulous at finding a man from such a strange and remote country in his company.

Why was he not at home among the icebergs; and how could he stand a warm summer's sun, and not be melted away? Besides, instead of icicles, there were earrings hanging from his ears; and he did not wear bearskins, and keep his hands in a huge muff; . . . .[20]

Although the other portraits are not so starry-eyed as the Greenlander's, Melville high lights the externals that a boy would be most likely to notice—the physical appearance, the clothes, the humorous eccentricities. Max the Dutchman (who incidentally scandalizes young Wellingborough by keeping one wife in New York and another in Liverpool) has red hair, red cheeks, red whiskers, and a red shirt, making him "altogether the most combustible looking man" that Redburn ever saw.[21] The Negro steward, a sentimental ladies' man, carries a lock of frizzled hair, which he exhibits with his handkerchief to his eyes. Jack Blunt doses himself constantly with horse salts and determines all future events by consulting his mysterious *Bonaparte Dream Book.* The former whaler, Larry, whose tales of primitive Madagascar Redburn loves to hear, lectures the boy on the evils of what he calls "snivelization." And the black cook, to Redburn's amazement, studies the Bible over his boiling pots.

Melville makes the sailors part of the boy's world; he also depicts them with sufficient skill to interest, if not to absorb, an adult audience. They are neither the literary creations of Scott, Marryat, and Cooper nor the actual personages of Dana, J. Ross Browne, Samuel Leech, George Little, and the other retailers of nautical reminiscences. They work upon the imagination without falling into the romantic attitudes of Bunce or Tom Coffin or Midshipman Easy. Yet they speak and act like real sailors, though they do not have the limitations of Dana's Tom Harris or the captain of the "Pilgrim." Dana, for example, takes eight pages to tell us only that Tom Harris had a wise mother, a remarkable memory, a strong constitution, and an unfortunate weakness for liquor and women. In the same space Melville takes us not only into Jackson's horrible past but also into every corner of his diabolical personality. Melville's superiority lies in his insight, in his imaginative choice of the most significant details. He makes the crew of the "Highlander" one of the most distinctive in the nautical literature of his day.

One reason for the power of Melville's characterization is the advance in style that with few lapses he achieves in *Redburn*. When he began the book he had developed two literary manners. In *Typee* and *Omoo,* written largely for entertainment, he was straightforward and pleasing enough but unable to make the most of his material.[22] Despite a wealth of exact and rich detail, his images were scarce, his allusions commonplace and sparse. His sentences were often self-consciously formal, and sometimes his paragraphs sagged into anticlimax.[23] Frequently his diction was either inflated or stereotyped.[24] In the first part of *Mardi,* however, Melville graduated from his apprenticeship. His style had lost its debt to tradition. A vigorous freshness breathed through the narrative of the escape from the "Arcturion" and the encounter with Samoa and Amatoo. After these introductory chapters, Melville's other style emerged, Carlylean in its inversions and involutions, gorgeous in its multiplicity of allusions and images, and often rhapsodic in tone. Its very excesses burned with the fire of a genius who has just discovered his deeper powers. However, such an exalted manner was unsuitable for the pedestrian narrative of a boy's first voyage, and though Melville could not resist indulgence in it on two occasions in *Redburn,* it was to a different style that he turned when he sent his hero off to Liverpool on the "Highlander."

The dominant manner of Redburn imitates through the very structure of sentence and paragraph the rhythms of an adolescent's eager, spontaneous flow of feeling. Of the many passages in which the boy's mental processes come to life on the page, that on the glass ship, which had so much influence in directing Redburn's thoughts to the sea, is one of the best.

> In the first place, every bit of it was glass, and that was a great wonder of itself; because the masts, yards, and ropes were made to resemble exactly the corresponding parts of a real vessel that could go to sea. She carried two tiers of black guns all along her two decks; and often I used to try to peep in at the portholes to see what else was inside; but the holes were so small, and it looked so very dark indoors, that I could discover little or nothing; though, when I was very little, I made no doubt, that if I could but once pry open the hull, and break the glass all to pieces, I would infallibly light upon something wonderful, perhaps some gold guineas, of which I have always been in want, ever since I could remember. And often I used to feel a sort of insane desire to be the death of the glass ship, case and all, in order to come at the plunder; and one day, throwing out some hint of the kind to my sisters, they ran to my mother in a great clamor; and after that, the ship was placed on the mantelpiece for a time, beyond my reach, and until I should recover my reason.[25]

In a formal composition this hodgepodge would sound incoherent. The second sentence sets forth two sequent thoughts, followed by a contrasting statement, which in turn is qualified, and the qualification leads to a subject and a time situation quite different from those with which the sentence began. But in the reminiscences of Redburn, the paragraph is a triumph of artistic skill, reproducing with ease the natural digressiveness of a youthful mind. Through many artfully constructed ramblings like this, Melville mirrors not only a young boy's ideas but also their movement. The effect is a psychological realism that takes us into the inner nature of the hero. We know what he thinks, and we know the manner of his thinking.

This style predominates in *Redburn,* carrying the story for chapter after chapter, but it is not the only one. Often when Melville wants to relate a dramatic incident or scene, he records it not in terms of Redburn's adolescent observation but objectively, as the quality of the incident demands. Such are the descriptions of a starving woman and children in Liverpool and the death of Jackson, the account of the wreck that the "Highlander" passes at sea, the narrative of the cholera among the immigrants, and the horrible description of the burning corpse. Economy and a starkness in physical realism more plain than anything that marked Melville in his previous books are the stylistic qualities of these and many other scenes. The same element of terseness permeates the colloquial dialogue, as in the speech of the mate when Redburn fails to understand his order to slush down the topmast.

> "Green as grass! a regular cabbagehead! A fine time I'll have with such a greenhorn aboard. Look you, youngster. Look up to that long pole there—d'ye see it? that piece of a tree there, you timberhead—well—take this bucket here, and go up the rigging—that rope-ladder there—do you understand?—and dab this slush all over the mast, and look out for your head if one drop falls on deck. Be off now, Buttons." [26]

These are the unquestioned accents of a rough, uneducated man, irked at having to explain what is so obvious to himself but clear and earthily emphatic in his explanation. And all the other sailors talk with the same crisp forcefulness as the mate.

The simple diction of such passages echoes throughout the book. It is incomparably better than the innumerable contemporary reminiscences of old tars who manufacture dialogue by the page but tell less about the sailor than Melville does in a phrase or two.[27] It is also more convincing than the stage dialogue of Cooper, Captain Chamier, and Marryat, Melville's nearest rivals, for it rings truer and at the same time it is artistically selected and molded.

The simplicity of a boy and the terseness of a mariner, then, are the elements of style in *Redburn*. But Melville did not entirely forsake the grand manner he had developed in

Mardi. He carried over, for example, the use of allusions, with which he had so liberally strewn his gigantic allegory. For a simple tale of a boy's first voyage, *Redburn* is surprisingly studded with a variety of decorative references, Biblical, geographical, literary, and philosophical. Melville's familiarity with Scripture supplies him with many a commonplace reference to Job, the wise virgins, Sodom and Gomorrah, and the lion and the lamb.[28] His personal experiences together with his reading enable him to exploit places as remote as Lima, Aroostook, the infamous North Corner in Plymouth, Pegu, and Nova Zembla. His literary allusions include a number of minor authors like Mrs. Ellis, Joel Barlow, Lavater, William Roscoe, and the sea poets Dibdin and Falconer, and writers of higher rank like Le Sage, Froissart, Johnson, Addison, Moore, Ossian, Smollett, Milton, and of course Shakespeare, whom he had been reading heavily just before writing *Redburn.* His recent reading of the classics furnished him with ready references to Homer, Livy, Martial, Petronius Arbiter, Seneca, Suetonius, Tacitus, Varro, and Tiberius at Capreae, while other references show his irrepressible interest in the lives or philosophies of Aristotle, Socrates, Paracelsus, Campanella, Hume, and Kant.

Despite the number and extent of these allusions, they give no evidence of extended indebtedness to any one author, nor even of any great amount of learning. Melville's knowledge was not deep but eclectic. Although he had acquired some familiarity with the classics, he was no more a scholar in his thirties than he had been in his teens. He was a wide reader with a brilliant memory who abstracted with rare perception the quintessence of what he read. Instinctively, he avoided mere window-dressing pedantry. His illustrations are almost always appropriate. Whole chapters go by without a single allusion, if the aim is physical realism and if decoration would be out of place. But he uses allusions liberally wherever they help to broaden or intensify the immediate meaning or supply color to an incident that requires it. Redburn's meditation on the old Liverpool guidebook, which he has suddenly discovered to be useless, is typical:

> Smell its old morocco binding, Wellingborough; does it not smell somewhat mummyish? Does it not remind you of Cheops and the Catacombs? I tell you it was written before the lost books of Livy, and is cousin-german to that irrecoverably departed volume entitled, "*The Wars of the Lord*," quoted by Moses in the Pentateuch. Put it up, Wellingborough, . . . and hereafter follow your nose throughout Liverpool; it will stick to you through thick and thin: and be your ship's mainmast and St. George's spire your landmarks.[29]

The range of references here conveys exactly the intensity of the almost cynical disillusionment Redburn has just experienced.

In general, however, Melville is most allusive in those sections of *Redburn* that reflect his mature mind and interests rather than Redburn's impressions. His reference to Salvator Rosa's "lowering sea-pieces" and his catalogue of paintings in the gambling house parallel his interest in art awakened by George Duyckinck's circle and the exhibitions at the American Art Union. He writes of pictures like those in the Temple of Ammon in the Libyan oasis, in the shrine of Quetzalcoatl at Cholula, in the house of Pansa at Pompeii, in the private room of Tiberius, and in the secret side gallery of the Temple of Aphrodite in Corinth.[30] The inclusion of a blatantly pornographic picture is one measure of Melville's sophistication. If most of the allusions are to nonexistent works of art, they are further evidence that Melville could not confine himself to strict realism indefinitely.[31] He could not suppress the instinct for decorating his story with the strange and the wonderful, which he had indulged for many chapters in *Mardi*.

It was undoubtedly the need for satisfying this instinct that impelled Melville to write the chapter on Carlo, a fantastic, dreamlike effusion on music that bespeaks the love of opera and symphony Melville had also developed through his association with the Duyckincks.[32] It is a dithyrambic, self-intoxicated piece of impressionism like the chapter on dreams in *Mardi*. Different kinds of music conjure up visions of Xerxes surrounded by his satraps, of the Fountain of Lions in the Alhambra, of "Medusa, Hecate, she of Endor, and all the Blocksberg's demons dire," and of "the inner palace of the Great Mogul." [33] Such stylistic extravagance, however artistically inappropriate in *Redburn*, is evidence of the poetic forces (many of its sentences scan perfectly) lying below the surface of Melville's consciousness and compelling him at times to jettison consistency.

In the prosaic story of Redburn, Melville's passion for allegorical or symbolical expression, which had blossomed suddenly in *Mardi*, is inevitably subdued. His figures are numerous but generally simple, in keeping with the character whose thoughts they are designed to convey. Occasionally, he contrives more arresting metaphors: a drowned sailor, with his up-rolled sleeve exposing his tattooed name and birth date, "seemed his own headstone." [34] For the relation of sailors and other workers to society, he creates a memorable image:

> There are classes of men in the world who bear the same relation to society at large, that the wheels do to a coach; and are just as indispensable. But however easy and delectable the springs upon which the insiders pleasantly vibrate; however sumptuous the hammercloth and glossy the door-panels; yet, for all this, the wheels must still revolve in dusty, or muddy revolutions. No contrivance, no sagacity can lift *them* out of the mire; for upon something the coach must be bottomed; on something the insiders must roll.[35]

If such extended imagery is rare, Melville occasionally employs symbols in *Redburn* in a way that looks forward to *Moby-Dick* rather than backward to *Mardi*, where, as Matthiessen observes, abstractions unrooted in sense experience impair both understanding and imaginative stimulation. Confined as he was in *Redburn* to a framework of reality, he had to draw his illustrations largely from fact and, conversely, to make his ideas grow out of real things. His technique varies. Sometimes he defines the relationship and deduces a single specific meaning. About an East Indian ship in Liverpool, where the English officers hold services in the cabin while "the heathen at the other end of the ship [are] left to their false gods and idols," Melville comments:

> As if to symbolize this state of things, the *"fancy piece"* astern comprised, among numerous other carved decorations, a cross and a mitre; while forward . . . was a sort of devil for a figure-head . . . .[36]

Sometimes he merely suggests the relationship of a single physical fact and a single spiritual fact. On the very day that Redburn leaves home, the figurehead on the little glass ship falls from its perch and "lies pitching head-foremost down into the trough of a calamitous sea . . . ."[37] At other times, Melville makes the physical object generate associations freely, giving it multiple links in time and space. In the central strand, or "heart," of an old piece of rope, he finds many "interesting, mournful, and tragic suggestions."

> Who can say in what gales it may have been; in what remote seas it may have sailed? How many stout masts of seventy-fours and frigates it may have stayed in the tempest! . . . What outlandish fish may have nibbled at it in the water, and what uncatalogued sea-fowl may have pecked at it, when forming part of a lofty stay or shroud?[38]

Such a passage, though severely limited when compared with the rich suggestiveness of chapters like "The Doubloon" in *Moby-Dick,* differs in degree rather than in kind. In each Melville uses the same method, seizing upon a concrete object and attaching to it as many associations as it can be made to suggest. Both here and elsewhere in *Redburn,* his technique of symbolism is proleptic, in that he elaborates his higher meaning from the foundation of real things.[39]

Taken as a whole, *Redburn* is stylistically an advance beyond Melville's first three books. His diction, stripped of the earlier artificiality and convention, is magnificently plain. Its range is small, but with apt choicc and skillful manipulation it conveys a diversity of powerful impressions. Melville's sentences and paragraphs are also simpler and firmer than they had been, for his eye for the significant detail is more searching and he avoids the clutter of irrelevance. The movement is swifter and smoother, the digressions fewer and less remote from the immediate subject. Only occasionally does he let himself wander away from a manner consistent with his material to stylistic extravagance. The mingling of form and matter in *Redburn* is the most nearly perfect in all of Melville's early work.

No good book, however, is merely a mechanism of style, or of characterization or structure, or of artistic manipulation of experience. Undertones and overtones of feeling and thought, the chiaroscuro of mood and theme play through its pages to make up what may be called its personality. And *Redburn* has something of this inner quality of complexity, of diverse strains that will not, happily, submit to a formula. The fruits of Melville's manifold experience, both sensuous and intellectual, were ripening with tropical speed when he wrote *Redburn,* and every inspiration brought its plenteous windfall. This is why the book has more than one level of mood and more than one angle of vision. Both the inside world of emotion and spirit and the outside world of society spurred Melville's energies. They had driven him to the brilliant if not completely achieved ambitions of *Mardi,* and despite the demands of personal finances, which could be satisfied by a mere potboiler, they shared in the molding of *Redburn.*

One vein that runs through the book to invest it with something of this diversity is Melville's humor. It is a quality the twentieth century has consistently ignored, though Melville's contemporary reviewers relished it, and his friend Joann Miller considered *Redburn* "as finished a piece of humour" as she had ever seen, and she read a chapter of it aloud to "a merry auditory." [40] His intention of presenting the comedy of a young boy at sea gave rise to the many incidents exploiting Redburn's greenness. But Melville, who had learned to laugh at the foibles of men as well as to pity them in failure and weep for them in defeat, had other resources—of irony, satire, and burlesque, of jollity and whimsy. These strains had appeared in the sailor portraits of *Omoo* and in the good fellowship and the ridiculous accounts of contemporary politics, society, and literature in *Mardi*. In *Redburn* they alternate with the somber passages, as Melville's mood fluctuates or his sense of proportion speaks out. Despite the brutality in the sailors' abuse of Redburn, he makes the young boy find a tolerant amusement for the cook's swearing when waves dash spray over his hot food or for the sociable way the crew break hard ship biscuits on his head. He gives a whole chapter, called "Some Superior Old Nailrod and Pigtail," to the sailors' frantic hunt for tobacco on the return trip, when they covet old chaws cast away under bunks on some previous voyage and ultimately come to nibbling the "tenderloin" or central strand of pieces of old rope. He sketches the multiple quirks of human character on land and sea, and we have the anxieties of a pale-faced fiddler when the cabin bucks ogle his unreluctant wife, the bewilderment of a nervous landlubber when the sailors play the traditional trick of spread-eagling him in the rigging, the comical embarrassment of one of the sailors as he is scratched, pummeled, and chewed by young boys whose mother's Bible he had thrown overboard.

Sometimes Melville's humor has the earthiness of Smollett or Fielding, as in Redburn's concern about having his "table linen" exposed when he is up in the rigging and in full view of the cabin or in the "frightful stories" the narrator might tell about sailors who take calomel off Cape Horn and then go on duty. The sailors' farewell to Captain Riga is written with a relish for healthy coarseness. When he appears on deck in answer to their summons, the crew, which has been lined up on the bulwarks, "suddenly wheeled about, presenting their backs; and making a motion, which was a polite salute to everything before them, but an abominable insult to all who happened to be in their rear, they gave three cheers, and at one bound, cleared the ship." [41]

But Melville found less opportunity for such scenes than

he did for comic irony and satire, which set the tone both of casual forays and of full offensives. Thus he pictures Redburn as whiling away the tedium of picking oakum by gazing through a porthole and reciting Byron's "Address to the Ocean." When Redburn is enticed to take a sip of rum to cure his first seasickness, Melville takes a sly dig at the rigidity of temperance pledges in Redburn's whimsical complaint that, when he signed the pledge, he should have "taken care to insert a little clause, allowing [him] to drink spirits in case of seasickness," and he advises temperance people to "attend to this matter in future . . . ." [42] Melville also took the opportunity to indulge in some literary satire. Hoping to learn how to retrieve the fortunes of his family, Redburn reads Adam Smith's *Wealth of Nations,* which his brother's friend Mr. Jones had given him, but despite "vague visions of future opulence" floating before him, the book gets "dryer and dryer," till Redburn wonders "whether anybody had ever read it, even the author himself; but then, authors, they say, never read their own books; writing them, being enough in all conscience." He finally uses the book only for a pillow but "sometimes waked up feeling dull and stupid; but of course the book could not have been the cause of that." [43] Melville has even more fun at the expense of the pretentious style and antique flavor of an epic poem on Liverpool in the old guidebook. He redecorates the editor's Introduction to mock the style of contemporary literary eulogies, confesses to the "uncharitable thought" "that the author of the guide-book might have been the author of the epic," and declares that the poet "breaks forth like all Parnassus" in his poetic praise of Liverpool. His only complaint is that though the author of the guidebook supplies the history of the town from the time of William the Conqueror, he betrays "a want of the uttermost antiquarian and penetrating spirit, which would have scorned to stop in its researches at the reign of the Norman monarch, but would have pushed on resolutely through the dark ages, up to Moses, the man of Uz, and

Adam; and finally established the fact, beyond a doubt, that the soil of Liverpool was created with the Creation." [44] Both this passage and the one on *The Wealth of Nations* break through the strictly logical limits of *Redburn* since the satire is adult, but like the others they are signs of robust energy and diversified talents. They have a decided value in offsetting the prevailing tone of somberness.

For despite the purpose Melville had in mind when he began *Redburn,* the book is his first to reveal a persistent and sometimes unrestrained bitterness. His major themes are the effects of poverty on a high-spirited and displaced young patrician and the disillusionments that shatter his pathetic naïveté. Although much of this is amusing, its overall effect is depressing to the point of morbidity. Only twice does he allow Redburn to find a bridge between his preconceptions and reality—when a farmer outside London spontaneously invites him to tea with his three daughters and when he feels for a time the exultant joy of the "glorious ocean life." [45] Otherwise, all is disenchantment, over which Melville ranges from casual to climactic events without exhausting himself but leaving the reader weary. Redburn's first sight of whales is a disappointment, he finds the Welsh coast depressingly like the Hudson and the Catskills, his boyish wonder at seeing his first live Englishman straight from England collapses when the pilot begins to swear and order men about just like Captain Riga. Countless similar shocks studding Redburn's history are merely the prelude, however, to the central incident, to which Melville, after careful preparation, devotes an entire chapter. When Redburn finds that the fifty-year-old guidebook, a treasured family possession on which he relies to lead him to the inn where his father had stayed, is quite useless since the inn has been razed, his whole vision of life crumbles. His boyish image of a concrete world unaffected by time yields to the knowledge that things are everlastingly mutable, that old must give way to new and new must become old, that the sacred, indissoluble bonds between father and son are illusory, that men, inns, cities, and all other organisms he had thought of as inexorably stationed in their proper places in the universe have no more permanence than clouds.

At this point Melville provides some resolution to Redburn's distressed realization of the truth, since he accepts things as they are. But the reader is more likely to remember the crises where no catharsis alleviates the suffering. "Such is boyhood," writes Melville in caustic summary of the chapter in which Redburn leaves home in tears, goes hungry all day, endures humiliations from his poverty, and travels for hours on the open deck in the cold, driving rain. At the end of his voyage, as we know, the rascally Captain Riga not only denies Redburn his paltry wages but demands reimbursement for the ship's equipment he has lost. Defeated and helpless, Redburn turns to go, thinking,

> Now, here was this man actually turning a poor lad adrift without a copper, after he had been slaving aboard his ship for more than four mortal months. But Captain Riga was a bachelor of expensive habits, and had run up large wine bills at the City Hotel. He could not afford to be munificent. Peace to his dinners.[46]

In bitterness of effect, the icy sarcasm of the last three sentences exceeds even some of the more extravagant emotional outbursts elsewhere in the book. Redburn's resentment is insoluble, forever hardened in a benediction whose inverted meaning carries a whole volume of scorn. It recalls Redburn's hopeless lament for his lost youth in the eloquent, much-quoted passage:

> Talk not of the bitterness of middle-age and after-life; a boy can feel all that, and much more, when upon his young soul the mildew has fallen; and the fruit, which with others is only blasted after ripeness, with him is nipped in the first blossom and bud. And never again can such blights be made good; they strike in too deep, and leave such a scar that the air of Paradise might not erase it.[47]

With such a conviction of irreparable calamity it is virtually inevitable that Redburn's story should have no over-all resolution. The body of the book is disfigured with wens, and morbid cysts lie embedded in its innermost tissues.

Thus, despite his humor, Melville invested his boy's book with the same unresolved conflicts, the same final frustration that finds both Taji and Ahab unreconciled to either heaven or earth. And in *Redburn,* as in *Mardi, Moby-Dick,* and *Pierre,* Melville gravitated almost by instinct to the theme of the frustrated quest to which he had been attracted in his very first writings. Frustration is the keynote of the chief episode, Redburn's quest for his father's ghost in Riddough's Hotel, an event untrue of Melville's own experience and hence a literary device. Melville concluded the Liverpool section, composing the second cycle of Redburn's adventures, with another frustrated quest. The chapter on the London gambling house crowns Redburn's oft-expressed hopes of seeing St. Paul's, Westminster Abbey, the tunnel under the Thames, and the lords and ladies in Hyde Park with a disappointment which the boy calls "almost distracting." Like the romantic poets, who liked to develop the theme of unfulfilled love, Melville habitually depicted the chasm between the real and the ideal in terms of a pursuit that fails to achieve its object.

With all tribute to the clarity with which Melville has traced the tortures of adolescence in *Redburn* and with all allowance for the impact of his own youth, it must be said that the hard, bitter core of the book interferes with its artistic success. The suffering is often meaningless. The disillusion, melancholy, and bitterness are overdone. Melville often exaggerates true sentiments into pathological extremes, as when Redburn indulges in an orgy of self-pity at the mere thought that the very father whose spirit he pursues in Liverpool had never even dreamed of his existence in those days long before. He seems to go out of his way to create harsh situations. Redburn is excluded from a reading room on his first day in Liverpool, but he tries only a few days later to enter another prompted by a course of reasoning that is sentimentally absurd, even for so naive a person as himself. "I'm a poor, friendless sailor-boy, [he thinks] and they cannot object; especially as I am from a foreign land, and strangers ought to be treated with courtesy." [48] No reader can be surprised when the strange youth in the old shooting jacket is thrust ignominiously out of doors. When Redburn's trials seem inevitable, they evoke sympathy, but Melville loses *vraisemblance* when he uses the same humiliation twice and under unconvincing circumstances. Even the most sensitive reader may justifiably feel that Melville is toying with his sympathies.

Perhaps one explanation for this defect is Melville's addiction to melancholy. The mood is pervasive in *Redburn,* whose hero often utters woebegone thoughts or indulges in bittersweet reverie. ". . . what a soft pleasing sadness steals over me," he says, in reflecting on the old guidebook, "and how I melt into the past and forgotten!" [49] If there is, in this quality, a note that recalls Lamb, of whom Melville had read a little,[50] there is also an apparent debt to other masters of romantic melancholy. The year before writing *Redburn* Melville had acquired a copy of *Fingal;* that he had read it is evident from his reference in *Redburn* to Ossian's ghosts,[51] which he had noted by penciled markings in Macpherson's text.[52] Among the many annotations is this significant comment upon a passage laden with Celtic sadness: "What can be finer than this? It is the soul of melancholy." [53] Melville was also a devotee of "Old Burton," as is well known,[54] and he thought well enough of Young to link him with Pascal and Rousseau.[55] In his youth, and probably later, he had read Byron, who had developed, as Cazamian remarks, "The specially Byronic theme of a melancholy that is disenchanted and associated with all the vanity of human endeavor . . . ." [56] Melville was unquestionably influenced by the literary tradition of the minor key. It may be relied upon to account in some measure for one of the principal moods in *Redburn.*

The link with Byron, Young, and Pascal as well as Melville's religious training and constant exposure to his mother's moralizing help to explain the presence of another supporting theme in *Redburn,* the vanity of human wishes.

This provides a point of secure retreat after many a disillusionment. Melville's method in embodying the idea is like his technique of symbolism, for he works from real incidents or objects to general moral implications. The near shipwreck of the "Highlander" suggests shipwrecks in general, and Melville applies their lesson to the lives of "some lordly men, [who] with all their plans and prospects gallantly trimmed to the fair, rushing breeze of life, . . . suddenly encounter a shock unforeseen, and go down, foundering, into death." [57] In monuments that merely commemorate a hero's death instead of celebrating his life, Melville finds an absurd vanity. And when he ponders on the proud allusion in the old guidebook to the immense grandeur of Liverpool and then considers how its present inhabitants must look back on the former era with "immeasurable superiority," he is "filled with a comical sadness at the vanity of all human exaltation," for

> . . . The cope-stone of to-day is the corner-stone of tomorrow; and as St. Peter's church was built in great part of the ruins of old Rome, so in all our erections, however imposing, we but form quarries and supply ignoble materials for the grander domes of posterity.[58]

The *vanitas vanitatum* theme in *Redburn* constitutes one more link with Melville's other work, especially *Moby-Dick*, where it trumpets forth at the end of "The Try-Works" chapter:

> The truest of all men was the Man of Sorrows and the truest of all books is Solomon's, and Ecclesiastes is the fine hammered steel of woe. 'All is vanity.' ALL.[59]

These are the grand organ tones of Melville's mood, but they differ only in degree from Redburn's world-weariness, and the technique by which they are evolved is already present in the earlier book.

What this ability to project the personal sufferings of Redburn into generalizations about vanity furnishes Melville is a natural bridge to a wider concern with the less personal and more social implications in experience. The ease with which he [obscured] destroyed the unity of *Redbu* [obscured] ts some of the most sardonic [obscured] es on social evils in the whole body of Melville's work. He had combined social protest with fiction and fact in each of his previous books, and in *White-Jacket* he would help crystallize the national conscience by expressing the general conviction of the dignity of man in his ferocious assault upon flogging in the Navy. His mood had been satirical and reformist for three years, and it is not surprising that he wove into Redburn's story implied and outright criticisms that make the book a kind of "novel" of purpose.

His principal target was the appalling dearth of real brotherhood, human sensitivity, and charity in the Christian world of the mid-nineteenth century. For the phenomenon of exclusiveness in society as a whole Melville invents a fitting symbol in the rope that is passed across the middle of the "Highlander" to protect the fifteen cabin passengers from the five hundred immigrants.

> Lucky would it be [he says] for the pretensions of some parvenus, whose souls are deposited at their banker's, and whose bodies but serve to carry about purses, knit of poor men's heart-strings, if thus easily they could precisely define, ashore, the difference between them and the rest of humanity.[60]

Melville sees the same withholding of human kindness in the attitude of society toward the sailor.

> What [he demands] in your heart do you think of that fellow staggering along the dock? Do you not give him a wide berth, shun him, and account him but little above the brutes that perish? Will you throw open your parlors to him; invite him to dinner? or give him a season ticket to your pew in church?—No. You will do no such thing; but at a distance you will perhaps subscribe a dollar or two for the building of a hospital to accommodate sailors already broken down; or for the distribution of excellent books among tars who cannot read.[61]

Even though he admits that the bad condition of sailors comes "under the head of those chronic evils which can only be ameliorated . . . by ameliorating the moral organization of all civilization," [62] he is not justifying the aloofness of society but suggesting that in its very heart lies an unforgivable defect in brotherly love. It is especially in the higher social strata that active charity is lacking, and this sin Melville exposes with Swiftian acerbity. At the end of the voyage to Liverpool, a purse is made up for a charming little six-year-old stowaway, and, says Melville, "the captain, officers, and the mysterious cabin passenger [contributed] their best wishes, and the sailors and poor steerage passengers something like fifteen dollars . . . ." [63] He strikes exactly the same note in describing the charity offered on the return trip to six poor boys in the steerage. "When a collection was taken up for their benefit among the magnanimous passengers [it] resulted in starting all six boys in the world with a penny apiece." [64] Melville admits an uncharitable disposition toward the inmates of the cabin, but, as he states significantly, it was "not because they happened to be cabin passengers; not at all; but only because they seemed the most finical, miserly, mean men and women that every stepped over the Atlantic." [65]

Melville's picture of the human heart is not, to be sure, entirely black. The sailors give alms when they can; the coarse, profane mate ignores his own health to minister to the fever-stricken immigrants; Handsome Mary, matron of the sailors' boardinghouse, refuses bread for a starving family, but at least she can offer the excuse that she takes care of the beggars in her own street. Even the man-hating, God-hating Jackson, as Melville conscientiously relates, makes several attempts to befriend the little stowaway. Mankind, he implies, is not wholly bad, for even the vilest character has some warmth of heart. But the immediate picture is, on the whole, pessimistic. The existence of the thousands of beggars in Liverpool and the monstrous devices they employ to attract charity make up for Melville "a picture of all that is dishonorable to civilization and humanity." [66] And though he says that "everyone in this world has his own fate entrusted to himself," [67] he makes it clear in an episode of terrifying realism that Christian society is morally calloused in denying recognition to suffering and solace to its victims. In Launcelott's Hey, a street leading from the docks to the sailors' boardinghouse, Redburn one day hears the hopeless wail of a woman who has crawled, with her three children, into a vault below the sidewalk to die. Three old ragpickers in the neighborhood refuse to help: "that Betsey Jennings desarves it," snarls one; "was she ever married? tell me that." [68] A porter for the warehouse of Perkins and Wood refuses to open the doors for shelter, and a policeman in the next block says it is none of his business, for he does not belong to that street. Redburn brings water and stolen bread, but the four are too weak even to eat. Only thoughts of the law deter him from putting a merciful end to their horrible lives:

> . . . I well knew [he says] that the law, which would let them perish of themselves without giving them one cup of water, would spend a thousand pounds, if necessary, in convicting him who should so much as offer to relieve them from their miserable existence.[69]

In three days, the wretched starvelings have perished, and in their place a heap of quicklime glistens.

> Ah! what are our creeds, and how do we hope to be saved? [exclaims Melville]. Tell me, oh Bible, that story of Lazarus again, that I may find comfort in my heart for the poor and forlorn. Surrounded as we are by the wants and woes of our fellow-men, and yet given to follow our own pleasures, regardless of their pains, are we not like people sitting up with a corpse, and making merry in the house of the dead? [70]

Melville's moral conscience is aroused by the obdurate soul of the Christian world in the nineteenth century just as Carlyle's was and Ruskin's and Arnold's were to be. Indeed, Melville's starving family is the equal to Carlyle's Irish widow, of Ruskin's "translator of boots," and of Arnold's unfortunate Wragg as a symbol of abominable neglect in a heartless, industrialized society.[71] And like Victorian reformers in England, Melville attacks specific as well as general evils. On two of the debated questions of the late 1840's, immigration and the conditions on immigrant ships, Melville lashed out with forthright views. Nativism, which included opposition to immigration, especially of Irish Catholics, had been an issue as early as 1835, when Samuel F. B. Morse published *Imminent Dangers to the Free Institutions of the United States through Foreign Immigration.* In the next two decades, nativism was one of the principal sources of contention in American politics.[72] True to his democratic feelings, Melville opposed the movement.

> Let us waive [he said] that agitated national topic, as to whether such multitudes of foreign poor should be landed on our American shores; let us waive it, with the one only thought, that if they can get here, they have God's right to come; though they bring all Ireland and her miseries with them. For the whole world is the patrimony of the whole world; there is no telling who does not own a stone in the Great Wall of China.[73]

From this point he plunges into a denunciation of the conditions aboard the vessels by which such emigrants came to America. After detailed pictures of the miseries aboard the "Highlander" he protests both the nonenforcement of a recent Congressional law and the law's startling inadequacies:

> What ordinance [he asks] makes it obligatory upon the captain of a ship to supply the steerage passengers with decent lodgings, and give them light and air in that foul den, where they are immured . . . ? What ordinance necessitates him to place the *galley* . . . in a dry place of shelter, where the emigrants can do their cooking during a storm, or wet weather? . . . There is no law concerning these things. And if there was, who but some Howard in office would see it enforced? and how seldom is there a Howard in office![74]

This shrill protest marks the peak of Melville's propagandist expression in *Redburn.* Like his peroration in behalf of merchant sailors, it calls for the application of active humanitarianism to a specific evil in contemporary affairs. Significantly, the source of his indignation was not his own experience on the "St. Lawrence" but the conditions prevailing at the very time he was writing. But in *Mardi* Melville had evolved the technique of assimilating into his story the events of the day—the Revolution of 1848 in France, the gold rush in America—and satirizing the men who created them. In *Redburn* he continued the technique, adapting the topic of immigration to his underlying theme of the need for more Christian charity in the contemporary world.

Melville's social point of view in *Redburn* rests on his concept of equality, which insists that since all men are human beings they have the same basic rights. The freedom with which the Negro was allowed to go about the streets of Liverpool, even in the company of whites, surprised Redburn at first,

> but a little reflection showed that, after all, it was but recognizing his claims to humanity and normal equality; so that, in some things, we Americans leave to other countries the carrying out of the principle that stands at the head of our Declaration of Independence.[75]

Melville does not support radical reform as a means of securing equality: the Chartist reformer in Liverpool is represented as a political desperado. But he recognizes a native nobility that creates claims superior to all the artificial or hypothetical standards of aristocracy. Recalling the Eastern potentate who said Lord Byron's hand furnished indubitable evidence of his noble birth, Melville says:

> And so it did; for Lord Byron was as all the rest of us—the son of a *man*. And so are the dainty-handed, and wee-footed half-cast paupers in Lima; who, if their hands and feet were entitled to consideration, would constitute the oligarchy of all Peru.
>
> . . . Dandies! amputate yourselves, if you will; but know, and be assured, oh democrats, that, like a pyramid, a great man stands on a broad base.[76]

In Melville's conception men have the birthright of equality. There are degrees of excellence: Melville never insisted on what Thorp has called "the superstitions of the extreme Jacksonian democrats";[77] one bears in mind his remark that "hell is a democracy of devils, where all are equals."[78] But rank arises not from imposed restrictions, like the rope on the "Highlander," but from inner merit—the "broad base" upon which the great man stands.

The maturity of Melville's thought on social equality does much to offset the snobbish standards the young Redburn applies to the world aboard ship with such disastrous effects. At the same time it is another contradiction in a book full of contradictions, for with few exceptions Redburn does not relinquish his convictions of superiority based on the artificial distinctions of lineage and clothes. The point re-emphasizes the dual angle of vision in the book. Melville's assertion of what he would later describe to Hawthorne as the "unconditional democracy in all things" [79] does not apply when the grandnephew of Senator Wellingborough sits down among sailors. The disparity is partially one of a gap between the fictional boy who experiences and the man who reflects. But it belongs too to a basic paradox in Melville's social thinking, for he also confessed to Hawthorne "a dislike to all mankind—in the mass." [80]

Such paradoxes mark his thinking about religion and the church in *Redburn,* which carries on his deep concern with these matters in his previous books. Although he complains that the money used in building fine cathedrals might be better employed in founding charities, yet he says that since they are built they might as well be used for the benefit of sinners. The fact that all churches, from St. Peter's in Rome to the Broadway Tabernacle, are constantly open for those who wish to use them draws his strong approbation. "I say, this consideration of the hospitality and democracy in churches is a most Christian and charming thought. It speaks whole volumes of folios, and Vatican libraries, for Christianity . . . ." [81] He also speaks with admiration of the clergymen of the Church of England in Liverpool who mount casks near the docks and preach homely "demonstrations of the miseries of sin" to the foregathered sailors and prostitutes.

> Is not this as it ought to be? [he asks] Since the true calling of the reverend clergy is like their divine Master's;—not to bring the righteous, but sinners to repentance . . . . Better to save one sinner from

an obvious vice that is destroying him, than to indoctrinate ten thousand saints. And as from every corner, in Catholic towns, the shrines of Holy Mary and the Child Jesus perpetually remind the commonest wayfarer of his heaven; even so should Protestant pulpits be founded in the market-places, and at street corners, where the men of God might be heard by all of his children.[82]

These two passages reflect ideas Melville had already set forth in chapter clxxxvii of *Mardi* in his description of the religious principles of the Serenians. There are no temples in Serenia, for Christ himself had preached in the open.

'Tis by not building *them,* that we widen charity among us [says the spokesman]. The treasures which, in the islands round about, are lavished on a thousand fanes;—with these we every day relieve the Master's suffering disciples.[83]

Similarly the Serenians accept the ideas of sin, salvation, immortality, and the divinity of Christ, which, for the most part, are typical of Melville's orthodox religious attitude in *Redburn*. The ideas of God as creator and as omnipotent and benevolent deity appear regularly. "Only He who made us," says Melville, can explain the contradictions in men's lives.[84] " . . . we feel and we know that God is the true Father of all, and that none of his children are without the pale of His care." [85] He carries on the implicit acceptance of the concept of sin in making Jackson's death the "wages of sin" and the notion of a life after death when he suggests that because of our indifference to human suffering the Turks and cannibals whom we abhor may go to heaven before us.

But contrasting with the fundamentalist implications of these phrases are two passages that imply doubt in the author's mind about the immortality of the soul. Moved by the memory of the dock-wall beggars, Melville exclaims: "Adam and Eve! If indeed ye are yet alive and in heaven, may it be no part of your immortality to look down upon the world ye have left." [86] And commenting on the death of Harry Bolton, he queries:

But why this gloom at the thought of the dead? And why should we not be glad? Is it, that we ever think of them as departed from all joy? Is it, that we believe that indeed they are dead? They revisit us not, the departed; their voices no more ring in the air; summer may come, but it is winter with them . . . .[87]

And he goes on to suggest that the only immortality lies in the memory one leaves behind him.

These liberal questionings about a belief that is just as much a part of the Christian credo as the idea of God the Father and of sin and repentance reveal a continuation of that inner conflict in personal faith which had appeared on a much wider scale in *Mardi* and which was to vex Melville for the rest of his life.[88] Still, it does not seem justifiable to agree with the conclusion that in *Redburn* Melville adopted Christian terminology "to his own purpose, pleading with orthodox Christians as though their beliefs were his own." [89] The orthodoxy is so firmly imbedded, so spontaneous in expression, and so preponderant that it must have been central in Melville's religious feeling.[90] The two questionings of immortality are the only departures, and it must be recalled that many liberal Christians, especially among Unitarians, whose influence Melville had known from his childhood, were about to make similar queries while retaining their essential Christian credo.[91] It is probable, then, that at the time he wrote *Redburn* Melville was in the position of the Christian rebel who adheres to the basic doctrines of Christianity but who freely explores along his own lines of thought some of the problems it implies.

But regardless of implied doubts in Melville's religious position, the Christian ethical beliefs that appear throughout the book form a logical framework for Melville's active humanitarianism. The vice, the poverty, the coldness in the world, he views in terms of the promise that lies in carrying out the Christian ideal, in working for the social and religious state he had so clearly described in Serenia, the one island in the world of *Mardi* where an honest attempt was made to love God and to live according to the Sermon on the Mount. And in an optimistic passage that antedates the visions of Whitman, Melville holds up America as the land where Serenia may turn from a symbol into actuality. After pointing out that America, with its mingling of English, French, Danes, Scots, and others, is international rather than national and that its "ancestry is lost in the universal paternity," [92] he adds:

> The other world beyond this, which was longed for by the devout before Columbus' time, was found in the New; and the deep-sea lead, that first struck these soundings, brought up the soil of Earth's Paradise. Not a Paradise then, or now; but to be made so, at God's good pleasure, and in the fullness and mellowness of time. . . . Then shall the curse of Babel be revoked, a new Pentecost come, and the language they shall speak shall be the language of Britain. Frenchmen, and Danes, and Scots; and the dwellers on the shores of the Mediterranean, and in the regions round about; Italians, and Indians, and Moors; there shall appear unto them cloven tongues as of fire.[93]

Did Melville mean that the only afterworld was a better material one? That the spiritual heaven, which was "the other world beyond this" of the "devout" who lived before Columbus, could be made real only in a Utopian social state here below? It is impossible to decide. But at least he makes a resounding affirmation that there is potential happiness and a cure for the world's ills here below and that it is within the power of a benevolent God to reward man's attempts to achieve it. The paragraph is perhaps one of the most significant in *Redburn,* for its fervor provides a hopeful balance to the pessimistic picture crowded with the world's beggars, suicides, immigrants, and merchants of dead bodies, its Ishmaels, Timons, and Levites.

Three months after finishing *Redburn* Melville wrote to his father-in-law, Judge Shaw:

> For Redburn I anticipate no particular reception of any kind. It may be deemed a book of tolerable entertainment;—and may be accounted dull. As for the other book, it will be sure to be attacked in some quarters. But no reputation that is gratifying to me, can possibly be achieved by either of these books. They are two *jobs,* which I have done for money—being forced to it, as other men are to sawing wood.[94] And while I have felt obliged to refrain from writing

the kind of book I would wish to; yet, in writing these two books, I have not repressed myself much—so far as *they* are concerned; but have spoken pretty much as I feel.—Being books then written in this way, my only desire for their "success" (as it is called) springs from my pocket, & not from my heart. So far as I am individually concerned, & independent of my pocket, it is my earnest desire to write those sort of books which are said to "fail."

Pardon this egotism.[95]

Melville's sense of artistic frustration and his equal determination to make even his minor pieces carry weight, both so powerful as to sweep past the barriers of decorum that stood between him and his relatives, make important conditions under which it is necessary to judge *Redburn* as a work of art. He was catering deliberately to the general public rather than to those whom Arnold Bennett calls "the passionate few." What he really wanted to write was "such things as the Great Publisher of Mankind ordained ages before he published 'The World,' " as he expressed it to Duyckinck in December.[96] Yet in *Redburn* he spoke pretty much as he felt. What he meant in detail may be debated interminably (to what extent does his statement apply to the boyish emotional moods? to the religious orthodoxy?); in general he seems to have meant that he held true to his artistic vision of life, to his awareness of the chasm between the ideal and the real and of the necessity of publishing the multifarious evils of society. Even within the limits of a book designed to entertain, Melville aimed at the ultimate frankness he had found wanting in Shakespeare.[97]

Conscious as one must be of the diversity of elements in *Redburn,* we may justly ask what achievement it constitutes as art. One answer is that in its own genre, at least, *Redburn* is pre-eminent. The humble materials of an Atlantic voyage and a sojourn in Liverpool it translates into literature as no one before Melville had succeeded in doing. Dozens of writers had crossed the Atlantic, inspected the dull and sordid city, and returned with nothing to say. In addition to Nathaniel P. Willis, Bayard Taylor, and other gentlemen voyagers whose accounts are singularly barren,[98] former sailors like Nathaniel Ames, Charles F. Briggs, Samuel Leech, and William Torrey, and other writers, such as C. S. Stewart and Timothy Flint, had treated the passage and the city of Liverpool with neither originality nor vision.[99] But Melville, infusing his experience with imagination and calling on suitable literary sources, created a book that bodies forth both beauty and truth. The ship and the ocean as they seem to a young and tenderhearted boy, the simplicity, humor, and tough likableness of merchant sailors, the charm of ships from distant ports in the docks of Liverpool, the sight of death, slow and painful or sudden and spectacular, the harrowing ordeals of diseased multitudes—all these and many other aspects of life Melville treats with an unrivaled skill.

Melville's predecessors in the nautical reminiscence wrote on only two planes, the factual and the melodramatic. They pictured a sailor's life aboard ship with the fidelity of a logbook, noting every shift of the wind and alteration of the course with a stubborn determination to tell all. They cluttered their pages with a mass of technical language, familiar to the mariner but bewildering to the general reader. The goal was realism; the effect was often dullness, for the emotions of the actor were seldom woven into the bare fabric of physical detail. Even Dana, despite his memorable account of rounding the Horn and of the flogging, could not tell his story without undue resort to nautical technology. On the other plane, the school of marine romancers filled their pages with sensational action and exotic backgrounds like Bombay, Shanghai, Madagascar, Lima, and the Pacific islands. Except for Dana, and Michael Scott, no one told his story in anything resembling an artistic style, and some, like William Torrey, were only partially literate. The nearest that former sailors came to impassioned writing was in their denunciation of conditions in the merchant marine. No one neglected to decry the tyranny of ship captains, the greed of owners, the filthiness of dark, wet forecastles, and the wretchedness and inadequacy of the worm-eaten biscuits and ancient meat that formed the daily fare.[100]

To all these accounts of life at sea and on land, *Redburn* is unquestionably superior. Melville saw more, felt more, and looked deeper into things, and he embodied his perceptions in moving prose. He brought a first voyage into the immediate experience of his reader by relating it to the emotions of his hero. We share Redburn's feelings at leaving home, his fright at the suicide, his mystification at the strange names of things aboard ship, his sense of triumph when he first performs a man's duty by loosing the skysail, his trembling fear of Jackson's snakelike glance. Among Melville's own books, *Redburn* has more of this quality of empathy than anything before *Moby-Dick* and *Pierre,* since Melville focuses so unblinkingly on the narrator's emotions. And though Ahab and Pierre are much deeper characters than Redburn, the earlier book adumbrates the psychological penetration of the later ones in its acute revelation of human motives.

In another sense as well, *Redburn* points forward. It is true that it has no second level of meaning, no symbolical illumination of life rising out of the literal story as have *Mardi* and *Moby-Dick*. But let us suppose that circumstances had permitted Melville to write another *Mardi*. There is no reason to believe that such a work would have furthered his artistic development at all. In *Mardi* he had not yet learned how to ballast his abstractions and the result was a nebulous, intangible allegory, lacking the necessary *vraisemblance,* the illusion of reality, to support the higher meaning. Before he could write *Moby-Dick,* with its perfect blending of "blubber" and "poetry," [101] he had to master a literal depiction of men and things. He had, for example, to weave his story about the lives of real persons. In *Mardi* he had neglected to do this, and if the "Pequod" had been peopled with apparitions like Babbalanja, Media, Yoomi, and the other mouthpieces for Melville's speculations and satire, *Moby-Dick* would have been a spirit without a body. But in the need of securing credibility for Redburn, Jackson, Bland, Jack Chase, Captain Claret, and the other human beings in *Redburn* and *White-Jacket,* Melville underwent a highly necessary discipline. Thus the two romances were practice sessions, arduous and detestable to their author but essential to the fruition of his talents.

But while *Redburn* served to train its author in the techniques of his craft, it would be unjust to a good book to look upon it as mere apprenticeship. It has a variety of merits. In its tender and varied depiction of the woes of a disappointed adolescent, it is second only to such works of its time as *David Copperfield.* Instead of the externalization and sentimentalism of most contemporary treatments of youth, *Redburn* has a penetrating psychological realism and a true pathos. Its scenes of physical realism, well wrought, vivid, and yet restrained, are masterpieces of their kind, not so detailed, perhaps, as Conrad's but almost as compelling. Its most memorable character, the sailor Jackson, is also one of the most fearful characters in fiction. In style, *Redburn,* with a few exceptions, has a compact, direct, limpid English which was so effective that contemporary critics, in their eagerness to illustrate it and the events it set forth, quoted collectively about an eighth of the entire book.[102] The sense of sin, evil, and tragedy in the book is balanced by a sense of humor and of comedy. Byron's romantic extravagance, melancholy, and loneliness combine with an active humanitarianism and moral indignation like Carlyle's and a sense of brotherhood and love like Whitman's. If *Redburn* lacks the poetry and the symbolism that load *Moby-Dick, Pierre,* and *Billy Budd* with multiple meanings, it still offers a host of pictures from life invested with human sympathy, moral earnestness, and vigorous creative power.

Redburn cannot shake its defects: imperfect characterization, inconsistency, and melodramatic excess. The lack of a plot will keep it from competing with many other creative works on the level of the novel, though certainly not with such superficial stories as those of Marryat. But it is superior to anything within its genre, and many single chapters or groups of chapters are superior to things outside the genre. We may expect the exotic settings of *Typee* and *Omoo* to gain them precedence with the ordinary reader, but *Redburn,* as a work of art, is superior. Through those readers who judge more by creative accomplishment and stylistic excellence, *Redburn* may well come to achieve the higher rank to which it is entitled, not alone among Melville's books, but also in the literature of nineteenth-century America.[103]

APPENDIXES

Appendix A

The Philo Logos Controversy*

The *Albany Microscope* for 1838 printed eight letters which are concerned in one way or another with Melville and the Philo Logos Society. These are:

1. The "Sandle Wood" letter, February 17 (see p. 91)
2. Melville's reply to "Sandle Wood," signed "Philologian," February 24
3. Charles Van Loon's reply to Melville, signed "Ex-President," March 10
4. Melville's reply to "Ex-President," divided by the editor into two parts: Part I, signed "Philologian," March 17, and Part II, signed "Philologean," March 24
5. Van Loon's reply to the two-part letter, signed "Ex-President," and also printed by the editor in two sections, March 31 and April 7
6. Melville's letter appealing for more support of debating, signed "Philologean," March 31 (see p. 95)
7. The peacemaking letter of "Americus," April 7 (see p. 94)
8. Van Loon's final statement, signed "Ex-President," April 14

Of these letters, the texts of the most significant are here reprinted for the first time. Unmistakable typographical errors have been corrected; otherwise the texts are unchanged.

Letter 2, from the Albany Microscope, *February 24*

Mr. Editor:—In every community there is a class of individuals, who are of so narrow-minded and jealous a disposition that deserving merit when developed in others, fills their bosoms with hatred and malice. And where a number of men having labored in the erection of some commendable institution are tendered the applause which their actions deserve, their breasts swell with envy, and they endeavor to villify and abuse what, if they could partake the admiration paid these, they would be as extravagant in eulogising and applauding as they were before clamorous in traducing and decrying.

Fortunate is it, however, for society, that their malignant efforts are

* See pages 90 ff.

generally powerless and feeble, and are not accompanied with that gratifying success, which in the accomplishment of a good object, is the source of the highest felicity.

Indeed, in the majority of instances the world is supremely indifferent as to which side of a cause they espouse, since they are frequently more annoying to their friends than troublesome to their enemies. They may be considered as a band of moral outlaws, the interdicted weapons they employ are falsehood and deceit, but so blunted and dulled by long service and ill-usage, that it is with extreme difficulty that they can be made to inflict a serious injury. Truly, so harmless have they become, that society with a mildness and lenity quite praiseworthy, tolerates them in all their inoffensive doings and smiles with derision at their ineffectual attempts to wound the sanctity of private reputation, or to plunge their wooden daggers in the side of public virtue.

Nor does their impotency proceed from the lack of ingenuity to plan, or the will to perform, but from their utter destitution of the ability to do. Surely were their weapons as sharp as their purpose, the number of murdered reputations would exactly correspond with the stabs of their slanderous poignards.

In the *van* of these notable worthies stands pre-eminent, that silly and brainless *loon* who composed the article in your last week's paper, denying the existence of the Philo Logos Society, the legality of its recent election, and its alleged possession of a room in Stanwix Hall.

I have only to remark in relation to this interesting production, that it is not more inelegant in style than wanting in truth and veracity. It is a complete tissue of infamous fabrications, and is as destitute of a single fact as is the author of parts. I refrain from enlarging upon what probable motives induced the writer to the publication of his miserable effusion. I will not say it proceeded from the pique of mortified pride, or from an unhallowed and foolish envy, but will merely remark that from whencesoever it derived its origin, it is contemptible, dastardly and outrageous.

Any individual calling at No. 9 Gallery, Stanwix Hall, next Friday evening at 7 o'clock, will receive indubitable evidence of the utter fallacy of "Sandle Wood's" statement, and will see the society in full operation, the officers (of whose election the public was notified in the Evening Journal,) in the act of discharging their respective duties, and as well furnished a room as is "owned, rented, or any manner used," by the most flourishing debating institution of which old Gotham may boast.

PHILOLOGIAN.

Letter 3, from the Albany Microscope, *March 10*

PHILO LOGOS SOCIETY.

Mr. Editor:—The basest villifacation does not unfrequently find a transitory lodgment in the public breast; the most fragile mesh of sophistry does not fail to ensnare for a moment the public mind; but, it is for the hand of truth and reason to raise the veil of black hypocrisy, to brush away the cobweb net, and expose the coward slanderer in all the shameful nakedness of vice, and unseemly deformity of guilt.

Regard for the welfare of society, and a sense of what is due to myself as an individual, impel me to hold up to the scorn and execration of the good and virtuous, the author of a foul, dastardly attack upon my character, in your paper of the 24th inst. As the name of this individual does not admit of an ingenious analytical introduction into the columns of the Microscope, I will inform the members of the Philo Logos Society, that it is none other than he, whose "fantastic tricks" have earned for him the richly merited title *"Ciceronian baboon";* but I shall lead him up before the public under the more romantic appellation of Hermanus Mel*villian.* Hermanus Melvillian, a moral Ethiopian, whose conscience qualms not in view of the most attrocious guilt; whose brazen cheek never tingles with the blush of shame, whose moral principles, and sensibilities, have been destroyed by the corruption of his own black and bloodless heart. With regard to his billingsgate effusion in the Microscope, I as heartily repel its infamous allegations, as I despise the character, and detest the principles of its infamous author. Reserving a more explicit statement of particular transactions (if it be demanded) for another number, I shall now proceed to state a few facts, and leave the public to judge who is destitute of truth and veracity, and "who the author of infamous falsehoods." At a time when the Philo Logos Society, watered by the refreshing showers of public admiration, and cheered by the cordial "God speed" of private friendship, was fast rising to the elevation of her elder sisters, and bid fair to fulfil a career of honorable usefulness; Hermanus Melvillian entered her happy domain, and with a ruthless hand severed the ties of friendship, wantonly injured the feelings of her most estimable members, incessantly disturbed the equanimity of her proceedings, abused her unsuspecting confidence; and forever destroyed her well earned reputation. The society forbore with long suffering; reproving, exhorting and beseeching, until "forbearance ceased to be a virtue," and then did she declare in a voice of thunder, that *"the conduct of Hermanus Melvillian was disgraceful to himself, discreditable to the society, and insulting to the chair."* In the course of time Mr. Melvillian left the city; but not until the Society, whose infant bloom and youthful vigor, gave promise of a long and useful existence, enervated by the repeated "stabs" of the assassin's poignard, dipped in the venom of his own heart, stood with her wasted form and haggard visage tottering over the grave of oblivion. Repeated attempts were made by the few whom repeated insult, and vile defamation had not provoked to recede in disgust, to revive the dying flame, and restore the society to its wonted strength, and pristine glory. But that untiring perseverence, that generous devotion which once characterized these individuals, was no longer exercised; and their laudable, though imbecile efforts, proved worse than in vain. The Society lingered on between life and death, when the prodigal Melvillian returned, with the face of a saint and the heart of a devil, to grieve over the ruins of the Society, and to water his victim with the tears of a human crocidile. But to "weep in vain," so thought Melvillian, and set about applying the remedy—persevering exertion. The little dispirited remnant of members were got together; a committee appointed to draft a new constitution; and it was resolved that at the next meeting the society should go into a new election. The then President having signified his intention of resigning; the devoted, penitent, leisureful Melvillian was nominated by a committee of two (himself being one) to fill the chair. Authorized by the President, Mr. M. was to have called a meeting on a specified Tuesday; but took the liberty of calling the meeting at a different time from that specified, without the consent and without notifying the President. At this unauthorized and unconstitutional meeting, Mr. M. was DULY elected President. Justice, to myself and the Society called upon me to expose this base treachery, and ungown this fawning hypocrite; which I did in the presence of the Society; detecting in his contemptable, abortive defence, the most absurd contradictions and abominable falsehoods. For the present I have done with Hermanus Melvillian. His abusive language in the last Microscope, is but the raving of an unmasked hypocrite, the "wincing, of a gall'd jade." I am not accountable for the "inelegancies" or "fabrications" of "Sandle Wood"; for myself I will say, I do not want "the ability" to defend myself against the dastardly attacks, of Hermanus Melvillian, (*alias* Philologean,) or the moral courage to expose vice, and "lash a rascal naked through the world."

EX-PRESIDENT.

Letter 4, Part I, from the Albany Microscope, *March 17*

Mr. Editor:—I had not intended again to obtrude myself upon your columns, when I penned my last communication, but circumstances which I need not mention having altered my determination, I beg of you to excuse the liberty I take, when I request you to insert the following epistle, which, if it be rather long you must not demur, as it is the last I shall inflict upon your patience. I am at a loss to account for the avidity with which Mr. C*****s V*n L**n seeks to drag before the public a distorted narative of the transactions of a private society; unless it be a mere feint or strategem, under which he advances towards the overthrow of my reputation. However, as he lays down many grave and serious charges, I am constrained to reply thereto, in the hope of exculpating myself from allegations the most unfounded and malignant. I am aware that my communication is somewhat long and tedious, but as Mr. C*****s V*n L**n intimates his design of publishing a series of articles upon the subject, and being unwilling to parade myself before the public in a subsequent number—I have seen fit to obviate the necessity alluded to by giving a faithful account of the affair, together with a few reflections thereon, in one comprehensive survey.

*To Mr. "Sandle Wood" alias "Ex-President" alias C*****s V*n L**n.*

Sir,—Without venturing to criticise the elegance of your composition, the absurd vagaries of your imagination, or impeaching the taste you have displayed in the abundance, variety and novelty of your scopes [tropes?] and figures, or calling into question the accuracy of your mode of Latinising English substantive[s], I shall without further delay, proceed to consider the merits of your late most fanciful performance. And I cannot but sincerely deplore the rashness with which you have published a production evidently composed in the heat and turmoil of passion, and which must remain without the sanction of your cooler judgement, and the approval of your otherwise respectable understanding. To no other cause can I impute that vile scurrility, that unholy defamation, and that low and groveling abuse which are the distinguishing characteristics of your late unfortunate attempt to asperse, through its chief officer, the institution over which I have the honor to preside. In all your ribaldry and villification there lurks a spirit of implacable rancour and hate, which afford the most delightful commentaries upon the dignity of your christian character. Alas! that your discretion should have been so little consulted when this evidence of the rabidness of your vindictive nature should have been suffered to escape in the moment of your ungaurded wrath, which must ever remain to demonstrate the hollowness of your religious professions of meekness, forbearance and love. Nor can I pass over without comment, the multitude of those blackguard epithets, which dance in sweet confusion throughout the whole extent of your recent production. *Here,* sir, are you upon vantage ground! I will not contend with you for the palm of vulgarity, nor seek to emulate the Billingsgate volubility of abuse in which you practice to perfection. Ah! what toilsome hours of study, what turning over of the leaves of Bee's Slang Dictionary, what studious attention to the lessons of the most accomplished masters of this divine art must have been required, ere you could have made way to that wonderful proficiency, which you seem to have attained in your late most brilliant communication. I have understood that the fish-women of Paris and the Thames were considered as the models of a regular blackguard style, as the standard and criterion by which all excellence in that department of polite literature was to be judged; and that for a readier flow of insolence, shamelessness and scurrility they proudly challenged the world. But I doubt whether the annals of Billingsgate itself, the posthumous papers of the renowned Peter Porcupine, or any of those interesting works which have been burned by the hands of the common hangman can match in purity of style and delicacy of phraseology, that valuable article which if it be destitute of every other excellence, must still be considered as the *chef-d'ouvre* of loafer eloquence. In this respect, I renounce, if ever I cherished all claims to superiority; and surely if laurels are to be reaped in such encounters—your brow is crowned with many a sprig. In regard to the hatred which you express towards me—I return it with no kindred detestation, but contemplate it with that mild and frigid contempt which it so richly deserves, and in common with the few who perused your performance, smiled at the folly which could prompt the utterance of personal dislike, and commiserate the headlong inconsiderateness which hurried you prematurely on to so public an avowal. If, however, you flatter yourself that you have bullied me into silence, or that the menaces which hang in terrorum over my devoted head, are objects of annoyance; I pray you to undeceive yourself, and rest assured, that I hold your abusive calumnies to be the outpourings of a causeless animosity, and your threats of defiance, as an idle and empty bravado. Under the dominion of temper and transported with fury, you have indulged in a vein of remarks, which with all the malice and acrimony of Junius, possess nought of that brilliancy of wit, that pugnancy [pungency?] of satire and force, and beauty of expression which redeemed him from the charge of vulgarity. His malevolence, his rancour and vindictiveness, were in a manner assuaged by the polished elegance of his style and the splendor of his diction. Instead of knocking down his man with savage ferocity, he skillfully parries his furious lounges, watches his opportunity, and runs him through the body, to the satisfaction of every beholder. But you have neither the bravery nor the strength to perform the one, nor the address and dexterity to achieve the other. Again, sir, I beg of you to accept my condolements upon your pitiable failure to substantiate your infamous allegations; my regret that so much good stationary should have been squandered in the prosecution of your charges; and my utter and profound indifference to all your professions of hatred, hostility and revenge. May these truly christian attributes cling around the sacred lawn with which you are hereafter to be invested, and your angelic nature be a fit illustration of the peaceful spirit of the gospel you profess.

PHILOLOGIAN.

Letter 4, Part II, from the Albany Microscope, *March 24*

Startle not, most amiable sir, when I inform you of what you are already apprised, that in your animadversions upon the relations which subsist between myself and the Philo Logos Society, you have shown yourself a stranger to veracity, to the truth of genuine narrative, and utterly disregardful of the feelings of my fellow members, and careless of the best and truest interests of the institution which you ostensibly defend. Now, therefore in behalf of the society, its members and myself, I feel bound by imperative necessity, to undertake your many fallacious positions, and to tear up and destroy that puny breast-work of sophistry and error, behind which you entrench the poverty and nothingness of your pretensions. At the solicitation of several of the Philo Logos Society, I became a member. Things proceeded with the utmost tranquility and order, until yourself indulging in a train of bitter and caustic personalities, drew upon yourself the bolts of my indignation, whereas frantic with rage, and burning with resentment, you moved that "the conduct of H—— M——— be considered as disgraceful to himself, &c."—Abortive attempt! Your motion was rejected, *viva voce* and yourself condemned to the pangs of mortified pride and foiled ambition. And yet with a hardihood, unparrellelled and barefaced, you endeavor to palm upon the public a palpable misrepresentation of the facts of this transaction, if mention whereof be made, it must redound to your lasting discredit. Thus much for the vote of censure which you allege was passed upon my conduct by the P. L. S. Called from town for a few months, I left the society in an apparently healthful and prosperous condition; on my return, however, my astonishment was unlimited, when I beheld our institution, which whilom flourished like a young cedar, in the last stages of a rapid decline. Immediately I instituted vigorous efforts for its resusitation, in which I was assisted by several prominent members, who all co-operated in the laudable design of reviving the ancient spark; we succeeded; obstacles were brushed aside, difficulties surmounted, and our labors crowned with gratifying success. In the midst of our generous endeavors, yourself being president of the P. L. S. was repeatedly importuned to unite with us in our operations—and having uniformly held yourself aloof—hereby showing none of that interest for the society which was to be expected from its chief officer, was tacitly and virtuously deposed and the few who then stood by the Assistant, resolved, to hold a new election; to that end they called meeting after meeting, but in vain! so few attended that the project was almost thrown up in despair. As a last attempt, however, it was decided, that if a certain number should be present at the next session, hereafter ensuing—the election should be proceeded with. Our expectations were realized, and at the first meeting of the society, subsequent to its restoration, the present incumbent was unanimously preferred to the presidency. Through my endeavors, a large and elegant room was obtained in Stanwix Hall, together with suitable furniture to the same, free from all expenses to the society. By virtue of my office, I convened the As[sociation?] at an early day, to adopt measures for the future course of the institution. My invitation was responded to, with alacrity by all the members of the society, which mustered in strong force as to a grand military review. The meeting progressed with the utmost harmony and good feeling, when yourself stung with dissapointment, smarting with envy, and boiling with wrath, sailed with all the majesty of offended pride into the midst of the assemblage, and pronounced [t]his recent election to have been unconstitutional and corrupt, becoming, however, rather unruly, you were called to order, and mildly requested to resume your seat; deeming this an outrage upon your dignity, with stentorian lungs you bellowed forth an appeal from the decision of the chair; when the society, disgusted with your insolence, by a large and triumphant majority vindicated the course of its president, ratified his election, and freely censured your intemperate and ungentlemanly behavior.

Frustrated then in your every endeavor to gratify the pique of private hostility—in order still to accomplish your iniquitous designs, you published under the signature of "Sandle Wood" a vile calumny upon the Ass., to which I indignantly rejoined, denying the slanderous accusations prefered, and insinuating yourself to be the author of the malignant effusion. Detected then, where you had every reason to suppose entire secresy would be observed, your anger knew no bounds, and disdaining all concealment and throwing off the mask entirely you hastened to give free vent to it, through the columns of the *Microscope,* in a tirade of obscenity and abuse, in which it is your peculiar province to excel.

It has not been, I can assure you, without reluctance that I have been drawn into any public disputation with one of your stamp, but a regard for my own reputation impelled me to expose the malevolence of your intentions; my only motive being then removed, I cheerfully bid a long good night to any further newspaper controversy with you, and subscribe myself,

Very respectfully
Your obedient servant
PHILOLOGEAN.

N.B. Your incoherent ravings may be continued if you choose; they remind me of the croakings of a Vulture when disappointed of its prey.

Letter 5, Part I, from the Albany Microscope, *March 31*

THE EXTINGUISHER.

Mr. Editor:—Had not the late malicious attacks of Herman Melville upon my honor and integrity, extended beyond the pales of the Philo

Logos Society or the circle of my acquaintance; I should have treated them with the silent contempt they so richly deserve; but having been perused by those, with whom the author and myself have yet to become acquainted; such silence though abundantly justified by the falsity and illiberality, might be construed into a tacit admission of their truth. This is my apology for again soliciting the favor of your columns. To Herman Melville—Sir,—the sensible Hudibras has well observed, that, there is no kind of argument like matter of fact; now, in my own opinion, he, who after announcing his intention of giving a general survey of particular transactions; indulges at the expense of an entire sheet, in contemptible critiscisms, displaying all the stiffness and swelling bombast of Johnson, to the entire exclusion of his irresistable reasoning and beautiful thoughts; is not only guilty of an unpardonable sacrifice of valuable stationary, but evinces a miserable destitution of that substantial matter, which should constitute the broad basis of every discussion. A reflection or two on your dastardly attempt at a retreat beneath the shadow of my principles and professions, and I shall proceed to deliver a round unvarnished tale of your whole course of—hypocrisy. As in the society when the unprovoked thunderbolt hurled by your own reckless hand, has recoiled, and wasted its fury upon your own head; so in this public contest, beaten with the rod of indignant truth, you have attempted a retreat to the old quarters, (my principles) and will assuredly meet with the same gracious reception. The charge, that in defending myself against your libellous reflections upon my character; and in using severe and pointed language in pourtraying yours, I have done violence to the meek and charitable spirit of the gospel I hold in the most *"frigid contempt."* Sir, in the principles avowed by me I glory: but, if those principles, demand the sacrafice of my dearest right, the right of free discussion; if those principles involve the necessity of surrendering my character to the "tender mercies" of an unprincipled foe; if those principles demand that—I should suffer hypocrisy to hold her masked sway unreproved; or finally, if those principles demand that I should call "bitter sweet, and sweet bitter," then sir, by me those principles shall be disavowed, "henceforth and forevermore." But, sir, I have yet to learn that when I intend to speak of the wily serpent or the ravening wolf, I am out of respect to my principles and professions, to style him the harmless dove, or the gentle lamb. If, however, (for we are falible mortals) in denouncing you as a "moral Ethiopean, whose conscience qualms not in view of the most attrocious guilt, whose brazen cheek never tingles with the blush of shame," I have done violence to the spirit of the gospel, most cordially do I recall the objectionable language, and in the meek and charitable spirit of Peter the Apostle, honestly and conscientiously pronounce you Herman Melville, a "child of the devil, full of all subtility and all mischief." So much, sir, for my inconsistency and want of charity. Having thus cursorily noticed your introduction (constituting two thirds of your article) I shall proceed to prove, beyond a question of doubt, not that you have given an exaggerated review of the late proceedings of the society, but that you have wilfully perpetrated the most abominable falsehoods. In denying the charge made by me, that you forever destroyed the well earned reputation of the society, you aver, that *"when called from town for a few months, you left the society in an apparently healthy and prosperous condition."* The following extract of a letter received from you during that absence and now in my possession will stamp false upon the declaration, *"but I have been digressing from the beginning of my letter my object is to know the existing situation of the society; whether it is on the rapid decline I left it in, or whether like the Phoenix it hath risen from its ashes, &c., &c."* In your communication to the Microscope, you deny with unparalleled effrontery, that in consequence of your gross misconduct and incessant violation of its wholesome laws, the society was obliged to pass upon your *riotous* proceedings the severest censure. Sir, among the barefaced falsehoods perpetrated, the secretary's accompanying certificate will abundantly prove, that this the paragon stands in bold relief:—*I do hereby certify that a resolution was adopted in the Philo Logos Society pronouncing the conduct of H. Melville "disgraceful to himself, discreditable to the society, and insulting to the chair," and that, the resolution stands in full force at this date.*

EX-PRESIDENT.

Letter 5, Part II, from the Albany Microscope, *April 7*

Lotus Niles,[1] Sir—Having thus convicted you of two absolute falsehoods, and these forming the pillar of your defence, and the only *points* in your communication, I shall now give a faithful sketch of the memorable altercation which ensued between us at the "debut" of the society in Stanwix Hall; now, sir, you know, that, so far from "sallying with all the dignity of offended pride into the midst of the assemblage" when "the meeting progressed with the utmost harmony and good feeling," I entered the Hall before the deliberations of the society had commenced; that (the secretary being absent) at your request I read the minutes, and that on miscellaneous business being called for, I arose with calm dispassion, and proposed the following interrogatory to the chair: Mr. Chairman—"will you be so good as to inform me, by what authority a meeting of this society was called, and an election holden, on Friday evening last?" To which you replied, after some hesitation, "extraordinary circumstances demand extraordinary action; the members of the society being together, and some of the officers being present, it was thought expedient to go into a new election; and beside this, those of the society, who had absented themselves twice successively, were by virtue of the constitution expelled."

To which I rejoined, "Sir, out of your own mouth shall I condemn you; you have intimated that I, the president being no longer a member of the society, had no longer the authority to call a meeting, and hence the fact that I did not authorise the meeting holden on Friday evening, did not effect its constitutionality; but, sir, my name has just been called from your roll, and I am now officiating in the capacity of Secretary." And here I divulged the fact; that you have been authorised by me to call a meeting of the society on *Monday* evening, but, that from motives not understood by me, you have taken the liberty of calling a meeting on Friday evening, without my knowledge or consent. After this unpleasant *expose* you remarked, that, "you understood me to invest you with authority to call a meeting upon any evening of the week deemed most suitable by yourself." To this I replied; Sir, in answer to my first interrogatory, you intimated very clearly, that I was no longer a member of the society; and not a syllable did you utter in relation to the power vested in you by the President; but, now, would you make it appear, that I, who by virtue of the constitution am expelled; authorised the call of that unlawful meeting. Sir, "there is something rotten about Denmark." At about this point as the last resource in your perilous plight, I was called to order. Appealing from the decision of the chair, it was sustained by the bare majority of one. I must here do my fellow members of the society the justice to remark; that the decision of the chair was sustained, as I have since been assured, not from disrespect to me whom they have for two years sustained in the Presidency, and who but for *positively* declining would have still occupied the chair; but, because the affair was at first considered of a somewhat personal character, and because they were not willing to postpone the discussion of "the question" then before the society. Sir, notwithstanding, your imbecile efforts to avoid another harsh encounter; at the close of the regular debate it was unanimously resolved, that I should be at liberty to pursue the scorching enquiry, and "bring to light the hidden things of darkness." I have observed that when called to order, I left you in an unhappy predicament, and at the close of the protracted discussion which ensued on the passage of the resolution referred to, you remained, sir, in *"statu quo"*. Since, that dreadful night you have stood almost alone in your glory; some half dozen solitary individuals have occasionally congregated in "that dismal place," not "as to a grand military review," but "as to the chamber of a dying friend"; not to engage in those spirited debates, so admirably combining *"utile cum dulces,"* but *again to censure your disgraceful conduct.* Sir, if the nature of your steel heart does not forbid shame, and repentance let your head be a fountain of tears, and let your body be clothed in sackcloth and ashes. I have been obliged to speak the unwelcome truth, I have vindicated my own character, and you have been convicted of falsehood and hypocricy.

Sir, I will not glory vainly in your downfall. It dont become me to hate the man, though I detest his principles. Had your ability been equal to your zeal, I should weep over the ruins of an unsullied reputation; and yet cordially do I forgive the injustice committed; and earnestly do I entreat you to devote the talents thus basely prostituted in the service of satan; to higher, nobler, and more honorable purposes.

I am Sir,
Your friend,
Ex-President.

P.S. I deny the most distant relationship to "Sandle Wood." If I was the author of an article over that signature the Editor of the Microscope is at liberty to publish the fact.

E. P.

Letter 6, from the Albany Microscope, *March 31*

YOUNG MEN'S ASSOCIATION.

Mr. Editor:—Aware that your paper is read by a large portion of the young men of Albany, I have been induced to solicit a small space, for the purpose of directing their attention to an institution, with which their honor as well as interest is deeply involved, I allude to the debating society attached to the Young Mens' Association. It is unnecessary to say that the Association, (as a whole) is sustained in a manner highly creditable to the young men of this city. The public spirit and laudable ambition that effected its organization, has increased with its onward progress, and we feel fully assured that the Young Mens' Association, is destined to awaken deeper and deeper interest, as years more and more develop its happy and benign influences. But we regret that what can be told of the whole cannot be said of its parts; the debating society does not receive that attention which its importance demands. It is unnecessary to speak of its advantages; they must be familiar to all, what doth it avail a man? though he possesses all the knowledge of a Locke or a Newton, if he know not how to communicate that knowledge. What? though he holds in his hand, "the sword of his country's defence" if he know not how to wield the "trusty steel." The former would be often more practical use, than a true honored volumn reposing in eternal obscurity, and the latter of no greater prowess than a man of straw. We ask no higher testimony in favor of its advantages, than the recorded opinions of all great men, Burke, the English Orator and Statesman acknowledged that the first spring which moved him on in a career of fame and honor, was the fostering encouraging effect of a literary club, our own Clay had revealed to him the latent powers of a giant mind in a like institution, and Franklin the philosopher and sage attributed the early development of his natural resources to the same mind stirring soul animating cause, but why specify? The learned are as one man, in their opinion of the importance of debating societies in developing the mind, and prompting to greater and higher efforts, may we not entertain then a confident hope that the young men of Albany, true to their interest and jealous of their honor, will devote that attention to this branch of the Association, which its importance so richly deserves; and may we not confidently anticipate the uniform attendance and efficient co-operation of our newly elected managers in reviveing the society, and multiplying its usefulness.

PHILOLOGEAN.

Appendix B

The Lansingburgh Fragments*

Melville's first compositions were discovered among his papers by Raymond M. Weaver in 1919. Of them he writes:

> These appeared in *The Democratic Press and Lansingburgh Advertiser* for May 4, and May 18, 1839. The first is signed "L. A. V."; the second, known to exist only in a single mutilated clipping, in lacking the closing paragraphs, can give no evidence as to concluding signature. Copies of these two articles are preserved among Melville's papers, each autographed by him in faded brown ink.[1]

There is much amiss about these statements. The copies of the articles bear Melville's name, but the autographs are not his, and of the three signatures, two are in blue ink and only one in faded brown ink. Weaver found three printed texts, two being those of "Fragment No. 1" and one of "Fragment No. 2." What may be called the A text is that of "Fragment No. 1," cut up at different points and pasted onto six pages of typewriter paper, about half of a newspaper column to a page. About eight inches of the date line, reading "Lansingburgh, N. Y., May 4, 1839," are retained with the first clipped section. To the right of "1839" appears "By Herman Melville," written in faded brown ink. A crudely drawn hand points down and back to the title of the fragment. The "Melville" of this signature resembles the "Melville" as signed by Herman's wife in the flyleaf of Melville's "Journal Up the Straits," 1856 (M). The most distinguishing feature is the "M," the first line of which begins at the bottom of the letter. Melville never began a capital "M" in this way in any manuscript I have ever seen, nor does the "Herman" of the signature correspond to anything in his hand.

The second text (A-1) is the entire issue of the *Democratic Press and Lansingburgh Advertiser* for May 4, 1839, with "Fragment No. 1" occupying almost three of the six columns on page one. "By Herman Melville" is written on the date line in blue ink, and a crude hand points to the title of the piece. Again, this writing does not correspond to Melville's. However, it is very much like his wife's in her later years, as is the signature on the B text, which is that of "Fragment No. 2," cut up, like the A text, and pasted on typewriter paper.

It seems, then, that Melville's wife identified these articles as her

* See pages 108 ff.

husband's work. If this identification appears to be tenuous, one must still allow much weight for the fact that the sketches were found among Melville's papers and that the style clearly adumbrates his future work. There is no sound reason to doubt Melville's authorship.

The ending of "Fragment No. 2," which Weaver says is lacking, was actually on the back of that portion of the "Fragment" that was pasted on page 6 of the typewriter paper. The sketch filled half of column 3 and all of columns 4, 5, and 6 on the front page, and the last paragraphs were printed at the top of page 2, column one. Like "Fragment No. 1," the second sketch is signed "L. A. V."

In reproducing for the first time the full and correct text of "Fragment No. 2," I have employed a copy of the original newspaper now in the Troy Public Library. I have made some corrections of what seemed to be obvious typographical errors, but I have indicated in the footnotes all deviations from the original since such spellings as "chord" for "cord" and "griped" for "gripped" may be Melville's rather than the compositor's. The latter, it must be pointed out, was careless and inconsistent; other articles in the same issue of the paper contain errors like "toscin" for "tocsin" and "HEMOLCK" for "HEMLOCK" as well as "skelleton," "unquialified," "superintendant," and "domicils." On the other hand, "heighth" for "height" is probably Melville's misspelling.

For the Democratic Press.

Fragments From a Writing Desk.

No. 2.

"Confusion seize the Greek!" exclaimed I, as wrathfully rising from my chair, I flung my ancient Lexicon across the room, and seizing my hat and cane, and throwing on my cloak, I sallied out into the clear air of heaven. The bracing coolness of an April evening calmed my aching temples, and I slowly wended my way to the river side. I had promenaded the bank for about half an hour, when flinging myself upon the grassy turf, I was soon lost in revery, and up to the lips in sentiment.

I had not lain more than five minutes, when a figure effectually concealed in the ample folds of a cloak, glided past me, and hastily dropping something at my feet, disappeared behind the angle of an adjoining house, ere I could recover from my astonishment at so singular an occurrence.—"Certes!" [2] cried I, springing up, "here is a spice of the marvelous!" and stooping down, I picked up an elegant little, rose-coloured, lavender-scented billet-doux, and hurriedly breaking the seal (a heart, transfixed with an arrow) I read by the light of the moon, the following:

"Gentle Sir—

If my fancy has painted you in genuine colours, you will on the receipt of this, incontinently [3] follow the bearer where she will lead you.

Inamorata."

"The deuce I will!" exclaimed I.—"But soft!"—And I reperused this singular document, turned over the billet in my fingers, and examined the hand-writing; which was femininely delicate, and I could have sworn was a woman's. Is it possible, thought I, that the days of romance are revived?—No, "The days of chivalry are over!" says Burke.[4]

As I made this reflection, I looked up, and beheld the same figure which had handed me this questionable missive, beckoning me forward. I started towards her; but, as I approached, she receded from me, and fled swiftly along the margin of the river at a pace, which, encumbered as I was with my heavy cloak and boots, I was unable to follow; and which filled me with sundry misgivings, as to the nature of the being, who could travel with such amazing celerity. At last perfectly breathless, I fell into a walk; which, my mysterious fugitive [5] perceiving, she likewise lessened her pace, so as to keep herself still in sight, although at too great a distance to permit me to address her.

Having recovered from my fatigue and regained my breath: I loosened the clasp of my cloak, and inwardly resolving that I would come at the bottom of the mystery, I desperately flung the mantle from my shoulders, and dashing my beaver to the ground, gave chase in good earnest to the tantalizing stranger. No sooner did I from my extravagant actions announce my intention to overtake her, than with a light laugh of derision, she sprang forward at a rate, which in attempting to outstrip, soon left me far in the rear, heartily disconcerted and crest-fallen, and inly cursing the ignis fatuus,[6] that danced so provokingly before me.

At length, like every one else, learning wisdom from experience; I thought my policy lay in silently following the footsteps of my eccentric guide, and quietly waiting the denouement [7] of this extraordinary adventure. So soon as I relaxed my speed, and gave evidence of having renounced my more summary mode of procedure; the stranger, regulating her movements by mine, proceeded at a pace which preserved between us a uniform distance, ever and anon looking back like a wary general to see if I were again inclined to try the mettle of her limbs.

After pursuing our way in this monotonous style for some time; I observed that my conductress rather abated in her precautions,[8] and had not for the last ten or fifteen minutes taken her periodical [9] survey over her shoulder; whereat, plucking up my spirits, which I can assure you courteous [10] reader, had fallen considerably below zero by the ill-success of my previous efforts,—I again rushed madly forward at the summit of my speed, and having advanced ten or twelve rods unperceived,[11] was flattering myself that I should this time make good my purpose; when, turning suddenly round, as though reminded of her late omission, and descrying me plunging ahead like an infuriated steed, she gave a slightly audible scream of surprise, and once more fled, as though helped forward by invisible wings.

This last failure was too much. I stopped short, and stamping the ground in ungovernable rage, gave vent to my chagrin in a volley of exclamations: in which, perhaps, if narrowly inspected, might have been detected two or three expressions which savored somewhat of the jolly days of the jolly cavaliers. But if a man was ever excusable for swearing; surely, the circumstances of the case were palliative of the crime. What! to be thwarted by a woman? Peradventure, baffled by a girl? Confusion! It was too bad! To be outgeneraled,[12] routed, defeated, by a mere rib of the earth? It was not to be borne! I thought I should never survive the inexpressible mortification of the moment; and in the height [13] of my despair, I bethought me of putting a romantic end to my existence upon the very spot which had witnessed my discomfiture.

But when the first transports of my wrath had passed away, and perceiving that the waters of the river, instead of presenting an unruffled calm, as they are wont to do on so interesting an occasion, were discomposed and turbid; and remembering, that beside this, I had no other means of accomplishing my heroic purpose, except the vulgar and inelegant one, of braining myself against the stone wall which traversed the road; I sensibly determined after taking into consideration the aforementioned particulars, together with the fact that I had an unfinished game of chess to win, on which depended no inconsiderable wager, that to commit suicide under such circumstances would be highly inexpedient, and probably be attended with many inconveniences.—During the time I had consumed in arriving at this most wise and discreet conclusion, my mind had time to recover its former tone, and had become comparatively calm and collected; and I saw my folly in endeavoring to trifle with one, apparently so mysterious and inexplicable.

I now resolved, that whatever might betide, I would patiently await the issue of the affair: and advancing forward in the direction of my guide, who all this time had maintained her ground, steadfastly [14] watching my actions,—we both simultaneously strode forward, and were soon on the same footing as before.

We walked on at an increased pace, and were just passed the suburbs of the town, when my conductress plunging into a neighboring grove, pursued [15] her way with augmented speed, till we arrived at a spot, whose singular and grotesque beauty, even amidst the agitating occurrences of the evening I could not refrain from observing. A circular space of about a dozen acres in extent had been cleared in the very heart of the grove: leaving, however, two parallel rows of lofty trees, which at the distance of about twenty paces, and intersected in the center by two similar ranges, traversed the whole diameter of the circle. These noble plants shooting their enormous trunks to an amazing height,[16] bore their verdant honors far aloft, throwing their gigantic limbs abroad and embracing each other with their rugged arms. This fanciful union of their sturdy boughs formed a magnificent arch, whose grand proportions, swelling upward in proud pre-eminence,[17] presented to the eye a vaulted roof, which to my perturbed imagination at the time, seemed to have canopied the triumphal feasts of the sylvan god.—This singular prospect burst upon me in all its beauty, as we emerged from the surrounding thicket, and I had unconsciously lingered on the borders of the wood, the better to enjoy so unrivalled a view; when as my eye was following the dusky [18] outline of the grove, I caught the diminutive figure of my guide, who standing at the entrance of the arched way [19] I have been endeavoring to describe, was making the most extravagant gestures of impatience at my delay.—Reminded at once of the situation, which put me for a time under the control of this capricious mortal, I replied to her summons by immediately throwing myself forward, and we soon entered the Atlantian arbor, in whose umbrageous shades we were completely hid.

Lost in conjecture, during the whole of this eccentric ramble, as to its probable termination—the sombre gloom of these ancestral trees, gave a darkening [20] hue to my imaginings,[21] and I began to repent the inconsiderate haste which had hurried me on, in an expedition, so peculiar and suspicious. In spite of all my efforts to exclude them, the fictions of the nursery poured in upon my recollection, and I felt with Bob Acres in the "Rivals," that "my valor was certainly going." Once, I am almost ashamed to own it to thee, gentle reader, my mind was so haunted with ghostly images, that in an agony of apprehension, I was about to turn and flee, and had actually [22] made some preliminary movements [23] to that effect, when my hand, accidentally straying into my bosom, gripped [24] the billet, whose romantic summons had caused this nocturnal adventure. I felt my soul regain her fortitude, and smiling at the absurd conceits which infested my brain, I once more stalked proudly forward, under the overhanging branches of these ancient trees.

Emergent from the shades of this romantic region, we soon beheld an edifice, which seated on a gentle eminence, and embowered amidst surrounding trees, bore the appearance [25] of a country villa: although its plain exterior showed none of those fantastic devices which usually adorn the elegant chateaux. My conductress as we neared this unpretending mansion seemed to redouble her precautions; and although she evinced no positive alarm, yet her quick and startled glances bespoke no small degree of apprehension. Motioning me to conceal myself behind an adjacent tree, she approached the house with rapid but cautious steps; my eyes followed her until she disappeared behind the shadow of the garden wall, and I remained waiting her reappearance with the utmost anxiety.—An interval of several moments had elapsed, when I descried [26] her, swinging open a small postern, and beckoning me to advance. I obeyed the summons, and was soon by her side, not a little amazed at the complacency, which after what had transpired, brooked my immediate vicinity. Dissembling my astonishment, however, and rallying all my powers, I followed with noiseless strides the footsteps of my guide, fully persuaded that this mysterious affair was now about to be brought to an eclaircissement.

The appearance of this spacious habitation was any thing but inviting; it seemed to have been built with a jealous eye to concealment; and its few, but well-defended windows were sufficiently high from the ground, as effectually to baffle the prying curiosity of the inquisitive stranger. Not a single light shone from the narrow casement; but all was harsh, gloomy and forbidding.[27] As my imagination, ever alert on such an occasion, was busily occupied in assigning some fearful motive for such unusual precautions; my leader suddenly halted beneath a lofty window, and making a low call, I perceived slowly descending therefrom, a thick [28] silken cord,[29] attached to an ample basket, which was silently deposited at our feet. Amazed at this apparition,[30] I was about soliciting an explanation: when laying her fingers impressively upon her lips, and placing herself in the basket, my guide motioned me to seat myself beside her. I obeyed; but not without considerable trepidation: and in obedience to the same low call which had procured its descent our curious vehicle, with sundry creakings, rose in air.

To attempt an analysis of my feelings at this moment were impossible. The solemnity of the hour—the romantic nature of my present situation—the singularity of my whole adventure—the profound stillness which prevailed—the solitude of the place, were enough of themselves to strike a panic into the stoutest heart, and to unsettle the strongest nerves.[31] But when to these, was added the thought,—that at the dead of night, and in the company of a being so perfectly inexplicable, I was effecting a clandestine entrance into so remarkable an abode: the kind and sympathising reader will not wonder, when I wished myself safely bestowed in my own snug quarters in ——— street.

Such were the reflections which passed through my mind, during our aerial voyage, throughout which my guide maintained the most rigid silence, only broken at intervals by the occasional creakings of our machine, as it rubbed against the side of the house in its ascent. No sooner had we gained the window, than two brawny arms were extended circling me in their embrace, and ere I was aware of the change of locality, I found myself standing upright in an apartment, dimly illuminated by a solitary taper. My fellow voyager was quickly beside me, and again enjoining silence with her finger, she seized the lamp and bidding me follow, conducted me through a long corridor, till we reached a low door concealed behind some old tapestry, which opening to the touch, disclosed a spectacle as beautiful and enchanting as any described in the Arabian Nights.

The apartment we now entered, was filled up in a style of Eastern splendor, and its atmosphere was redolent of the most delicious perfumes. The walls were hung round with the most elegant draperies, waving in graceful folds, on which were delineated scenes of Arcadian beauty. The floor was covered with a carpet of the finest texture, in which were wrought with exquisite skill [32] the most striking events in ancient mythology. Attached to the wall by cords [33] composed of alternate threads of crimson silk and gold, were several magnificent pictures illustrative of the loves of Jupiter and Semele, Psyche [34] before the tribunal of Venus, and a variety of other scenes, limned all with felicitous grace. Disposed around the room, were luxurious couches, covered with the finest damask, on which were likewise executed after the Italian fashion the early fables of Greece and Rome. Tripods, designed to represent the Graces bearing aloft vases, richly chiseled in the classic taste, were distributed in the angles of the room, and exhaled an intoxicating fragrance.

Chandeliers [35] of the most fanciful description, suspended from the lofty ceiling by rods of silver, shed over this voluptuous scene a soft and tempered light, and imparted to the whole, that dreamy beauty, which must be seen in order to be duly appreciated. Mirrors of unusual magnitude, multiplying in all directions the gorgeous objects, deceived the eye by their reflections, and mocked the vision with long perspective.

But overwhelming as was the display of opulence, it yielded in attraction to the being for whom all this splendour glistened; and the grandeur of the room served only to show to advantage the matchless beauty of its inmate. These superb [36] decorations, though lavished in boundless profusion,[37] were the mere accessories of a creature, whose loveliness was of that spiritual cast that depended upon no adventitious aid, and which as no obscurity could diminish, so, no art could heighten.

When I first obtained a glimpse of this lovely being, she lay reclining upon an ottoman; [38] in one hand holding a lute, and with the other lost in the profusion of her silken tresses, she supported her head.—I could not refrain from recalling the passionate exclamation of Romeo:

> "See how she leans her cheek upon her hand;
> Oh! that I were a glove upon that hand,
> That I might kiss that cheek!"

She was habited in a flowing robe of the purest white, and her hair, escaping from the fillet of roses which had bound it, spread its negligent graces over neck and bosom and shoulder, as though unwilling to reveal the extent of such transcendent [39] charms.—Her zone was of pink satin, on which were broidered figures of Cupid in the act of drawing his bow; while the ample folds of her Turkish sleeve were gathered at the wrist by a bracelet of immense rubies, each of which represented a heart pierced thro' by a golden shaft. Her fingers were decorated with a variety of rings, which as she waved her hand to me as I entered, darted forth a thousand coruscations, and gleamed their brilliant splendors to the sight. Peeping from beneath the envious skirts of her mantle, and almost buried in the downy cushion [40] on which it reposed, lay revealed the prettiest little foot you can imagine; cased in a satin slipper, which clung to the fairy-like [41] member by means of a diamond clasp.

As I entered the apartment, her eyes were downcast, and the expression of her face was mournfully interesting; she had apparently been lost in some melancholy revery. Upon my entrance, however, her countenance [42] brightened, as with a queenly wave of the hand, she motioned my conductress from the room, and left me standing, mute, admiring and bewildered in her presence.

For a moment my brain spun round, and I had not at command a single [one] of my faculties. Recovering my self possession however, and with that, my good breeding,[43] I advanced en cavalier, and gracefully sinking on one knee, I bowed my head and exclaimed—"Here do I prostrate myself, thou sweet Divinity, and kneel at the shrine of thy [44] peerless charms!"—I hesitated,—blushed, looked up, and beheld bent upon me a pair of Andalusian eyes, whose melting earnestness of expression pierced me to the soul, and I felt my heart dissolving away like ice before the equinoctial heats.

Alas! For all the vows of eternal constancy I had sworn to another!—The silken threads were snapped asunder; the [45] golden cords [46] had parted! A new dominion was creeping o'er my soul, and I fell, bound at the feet of my fair enchantress. A moment of unutterable [47] interest passed, while I met the gaze of this glorious being with a look as ardent, as burning, as steadfast as her own.—But it was not in mortal woman to stand the glance of an eye which had never quailed before a foe; and whose fierce lightnings were now playing in the wild expression of a love, that rent my bosom like a whirlwind, and tore up my past attachments as though they were but of the growth of yesterday.—The long dark lashes fell! smothered were the fires, whose brightness had kindled my soul in flames! I seized the passive hand, I lifted it to my lips and covered it with burning kisses! "Fair mortal!" I exclaimed, "I feel my passion is requited: but, seal it with thy own sweet voice, or I shall expire in uncertainty!"

Those lustrous orbs again opened on me all their fires; and maddened at her silence, I caught her in my arms, and imprinting one long, long kiss upon her hot and glowing lips, I cried "Speak! Tell me, thou cruel! Does thy heart send forth vital fluid like my own? Am I loved,—even wildly, madly as I love?" She was silent; gracious God! what horrible apprehension crossed my soul?—Frantic with the thought, I held her from me, and looking in her face, I met the same impassioned gaze; her lips moved—my senses ached with the intensity with which I listened,—all was still,—they uttered no sound; I flung her from me, even though she clung to my vesture, and with a wild cry of agony I burst from the apartment!—She was dumb! Great God, she was dumb! DUMB AND DEAF!

L. A. V.

Appendix C

Jackson and Ahab

The resemblances between Jackson and Ahab, only partly noticed, suggest that well before the composition of *Moby-Dick,* a partial vision of Ahab had begun to take shape in Melville's mind. If it is Jackson's diabolism that recurs most clearly in Ahab, other marks and qualities have their growth there too. Jackson is "branded on his yellow brow with some inscrutable curse"; [1] Ahab has a brand that runs, some say, from head to heel. Jackson is a tyrant, despite physical weakness; so is Ahab, though he has an artificial leg. Jackson's practical knowledge, cleverness, and shrewd perception of human weakness all turn up in Ahab; in both men they help establish leadership. The power of each over other men is partly sinister and inexplicable. Jackson perpetually insults the sailors, jeering at them for "lily-livered poltroons," and despite their resentment and occasional mutinous conspiracies, which they never dare bring to a head, they not only submit to his savage lordship but minister to him. Similarly, Ahab insults Stubb, but Stubb, ruled by some occult power, is nearly persuaded to pray for Ahab; the other men of the "Pequod" sometimes feel rebellious, but they fear Ahab more than they fear Fate. Jackson continually terrifies Redburn, yet the boy finds in him a subject for pity.

> There seemed [he says] even more woe than wickedness about the man; and his wickedness seemed to spring from his woe; and for all his hideousness there was that in his eye at times that was ineffably pitiable and touching; and though there were moments when I almost hated this Jackson, yet I have pitied no man as I have pitied him.[2]

Ahab, too, is a "man of sorrows," deeply beset by some inner woe, and Starbuck's feeling about him is, with some variation, the feeling of Redburn and the crew toward Jackson:

> Oh! I plainly see my miserable office,—to obey, rebelling; and worse yet, to hate with a touch of pity! For in his eyes I read some lurid woe would shrivel me up, had I it.[3]

Redburn often thinks that Jackson is crazy; Ahab's officers believe him mad. Both men have been physically wounded by life, and both are beset by a colossal grievance. Jackson's vices have left him with diseased lungs, and he is "full of hatred and gall against everything and everybody in the world; as if all the world was one person, and had done him some dreadful harm, that was rankling and festering in his heart."[4] Ahab's leg has been bitten off in his first attack upon Moby-Dick, and he shares with Jackson the sense of active malice in the universe. The difference is that by 1851 Melville could see how to dramatize this general hatred of "everything and everybody" by giving it a specific object which was both real and almost infinitely symbolic. Thus, for Ahab the white whale became "the incarnation of all those malicious agencies which some deep men feel eating in them, till they are left living on with half a heart and half a lung."[5] Finally, both men go unregenerate to their doom, Jackson with a curse in his teeth, Ahab spitting hate and defiance from the brink of hell.

As a character, Jackson cannot, of course, compare with the monumental figure of Captain Ahab. "The infernal nature," Melville noted in his copy of *King Lear,* "has a valor often denied to innocence," but in 1849 he was not ready to embody this idea in character. In fact, he specifically makes Jackson's Satanism loathsome, though in Ahab he invests it with an irresistible magnetism. Jackson is the detailed etching of a man whose malevolence is only occasionally translated into dramatic action, whereas Ahab's Titanic passions motivate action on an epic scale. Melville called upon many other sources for his concept of Ahab—King Ahab of old, King Lear, Byron's and Shelley's Satanism, Prometheus, Lucifer, the Persian fire worshipper, and others. But the parallels between the tyrant of the "Highlander" and the tyrant of the "Pequod" are so numerous that the line of descent seems unquestionable.

Appendix D

The Reputation of *Redburn* [1]

The formal history of the reputation of *Redburn* falls into four periods. On publication it received a warm welcome from critics and public alike and rapidly outsold its allegorical predecessor, *Mardi.*[2] For the rest of the nineteenth century and well into the twentieth it was almost totally forgotten. After Raymond Weaver's biography of Melville in 1921, interest in *Redburn* revived and several new editions appeared. But this interest was largely biographical, and not until the last decade or so has it attracted the attention as an artistic work which it deserves.

Redburn made its first appearance in England, on September 29, 1849, in a handsome two-volume edition, printed in large, clear type, and bound in blue cloth.[3] Richard Bentley, the publisher, advertised it prominently in the *Spectator* and the *Athenaeum,*[4] though his price of a guinea, five times the American cost, must have discouraged large sales.[5] On November 10 Evert Duyckinck's *Literary World,* which had already informed the reader of *Redburn*'s progress toward the press,[6] whetted public taste with a eulogistic notice and two full chapters, the attempt of Redburn to call on the captain and the account of the burning corpse. The book was "eminently attractive," wrote the reviewer, probably Duyckinck himself; it showed that "there is no such thing as exhausting nature while there is reality in the description. . . . Mr. Melville proves himself in this work the DeFoe of the Ocean." [7] With this advance praise, *Redburn* appeared a few days later on the booksellers' shelves in a single volume selling for a dollar in muslin and seventy-five cents in paper.[8] Harper, the publishers, took a half-page advertisement for it in the *Literary World* and continued to publicize it until the end of the year.[9] Other places, especially those that could lay claim to some association with Melville, also heralded *Redburn.* In Albany three booksellers featured *Redburn* as "Melville's New Book," [10] and Thurlow Weed, influential editor of the *Evening Journal* and an acquaintance of Melville's, gave the book his personal commendation,[11] with the result that it sold "like hot cakes." [12] The *Lansingburgh Gazette* affirmed that "certainly the writings of Herman Melville should be sought with filial interest by the people of Lansingburgh." [13] Newspapers in Boston, Worcester, Hartford, Philadelphia, Baltimore, and Richmond applauded it.[14] Thus *Redburn* was launched with sufficient fanfare on both sides of the Atlantic to secure a just reception.

To the anticipatory review of *Redburn,* the first in America, Duyckinck's *Literary World* added a longer and even more laudatory criticism on November 17.[15] Throughout it emphasized the "thorough impression and conviction of reality"[16] and the naturalness of incident and character. "We are among sailors with the tar on them, not stage sailors, or missionaries' sailors . . . ," said the reviewer, quoting much of the description of Jackson in evidence.[17] In recognition of the surplus of affected sailor lingo in current sea novels, the writer remarked, with some acumen: "This sailor's use of language, the most in shortest compass, may be the literary school which has rescued Herman Melville from the dull verbosity of his contemporaries."[18] He also found a strong suggestion of Smollett in the description of the sailors' boardinghouse and other sordid scenes in Liverpool. Perhaps the most characteristic compliment was bestowed on the death of Jackson, which was quoted in full as an example of "strong writing" with "the outlook of a man who sees the world and life in their intensity, with no partial exaggeration, or morbid feeling, but with a manly sense of the actuality."[19] The critic also liked the originality of the central situation, involving the son of a gentleman turned sailor. The book as a whole he recommended in the warmest, most sweeping terms, for it had "the lights and shades, the mirth and melancholy, the humor and tears of real life."[20]

The value of this enthusiastic review is somewhat reduced by the lack of critical detachment. Not a single word of adverse comment escaped the writer, though if Melville had not been such a good friend of Evert Duyckinck, the *Literary World,* which prided itself upon some discernment, must certainly have remarked upon some of the less convincing scenes, like that in the London gambling house. But the review underlines the chief appeal of *Redburn* for most critics—the extraordinary sense of reality, of eyewitness reporting that Melville created.

Thus the *Southern Literary Messenger*'s review began:

> If this volume be an imaginary narrative then is it the most life-like and natural fiction since Robinson Crusoe's account of his life on the island of Juan Fernandez . . . . No one . . . can find in this sailor-boy confession any incident that might not have happened—nay, that has not the air of strict probability.[21]

Having already praised the book as one in which Melville "made ample amends . . . for the grotesqueness and prolixity of *Mardi,*"[22] the review urged Melville to continue in the vein of *Redburn* and strangely enough, considering the universal popularity of *Typee,* to "let Polynesia alone."[23] Like the other two magazines, the *Albion* extolled Melville's exact pictures of ships and sailors, adding that he revealed more talent than his predecessors, who wrote of the picturesque while Melville often chose unpromising or even repulsive scenes and treated them cleverly.[24] The *Albion* also noted the "unusual gravity of the book," overshadowing its "quiet, subdued humor," and it agreed with others that in the London episode Melville was "out of his own walk" and that he was as inept as Dickens in treating high life.[25] The *Literary American* observed in *Redburn* a power Melville had not displayed before "of drawing the darker pictures, the shadows, of life, with a sombre reality," and it thought the plot more interesting and the style more nervous though less imaginative than Melville's previous work.[26] The review in N. P. Willis' *Home Journal,* perhaps written by Willis himself, who knew Melville, struck an unusual note by linking *Redburn* with Rousseau's *Confessions* and Lamartine's *Confidences.*[27] The writer also took issue with most of his fellow critics by observing that *Redburn,* however popular it might be, would probably "not raise the author's literary reputation from the pinnacle where *Mardi* placed it." [28]

Several briefer notices praised the vivid realism in *Redburn,* compared Melville favorably with Defoe and Marryat, and commended its humor, charm, pathos, and originality. "It is written for the million," said *Noah's Times and Messenger,* "and the million will doubtless be delighted with its racy description of the life of a young sailor." [29] The *Boston Post* was deeply impressed because *Redburn* "seemed to be fact, word for word." [30] The *Baltimore American* saw in it an abundance of "freshness," "humor," and character description which maintained Melville's reputation as "the Defoe of the Sea." [31] The *Hartford Republican* thought *Redburn* had "higher merits than any other volume from the same pen." [32] Melville does "nothing *secundum artem,*" wrote the reviewer in *Sartain's Union Magazine:*

> He imitates nobody; he is evidently "a law to himself." Surely it is refreshing in this age of stereotyping and fac-similes, to meet with one so unique, so perfectly individual.[33]

A succinct notice in *Graham's Magazine,* while agreeing that Melville should be called the Defoe of the ocean, drew attention to his "deviltry," a quality not found in Defoe. The critic thought that *Redburn* lacked the "intellectual merit" of *Mardi* but that it was more interesting. He commended its "rapidity of movement" and its value to other greenhorns like the hero and pronounced that it should become one of the most popular books of the sea.[34] Finally, the *United States Magazine and Democratic Review* said that in *Redburn* Melville triumphed "as the most captivating of ocean authors." [35] The chorus of praise, though often superficial or indiscriminate, was sung from Boston to Washington and from New York to Albany and tiny Lansingburgh.[36]

On the other hand, *Redburn* did not escape indifference or even adverse criticism among Melville's compatriots. The influential *North American Review* and the *Knickerbocker Magazine* ignored it, though the latter, in a review of *White-Jacket,* confessed to being reassured by *Redburn,* after the "pseudo-philosophical rifacciemento [*sic*] of Carlyle and Emerson in *Mardi.*" [37] The writer of the notice in the *Southern Quarterly Review,* besides thinking *Redburn* a much lesser work than the "wild, warm, and richly fanciful" *Mardi,* pointed out certain weaknesses. The hero, he complained, is not "symmetrically drawn. He forgets his part at times; and the wild, very knowing and bold boy ashore, becomes a sneak and a numbskull aboard ship." [38] If this overstates the case (Redburn is never a sneak), it is still basically true. The writer also objected to "all that foreign graffing" of Harry Bolton in the gambling house and in "sundry fantastic scenes" aboard ship. But the explanation of these aberrations was both sympathetic and perspicacious:

> The truth is, the author has an imagination which naturally becomes restive in the monotonous details of such a career as that of Redburn, and, in breaking away from bounds self-imposed, does not suffer him to see how much hurt is done to his previous labors.[39]

Melville himself would probably have been the first to agree with this.

The most severely critical of the American reviews was the one in *Holden's Dollar Magazine.* The editor, Charles F. Briggs, had been a sailor before the mast, had known Liverpool, and had written amusing if superficial tales of his experiences.[40] If he was the author of the article, it represented the objections of the only critic who could meet Melville on both literary and nautical grounds, and since it displays familiarity with the forecastle and Liverpool, Briggs probably wrote it.[41] At any rate, the writer challenged the authenticity of the book as personal experience. Many of the incidents, he said, must have happened to the author, but there were also "many forecastle traditions familiar to every sailor, which the author claims as his own, that tend to create a suspicion of the actuality of the occurrences which befel him." [42] He objected to the rhapsodical sections, like that on the hand organ, and declared that Melville would have produced a better book by confining himself to a simple record of facts. But though he discovered many faults and denied that Melville had Defoe's simplicity and artistic accuracy, he still found the book worthy: "for clothed in the fresh and poetic style of the author, the incidents of his first voyage charm us more than novelties would in a less beautiful dress." [43]

Thus Melville's American critics received *Redburn* warmly and with only few dissonant notes. In England the book won somewhat less favor. The *Critic,* which habitually reviewed almost everything the publishers sent in, ignored it. *Blackwood's Edinburgh Magazine,* it is true, gave thirteen pages to *Redburn,*[44] and since the magazine ordinarily reviewed only one or two books each month of the rank of Chateaubriand's *Memoirs* or Lord Baybrook's edition of the *Diary of Samuel Pepys,*[45] this attention was flattering indeed. Yet most of the criticism, typically stilted and patronizing, exposed Melville's defects. "A good deal of detail and ingenuity," it declared, were "necessary to fill two volumes" about a "hardy wrong-headed lad" whose adventures were neither numerous nor extraordinary.[46] Recalling Redburn's leaving home with a meager outfit and no food, the review said:

It seems the author's aim to start his hero in life under every possible circumstance of disadvantage and hardship; and to do this, he rather loses sight of probability.[47]

The writer then scored the inconsistency in Redburn's characterization. "A sharp enough lad on shore" and "altogether precocious in experience of the world's disappointments," he "seems converted, by the first sniff of salt water, into as arrant a simpleton as ever made mirth in a cockpit." Melville must surely have been thinking of Peter Simple when he contrived the deck-washing scene, but it was "altogether out of character." [48] So was Redburn's naïveté in his attempt to evangelize the sailor and to visit the captain.

After guarded approbation of Melville's sailor sketches, the review went on to deride most of the Liverpool and London scenes. While it paid grudging tribute to Melville's ability to make the commonplaces of boardinghouses and emigrant ships interesting, it laughed sarcastically at the picture of English clergymen preaching "in full canonicals" at street corners and condemned the Launcelott's Hey chapter as "utterly absurd." [49] Melville's account of the English aristocracy seemed to be based "upon the revelations of Sunday newspapers, and upon that class of novels usually supposed to be written by discarded valets-de-chambre." [50] Like most of the reviews, it attacked the gaming-house chapter ("fantastical . . . rubbish" [51]), and it sneered at Harry Bolton as a specimen of the English aristocrat.

From this broad revelation of "Mr. Melville's defects," the review turned in self-confessed fairness to examples of "his happier manner," like the deaths of Miguel and Jackson, which it quoted at length. This was "plain, vigorous, unaffected writing." Mr. Melville was most effective in such passages, and if he would "put away affectation and curb the eccentricities of his fancy," he might become "an agreeable writer of nautical fictions," though never as potent as Cringle or Marryat.[52] After disapproving of Harry Bolton's death as "a most lame and impotent conclusion," the review closed with a paternal admonition to Melville to mend his faults and live up to the promise which "Maga" had hitherto found in him.

This painstaking exposition of *Redburn*'s faults could not have helped sales very much, but most of the other English notices and reviews would have counteracted it. The *Athenaeum* charged that the humor in *Redburn* was derived from *Peter Simple* and seemed pale beside Marryat's. Yet it also quoted numerous scenes as evidence of better writing than *Typee* and *Omoo* and of striking improvement over *Mardi*.[53] A single-paragraph notice in *John Bull* commended the "diversity" and the "liveliness of tone and graphic power of delineation" and avowed that Melville promised to fill the void left by the death of Marryat.[54] To the *Spectator, Redburn* was "even more remarkable than [Melville's] stories 'founded on fact.'"[55] Redburn's character was inconsistent at times, but even if the idea of placing a simple-minded lad from a decent home in the rude surroundings of a ship appeared in *Peter Simple,* Melville had handled it with originality. The book's interest, concluded the *Spectator,* lay in its "quiet naturalness. It reads like a 'true story'—as if it had all taken place."[56]

To this measured but sincere approval, *Bentley's Miscellany* added an even more sympathetic criticism. The critic valued *Redburn* higher than its predecessors and alone among contemporary readers, he brought to light the central theme. With a singular sensitivity he pointed out that the hero, a son of a gentleman, goes to sea with delightful expectations of travel and with no suspicion of shipboard drudgeries and the little respect accorded social rank. "The interest of the book," he wrote, "consists in the details of the process by which, item after item, he is disenchanted of these pleasant delusions."[57] If the action was slight, it was full of charm derived from the vitality and minuteness of the descriptions and "the natural feelings of the boy throughout the startling ordeal of his first cruise."[58] The gambling episode was "perhaps a little in excess," but a spice of such romanticizing was a welcome contrast. Like all reviewers, the author emphasized the "sense of reality" as constituting "the paramount merit of the work."[59] It remained for the critic in the *Literary Gazette,* who also praised Melville's graphic depiction of common life, to call *Redburn* "as perfect a specimen of the naval yarn as we ever read."[60]

In many respects the comments of these early reviewers, both English and American, constitute better literary criticism than *Redburn* has received from modern observers. Whether they considered it fact or fiction or a mixture—and there was every shade of opinion about this matter—they focused on the book itself as literature, not as autobiography. They remarked the improvement in style over Melville's previous works and his extraordinary capacity for erecting the illusion of reality. They quoted memorable scenes, not as evidence of what happened to the author, but as specimens of his artistic power in depicting life. Unlike many modern authorities on Melville, they knew Marryat well, and whatever their opinions of the comparative merits of the two, they were quick to detect Melville's indebtedness to *Peter Simple.*[61] Thus they saw what has been largely overlooked in the twentieth century: that many of the scenes, instead of being personal history, were contrived for humor. Indeed, one has to look back to these writers almost exclusively to find any mention whatsoever of the humor in *Redburn,* an oversight that makes most modern authorities look somewhat obtuse. Finally, the critic who seems to have known most about the sea accused Melville of representing well-known forecastle traditions as his own experience. The observation receives support from another critic who wrote a few years later:

> We do not think there is any living author who rivals [Melville] in his peculiar powers of describing scenes at sea and sea-life in a manner at once poetical, forcible, accurate, and, above all, original. But it is his *style* that is original rather than his *matter*. He has read prodigiously on all nautical subjects—naval history, narratives of voyages and shipwrecks, fictions, &c.—and he never scruples to deftly avail himself of these sources of information.[62]

The emphasis on originality in this last quotation is also common to most of the other criticisms. It is the mark of the reader who knew well the literature of the sea up to the time Melville wrote. In failing to recognize this originality in the use of traditional materials, modern critics have made a tacit confession of ignorance, at the same time undervaluing Melville as an imaginative artist.

The immediate enthusiasm for Redburn in 1849 and 1850 was somewhat tempered a few years later. In 1853, "Sir Nathaniel," reviewing Melville's achievement in the *New Monthly Magazine,* described the book as "prosy, bald, and eventless," [63] and Fitz-James O'Brien virtually ignored it in a survey of Melville's work.[64] Later he wrote that though *Redburn* was a rather clever work, it contained an "extraordinary mixture of sense and nonsense, of accuracy and extravagance, of exact portraiture, and of incredible caricature . . . ." [65] The extravagance lay in Melville's misrepresentation of the habits of English aristocrats, in the gambling-house episode, and in some fantastic metaphors, but beside all this was "the freshest and finest writing— . . . stories of nautical adventure, told with a grace that Marryat never approached, and a fire that Cooper never surpassed." [66]

O'Brien's notes on *Redburn* were almost the last criticism the book received in the nineteenth century in America.[67] In England, the last of the contemporary evaluations was even more severe. The anonymous author of "A Trio of American Sailor Authors" in the *Dublin University Magazine* for January 1856 found some clever chapters in the book but repeated earlier denunciations of many of the Liverpool scenes and the London chapter as "outrageously improbable." [68] The reviewer was wrong in stating that *Redburn* "neither obtained nor deserved much success," but he had virtually sealed the book in its tomb, where except for a single tribute it would rest almost unnoticed for nearly two generations.

In the record of sales and editions of *Redburn* until 1887 lies further evidence of its obscurity after the middle of the century. Following its initial success, Harper reissued it in 1850 and again in 1855, after the fire two years before that destroyed 296 of the 427 copies on hand.[69] But after the Harper reprint in 1863, it was nearly sixty years before the next American issue came off the press. The sales figures tell the same story of neglect. By March 4, 1852, Richard Bentley, having regained only a quarter of the £100 he had advanced Melville on account of half profits on *Redburn,* had a deficit of over £76.[70] There is evidence, too, that he was forced to remainder some of the 415 copies then on hand.[71] At any rate, he did not reprint it, and it was seventy-three years before another English edition came out.[72] In America, after selling 3,695 copies from November 1849 to April 1851, *Redburn* averaged only 28 sales a year for the next thirty-six years, ranging from 171 in 1853 to 1 in 1876.[73] It is true that *Typee* and *Omoo* were Melville's best sellers; yet *Redburn* ran close to *White-Jacket* in the second rank and sold much better than *Mardi* or *Moby-Dick.*[74] But a novel that sells only a thousand copies in thirty-six years cannot be said to have made an enduring mark on its century. Richard Henry Dana, Jr., had liked it;[75] Lowell owned a copy;[76] and Hawthorne wrote to Duyckinck that "no writer ever put the reality before his reader more unflinchingly than [Melville] does in 'Redburn,' and 'White Jacket.'"[77] But the public showed no permanent interest, and the retrospective depreciations of the critics in the middle fifties apparently reflected the general judgment.

For nearly thirty years after Fitz-James O'Brien's criticisms of Melville in 1857, *Redburn* seems to have escaped mention in the public press. In the leanest years of Melville's reputation, only a solitary Englishman raised his voice to hail Melville as an author. To W. Clark Russell, the English writer of scores of nautical tales and an ardent propagandist for the sailors in the merchant service, where he had served for eight years, Melville held first place among the "poets of the deep."[78] He praised *Redburn* for its mingling of realism with "the finest fancy" and for its accurate pictures of English and Yankee sailors and of the horrors in the steerage.[79] Four years later Russell wrote directly to Melville in words that must have reminded him of a ghost:

> Quite recently I have been reading your "Redburn" for the third or fourth time and have closed it more deeply impressed than heretofore with the descriptive power that vitalizes every page, especially with your marvellous creation of the man Jackson whose character I know to be absolutely true to forecastle life.[80]

In 1892 Russell brought Melville once more before the public in an article in the *North American Review,*[81] whose august editors had never taken the slightest notice of Melville during the years of his fame. Russell affirmed that Melville, with Dana, had "expanded American literature immeasurably" by being the "first to lift the hatch and show the world what passes in a ship's forecastle." "No such book" as *Redburn,* he thought, "was to be found in literature in the English language." It seemed to him that Melville had said to himself, " 'I, too, have suffered and seen and know' " and that he had determined to throw open the forecastle and help make all English readers understand "that we merchant seamen form a great world of human beings . . . ."[82]

Russell's tribute to Melville emphasized its value as propaganda rather than as art. But despite his latter-day eulogy, *Redburn* did not figure in the revival of Melville's works following his death in 1891, when *Typee, Omoo, Moby-Dick,* and *White-Jacket* were reissued in numerous editions in the course of the next three decades. In this period, criticism of Melville began to stir into wakefulness, and occasionally a few verdicts about *Redburn* were heard—from H. S. Salt,[83] F. J. Mather, Jr.,[84] and John St. Loe Strachey[85]—while John Masefield confessed to loving *Redburn* best among Melville's writings.[86] But almost no one else from 1891 to 1921 noticed the book.[87] It remained for the critics of the next fifteen years to revive it, though with harmful results to its proper position as a work of art.

The modern interest in *Redburn* began with Raymond Weaver's biography of Melville in 1921. His assertion that "despite its unaccountable neglect, . . . it is none the less important in the history of letters as a very notable achievement,"[88] and his reproduction of numerous pages of the text laid the foundation for a renewed attention to the book. With the publication of the Constable edition of Melville's complete works in 1922-1924, *Redburn* was again available for the first time in nearly sixty years.[89] Weaver's pioneering biography also led to other editions, of which fourteen separate ones have been issued since 1922, far fewer, of course, than those of *Moby-Dick* and *Typee* but close to those of *Omoo* and *White-Jacket.*[90]

Most modern criticism of *Redburn* has fallen, like Weaver's, into the biographical fallacy described in my Introduction. It has focused less on the book's merit than on its supposed record of Melville's real or spiritual history. But many victims of the fallacy and others less credulous have uttered critical judgments that in the aggregate compose its present reputation. John St. Loe Strachey, an admirer of Melville's for thirty years, struck an early blow for objective criticism of *Redburn* by citing passages from the book as examples of good writing rather than as illuminating autobiography.[91] Van Wyck Brooks, though assuming that *Redburn* was "the account of Melville's first voyage," praised the description of the burning corpse and the "masterly portrait" of Jackson and noted the "delight in health and physical beauty" that linked Melville with Whitman.[92] In 1924 H. P. Marshall contributed the original comment that *Redburn* was more human than Melville's previous works, its emotions being more within the range of the reader's experience.[93] In remarking that the sympathy Melville arouses for young Redburn in his disillusion makes the story "an intimate, personal affair," [94] he hinted at one of the qualities least noted in the book, the directness and psychological truth with which it conveys a boy's passionate feelings.

In contrast to these observations was the introduction to a new edition of *Redburn* by Preston H. Early, who played sedulous ape to Weaver and passed *Redburn* off as a "complete return to the autobiographical manner." [95] The judgment represents a typical opinion of the critics. John Freeman, for example, admired the story as "a chapter of innocent autobiography." [96] However, he also took time to extol the "unaffected and pure English" of *Redburn* [97] and the "growth in literary grace" by which it excelled *Typee* and *Omoo*.[98] Lewis Mumford, to whom *Redburn* was "autobiography with only the faintest disguises," [99] also considered it a "sound, well-written book" [100] and "an honest narrative, with none of the mildewed rainbows . . . that usually characterize such efforts." [101] Like Weaver, he pointed out Melville's superiority over Dana in subordinating recondite nautical description to the creation of the ship that formed part of the sailor's consciousness and in embodying characters rather than merely describing them.[102] However, his admiration for the skill with which Melville presents "a boy's consciousness of the world" [103] is only unwitting tribute to Melville as an artist since Mumford believed that Melville was merely reproducing his own sensations.

Other followers of the Weaver school continued to overemphasize the biographical element in *Redburn* during the next decade, but the period also saw a new trend in Melville scholarship designed to reveal the fiction lying behind the supposed facts in his personal narratives. The work of Forsythe, Anderson, Thorp, and others from 1935 to 1939 showed Melville's methods in using sources and romanticizing his career in the South Seas and at the same time drew more attention to Melville's achievements as an artist.[104] Thorp was the first scholar who actually discovered a literary source for *Redburn*. With this information, he treated the book as fiction in which Melville aimed at two effects:

> to simulate the naiveté of a proud, innocent, and romantic boy and to make the dominant theme of the story the pathetic instance of a gentleman's son forced by poverty to endure the squalor of life in the fo'c's'le of the *Highlander*.[105]

His exposition of the manner in which Melville pillaged the Liverpool guidebook for Redburn's "true experiences" reinforces his assumption about the nature of the book and his dicta that "Melville was not telling the story of his life in *Redburn*" and that Redburn was a created character.[106] Despite such scholarly discoveries, Jean Simon treated *Redburn* as the revelation not only of Melville's youth but also of the bitterness he felt at the time of writing the book.[107] Yet, with much critical acumen, he observed Melville's sensitive depiction of the emotions of a young boy. From the purely artistic point of view, he wrote, and quite aside from the biographical interest, Redburn is a striking figure of a child whose eyes have been opened to the sorrows and evils of the world but who still keeps looking for love. Although Melville arouses our pity almost in spite of himself, he has created a child so moving that we think of those of Dickens and Daudet.[108] Simon also saw that *Redburn* was more carefully constructed than anyone had supposed, with the descriptive chapters carefully framed by the narrative.[109]

The criticism of F. O. Matthiessen, though unsystematic and inconveniently dispersed through many pages of his *American Renaissance,* is within its limits perhaps the best now extant. At least it resists the biographical fallacy completely and attempts to state the significance of *Redburn* in relation to the growth of Melville as an artist, as a maker of tragedies, and as a political and social observer. Treating it mostly under a section called "The Economic Factor," he sees in it "the waking of Melville's tragic sense," the miseries of the world having been so impressed on him that no optimistic contemporary palliatives could wash them away.[110] He notes that it is a study in disillusion, of "innocence confronted with the world," but that unfortunately Melville does not hold the line since he allows the thoughts of a much older person to replace the revelation of Redburn's inexperience.[111] He sees poverty as the most recurrent theme, and he sees too its benefits for Redburn, who grows beyond self-pity as he learns about other poor people. In his awareness of Melville's tragic powers, he perceives the unsentimental treatment of the immigrants which shows that Melville had developed "the balance that is indispensable for the writer of tragedy." [112]

Matthiessen also finds in the contrast of Redburn and Jackson the problem that was to plague Melville's mind until *Billy Budd:* "the opposition between the generous heart and the ingrown, self-consuming mind." [113] In Redburn's pity for the evil tyrant of the "Highlander," as in the representation of tenderness in the wicked Claggart, Matthiessen sees further evidence of Melville's tragic vision, which faced the evil in men squarely but viewed it with compassion.[114] He holds that *Redburn,* like *White-Jacket,* was written before Melville had learned how to employ symbols in fusing the abstract and imaginative elements, which he had handled unsuccessfully in *Mardi,* with the immediate, concrete experience in order to express the "intricate correspondence between matter and spirit" which emerges in *Moby-Dick.*[115] Finally, he mentions what no previous critic had touched on: Melville's "belief in the potential good of democracy," expressed through the passage in *Redburn* that celebrates "the opening promise of America, the free mixture of bloods which would make us not a mere nation but a world." [116]

Matthiessen's criticism of *Redburn* uncovers many powers previously slighted, and for the first time it views the book with the perspective of a man familiar with the discoveries of Melville scholars in the 1930's. Yet in his search for the higher artistic and social meanings he ignores or glosses over many of *Redburn*'s virtues, like the remarkable evocation of a young boy's tender emotions, the sturdy fabric of its style, and its vivid realism. He considers it the "most moving of its author's books before *Moby Dick,* since it does not read like a journal of events,"[117] but he says also that it has "the quality that comes when material is not written off the top of the mind but rises to the surface through assimilated memories."[118] This is partially true, to be sure, since Melville unquestionably relied on his memory in *Redburn,* but it leaves little room for the intricate transformations of experience, the reworkings of sources, and the pure invention that form almost as much of the texture of *Redburn* as they do of *Moby-Dick.*

Matthiessen's concentration upon the tragic quality in *Redburn* paved the way for another similar approach, that of William Ellery Sedgwick. He treats it along with Melville's other works as part of the "unfolding development" of the tragic drama of Melville's mind as it tried to preserve equilibrium before the necessity of apprehending "'the absolute condition of present things,' regardless of the desolation that this invariably brings."[119] Thus the book must reveal Melville's perceptions of evil at the time of writing. However, by identifying Redburn with his creator, Sedgwick falls into a bewildering ambiguity. For example, we have his judgment on the guidebook incident, "a crucial episode":

> Whether the episode is fiction or not, the discovery that this book on which he had relied so much, "the book full of fine old family associations . . . was next to useless," shows that Melville had glimpsed, in his initial experience of the world, that his father's world of social privilege and economic security, of right and wrong firmly established by the sanctions and prescriptions of Presbyterian orthodoxy . . . did not rest on immutable foundations.[120]

But the statement is logically confused, for it says in effect that whether the hotel incident happened or not, it happened.[121] Besides, its bifocal time perspective debases the value of Sedgwick's interpretation; at one and the same time he sees the boy passing consciously through tragic adventures and the mature author just discovering the tragic implications of his supposed adventures.

Sedgwick's line of thought becomes impossible to follow when he asserts that

> while still in his formative years, [Melville's] notion of original sin was horribly realized for him in the impressions which he drew from his characterization of the sailor Jackson.[122]

But the characterization of Jackson was made in 1849; the impressions, if true, were obtained in 1839; and Melville most certainly did not, in his formative years, realize a notion of original sin from a characterization that he wrote ten years later. Sedgwick's interpretation of *Redburn* is thus badly blurred and logically indefensible because of his failure to disassociate author and narrator, artist and artistic creation. There is tragic vision in *Redburn,* as Matthiessen makes quite clear, but Sedgwick's handling of the book adds little to his complex thesis.

Three recent studies of Melville have in one way or another contributed something to the interpretation and standing of *Redburn.* The most original is Richard Chase's assimilation of incidents from the book into his picture of a mythological, Protean Melville. Chase reads *Redburn* only as "the first large-scale portrait of Melville's Ishmael,"[123] as the depiction, that is, of one of the two basic types of hero in Melville's works. The other is Prometheus, whom Redburn also resembles, it seems, for his very name "is apparently meant to signify 'the Promethean fire.'"[124] This specialized treatment of the book is not concerned about distinctions between Melville and Redburn, both of whom are stripped of individual features and melted down, along with Ishmael, Prometheus, and "the Handsome Sailor" found often in Melville, into a generic figure called "the young man." The interpretation is perhaps provocative, though why "Redburn" does not just as apparently signify blushing innocence is not clear. At any rate, one hears no qualitative judgments from Chase about form, imaginative power, interest, or style. A few such judgments do appear in Geoffrey Stone's study, chiefly on style, which impresses him deeply. In its coolness, in the poignancy it gives to adolescent experience, in the safeguards it provided against ornamentation, and in its poetic quality, Melville had an instrument, thinks Stone, that was "capable of further extension than he realized."[125]

It is in the latest critical study of Melville that *Redburn* receives something like its due. Newton Arvin forthrightly ranks the book as deeper in substance, feeling, complexity, and connotation than *Typee* and *Omoo* and more mature and expert in style. Its subject, "the initiation of innocence into evil," is more profound, and it is a theme, Arvin reminds us, that has a "peculiarly American dimension" so that Redburn deserves a place beside *Ormond, The Marble Faun,* and *What Maisie Knew.*[126] The evil in man is concentrated in Jackson, whom Melville has made so wicked as to give him almost heroic stature. The evil in society is crystallized in the infernal city of Liverpool, of which Melville's picture is equal in power to those of the Paris of Balzac and Beaudelaire, the London of Dickens, and the Dublin of Joyce. Arvin points out that though all this evil is in some measure balanced by "the moral relief of goodness,"[127] the goodness is only passive, since the hero is chiefly a victim. In asserting the superiority of *Redburn* over *Typee* and *Omoo* in its symbolic elements, Arvin treats a long series of pretty plain events, like collisions at sea and the plague on the "Highlander," as "images," and he elevates the voyage to "a metaphor of death and rebirth";[128] but he also perceives Melville's power, first displayed in *Redburn,* of "endowing ordinary objects, ordinary incidents, with a penumbra of feeling and suggestion that imparts to them a symbolic character."[129] He recognizes too the vivacity and the humor of Redburn, which temper its pessimism. He is among the first to rate the book above *White-Jacket* because the latter suffers from imaginative fatigue and hasty composition. On the whole, Arvin concludes, in style, imagery, metaphor, and form, *Redburn* is rather a segment of the spiral rise toward *Moby-Dick* than a descent to *Typee* and *Omoo*.[130]

With Arvin's criticism, *Redburn* comes pretty well into its own. The forthcoming scholarly edition of the book by Willard Thorp should also increase its stature. A widened knowledge of the extent of Melville's creative achievement in *Redburn* should help place it at its proper level.

This survey of *Redburn*'s reputation is a miniature history of taste and criticism in the last hundred years, reflecting as it does the changing standards, interests, and methods of three or four generations. The nineteenth century was concerned largely with the surface meaning. It liked the comic spirit of the book and its apparently literal truth. It relished the sense of sharing real adventures and of meeting real people. In its bias toward optimism, it ignored, on the whole, the tragic notes, the social and economic criticism, and the humanitarianism. The twentieth century, with its awakened social consciousness and its sharpened sense of the split between the modern individual and his environment, has quite naturally laid heavy stress on these elements. Characteristically humorless, it has been mostly blind to the comedy of *Redburn,* but its earnestness has at least been able to lay bare the moral conflict between innocence and evil. Inevitably, it has tried to be "scientific": it has applied its understanding of psychology and psychoanalysis to the interpretation of the book, perhaps with more self-assurance than persuasiveness. Its wide knowledge of Melville's works has enabled it to see *Redburn* in terms of his total achievement, to trace theme and pattern in evolution. Its limited knowledge of Melville's early life has generally provoked intuitive rather than inductive criticism. Frequently, it has treated Melville and Redburn as though they were but two plates of a stereopticon slide that must form a clear, three-dimensional image if viewed through the lenses of Freud. In treating Redburn only as Melville's anima it has overlooked such forces as the traditions of previous sea literature, the taste of the public, Melville's supple powers of invention, and his need for cash. Like the nineteenth century, it has done its best work when it has treated *Redburn* as a work of art in itself, in relation to Melville's other works, and in relation to comparable works in the whole history of literature.

NOTES

Notes to Introduction

1. Bertrand M. Wainger, "Herman Melville: A Study in Disillusion," *Union College Bulletin,* XXV (January 1932), 41.

2. Charles R. Anderson, *Melville in the South Seas* (New York: Columbia University Press, 1939); Russell Thomas, "Yarn for Melville's *Typee,*" *Philological Quarterly,* XV (January 1936), 16-29; Robert Forsythe, "Herman Melville in the Marquesas," *ibid.,* 1-15.

3. *Herman Melville, Mariner and Mystic* (New York: George H. Doran & Company, 1921), p. 72.

4. *Ibid.,* p. 81.

5. *Ibid.,* p. 77.

6. *Herman Melville* ("English Men of Letters Series" [New York: The Macmillan Company, 1926]), p. 7.

7. *Ibid.,* p. 11.

8. *Herman Melville* (New York: Harcourt, Brace and Company, 1929), p. 109.

9. Ludwig Lewisohn, *Expression in America* (New York: Harper and Brothers, 1932), pp. 187, 190. For a psychoanalytical interpretation of *Redburn,* see Frederick Rosenheim, "Flight from Home," *The American Imago,* I (December 1940), 1-4.

10. *Herman Melville, marin, metaphysicien, et poète* (Paris: Boivin et Cie., 1939).

11. "Herman Melville," *Dictionary of American Biography,* XII, 522. See also Brooks's *Emerson and Others* (New York: E. P. Dutton and Company, 1927), pp. 174, 187-88.

12. *Herman Melville, The Tragedy of Mind* (Cambridge: Harvard University Press, 1944).

13. Geoffrey Stone, *Melville* (New York: Sheed and Ward, 1949); Newton Arvin, *Herman Melville* ("American Men of Letters Series" [(New York): William Sloane Associates, 1950]), p. 42; Richard Chase, *Herman Melville, A Critical Study* (New York: The Macmillan Company, 1949), p. 2. *Whitaker's Cumulative Book List,* a register of all books published in England during 1949, offers us a final instance of the biographical fallacy, at the popular level. It lists *Redburn* simply as "biog."

14. "Melville's Use of Autobiographical Material in Redburn" (Master's thesis, University of Chicago, 1938), pp. 27-28.

15. *Herman Melville: Representative Selections* (New York: American Book Company, 1938), p. xlviii.

16. "Redburn's Prosy Old Guidebook," *PMLA,* LIII (December 1938), 1146-56.

17. *American Renaissance* (New York: Oxford University Press, 1941), pp. 396-99 and *passim.*

18. Although the time limits of this study extend some fifteen months beyond the period of Melville's youth that relates, strictly speaking, to *Red-*

burn, it has seemed reasonable to follow his story to the natural termination of his early years. I have deliberately sought out every new fact that might add to the present knowledge of his life, with the result that the biographical portions of this book exceed the critical. But students of Melville will perhaps condone the excess on the grounds that no existing account of his youth makes full use of the legitimate sources—and that for the understanding of Melville's complex personality and genius every fact has either actual or potential meaning.

Notes to Chapter I

1. *Moby-Dick,* I, 6. Unless otherwise indicated, all references to Melville's works are to the Standard Edition (16 vols.; London: Constable and Company, 1922-1924).

2. I am indebted to the kindness of Jay Leyda for this information.

3. Allan Melvill to Peter Gansevoort, August 2, 1819 (G-L). Allan Melvill never spelled his name with an *e* at the end; Herman was actually born "Herman Melvill." But since Herman, his mother, and his brothers and sisters all added the *e* at a later date, I have followed their practice, though preserving Allan's spelling when referring to him alone.

4. Herman Melville to Lemuel Shaw, September 10, 1849 (S).

5. The Gansevoort-Lansing Collection contains his writing books dated "West Boston School, November 22, 1790," "Amherst Academy, January 3, 1792," "West Boston Academy, September 24, 1793," and a fourth, for which no school is given, dated "November 1st, 1794." In this he copied a poem "Swearing," which concludes:

> "For 'tis a wicked and a great offence
> To call on GOD for each Impertinence."

6. Allan Melvill's Journal, August 22-September 3, 1801 (M).

7. *Ibid.,* January 15, 1811.

8. In 1806, Count Rumford, the physicist, essayist, and count of the Holy Roman Empire, requested him to bear certain important papers from Paris to his daughter in England. (The Count's note, dated July 22, 1806, is in G-L.)

9. Allan Melvill's Journal, April 6, 1811 (M).

10. *Ibid.,* June 27, 1811.

11. The portrait is now in the Metropolitan Museum in New York. Weaver's statement that it was painted in Paris must be weighed against the fact that Allan Melvill was in America from 1807 to 1811 (see his Journal).

12. Weaver, *Herman Melville, Mariner and Mystic,* pp. 56-57; Mumford, *Herman Melville,* pp. 13-14; Simon, *Herman Melville, marin, metaphysicien, et poète,* pp. 28-29.

13. Copy of letter of Thomas Melvill to David Swan, May 6, 1811 (G-L).

14. This sister died in 1812.

15. A few lines from Allan's letter to Lemuel Shaw of April 28, 1804 (M), illustrate what talents he had:

> "Ye powers that rule the pen, if such there be,
> Inspire, enliven, and bestow on me,
> The gift of wielding it with ease and grace,
> Not the dull pedant's systematic grace."

16. Allan Melvill to Lemuel Shaw, April 28, 1804 (M).

17. See the volume of Akenside's *The Pleasures of the Imagination* (n.p., 1813), inscribed "Miss Maria Gansevoort from her friend A M" (M); John M. Bradford, *The Fear of the Lord, the Hope of Freedom, A Sermon* . . . (Albany, February 18, 1814), inscribed "from Miss M G—A M" (G-L); and Thomas Campbell, *The Pleasures of Hope* (New York, 1811), inscribed "Miss Maria Gansevoort from her friend A M Albany March 11 1814" (G-L). The latter volume is annotated.

18. The volume is in M.

19. Records of the First Reformed Dutch Church of Albany and the Melville family Bible (G-L).

20. Allan Melvill to Catherine Van Schaick Gansevoort, Maria's mother, October 20, 1814 (G-L).

21. *Ibid.*

22. Maria Gansevoort was born in Albany, April 6, 1791. The Assessment Rolls for the City of Albany, 1812 (in the County Clerk's Office in Albany), show that only half a dozen individuals paid higher taxes than General Peter Gansevoort. It was Herman Melville's opinion that the large tract of land in Northumberland County, which increased the General's wealth considerably, was granted to him for his military services (Elizabeth Shaw Melville to Catherine Gansevoort Lansing, May 28, 1891, printed in V. H. Paltsits, *Family Correspondence of Herman Melville, 1830-1904, in the Gansevoort-Lansing Collection* [New York: New York Public Library, 1929], p. 65).

23. Bills for tutoring in these subjects, dated from 1804 to 1814, survive in M and G-L.

24. Mrs. Eleanor Melville Metcalf, Melville's granddaughter, has kindly supplied the information about her great grandmother's piano.

25. See the invitation to Miss Gansevoort to a ball in honor of Commodore Perry, Albany, November 8, 1813 (G-L). In a letter to Peter Gansevoort, January 22, 1823 (G-L), she speaks of attending assemblies in her youth.

26. Peter Gansevoort to Leonard H. Gansevoort, December 30, 1805 (G-L).

27. There is a photograph of the portrait reproduced in Weaver, *Herman Melville, Mariner and Mystic,* opposite p. 64, in G-L.

28. Melville family Bible (G-L). Helen Maria was born August 4, 1817.

29. The *Albany Directory* for 1816 lists Allan Melvill and Catherine Gansevoort at the same address, 316 North Market Street. See also the receipt signed by Allan Melvill, Albany, May 6, 1816, for $675 for the board of Mrs. Catherine Gansevoort and servant for nine months (M) and the invitation to dinner from Governor Clinton to Allan Melvill, February 26, 1818 (G-L).

30. Draft of letter of Allan Melvill to J. S. Cast, October 31, 1817 (M).

31. This and subsequent debts of Allan Melvill to Thomas Melvill are itemized in the copy of an "Action by John D'Wolf and Lemuel Shaw before the Supreme Judicial Court in Suffolk County [Massachusetts]," February 19, 1834 (G-L).

32. In 1811 the Reverend David Swan of the parish of Scoonie, Leven, Fifeshire, Scotland, where Thomas Melvill's grandfather had been pastor for many years, wrote to Thomas that he was entitled to a share in the estate mentioned, being next of kin. Thomas wrote immediately to Allan, then abroad, but the letter failed to reach him before he embarked for America. When Allan went to Europe again in 1818 he undertook the mission referred to. See letters of David Swan to Thomas Melvill, January 7, 1811, Thomas Melvill to Allan Melvill, May 6, 1811, and Allan Melvill to Thomas Melvill, May 31, 1818 (G-L).

33. Allan Melvill to Thomas Melvill, May 14, 1818, added to letter of May 12, and to Maria Melville, May 28, 1818, added to letter of May 21 (G-L).

34. Allan Melvill to Maria Melville, June 14, 1818, and to Thomas Melvill, July 5, 1818 (G-L).

35. Allan Melvill to Thomas Melvill, May 31, June 27, and July 5, 1818 (G-L).

36. Allan Melvill to Maria Melville, May 17 and June 8, 1818 (G-L), and Journal, June 8, 1818 (M).

37. Allan Melvill to Thomas Melvill, May 31, 1818 (G-L).

38. *Ibid.*

39. Allan Melvill to Maria Melville, May 14, 1818, added to letter of May 12 (G-L).

40. Allan Melvill to Maria Melville, April 19, 1818 (G-L).

41. Allan Melvill to Maria Melville, May 14, 1818, added to letter of May 12 (G-L).

42. Allan Melvill to Maria Melville, May 17, 1818 (G-L).

43. Alarmed at news of her ill health, he once wrote: "For Gods sake Maria take care of yourself, your welfare is too important to be neglected, my happiness depends upon it & to our children it is invaluable" (June 18, 1818, G-L). This is the only occasion in all his letters when the name of God does not appear in his schoolboy capitals.

44. Allan Melvill to Maria Melville, May 31, 1818 (G-L).

45. From a copy of his advertisement (G-L).

46. Allan Melvill to Peter Gansevoort, October 13, 1820 (G-L).

47. Allan Melvill to Thomas Melvill, June 27, 1818 (G-L).

48. Maria Melville to Peter Gansevoort, December 24, 1822, quoted by permission from Jay Leyda, "The Melville Log," to be published by Harcourt, Brace and Company.

49. The invoice is in G-L. Although Allan Melvill may have imported the books for retail sale, it is more than likely that he kept some titles for his own library.

50. Allan Melvill to Lemuel Shaw, May 25, 1823 (S).

51. In a copy of Burton's *Anatomy of Melancholy* (London, 1801) (M), there appears the autograph, "A. Melvill, 1816," and the following inscription in Herman Melville's hand: "I bought this book more than four years ago at Gowan's Store in New York. Today, Allan in looking at it, first detected the above pencil signature of my father's; who,—as it now appears—

must have had the book, with many others, sold at auction, at least twenty five years ago.—Strange! Pittsfield, July 7th, 1851."

52. Allan Melvill to Lemuel Shaw, June 20, 1804 (M).

53. Allan Melvill to Peter Gansevoort, October 17, 1829 (G-L).

54. Allan Melvill to Peter Gansevoort, September 4, 1830 (G-L).

55. Allan Melvill to Peter Gansevoort, March 11, 1822 (G-L).

56. The notes are in G-L.

57. One of the books that remained in Allan Melvill's library was *The Principles of Politeness and of Knowing the World, By the Late Lord Chesterfield, Methodised and Digested under Distinct Heads, with Additions,* by the Reverend Doctor John Trusler (Portsmouth, N.H., 1786) (M). His attitudes from the time he acquired this volume at the age of ten show a thorough mastery of its contents.

58. Allan Melvill's passport, February 28, 1818 (G-L), furnishes some of the details; the rest appear in a photograph of the portrait by Ezra Ames, now in the Huntington Library.

59. See Weaver, *Herman Melville, Mariner and Mystic,* pp. 61-62, 338.

60. In 1823, when Thomas I. Rogers was preparing an encyclopedia of biography, Allan Melvill urged him to include a sketch of General Peter Gansevoort. To his brother-in-law Allan wrote: "I feel a deep personal desire that the 'Hero of Fort Stanwix' should attain his proper station in every future American History descriptive of the Wars of the Revolution . . . . Such a man as your father, is a model for the imitation of his offspring, & was born for the contemplation of after ages . . ." (to Peter Gansevoort, February 28, 1823 [G-L]). Allan refers frequently in his letters to his wife's illustrious ancestry, but Maria does not mention it.

61. Maria Melville to Peter Gansevoort, January 22 and May 11, 1823 (G-L). In the former she agrees with him that nothing was wanting to his supper party but her *"imposing* presence" but thinks it "very fortunate considering the squeeze . . . that [she] was not there, as [her] enbonpoint might have excluded many more deserving & agreeable guests . . . . " In the latter she tells him that she has "increased in breadth most astonishingly."

62. Maria Melville to Peter Gansevoort, November 28, 1828 (G-L). She writes of berating a coachman for refusing to obey her instructions. See also her letter quoted in part on page 20.

63. Maria Melville to Peter Gansevoort, September 23 and December 29, 1824, and February 20, 1827 (G-L).

64. Maria Melville to Peter Gansevoort, December 8, 1826 (G-L).

65. Maria Melville to Peter Gansevoort, June 26, 1823 (G-L).

66. Allan Melvill to Peter Gansevoort, October 21, 1828 (G-L).

67. Allan Melvill to Peter Gansevoort, November 9, 1824, June 14, 1826, and May 19, 1827 (G-L). In the last he writes: "Our dear Maria is still in the agonies of a genuine dutch vernal housecleaning which you well know in New York as in Albany, is a most alarming & formidable operation." If Herman Melville ever read Irving's burlesque of Dutch house cleaning, he probably found it all too accurate (see the *Knickerbocker History of New York,* Bk. III, chap. iii).

68. Only once after marriage does she refer in her letters to books, when she recommends "Memoirs of Marie Antoinette—written by Madame Campan—Sister of Our Old Friend, Monsieur Genêt" (to Peter Gansevoort, November 21, 1823 [G-L]). In the winter of 1819-1820, a friend read a French novel to her, "translating every sentence" (to Catherine Gansevoort Lansing, May 24, 1866 [G-L]). Her surviving books are *Justine, or The Will,* Lady Sydney (Owenson) Morgan's *The Wild Irish Girl,* John Aikin's *Letters to a Young Lady on a Course of English Poetry,* Mark Akenside's *The Pleasures of Imagination,* Thomas Campbell's *The Pleasures of Hope,* Hester Chapone's *Letters on the Improvement of the Mind,* and *Cheap Repository Tracts: Entertaining, Moral, and Religious,* by Hannah More and Others, as well as an English and a Dutch Bible (see Merton M. Sealts, "Melville's Reading: A Check-List of Books Owned and Borrowed," *Harvard Library Bulletin,* II (1948), 141-63, 378-92; III (1949), 119-30, 263-77, 407-21; IV (1950), 98-109. These articles have been collected in a pamphlet with the same title and published by the Harvard University Press in 1950.

69. Maria Melville to Peter Gansevoort, January 22, 1823 (G-L).

70. Mary A. Gansevoort to Peter Gansevoort, August 20, 1826 (G-L). Mary was the widow of Maria's brother Leonard.

71. Allan Melvill to Peter Gansevoort, August 23, 1829 (G-L).

72. Peter Gansevoort to Catherine Van Schaick Gansevoort, November 19, 1819 (G-L).

73. Allan Melvill to Thomas Melvill, August 15, 1820 (Leyda, "The Melville Log").

74. Allan Melvill to Thomas Melvill, September 14, 1819 (G-L).

75. Allan Melvill to Peter Gansevoort, October 7, 1820 (M).

76. Allan Melvill to Peter Gansevoort, November 3, 1821 (G-L).

77. Peter Gansevoort to Catherine Van Schaick Gansevoort, August 9, 1824 (G-L).

78. Mary A. Gansevoort to Peter Gansevoort, June 5, 1825 (G-L).

79. Maria Melville to Peter Gansevoort, August 2, 1825 (G-L).

80. Maria Melville to Peter Gansevoort, July 15, 1829 (G-L).

81. Maria Melville to Peter Gansevoort, December 8, 1826, August 31, 1829, and August 17, 1831 (G-L).

82. Allan Melvill to Lemuel Shaw, August 8, 1820 (S).

83. Allan Melvill to Peter Gansevoort, April 5, 1823 (G-L).

84. *Ibid.*

85. Allan Melvill to Peter Gansevoort, September 14, 1826 (M).

86. Allan Melvill to Peter Gansevoort, September 12, 1826 (M), reprinted in part, with some errors, by Weaver, *Herman Melville, Mariner and Mystic,* p. 67.

87. Allan Melvill to Peter Gansevoort, May 3, 1823 (G-L).

88. Draft of letter of Peter Gansevoort to Allan Melvill, April 1818 (G-L).

89. Allan Melvill to Peter Gansevoort, April 5, 1823 (G-L).

90. See Mary A. Gansevoort to Catherine Van Schaick Gansevoort, July 1, 1828; receipted bills to Mrs. Gansevoort from the Reformed Dutch Church of Albany for pew rent and "Subscription for Repairs to Church," Albany, July 1, 1826, and for subscription of $150 for the "Third Professorship in

the Theological College of New Brunswick," September 21, 1827; and the Partial Inventory of Household Furniture of Catherine Van Schaick Gansevoort (G-L).

91. Peter Gansevoort to Catherine Van Schaick Gansevoort, July 21, 1819 (G-L).

92. Maria Melville to Peter Gansevoort, October 22, 1823, and September 17, 1826, and to Catherine Van Schaick Gansevoort, December 7, 1828, and Mary A. Gansevoort to Peter Gansevoort, September 1825 (G-L).

93. Maria Melville to Peter Gansevoort, September 3, 1824 (G-L), on his restitution to health.

94. Maria Melville to Peter Gansevoort, March 8, 1825 (G-L).

95. Maria Melville to Peter Gansevoort, May 11, 1823 (G-L).

96. Maria Melville to Peter Gansevoort, August 2, 1825 (G-L).

97. Thomas Melvill's miscellaneous papers, 1831-1832 (S), contain receipts for pew rent in the Brattle Square (Unitarian) Church in Boston and for subscriptions to *The Christian Register*. A letter of Thomas Melvill, Jr., to Lemuel Shaw, May 21, 1833 (S), refers to a "volume of Buckminster's Sermons much used by my parents."

98. Allan Melvill to Peter Gansevoort, January 18, 1827, added to letter of January 17 (G-L). He once noted down the following formula: "'Universal nature' must have had an origin; that origin must have had a cause; that cause must have been intelligent; that intelligence must have been efficient; that efficiency must have been ultimate; that ultimate power must have been supreme & that which always was & is supreme we call God the 'great spirit or the Eternal'" (memorandum in G-L).

99. Allan Melvill to Peter Gansevoort, April 1, 1824 (M).

100. Allan Melvill to Peter Gansevoort, March 2, 1826 (M).

101. Allan Melvill to Peter Gansevoort, January 20, 1818, and November 9, 1824 (G-L).

102. Allan Melvill to Peter Gansevoort, March 10, 1828 (G-L).

103. Copy of letter of Allan Melvill to Guert Gansevoort, October 27, 1824 (G-L).

104. The manifold effects of the Bible on Melville's thinking and on his art have been traced in William Braswell, *Melville's Religious Thought* (Durham: Duke University Press, 1943), and Nathalia Wright, *Melville's Use of the Bible* (Durham: Duke University Press, 1949).

105. *Journal Up the Straits,* ed. Raymond M. Weaver (New York: The Colophon, 1935), p. 107.

106. *Moby-Dick,* II, 264.

107. See the receipt for these commodities, dated New York, August 18, 1819 (G-L).

108. No Melvilles are listed in the roster of the school of the Collegiate Reformed Dutch Church, the only school sponsored by the church in New York City (*History of the School of the Collegiate Reformed Dutch Church in the City of New York from 1633 to 1883* [2d ed.; New York, 1883]).

109. In the Reformed Church it was the duty of parents not only to "instruct their children . . . in the principles of the Christian religion" but also to take them to church, to "require an account of the sermons they hear,"

and to "assign them some chapters of Scripture to read, and certain passages to commit to memory" (from the Decrees of the Council of Dort, quoted in David D. Demarest, *History and Characteristics of the Reformed Protestant Dutch Church* [New York, 1856], p. 165).

110. According to Melville's granddaughter, Mrs. Eleanor Melville Metcalf, his mother observed the Sabbath in her later years with just such rigor as this. (See Braswell, *Melville's Religious Thought,* p. 6.)

111. *Last Days of Knickerbocker Life in Old New York* (New York: G. P. Putnam's Sons, 1897), pp. 6-7.

112. *Ibid.,* pp. 8, 9, 10.

113. *Ibid.,* p. 11.

114. *Minutes of the Common Council of the City of New York, 1784-1831* (New York, 1917), XII, 587, 589. The privies of eighty-six other residents of the Cortlandt Street area were condemned at the same time.

115. Allan Melvill to Peter Gansevoort, April 1, 1824 (M).

116. Allan Melvill to Peter Gansevoort, October 25, 1825 (G-L).

117. Allan Melvill to Peter Gansevoort, April 1, 1824 (M).

118. Maria Melville to Peter Gansevoort, March 11, 1824 (M).

119. Allan Melvill to Peter Gansevoort, April 1, 1824 (M).

120. Maria Melville to Peter Gansevoort, December 29, 1824 (M).

121. Maria Melville to Peter Gansevoort, January 22, October 22, and November 21, 1823, and September 3, 1824 (G-L).

122. Maria Melville to Peter Gansevoort, December 29, 1824 (M).

123. Allan Melvill to Peter Gansevoort, April 19, 1826, and Herman Gansevoort to Peter Gansevoort, April 21, 1826 (G-L).

124. Allan Melvill to Peter Gansevoort, September 2, 1826 (Leyda, "The Melville Log").

125. Allan Melvill to Peter Gansevoort, August 10, 1826 (M). Printed, with some errors, in Weaver, *Herman Melville, Mariner and Mystic,* p. 66.

126. Allan Melvill to Peter Gansevoort, February 10, 1827 (G-L).

127. Allan Melvill to Peter Gansevoort, February 23, 1828 (G-L).

128. See the receipt dated New York, June 18, 1829, to Allan Melvill from the New-York Male High School for "the Tuition of Herman & Allan" from May 1 to August 1, 1829 (G-L). Allan Melvill is listed as a stockholder and one of the twenty-five trustees in *The Second Annual Report of the Trustees of the High-School Society, of New-York, Made on Monday, November 13, 1826* (New York, 1826). Information about the school is derived from this and the following pamphlets: *The High School Society of New-York, A meeting of the Subscribers to a fund for the erection of a School . . . May 15th, 1824* [New York, 1824]; *Charter, By-Laws, and Regulations of the High School of New York* [New York, 1825]; *First Annual Report of the Trustees of the High-School Society in the City of New-York* (New York, 1825); *Fifth Annual Report of the High-School Society of New-York* (New York, 1829).

129. Allan Melvill to Peter Gansevoort, February 10, 1827, and to Thomas Melvill, May 20, 1830 (G-L).

130. Letter to Catherine Van Schaick Gansevoort (M).

131. Allan Melvill to Peter Gansevoort, May 20, 1830 (G-L).

132. Maria Melville to Peter Gansevoort, December 8, 1826, and February 28, 1828, and Allan Melvill to Peter Gansevoort, February 23, 1828, and to Thomas Melvill, May 20, 1830 (G-L).

133. Two illegible words in the MS.

134. Maria Melville to Peter Gansevoort, February 20, 1827 (G-L).

135. Gansevoort Melville to Maria Melville, October 6, 1826 (G-L).

136. Maria Melville to Peter Gansevoort, September 3, 1824 (G-L).

137. Maria Melville to Peter Gansevoort, February 28, 1828 (G-L).

138. The livery stable was at 661 Broadway; John Jacob Astor lived at 223, Philip Hone at 235, and the Depaus at 358 (*New York Directory*, 1827-1828).

139. Maria Melville to Peter Gansevoort, February 28, 1828 (G-L).

140. David S. Jones, a lawyer, lived at 37 Great Jones Street; William Astor, son of the millionaire, at 8 Bond Street; James G. King, member of the leading banking house of Prime, Ward, and King, at 12 Bond Street; and Jeremiah Van Rensselaer, a doctor, at 638 Broadway (*New York Directory*, 1827-1828). The Melville house was on Broadway between Great Jones and Bond Streets.

141. Maria Melville to Peter Gansevoort, February 28, 1828 (G-L).

142. *Ibid.*

143. Allan Melvill to Peter Gansevoort, May 10, 1828 (G-L).

144. Allan Melvill to Peter Gansevoort, October 22, 1823, and Maria Melville to Catherine Van Schaick Gansevoort, December 7, 1828 (G-L).

145. Maria Melville to Catherine Van Schaick Gansevoort, December 7, 1828 (G-L).

146. Allan Melvill to Peter Gansevoort, October 14, 1826 (Leyda, "The Melville Log").

147. Mary A. Gansevoort to Peter Gansevoort, August 20, 1826 (G-L).

148. Gansevoort Melville to Maria Melville, May 23, 1828 (G-L).

149. Allan Melvill to Peter Gansevoort, January 1, 1831 (G-L).

150. Allan Melvill to Peter Gansevoort, February 28, 1823 (G-L).

151. Allan Melvill's Journal, August 28, 1806, October 16, 1807, and January 15 and June 27, 1811 (M); and *Redburn*, p. 3.

152. Allan Melvill to Maria Melville, June 8, 1818 (G-L), describing his "five days street campaign" in London. Cf. *Redburn*, p. 3.

153. W. M. MacBean, *Biographical Register of the St. Andrews Society of New York* (New York: The Society, 1922-1925), XX, 79.

154. See Sealts, "Melville's Reading," *Harvard Library Bulletin*, IV (1950), 102, nos. 537 and 538, for the first two titles cited, which survive from Allan Melvill's library. Many other French works appear on a list of books imported by Allan Melvill in 1805 (see Sealts, *ibid.*, II [1948], 146). The volumes of [D'Alembert's] "Encyclopedie des Arts & Sciences" in this list recall that Redburn used to think "what a great man [he] would be, if by foreign travel [he] should ever be able to read straight along without stopping" in his father's copy of "D'Alembert in French" (*Redburn*, p. 6).

155. Some of Allan Melvill's guidebooks survive, like *The Picture of London* (London, 1818), in the collection of Melville's grandniece, Miss Agnes Morewood of Pittsfield, Massachusetts (see Sealts, "Melville's Reading,"

Harvard Library Bulletin, III [1949], 413). Unfortunately, *The Picture of Liverpool* (Liverpool, 1808), in the flyleaves of which Redburn scrawled "wild animals and falling air-castles" (*Redburn,* p. 183), has never been located among Allan's or Herman's books.

156. For a brief sketch of Herman's wife, Catherine Quackenboss (or Quackenbush) Gansevoort, see the letter of Elizabeth Shaw Melville to Catherine Gansevoort Lansing in Paltsits, *Family Correspondence,* p. 65.

157. Allan Melvill to Peter Gansevoort, October 25, 1824 (G-L).

158. Allan Melvill to Peter Gansevoort, August 30, 1827 (G-L). Herman was actually in Boston at this time, but Gansevoort, who was with Guert in Albany for about ten days after his return from the cruise on the "Constitution," probably relayed to Herman the career of their cousin. (See Allan Melvill to Peter Gansevoort, September 5, 1827, for Gansevoort's companionship with Guert.)

159. *Redburn,* p. 4.

160. Allan Melvill to Peter Gansevoort, October 27, 1828 (G-L). Allan's phrase inevitably suggests the first sentence of chapter ii in *Moby-Dick:* "I stuffed a shirt or two into my old carpet-bag, tucked it under my arm, and started for Cape Horn and the Pacific."

161. Maria Melville to Peter Gansevoort, November 26, 1826 (G-L).

162. Records of Peter L. Gansevoort, now in the Office of Naval Records and Library, Navy Department, Washington, D.C., and letter of Allan Melvill to Peter Gansevoort, December 3, 1828 (G-L). Peter was drowned on March 7, 1832, when a schooner on which he had taken passage went down in a storm.

163. Thomas' character is described in a letter of Thomas Melvill to Allan Melvill, June 30, 1819, and in one by Priscilla Scollay Melvill to Allan Melvill, September 30, 1831 (G-L).

164. *Redburn,* p. 44, and *Moby-Dick,* I, 261.

165. Calbraith Perry, *Charles D'Wulf of Guadaloupe, His Ancestors and Descendants* (New York: T. A. Wright, 1902), pp. 1-50.

166. John D'Wolf visited the Melvilles in New York in 1828 and in Albany in 1831 (Allan Melvill to Peter Gansevoort, December 31, 1828 [G-L], and to Thomas Melvill, May 6, 1831 [M]). Another visit in New York is referred to in an undated letter of Peter Gansevoort's to Catherine Van Schaick Gansevoort (G-L).

167. Allan Melvill to Peter Gansevoort, August 7 and 20, 1828 (G-L).

168. Allan Melvill to Peter Gansevoort, February 2 and July 28, 1828 (G-L).

169. Allan Melvill to Peter Gansevoort, September 22, 1827, and September 26, 1829 (G-L).

170. Cuyler Reynolds, *Hudson-Mohawk Genealogical and Family Memoirs* (New York: Lewis's Historical Publishing Company, 1902), I, 62.

171. Annie Haven Thwing, *The Crooked and Narrow Streets of Boston* (Boston: Marshall Jones Company, 1920), p. 201.

172. It is well-known that Thomas Melvill's antique appearance inspired Oliver Wendell Holmes's "The Last Leaf."

173. *Boston Evening Transcript,* December 15, 1873.

174. Thomas Melvill, Jr., to Lemuel Shaw, May 21, 1833 (S).

175. Unidentified, undated newspaper clipping entitled "Here in Boston" (M).

176. Maria Melville to Peter Gansevoort, July 14, 1832 (G-L).

177. *Boston Evening Transcript,* December 15, 1873.

178. Priscilla Scollay Melvill to Allan Melvill, October 19, 1830 (G-L).

179. *Ibid.*

180. According to Weaver, *Herman Melville, Mariner and Mystic* (p. 258), Aunt Priscilla Melvill left Herman nine hundred dollars when she died in 1862. The Bible given Herman by Aunt Jean is in M.

181. Allan Melvill to Peter Gansevoort, September 26, 1829 (G-L).

182. Gansevoort Melville to Peter Gansevoort, October 4, 1826 (G-L).

183. Allan Melvill to Peter Gansevoort, September 22, 1827 (G-L).

184. Maria Melville to Peter Gansevoort, July 15, 1829 (G-L). The letter indicates that this was the first occasion on which Maria had asked her brother Herman to take his "namesake" for the summer. Her statement that she would not have hazarded the request could she have anticipated "the shadow of a refusal" suggests that she never repeated it. The point is of some importance to the interpretation of *Pierre* as veiled autobiography. The hero spends much of his youth in the family mansion, located in a rural area that could only be upstate New York. It has been assumed that in creating this background Melville was drawing upon his early memories of vacations at the Gansevoort family "mansion" in Saratoga, where Herman Gansevoort lived. Yet there is not a particle of evidence in the family letters to support the assumption, and the letter above, as well as positive proof that Herman spent his summers in Albany, Boston, Bristol, Hadley, or Pittsfield, argues against any early associations with the Gansevoort "mansion." (For further discussion of this point, see chap. ii, n. 17, p. 304-5.)

185. See, for example, her letter to Peter Gansevoort, August 25, 1826, and her addition to her husband's letter of September 17, 1826, also to Peter Gansevoort (G-L).

186. On February 10, 1827, he wrote to Peter Gansevoort describing a confidential connection he had just made with two men who were about to launch a jobbing business. He had promised to advance them ten thousand dollars which he did not have; from Gansevoort he then begged half that sum, declaring that without it "all, all [might] be lost . . . forever" and that he could procure the other half from another source. Gansevoort sent the sum requested, but when the other source, possibly Allan's father, failed, Allan asked Gansevoort for five thousand dollars more, by return mail. "As you esteem me," he wrote, "& love our dear Maria, do not I conjure you as a friend & Brother, disappoint me . . . or all will be lost even to my honour . . . " (letter of March 30, 1827 [G-L]). Peter Gansevoort favored this request also.

187. Draft of letter of Peter Gansevoort to Lemuel Shaw, February 20, 1834 (G-L).

188. Assignment of Allan Melvill to Peter Gansevoort, June 9, 1830 (G-L). When Peter asked Allan what had become of his profits in the firm, Allan gave him to understand that he had paid a large portion to his father (draft of letter of Peter Gansevoort to Lemuel Shaw, February 20, 1834 [G-L]).

189. Allan Melvill to Peter Gansevoort, July 15, 27, 29, and 31, 1830 (G-L).

190. Allan Melvill to Peter Gansevoort, June 28 and August 3, 1830 (G-L). It seems, however, that the furniture, or some of it at least, was not sold. See below.

191. Allan Melvill to Peter Gansevoort, August 11, 1830 (G-L).

192. *Ibid.*

193. Allan Melvill to John D'Wolf, September 22, 1830 (G-L).

194. Allan Melvill to Peter Gansevoort, August 21, 1830 (G-L).

195. Allan Melvill to John D'Wolf, September 22, 1830 (G-L).

196. Allan Melvill to Augusta Melville, September 2, 1830 (G-L).

197. Allan Melvill's Journal, October 9, 1830 (M).

Notes to Chapter II

1. Draft of letter of Peter Gansevoort to Lemuel Shaw, February 20, 1834 (G-L). In view of Allan Melvill's financial history in Albany, the "clerk's hire" was probably more substantial than it sounds (see n. 30, p. 306).

2. Allan Melvill to Peter Gansevoort, July 15 and 29, 1830 (G-L). Denison Williams was a New York firm dealing in furs. Allan Melvill entered the Albany branch of the company.

3. Materials on Albany in the 1830's are drawn from Arthur J. Weise, *History of Albany* (Albany, 1884); Joel Munsell, *Annals of Albany* (Albany, 1858); J. Silk Buckingham, *America, Historical, Statistic, and Descriptive* (New York, 1841); and Cuyler Reynolds, *Albany Chronicles* (Albany: J. B. Lyon Company, 1906).

4. *Albany Argus,* February 16, April 16, 20, and 22, November 7, December 2, 1835, and May 3, September 14, and October 10, 1836.

5. *Ibid.,* March 25, 1836, quoting an attack on the theater printed in the *National Intelligencer,* a temperance paper, which had ascribed the attack to the *Albany Evening Journal.*

6. *Ibid.,* December 8, 1835. Despite the murder of Duffy in 1836 the Albany Theater soon reopened and presented programs almost nightly during the season until 1839, when it was sold to a church (Munsell, *Annals,* X, 390).

7. They were the *Albany Literary Gazette,* September 3, 1831-April 7, 1832; *Albany Times and Literary Writer,* December 27, 1828-[?]; *The Zodiac,* July 25, 1835-January 1837; and *Albany Bouquet and Literary Spectator,* April-September, 1835.

8. Munsell, *Annals,* IX, 203-4. Munsell describes the society's concerts as "extremely popular." See also *Albany Argus,* March 11 and December 7, 1835, for concert programs.

9. *Albany Argus,* March 11 and December 7, 1835.

10. Peter Gansevoort's Account Book for Stanwix Hall, 1835-1854 (G-L), lists one sculptor and six portrait painters who had their studios in the building. Albany's best-known artist at the time was Ezra Ames (d. 1836), who had painted Allan Melvill's portrait.

11. Diary in the New-York Historical Society.

12. Reynolds, *Albany Chronicles,* p. 484.

13. Munsell, *Annals,* X, 282-83 and 392-93. The latter pages contain the English actor Tyrone Power's tribute to Cruttenden.

14. Mary Sanford to Edward Sanford, February 19, 1832 (G-L).

15. *Albany Argus,* January 6, 1835.

16. *Ibid.,* 1835 and 1836, *passim,* and *Albany Microscope,* 1836 and 1837, *passim.*

17. Leonard Gansevoort, 1751-1810, was among other things a delegate to the Continental Congress, 1787-1788 (Alfred Spencer, *Roster of Native Sons* [Bath, N.Y.: The Courier Press, 1941], p. 3). He is the model for Redburn's

great uncle, Senator Wellingborough. "Whitehall" may well be the original of Pierre's "manorial mansion." It was a building "one hundred and ten feet in front and seventy-five feet deep," set in an estate of 2,000 acres (Reynolds, *Hudson-Mohawk . . . Memoirs,* I, 131). The Gansevoort "mansion" at Gansevoort, thirty miles north of Albany, which has been generally taken as the scene of Pierre's (and Melville's) childhood, was a medium-sized farmhouse (see the drawing in Paltsits, *Family Correspondence,* opp. p. 64).

18. The letters of Allan and Maria Melville contain frequent references to personal and social connections with James Stevenson, mayor of Albany in 1826 and 1827-1828, Governor De Witt Clinton, and Governor Enos T. Throop. Maria was a distant relation of Stephen Van Rensselaer, last descendant of the first patroon and lord of the manor of Rensselaerwyck and its thousands of acres.

19. Letters of Wessel Gansevoort to Peter Gansevoort, January 5, 1814, and William Angel to Catherine Van Schaick Gansevoort, October 11, 1817 (G-L). The will of General Peter Gansevoort is in the Surrogate's Office, Albany, New York. Despite his disgrace, Wessel was not completely ostracized; he exchanged letters with Peter and sometimes called on Herman Gansevoort and Maria. A letter of Allan Melvill to Peter Gansevoort (January 8, 1825 [G-L]) records a brief call, but there is no other direct evidence in family papers or Melville's works that Herman ever saw his reprobate uncle.

20. Gorham A. Worth, who lived in Albany from 1800 to 1858, discusses the Van Rensselaers, the Ten Broecks, and other illustrious Albany families and then remarks: "In alluding to these ancient and wealthy families, that of the Gansevoorts should not be omitted; for it is connected with the patriotism and the triumphs of the Revolution. 'The hero of Fort Stanwix' has left to his descendants a time-honored name—a name that belongs to the history of the country, and to one of its most interesting and important periods" (quoted in Munsell, *Annals,* X, 199-200).

21. See Catherine Van Schaick Gansevoort's will (G-L). The drum was presented by Peter Gansevoort to the Albany Republican Artillery, February 22, 1832 (Reynolds, *Albany Chronicles,* p. 489). Fort Stanwix is now known as Fort Schuyler.

22. Peter Gansevoort to Allan Melvill, June 14, 1825 (G-L).

23. For Catherine Gansevoort's house, see the Inventory in G-L and *Albany Argus,* February 4, 1834; for the ostler, see a letter of Mary A. Gansevoort to Catherine Van Schaick Gansevoort July 25, 1827 (G-L). Melville mentions the house in *Redburn,* p. 204, and the ostler, p. 158, where he calls him Patrick Flinnigan.

24. List in G-L.

25. Advertisements inserted by Peter Gansevoort in the *Albany Argus,* February 4, 1834, and January 26, 1836.

26. A note in Maria Melville's hand, dated June 17, 1831 (G-L), acknowledges receipt of her full share in her mother's effects, including silver, beds, bolsters, and other furnishings.

27. Will of Catherine Van Schaick Gansevoort (G-L).

28. Peter Gansevoort's public career is sketched in William L. L. Peltz, *The Top Flight at Number One Lafayette Street* (Albany: Privately printed, 1939), p. 45. On January 27, 1838, the *Albany Microscope* printed an announcement of a series of lectures mocking those presented to the Young Men's Association. The heading was

Young Men's Optimist Association
For the Perfection of the Human Race
Arrangements for Lectures for February, 1838

Lecture 28 was "On the science of 'bowing.' P. G--nse--t." After Peter Gansevoort became a judge of the Court of Common Pleas in 1843, the following jingle was written about him:

"But this moss-covered knoll for another we'll keep,
For here polished Gansevoort shall take his last sleep—
The judge, whose respect for mankind, it is said,
Oft proves that his heart is too much for his head,
And thus while the one is expounding the laws,
The other, all glowing, pulls the fangs from its claws."

(From an undated pamphlet entitled "The Song of the Sexton Addressed to His Shovel, After the Dedication of the Albany Cemetery, by Old Mortality," in *College Pamphlets,* Vol. II, in the Yale University Library.)

29. Harold A. Larrabee, "Herman Melville in Albany," *New York History,* XV (April 1934), 144-59.

30. "My situation," he wrote his father on December 4, 1830 (M), "has become almost intolerable for the want of $500 to discharge some urgent debts, and provide necessaries for my Family." He says that daily expenses are being met by loans from Peter Gansevoort. It is not on record that he received the needed loan from his father. However, his next extant letter to his father, dated May 6, 1831 (M), says nothing of debts or overdue rents but talks confidently of the business boom in Albany. Further evidence of his temporary financial resurgence is available in the "Account Book with Allan Melvill" kept by Peter Gansevoort (G-L). Seven small loans were made between December 10, 1830, and January 31, 1831, amounting to $476.28, but the next entry is not until December 5, 1831. Meanwhile, Maria Melville was able to employ a maid, to whom she sends her regards in a letter written from Boston, August 17, 1831 (G-L).

31. Catherine Van Schaick Gansevoort and Peter Gansevoort lived at 316-318 North Market Street, halfway between Columbia and Steuben Streets. The Melvilles lived on the southeast corner of North Market Street and Steuben Street, at 338, and Allan's store was at 446 South Market Street. See the *Albany Directory* for 1831 and the Albany Assessment Rolls, Ward 3, No. 3, and Ward 4, No. 2, in the County Clerk's Office in Albany.

32. The corner where the Melville house stood is now occupied by the National Cash Register Company.

33. *The Celebration of the Seventy-Fifth Anniversary of the Founding of the Albany Academy, October 25, 1888* (n.p.), p. 149. The fees in 1831 were from twenty to twenty-eight dollars a year.

34. Munsell, *Annals,* IX, 275.

35. *An Address Delivered at the Public Exercises of the Albany Academy in the Second Dutch Church, August 6, 1835* (Albany, 1835), pp. 14-15.

36. A former student wrote in 1863: "No one can estimate the insensible and withal potent influence upon the minds of all those youths, of its beautiful exterior—of its large and lofty school-rooms—of its stately chapel—of its ample halls, filled with well arranged libraries and scientific collections" (*Celebration of the Semi-Centennial Anniversary of the Albany Academy* [Albany, 1863], p. 17). The building is still standing.

37. For all these details, see the pamphlet cited in n. 36.

38. See the *Statutes of the Albany Academy* (Albany, 1831), *passim.*

39. "Specimens of Penmanship in Albany Academy," March 1832, in the Albany Institute of History and Art. This book, like the others in the series, consists of original manuscripts written by the academy students for the semiannual prize examinations. Gansevoort Melville's examination appears in one of the volumes (it won a prize), but in binding the volume that probably contains Herman's the binder trimmed off the numbers by which the papers could be identified.

40. The date of entrance is given in Henry Hun, "A Survey of the Activity of the Albany Academy," an unpublished typescript dated 1934 and alphabetically arranged (in the New York State Library, Albany). Melville is listed in the fourth department in the *Albany Argus,* August 6, 1831. The quoted matter is from a report of a committee to observe the prize examinations, *Albany Argus,* March 5, 1831.

41. Hun, "A Survey." Carpenter had become city engineer by 1835, when he drew the official map of Clinton Square dated February 1835 and now in the County Clerk's Office, Albany.

42. *Albany Argus,* August 6, 1831.

43. Hun, "A Survey," *passim.* The *Albany Argus* of August 6, 1831, prints the names of a score or more students in the fourth department, and Hun supplies the biographical details.

44. Although the title page is missing, the book (in G-L) has been identified by Merrell R. Davis as the edition published in Canandaigua, New York, by J. D. Bemis and Company in 1819. On the inside of the front cover and on page xvii is the inscription "H Melvill" in Herman's formal, schoolboy hand. Inside the back cover he has written "H Melvill' [*sic*] Book." The volume contains only one marking, a penciled line in the margin opposite the following lines from Thomson's "Hymn on a Review of the Seasons":

> "Thy bounty shines in autumn unconfin'd,
> And spreads a common feast for all that lives.
> In winter, awful Thou! with clouds and storms
> Around thee thrown, tempest o'er tempest roll'd,
> Majestic darkness! On the whirlwind's wing,
> Riding sublime, thou bidst the world adore;
> And humblest nature with thy northern blast.
> Mysterious round! What skill, what force divine,
> Deep felt, in these appear!"

If the marking is Herman's, he appears to have been struck by the more melancholy and awesome aspects of God's majesty as it is revealed in nature.

45. *Albany Argus,* August 4, 1831, where the program for the exercises is given.

46. *Statutes,* p. 19. One premium was given in classes of six to ten students, two in classes of ten to fifteen, and three in classes of more than fifteen.

47. *Albany Argus,* August 6, 1831. The prize book is in the Yale University Library. The Library Committee has kindly allowed me to publish all inscriptions and marginalia in this volume.

48. Hun, "A Survey."

49. *Ibid.*

50. See "A Memorandum Book of Unsettled Accounts of the Albany Academy" kept by Peter Gansevoort, attorney for the school (G-L).

51. *Celebration of the Semi-Centennial Anniversary of the Albany Academy,* p. 47. Bradford attended the academy from 1825 to 1831.

52. After a student had completed the introductory studies of the fourth department, he could then take up any one of three main courses, the classical, the English, or the mercantile (*Statutes,* p. 24).

53. *Albany Argus,* March 5, 1831.

54. Hawley, *Address,* p. 18.

55. *Ibid.*

56. Matthiessen, *American Renaissance,* pp. 442-43.

57. "Sketch of Thomas Melvill Junior by a Nephew" (G-L). This is a manuscript copy, in an unknown hand, of an article Melville wrote in 1870, a portion of which was printed in J. E. A. Smith's *The History of Pittsfield* (Springfield, 1876), II, 399-400. Herman evidently forgot his first visit to Pittsfield in 1823, when he probably saw his uncle (Allan Melvill's Journal, August 25, 1823).

58. There had, however, been some friction in 1819 and 1821, when Thomas' "sheat," as his father termed it, resulted in a jail sentence for debt. Allan's attitude was unsympathetic and somewhat righteous. On the other hand, it is clear that Thomas's extravagant habits led him, in crises, to adopt methods that were somewhat less than ethical, such as selling farm tools that belonged to his father. (See Thomas Melvill to Allan Melvill, April 5 and 13 and May 8, 1819 [G-L]; Allan Melvill to Thomas Melvill, April 22, 1819 [M]; and Thomas Melvill, Jr., to Allan Melvill, May 12, June 24, and August 18, 1821 [S]. These last three were written from the jail in Lenox, Massachusetts.)

59. Letter to Peter Gansevoort, August 17, 1831 (G-L).

60. Draft of a letter of Peter Gansevoort to Thomas Melvill, Jr., January 10, 1832 (G-L). Allan's illness is first mentioned in a letter of Peter Gansevoort to J. L. Rathbone, January 8, 1832 (New-York Historical Society).

61. Thomas Melvill, Jr., to Lemuel Shaw, May 21, 1833 (S).

62. There is some evidence in Peter Gansevoort's papers that Denison Williams, the furriers for whom Allan was working, went bankrupt at this time.

63. Peter Gansevoort to Thomas Melvill, Jr., January 10, 1832 (G-L).

64. Thomas Melvill, Jr., to Lemuel Shaw, January 15, 1832 (M). Herman Gansevoort seems to have held a similar opinion; after seeing Melvill

January 17 or 18 he noted that "his case [was] hopeless" (Herman Gansevoort's "Checkbook and Remembrancer, 1823-1832" [G-L]). The exact cause of Allan Melvill's maniacal behavior cannot be ascertained. Maria Melville wrote of the "severe suffering" by which "my dear Allan was deprive'd of his Intellect" (Family Bible [G-L]), and Mr. Victor H. Paltsits has passed on to me a statement from Charlotte Hoadley, Melville's grandniece, that Allan died from pneumonia. In what testimony exists, there is no evidence of real insanity.

65. *Pierre,* pp. 96-99.

66. Allan Melvill to Peter Gansevoort, December [7], 1831 (G-L).

67. *Redburn,* p. 197.

68. *Ibid.,* p. 45.

69. One may judge the emotional effects of Allan Melvill's death by Maria's reactions six months later, after a visit to Allan's father in Boston: "Having never travelled from Boston to Albany or on this road without Mr Melvill every object served to remind me of him—The absence of one to whom I ever was most sincerely attached, render'd my journey to Pittsfield, & Boston rather painful, I had need of all my fortitude to repress my feelings before Strangers—but when I enter'd the old Mansion, it was silent & dark as night. my feelings got the better of all restraint & I wept Hysterically for some time unable to controul them" (letter to Peter Gansevoort, July 24, 1832 [G-L]).

70. Lemuel Shaw to Maria Melville, February 12, 1834 (G-L).

71. Peter Gansevoort's "Account Book with Allan Melvill, 1830-1834," and draft of a letter of Peter Gansevoort to Lemuel Shaw, February 20, 1834 (G-L).

72. Will of Catherine Van Schaick Gansevoort and legal papers of Peter Gansevoort (G-L). A sale of part of her estate in 1835 yielded over forty thousand dollars (*Albany Argus,* March 24, 1835).

73. In a letter to Lemuel Shaw, June 20, 1833 (M), Maria Melville says that when Allan died "my Brother was called upon to assist us immediately—for we had nothing."

74. As early as January 24, 1832, Gansevoort had paid the wages of one of his father's employees in the fur store (Peter Gansevoort's "Account Book with Allan Melvill, 1830-1834"). In a memorandum dated March 28, 1832 (G-L), Maria Melville certified that Gansevoort was "carrying on the Fur, and Cap business" on her account. The Assessment Rolls for the City of Albany, Ward 4, 1831 and 1832, show that 446 South Market Street, where Allan had his shop in 1831, was renumbered "364" in 1832, in which year Gansevoort is listed at that number. His personal card (G-L) indicates that he also manufactured fur caps, cloth caps, and other kinds. It was apparently at this time that he added an "e" to his name, which is spelled "Melville" on the card and in a letter to Peter Gansevoort, July[?], 1832 (G-L). As the son of a man who had died owing thousands of dollars to creditors in Albany and New York, Gansevoort may well have wished to hide his relationship so that his own business might escape being strangled at birth. His family ultimately took up his spelling of the name.

75. Memorandums of Maria Melville, dated September 24, 1832, and of Gansevoort Melville dated February 10, 1833 (G-L).

76. As early as 1833, when Gansevoort had been in business less than a year, he was appropriating one hundred dollars a month for "house expenses," not including rent (memorandum dated February 10, 1833 [G-L]).

77. Herman Melville's name appears among the list of clerks of the New York State Bank in the *Albany Directory* for 1832. Since this bears a Preface dated in June and since the academy term did not end until the last of July, Herman must have been taken out of school sometime in the spring.

78. Arthur Pound, *Murals in the State Bank of Albany* (Albany: The Bank, 1943), p. 21.

79. Hun, "A Survey," *passim.*

80. Diary, July 10, 1832 (New-York Historical Society).

81. Maria Melville to Peter Gansevoort, July 14, 1832 (G-L).

82. Maria Melville to Peter Gansevoort, August 7, 1832 (G-L).

83. Reynolds, *Albany Chronicles,* pp. 491-92.

84. See, for example, the reaction to the crowds of mendicants around the docks in Liverpool (*Redburn,* p. 242).

85. Maria Melville to Peter Gansevoort, July 24, 1832 (G-L). She added: "I am anxious about you & Herman, trust much to your prudence & leave the rest to Providence."

86. Maria Melville to Peter Gansevoort, August 7, 1832 (G-L).

87. Maria Melville to Peter Gansevoort, August 8, 1832 (G-L).

88. Gansevoort Melville to Peter Gansevoort, October 4, 1826 (G-L).

89. Gansevoort Melville's Journal, March 7, 1834 (Leyda, "An Albany Journal by Gansevoort Melville," *Boston Public Library Quarterly,* II [1950], 345).

90. Thomas Melvill, Jr., to Lemuel Shaw, September 2, 1833 (S).

91. The move had evidently been planned as early as January, when Horace Allen advertised as "To Let, the dwelling house at the corner of Steuben and North Market Sts., at present occupied by Mrs Melville" (*Albany Argus,* January 31, 1834). For the development of Clinton Square from a squalid area with low wooden houses to a handsome park with fine brick homes, see Munsell, *Annals,* IX, 178, 180, 189, and 329, and X, 232. The Assessment Rolls for the City of Albany, Ward 5, No. 1, 1815-1835, show that the house was built in 1834. The *Albany Directories* for 1834, 1835, and 1837 list the Melvilles at Number Three Clinton Square. (No *Directory* was published in 1836.)

92. The building, which is still standing, is now a rooming house. The principal evidence that the Melville family occupied the house from 1834 to 1838 lies in the history of the assessments of this and adjacent property. Had a new house been built on the lot at any time, the assessments would have shown a sudden increase over those of neighboring houses. But a careful study of the records beginning in 1835 shows that no increase was made in the assessment unless corresponding increases were made on the houses at Numbers One and Two. (The Assessment Rolls which I have consulted are in the Albany County Clerk's Office [1835-1849] and in the City Treasurer's Office in the City Hall [1850-1902]). Such increases occurred in 1841, when the original assessment of Numbers One, Two, and Three was raised from $2,500 to $4,000. In this year the house was first described as a three-

story brick house with a basement, a description which fits it at the present day. Five years later the assessment on Number Three was raised to $4,300, on Number Two to $4,500, and on Number One (a corner house) to $5,000; in 1849 the assessment on Number Three was raised to $4,500, bringing it equal to its neighbor. In 1850 each of the three houses was given another revaluation: $7,500 for Number One, $7,000 for Numbers Two and Three. In 1857 Numbers Three and Four, which had both been acquired by Samuel Anable, were assessed together for $10,000, the addition being, of course, the valuation of Number Four. For the next thirteen years the assessment for the two houses together remained at $10,000.

Although the assessments on Number Three continue until 1902 to reflect general rises in the valuation of property on Clinton Square rather than the erection of a new house, it is not necessary to trace their history beyond 1870. At this time John T. Bender, now living in Albany, was born at Number Three Clinton Square, and though he lived there only a few years, he assures me that the house in which he was born and the house now standing at that number are the same.

Collateral evidence in support of the identity of the present house with the one Melville lived in is found in the prices paid for the property when it changed hands. In 1839, when it was assessed for $4,000, it was sold by Richard Yates *et al.* to Mary Bradford and Louise R. Livingston for $9,500 (Albany County "Book of Grantors," LXVII, 256, in the Albany County Clerk's Office, Albany). In 1856 Mary Bradford sold it to Samuel Anable for $7,500 ("Book of Grantors," CXXXVIII, 381), and the decline in value again argues against any possibility that a new house had been constructed in the meantime. When Matthew Bender, the next owner, bought lots 3 and 4 together in 1868, he paid $16,500 for them ("Book of Grantors," CCXV, 155), which amounts to $8,250 apiece, or only a few hundred dollars more than the price in 1856. Here again there is no evidence of new construction on the property, which would have been reflected in a much higher purchase price.

In 1902 the house came into the possession of Daniel F. Nolan, whose widow has been kind enough to let me inspect it. If official records and personal testimony indicate that the house is of early date, the physical condition helps to confirm their evidence. The brownstone porch and threshold are worn deep, and the brownstone pillars are weathered and chipped. The ceilings in the front parlor are fourteen feet high and the front windows ten feet; the blinds are built into cases on the inside. The dining room is on the second floor rather than on the first. Such features alone would not, of course, establish the house as a hundred years or more old. But for further evidence, I have the opinion of Kenneth G. Reynolds, an Albany architect, who states in a letter of February 24, 1947: "I feel quite positive that the house that you refer to, No. 3 Clinton Square, is of the vintage of around 1838 . . . ; I know of other houses of similar type that are definitely of that era."

There can be no doubt that the house now at Number Three Clinton Square was the home of Herman Melville during his youth in Albany.

93. The stable is mentioned in an indenture made June 1, 1835, among Richard Yates, Ambrose Spencer, and John Woodworth (Albany County "Book of Deeds," L, 103), and by Gansevoort Melville in his Journal, March 9, 1834 (Leyda, "An Albany Journal by Gansevoort Melville," *Boston Public Library Quarterly,* II [1950], 345).

94. Their names are listed as winners of awards at the academy in the *Albany Argus,* July 21, 1835, and July 19, 1836.

95. The traditional date for Melville's sojourn on his uncle's farm has been taken from the sketch of Thomas Melvill, Jr., which he wrote in 1870 for Smith's *History of Pittsfield.* "In 1836," he writes, "circumstances made me for the greater portion of a year an inmate of my uncle's family and an active assistant upon the farm" (II, 399). But all available data argue that 1836 is either a printer's error or a slip in Melville's memory, like the two other dating errors in the sketch, 1845 instead of 1846 for the date of his uncle's death and 1841 for an inland voyage when Melville was actually far at sea. On January 16, 1836, he was working in Albany (see n. 123, p. 314). On July 8 and September 1 he gave indications of continued residence in Albany during the summer (see n. 140, p. 315). On October 22 he was on hand to witness a mortgage made by his mother in Albany, though in the sketch mentioned above he recalls sitting frequently with his uncle "by the late October fire" in the farmhouse at Pittsfield (see the "Book of Mortgages," XXXVIII, 324, County Clerk's Office, Albany). This reminiscence could not have referred to the fall of 1837 or thereafter (see p. 90). It will shortly be seen that Herman was in Albany for most if not all of 1835. It seems impossible that he could have lived with his uncle for "the greater portion" of any year between 1835 and 1837.

1834 remains, a year in which the *Albany Directory* lists Herman Melville as a clerk in the New York State Bank in its alphabetical section. But in the list of bank officers in the introductory pages, where Melville's name appears in the *Directories* of 1832 and 1833, it has been dropped. Since the bank undoubtedly furnished the information to the *Directory,* its data are more reliable. Melville was therefore no longer working in the bank after the spring of 1834. In the absence of other records of his movements, it seems most likely that he spent the rest of that year in Pittsfield.

96. Melville, "Sketch of Major Thomas Melvill" (G-L); Allan Melvill to Thomas Melvill, March 11, 1822 (G-L); Van Wyck Brooks, *The World of Washington Irving* (New York: E. P. Dutton and Company, 1944), p. 75; Allan Melvill to Peter Gansevoort, March 26, 1830 (G-L).

97. David Cargill to Thomas Melvill, June 13, 1802 (M). There seem to be no grounds for the assertion that Thomas Melvill, Jr., made a disgraceful marriage (see Thorp, *Herman Melville, Representative Selections,* p. xii).

98. "Sketch of Major Thomas Melvill."

99. *Ibid.*

100. Eliza P. Curtis wrote Thomas Melvill, April 12, 1812 (M), that Madison had nominated Thomas Melvill, Jr., to the Senate, but that that group had opposed the President's will. Thomas' term in the Massachusetts Legislature occurred in 1832 (Reynolds, *Hudson-Mohawk . . . Memoirs,* I, 63). For one jail term, see n. 58. Thomas refers to his arrest for debt in Albany about

1819 in a letter to Lemuel Shaw, May 21, 1833 (S); in another letter to Shaw, October 25, 1835 (S), he says he has been jailed again, this time in Lenox (near Pittsfield) by the same creditor by whom he was "committed in the Summer."

101. "Sketch of Major Thomas Melvill."

102. Thomas Melvill, Jr., to Thomas Melvill, April 15, 1831 (M).

103. He wrote that "Mr Edward Ballard was our minister" in Pittsfield (to Lemuel Shaw, April 24, 1841 [S]). Edward Ballard was rector of St. Stephen's Episcopal Church in Pittsfield, 1831-1847 (Smith, *History of Pittsfield,* II, 456).

104. Thomas Melvill to Lemuel Shaw, May 15, 1842 (S).

105. "Sketch of Major Thomas Melvill."

106. *Ibid.*

107. Pierre François Henry Thomas Wilson Melvill (known as Thomas) was born in Paris, March 2, 1806; Priscilla Anne Mary, in Paris, November 5, 1810; Henry Dearborn in Pittsfield, July 17, 1812 (memorandum by Thomas Melvill, Jr. [M]).

108. Thomas Melvill's first wife died in Pittsfield in April 1814. On November 21, 1815, he married Mary Ann Augusta Hobart (Reynolds, *Hudson-Mohawk . . . Memoirs,* p. 63).

109. Anderson, *Melville in the South Seas,* pp. 18-20. However, Anderson's romantic picture of Thomas reciting his adventures to his wide-eyed young cousin in Pittsfield in 1836 and even charting Herman's future course through the South Seas on a map is founded on the false assumption that Thomas returned home in 1834 and lived there.

110. Records of Thomas W. Melvill (Office of Naval Records and Library, Washington, D.C.). Tom had been in trouble with the Navy before. He was suspended from duty in 1831 for striking an officer on the "Vincennes" and court-martialed in April 1832. But because of the "strong provocation" given him and his own "good character," he was released from further punishment with the admonition that "no circumstances can justify an officer in forgetting his dignity by yielding to a paroxysm of passion." (For this additional information about Thomas, I am indebted to Jay Leyda.)

111. In a letter to Lemuel Shaw, November 18, 1841 (S), Thomas Melvill, Jr., writes that he has just received the first letter from his son Thomas in about nine years. From this it seems that Thomas had not been home since 1832, in October of which year he was, according to his naval record, addressed at Pittsfield. In a letter to Lemuel Shaw, August 26, 1844 (S), Robert Melvill, Thomas' brother, speaks of a letter Thomas had written in 1841 in which Tom said "that he had left off his habit of drinking."

112. In a letter to Lemuel Shaw, November 15, [1835], which is misdated 1837 by a later hand (S), J. M. Wright stated that Thomas Melvill had been fitted out in New Bedford for a whaling cruise on the ship "Columbus." This ship left New Bedford (actually Fairhaven) June 7, 1835, and returned February 26, 1837. Thomas' name appears on the crew list of the whaling ship "Hydaspe," which left New Bedford June 23, 1837, and returned February 27, 1839. On June 10 of that year Thomas sailed on the whaling ship "Amazon" (letter of J. H. W. Page to Lemuel Shaw, July 9, 1839 [S]). The

"Amazon" returned on May 28, 1841. Finally, Thomas' name appears on the crew list of the "Oregon," which left New Bedford July 21, 1841, and returned March 31, 1845. He died on the ship September 26, 1844, and was buried in Lahaina in the Hawaiian Islands two days later. (For data on whaling ships, see Alexander Starbuck, "History of the American Whale Fishery," in *Report of the Commissioner* [of Fish and Fisheries], *Part IV, 1875-1876* [Washington, D.C., 1878]. The crew lists are in the Old Dartmouth Historical Society, New Bedford. For Tom's miserable history, see Jay Leyda, "Ishmael Melvill," *Boston Public Library Quarterly,* I [October 1949], 119-34.)

113. Thomas Melvill, Jr., to Lemuel Shaw, September 6, 1843 (S).

114. The letter is dated September 1847 (G-L).

115. Since this passage was written, further parallels between Priscilla and Isabel have been suggested by Henry A. Murray, in Introduction to Melville's *Pierre* (New York: Hendricks House and Farrar, Straus and Company, 1949), p. lxv.

116. Thomas Melvill, Jr., to Thomas Melvill, April 15, 1831 (M).

117. *Ibid.*

118. *Pierre,* ed. Murray, p. 457, n. 114.8.

119. Thomas Melvill to Allan Melvill, October 6, 1820 (G-L), referring to a letter from Thomas Melvill, Jr.

120. Thomas Melvill, Jr., mentions the fire in a letter to Lemuel Shaw, May 14, 1834 (S).

121. See *Albany Microscope,* 1837-1838, *passim,* and May 20, 1837, for a correspondent's letter complaining of the rats in front of 362 South Market Street.

122. Gansevoort Melville's Journal, January 7, 1834 (Leyda, "An Albany Journal by Gansevoort Melville," *Boston Public Library Quarterly,* II [1950], 332).

123. See the bill dated January 16, 1836 (G-L), for three boys' caps, purchased at various dates in 1835 by Isaiah Townsend, a prominent Albany merchant. The items are entered in the hand of Gansevoort Melville, but the receipt of payment is acknowledged by "H Melvill." Herman had not yet adopted the final *e.*

124. Advertisements inserted by Gansevoort Melville in the *Albany Argus,* 1834-1835, *passim.*

125. Gansevoort paid other employees at this rate, according to his letter to Peter Gansevoort, August 2, 1832 (G-L).

126. "In 1835," wrote J. E. A. Smith, "Professor Charles E. West . . . was president of the Albany Classical Institute for boys, and Herman Melville became one of his pupils" (*Herman Melville* [Pittsfield, 1891], p. 6). He meant the Albany Classical School; the institute was not founded until 1842. Confirmation of the fact that West taught Melville at the Classical School appears in "Retirement of Dr. Charles E. West," *Pittsfield Sun,* July 11, 1889.

127. *Albany Argus,* April 27, 1835.

128. *Pittsfield Sun,* March 14, 1889, and Charles E. West, *An Address on the Fiftieth Anniversary of the Class of 1832* [of Union College] (Brooklyn, 1882), p. 4.

129. *Albany Argus,* November 10, 1837. (By this time the school had changed its name to the Albany Pearl Street Academy.)

130. West, *An Address,* pp. 4-7, and *Albany Argus,* April 30, 1834.

131. *Albany Argus,* November 17, 1835.

132. Smith, *Herman Melville,* p. 6. Smith adds that Herman was also, according to West, so "strict in truthfulness that when Professor West read *Typee* for the first time he was shocked that he should send out 'such a pack of lies,' and was greatly relieved when an 'ancient mariner' who was familiar with the Typee valley, assured him that they were not lies but veritable facts."

133. *Pierre,* p. 5.

134. Peter Gansevoort's borrowings for 1831 to 1836, listed by shelf number in the "Loan Book of the Albany Library, Vol. II" (New York State Library, Albany), include the novels of Scott and Maria Edgeworth. In some months the number of books withdrawn (54 in one instance) suggests that he shared his privilege as a borrower, and it is very likely that Gansevoort and Herman took advantage of it.

135. Gansevoort Melville's Journal, January 5 and 18, 1834 (Leyda, "An Albany Journal by Gansevoort Melville," *Boston Public Library Quarterly,* II [1950], 331, 333); and Sealts, "Melville's Reading," *Harvard Library Bulletin,* III (1949), 414, no. 406.

136. Gansevoort was particularly fond of the portrait of Zuleika in "The Bride of Abydos," just as Herman seems to have been (see pp. 117-18). See also Sealts, "Melville's Reading," *Harvard Library Bulletin,* III (1949), 418, no. 454.

137. He and James Stevenson dined with "our friend James Fenimore Cooper" in 1851, and he noted the death of "my old friend James Fenimore Cooper" (Diary, March 20 and September 15, 1851 [G-L]). Jay Leyda has kindly furnished these entries.

138. From a letter of Melville's in *A Memorial to James F. Cooper* (New York, 1852), p. 30, reprinted by John H. Birss, "A Letter of Herman Melville," *Notes and Queries,* CLXII (January 16, 1932), 39.

139. [Herman Melville], "A Thought on Book-Binding," *Literary World,* VI (March 16, 1850), 276-77 (a review of Cooper's *The Red Rover*).

140. The manuscript records of this association are now in the Harmanus Bleecker Library in Albany. In "Records," Vol. I, under the meeting of the Executive Committee on January 29, 1835, is this entry: "The following persons were admitted as Members, Henry Russell, David Murry, Anthony Ten Eyck, George H. Herker, John W. Pruyn, Herman Melville." The "Cash Book," 1833-1839, reveals the following payments of dues by Herman (or H.) Melville: "January 30, 1835, $1.50; December 2, 1835, $1.50; July 8, 1836, $1.00; September 1, 1836, 50 cents; January 5, 1837, $1.00." Dues were fifty cents a quarter, plus one dollar for initiation.

141. *Albany Express,* June and July 1850, in a collection of clippings on the history of the Young Men's Association, now in a scrapbook in the Harmanus Bleecker Library.

142. "Records," Vol. I. See also "Minutes of the Debating Society of the Albany Young Men's Association," in the Harmanus Bleecker Library.

143. *Albany Express,* June and July 1850, in a collection of clippings on the history of the Young Men's Association, now in a scrapbook in the Harmanus Bleecker Library.

144. *Ibid.*

145. A manuscript catalogue of the library exists in the collection of the association's records, from which was printed a *Catalogue of Books in the Library of the Young Men's Association of the City of Albany* (Albany, 1837). Although this was not published until after Melville's membership had ceased, all the books listed were in the library by February 15, 1837, while Melville was still a member. Unhappily, the withdrawal books which the association kept have disappeared.

146. See p. 86. The association library had a file of the *Edinburgh Review.* It is unlikely that Melville would have had access to any other file of the magazine.

147. *Omoo,* p. 119. Melville was prompted to this memory by seeing in Papeete Harbor a whaleship from Hudson, a town only a few miles below Albany. Since Anderson has shown that the very ship described was in the harbor at the time, Melville's reminiscence is almost certainly authentic (see *Melville in the South Seas,* p. 218).

148. In "The Fiddler" (1854), the narrator, Helmstone, meets, through his friend Standard, a man now reduced to teaching music from house to house, though he was once a renowned child prodigy, like Master Betty (W. H. W. Betty, 1791-1874, an English boy who, at the age of twelve, won acclaim in Dublin and London for his acting and retired in 1824). When Standard whispers the name of his friend to Helmstone, the latter says: "What! Oh, Standard, myself, as a child, have shouted myself hoarse applauding that name in the theatre." ("The Fiddler" is printed in *Billy Budd and Other Prose Pieces,* pp. 220-27.)

It is highly probable that Melville is referring here to Joseph Burke (1815-1902), who had captivated both England and Ireland by his impersonations and his skill as a violinist before coming to America in 1830. He made his first appearance here on November 22, 1830, in New York, after the Melville family had left the city. In January 1834 he was elected an honorary member of the Albany Young Men's Association, and on February 10 he was advertised to give a performance in Duffy's Theater. On January 12, 1838, he had a "benefit night" at the theater. For some years thereafter he lived in Albany, studying law and giving occasional concerts. (See *Biography of Master Burke* [7th ed.; Philadelphia, (1831)]; George C. Odell, *Annals of the New York Stage* [New York: Columbia University Press, 1928], III, 490; *Albany Argus,* February 10, 1834; *Albany Microscope,* January 13, 1838; and Harold W. Thompson, *Body, Boots, and Britches* [Philadelphia: J. B. Lippincott Company, 1940], pp. 367-68.) Evidence of interest in the theater in Melville's family appears in the fact that his Uncle Peter Gansevoort was one of the subscribers to a benefit performance for William Duffy announced for December 9, 1835 (*Albany Argus,* December 2, 1835).

149. See Gansevoort Melville's Journal, January 5 and 8 and February 27, 1834 (Leyda, "An Albany Journal by Gansevoort Melville," *Boston Public Library Quarterly,* II [1950], 331, 333, 340).

150. *Albany Argus,* July 2 and 6, 1836. One recalls that Herman paid his dues to the Young Men's Association on July 8.

151. Maria Melville to Peter Gansevoort, July 14, 1832 (G-L).

152. Maria Melville to Peter Gansevoort, June 26, 1833 (G-L).

153. Mary Sanford Gansevoort to Peter Gansevoort, August 20, 1835 (G-L).

154. *Ibid.*

155. Gansevoort Melville's Journal, January 26, 1834 (Leyda, "An Albany Journal by Gansevoort Melville," *Boston Public Library Quarterly,* II [1950], 337).

156. Maria Melville to Peter Gansevoort, August 17, 1831 (G-L).

157. Peter Gansevoort's miscellaneous papers (G-L) contain the following item, undated, but undoubtedly written during his courtship or shortly thereafter: "Whereas our dearly beloved brother has been unavoidably detained until this late hour—We the undersigned, do recommend him to the mercy of our beautious [*sic*] & tenderly beloved Mary. Done in the presence of Uncle Herman and Guert, Mary A. Gansevoort, C[onrad] Gansevoort, Maria G. Melville."

158. Gansevoort Melville's Journal, January 24, 1834 (Leyda, "An Albany Journal by Gansevoort Melville," *Boston Public Library Quarterly,* II [1950], 336).

159. Records of Commodore Guert Gansevoort, Office of Naval Records and Library, Washington, D.C.; see also Anderson, *Melville in the South Seas,* p. 17.

160. Hun Gansevoort, a fourth cousin of Herman's, was appointed an acting midshipman in 1832 at the age of fourteen and sent in 1833 to the Pacific on the U.S.S. "Vincennes," returning in June 1836 to enjoy a three months' leave. He was not ordered to duty in another vessel until February 1837 (Records of Hun Gansevoort, Office of Naval Records and Library, Washington, D.C.). He was undoubtedly at his home in Albany during part of the time when Herman was living there.

161. Gansevoort Melville records a visit to "Whitehall' with his mother (Journal, January 4, 1834, in Leyda, "An Albany Journal by Gansevoort Melville," *Boston Public Library Quarterly,* II [1950], 330).

162. It is clear from an inscription in Helen's copy of Mrs. Charles Sedgwick's *A Talk with My People* (New York, 1863) (G-L), that Mrs. Sedgwick had been Helen's teacher. A letter of Maria Melville to Peter Gansevoort, August 7, 1832 (G-L), describes a meeting with Miss Sedgwick, "the authoress," and her friends, who received Maria "in a flatering [*sic*] welcome manner, & beg'd [her] to visit them at New York & Stockbridge." Miss Sedgwick's sister and niece, Mrs. and Miss Frances Watson, were occasional visitors at Number Three Clinton Square (Gansevoort Melville's Journal, March 1, 1834, in Leyda, "An Albany Journal by Gansevoort Melville," *Boston Public Library Quarterly,* II [1950], 342).

163. Gansevoort Melville's Journal, March 1, 1834 (Leyda, "An Albany Journal by Gansevoort Melville," *Boston Public Library Quarterly,* II [1950], 342).

164. Helen Maria Melville to Peter Gansevoort, August 8, 1832 (G-L).

165. *Ibid.*

166. Berg Collection, New York Public Library.

167. See Priscilla Frances Melville's copy of the book (New York, 1823), with her note, "Mother read this alout [*sic*] to me—" (G-L).

168. Augusta Melville to Evert A. Duyckinck, December 30, 1859 (Duyckinck Collection, New York Public Library).

169. The compositions are in G-L.

170. Augusta Melville to Evert A. Duyckinck, June 14, 1863 (Duyckinck Collection, New York Public Library), and to Peter Gansevoort, February [?], 1841 (G-L).

171. Elizabeth Shaw Melville to Hope Savage Shaw, May 5, 1848 (M), and Peter Gansevoort to Allan Melville, Jr., September 20, 1848 (G-L), mentioning Augusta's long visit at the Van Rensselaer Manor House.

172. Augusta Melville to Catherine Van Schaick, June 23, 1846 (New York State Library, Albany).

173. Augusta Melville to Evert A. Duyckinck, September 30, 1850 (Duyckinck Collection, New York Public Library).

174. January 20, 1845 (G-L) (printed in Paltsits, *Family Correspondence,* pp. 7-9).

175. P. 81.

176. *Daily Union of Washington,* June [?], 1846. (I am indebted to Jay Leyda for this information.)

177. Gansevoort Melville's Journal, January 21, 1834 (Leyda, "An Albany Journal by Gansevoort Melville," *Boston Public Library Quarterly,* II [1950], 334).

178. See his letters to Peter Gansevoort, July [?] and August 1 and 2, 1832 (G-L).

179. "The Minutes of the Consistory of the First Reformed Dutch Church of Albany" note on April 6, 1832: "The following persons were admitted as members in full communion with this church on examination and confession of their faith, to wit, Maria Gansevoort widow of Allen [*sic*] Melville." On July 13, 1837, is the entry: "Miss Helen Melville received into the Communion of this church on Confession"; and on October 11, 1838: "Miss Augusta Melville admitted by profession to the communion of the church."

180. Gansevoort wrote in his Journal, Sunday, January 26, 1834, that of the household "Uncle Herman, Herman and Allan were all that went" to church that day (Leyda, "An Albany Journal by Gansevoort Melville," *Boston Public Library Quarterly,* II [1950], 337). See also *Albany Microscope,* February 4, 1832.

181. Maria Melville to Allan Melville, Jr., August 20, 1838 (Leyda, "The Melville Log"). She says in part: "My dear Allan, if you regularly attend the Sabbath School, & thereby obey your Mothers parting injunction, for be assured my beloved Boy the future usefulness of the Man depends much upon the foundation laid in boyhood. The instruction you receive in our Sabbath School is very important, you are away from a Mothers Care, under a comparatively strange roof . . . . "

182. March 2, 1834. Gansevoort noted on January 26 that the snow (which had fallen overnight) "prevented the female members of the family from

going to church." Since the church door was approximately fifty yards from their own, it would seem that religious fervor burned somewhat unevenly in the family.

183. E. T. Corwin, *Manual of the Reformed Dutch Church in America* (4th ed.; New York: Board of Publication of the Reformed Church in America, 1902), pp. 583-84. Gansevoort Melville twice records hearing Dr. Ludlow preach (Journal, March 9 and 23, 1834, in Leyda, "An Albany Journal by Gansevoort Melville," *Boston Public Library Quarterly,* II [1950], 346).

184. Maria Melville to Peter Gansevoort, June 26, 1833 (G-L).

185. Corwin, *Manual of the Reformed Dutch Church,* p. 883.

186. John H. Livingston, *The Psalms and Hymns . . . of the Reformed Dutch Church* (New York, 1832), *passim.* Herman and his family may have found the discipline of the First Dutch Church rigorous. As late as 1843, according to its records, the Consistory suspended a church member for intoxication and profane language while on a steamboat going to New York.

187. *Albany Argus,* March 10 and 14, 1836.

188. On June 17, 1836, she sold for a thousand dollars one of the fifteen lots she had received through her mother's will (Albany County "Book of Grantors," LVII, 167). On October 22 she granted for four thousand dollars a mortgage on eight other lots (Albany County "Book of Mortgages," XXXVIII, 324); and on December 31 she secured a little more than a thousand dollars on another lot (Albany County "Book of Mortgages," XXXVIII, 443).

189. Memorandum of Gansevoort Melville for Peter Gansevoort, November 29, 1836 (G-L).

Notes to Chapter III

1. See his General Assignment of all properties, real and personal, to Alexander W. Bradford and Benjamin Collier (G-L).

2. See her General Assignment to Conrad A. Ten Eyck, "City and County of Albany Book of Deeds," LXIII, 504-7, in the County Clerk's Office, Albany.

3. See Bond of Maria Melville to the New York State Bank, April 28, 1837 (G-L).

4. From statements made and signed by Gansevoort Melville, April 15, 1837 (G-L). The exact figures were $33,530.33 and $17,045.12.

5. The Gansevoort-Lansing Collection contains two slips of paper, dated May 1, 1837, by an unknown hand, one of which, written by Gansevoort Melville, lists the following items: "2 Silver Tea Pots, 1 Sugar Bowl, 1 Cream Pitcher, 1 Bowl, 6 Table Spoons, 12 Dessert Spoons, 2 Tumblers, 1 Soup Ladle, 2 Sauce Boats, 8 Tea Spoons, 1 Sugar Tongs, 1 Plated Cake Basket." The other, a note from Maria Melville to Peter Gansevoort, reads: "I have as well as I could estimated the value of the articles mentioned perhaps they may be less in reality—." The implication is strong that Maria was considering selling or pawning her silver service.

6. Gansevoort Melville to Peter Gansevoort, June 6, 1837 (G-L).

7. Gansevoort Melville to Peter Gansevoort, July 20 and September 27, 1837 (G-L).

8. Note in G-L.

9. Hun, "A Survey," says that Allan Melville left Albany Academy June 1, 1837. On July 12 he witnessed a power of attorney given to Peter Gansevoort by his law partner, John J. Hill (G-L), indicating that he was employed in his uncle's office by that date. In his Journal, begun July 16, 1843, Allan wrote that a "family council" decided that his tuition "ought to be saved to the limited exchequer of the family" (Leyda, "The Melville Log").

10. Records of the Town of Pittsfield, IV, 470 ff., in the Town Clerk's Office, Pittsfield.

11. The letter (G-L) is postmarked Pittsfield, December 30.

12. Robert Melvill, a son of Thomas Melvill, Jr., and Herman's first cousin, born June 20, 1817.

13. Although possibly a literary reference, this may refer to Leverett Cruttenden, "long and favorably known as Mine Host of the Hill" and proprietor of the Eagle Tavern in Albany (Munsell, *Annals*, X, 282). Tyrone Power, the English actor, referred to him twice as "mine host" (see chap. 2, n. 13, p. 304). Melville's allusion suggests an acquaintance with the good cheer for which the tavern was famous.

14. Washington Mountain, in the southeastern section of the township of Pittsfield.

15. For example, in the last paragraph Melville writes "refrained" but strikes it out in favor of "has not been deterred from," foreseeing that it will prevent using the phrase, "by any feelings of delicacy."

16. The volume is described only as *Self-Teacher—1834* (Sealts, "Melville's Reading," *Harvard Library Bulletin,* III [1949], 418, no. 456a). It is inscribed "Herman G. Melville from his aff Uncle Peter Gansevoort Albany Nov. 1837." There is no other indication anywhere that Herman had a middle initial.

17. The full title is *The District School, or, National Education.* I have used the third edition, published in Philadelphia by Carey, Lea, and Blanchard in 1835. However, the evils of the schools which I cite are also described in the preceding editions.

18. *The District School,* pp. 94-95, 296, 229-32.

19. Thorp, *Herman Melville, Representative Selections,* p. xv.

20. Taylor, *The District School,* p. 208. The school stood in the fork of the roads leading to New Lenox and to Washington County (see *Map of the County of Berkshire, Massachusetts* [Boston, 1858]).

21. Taylor, *The District School,* pp. 208-9, 213, 29, 114-15, and 116. Some of the evils Taylor mentions are also described by Thomas Melvill, Jr., in his report on Pittsfield schools (see p. 84).

22. *Herman Melville,* p. 8.

23. *Boston Museum,* January 31, 1832, quoted by S. Foster Damon, *American Literature,* II (November 1930), 282.

24. *Express* (Buffalo), September 19, 1899.

25. Lady Shelley (ed.), *Shelley Memorials: from Authentic Sources* (Boston, 1859), p. 16 (M).

26. The Journal is in M.

27. Thomas Melvill to Lemuel Shaw, June 3, 1837 (S).

28. The *Albany Evening Journal* printed this notice on February 13, 1838:

> "At a meeting of the Philo Logos Society of the City of Albany, held at their room in Stanwix Hall, on the evening of the 9th instant, the following gentlemen were unanimously elected to serve for the ensuing year:
>
> President..............Herman Melville.
> Vice President...............Lotus Niles.
> Secretary..............Daniel E. Bassett
> Treasurer...............Alfred Greene."

29. Hun, "A Survey."

30. *Albany Microscope,* February 17, 1838. For the text of the principal letters in the controversy, see App. A, pp. 251-63. I am indebted to Jay Leyda for calling my attention to these letters.

31. The following is a typical piece of *Microscope* humor:

> "*Figure of speech.* During the debate upon the bill in relation to 'the *rights* and *property* of married women,' Mr. *Smellfungus,* of one of the *three* houses, *delivered* himself as follows, viz: 'I am opposed to the passage of this bill, Mr. Speaker, because it places wives upon a *level* with their husbands, whereas, I am for keeping the women *under.* And besides, such a law would have a tendency to make all our wives *close corporations,* and hence, in my view, it would be clearly unconstitutional'" (May 6, 1837).

32. *Ibid.*, April 29, 1837.

33. *Ibid.*, February 24, 1838, in a letter from a subscriber printed directly underneath one of Melville's.

34. *Ibid.*, March 17, 1838.

35. Maria Melville to Peter Gansevoort, February 6, [1838] (G-L).

36. James J. Hill to Peter Gansevoort, May 29, 1838 (G-L).

37. Draft of letter of Peter Gansevoort to Lemuel Shaw, February 20, 1834 (G-L).

38. In a letter dated May 23, [1839], Maria Melville says that her rent is due on the first of May, and in a letter of August 2, 1838, she indicates that the rent was payable the day before. Since rents were paid in quarterly installments, these letters indicate that the Melvilles began to occupy the house either on August 1 or on May 1. But since another letter of Maria's is dated Lansingburgh, June 9, [1838], it is apparent that she had moved to the village about May 1.

39. Arthur J. Weise, *History of Lansingburgh* (Troy: W. H. Young, 1897), p. 39. Natives of the town called it "The Garden," or "The Garden of America." See a letter of H. R. Hawkins to Captain Esek Hawkins, Jr., *Lansingburgh Democrat,* March 14, 1850.

40. Although Lansingburgh was above the head of navigation and the Hudson had been dammed below the town some years before, a lock enabled boats of the classes mentioned to carry on trade.

41. *Democratic Press and Lansingburgh Advertiser,* May 18, 1839.

42. Ann Seelye to Sarah M. Seelye, Lansingburgh, February 15, 1844 (New York State Library, Albany).

43. Thomas F. Gordon, *Gazeteer of the State of New York* (Philadelphia, 1835), p. 644.

44. Gordon, *Gazeteer,* p. 644, lists fifteen factories and "about 500 dwellings, most of which are neat and commodious and some of them elegant." In 1900 Lansingburgh was incorporated into Troy, its rival to the south.

45. Maria Melville to Peter Gansevoort, June [9] and 16 and August 2, 1838, June 1, 1839, and May 16, 1841 (G-L).

46. Maria Van Schaick Peebles was the daughter of John Gerrit Van Schaick, brother of Maria Melville's mother, Catherine Van Schaick Gansevoort (Reynolds, *Hudson-Mohawk . . . Memoirs,* III, 993). Her house stood on the corner of North and Congress Streets in Lansingburgh (see Catherine G. Lansing's collection of photographs in "The Calico Book," p. 18 [G-L]).

47. The wills of Gerritt Peebles, who died January 23, 1841, and his wife Maria, who died in 1865, show substantial holdings in real and personal property, including Haver Island, near the confluence of the Mohawk and the Hudson. Maria Peebles made Maria Melville's daughters provisional legatees of Haver Island, and she gave them an equal share with her daughter-in-law in her jewelry, plate, horses, carriages, etc. (Wills in Rensselaer County "Book of Wills," County Clerk's Office, Troy.) Maria Melville speaks of borrowing money from Gerritt and Maria Peebles in letters to Peter Gansevoort, May 23 and December 14, 1839 (G-L).

48. Journal of Allan Melville, Jr. (Leyda, "The Melville Log"). The house is still standing, at 2—114th Street, Troy, formerly North Street. That it became the Melvilles' home in 1838 is clear from the following evidence.

On April 13, 1844, William Knickerbacker, of Lansingburgh, New York, bequeathed to his wife Eve "that certain dwelling house Barn and lot of land situate in the village of Lansingburgh and which are now occupied by me . . . ." He added: "I give and devise to my daughter Anna V. Knickerbacker that certain lot of land situate in Lansingburgh and now occupied by Mrs. Melville" (Will in Rensselaer County "Book of Wills," XXXVII, 86, Rensselaer County Court House, Troy). When he died, on July 11, 1846, an inventory of his personal property was made, which contained the following item: "6 Moths Rent on Mrs Melvils House $75.00" (inventory in Surrogate's Office, Rensselaer County Court House). These two references, together with Maria Melville's statement in 1840 that Mr. Knickerbacker was demanding her unpaid rent (letter to Peter Gansevoort, May 16, 1840 [G-L]), indicate that from 1840 to 1846 the Melvilles occupied a house owned by William Knickerbacker.

William Knickerbacker had bought his two houses in Lansingburgh on October 3, 1839, from John M. Caswell (Rensselaer County "Book of Deeds," L, 122, Rensselaer County Court House, Troy). One stood on lot 24, at the southeast corner of River Street and North Street and the other on lot 23, running back from River Street parallel to the first ("Book of Deeds," L, 122). The question regarding which family lived in which house appears to be settled by the "Census Records for the Town of Lansingburgh" for 1840 (now in National Archives, Washington, D.C.). The relevant section lists heads of families in the following order: "Wm Knickerbacker, Mrs. Melville, Josiah Jones, Robert Woodhill, Edward Chamberlain, Esek Hawkins, Jabez Hawkins, and Esek Hawkins 2d." The census takers were evidently working down River Street from North Street to Hoosick, the next street south, for Esek Hawkins owned the house that was the second north from the corner of Hoosick on River Street and his son, Esek Hawkins, Jr., owned a house south of his father's (Nathaniel Sylvester, *History of Rensselaer County, New York* [Philadelphia, 1880], p. 323. Sylvester says Esek, Jr., owned the next house south of his father's, and he does not list a house for Jabez Hawkins. He may, of course, have made an error, but the important point, that Esek Hawkins, Jr., lived south of Esek Hawkins, is clear). Furthermore, according to the original plat of Lansingburgh (now in New York State Library, Albany), there were eight lots on the east side of River Street between North and Hoosick, and there are exactly eight heads of families listed in the Census of 1840 beginning with William Knickerbacker and ending with Esek Hawkins, Jr. Therefore, it appears that the owner of Maria Melville's house was living on the corner of North and River Streets in the house on the lot numbered 24 on the plat and that Maria and her family were living in the house on lot 23.

Was this the house to which Maria moved in 1838 and from which Herman set out on the journey he made a year later? As we have seen, William Knickerbacker bought his two houses from John M. Caswell in 1839. Caswell, besides being a dealer in real estate (Assessment Rolls of Lansingburgh for

1835 and 1840, now in the New York State Library, show that John M. Caswell owned seven houses in 1835 and six in 1840), was a manufacturer of guns and rifles and, with his son, the only person in Lansingburgh engaged in that business (Sylvester, *History of Rensselaer County,* p. 325; and in the Lansingburgh census of 1850, the first to list individual manufacturers, John M. Caswell and his son, John W., are the only manufacturers of guns). In her first letter from her Lansingburgh home, Maria Melville says:

> "Will you be pleased to send me by to days mail if possible $100, I have promised my Landlord to advance him a half years Rent if he will put up blinds in front of the house *immediately* for the sun is pouring in with great power . . . he meant to postpone it untill he had more money, in the Autumn, his Rifles dont sell . . ." (letter to Peter Gansevoort, June [9], 1838 [G-L]).

This letter contains two clues to Maria Melville's residence. Since her landlord sold rifles, he must have been the John M. Caswell who owned the house in 1839. And Maria could not have been talking about the house on the corner lot (24), for the front of that house faces just east of north, and little sun comes into its windows. But the front windows of the house on lot 23 face southwest, where they receive the sun with increasing brightness all during the afternoon.

To these bits of evidence may be added the testimony of Charlotte Van Schoonhoven, a distant cousin of Herman Melville's. Mrs. Paul Cook, a resident of Troy, writes me:

> "My friend Charlotte Lansing Van Schoonhoven, who died at 96, a few years ago, told me once that Melville was a distant cousin, and that he lived for some years in a house on River Street (now 1st Avenue) Lansingburgh, a short distance from her home, and was said to have written 'Typee' there.
>
> "The house, a wooden one, is still standing, made into small flats, and has always been occupied" (April 7, 1946).

In a subsequent conversation, Mrs. Cook identified the house as the one standing on what is still lot 23 on First Avenue (formerly River Street).

That this house is of ancient construction is clear from its built-in Dutch oven, its wide, weather-beaten sidings, its hand-hewn rafters and beams in attic and basement, its brick vegetable bin, and its masonry walls three feet thick. The house on lot 24 has many of the same features, but it is much smaller, with only two bedrooms and a garret on the second floor. The eight Melvilles who were listed in the Census of 1840 could hardly have squeezed themselves into this space. The inventory of William Knickerbacker's effects lists enough house furnishings to have provided comfort in the small house but not in the large one ("Book of Grantors," LXVII, 256). By all the evidence it was in the latter that Melville lived after 1838. With the existence of the Lansingburgh Academy and several other houses in the neighborhood which were standing in 1838, the visitor to Lansingburgh (now the northern section of Troy) can form a good picture of the scenes Melville knew during his early manhood. For anyone who may wish to make a pilgrimage, it should be pointed out that Melville's old home is now numbered 2—114th Street.

49. *Lansingburgh Democrat,* July 11, 1846, and *Lansingburgh Gazette,* July 16, 1846.

50. Dr. Jeremiah Spofford, *A Genealogical Record . . . of . . . Descendants of John Spofford and Elizabeth Scott* (Boston, 1888), p. 156; Sylvester, *History of Rensselaer County,* p. 323.

51. Maria Melville to Peter Gansevoort, May 16, 1840 (G-L).

52. Maria Melville to Peter Gansevoort, June [9], 1838 (G-L).

53. Draft of letter from Peter Gansevoort to Maria Melville, June 20, 1838 (G-L).

54. Maria Melville to Peter Gansevoort, August 2, 1838. He noted on the letter: "1838 Aug 3 Asd enclosing check $100" (G-L).

55. Maria Melville to Peter Gansevoort, August 2, 1838 (G-L).

56. They evidently traveled to New Orleans and up the Mississippi, arriving in Galena about October 20, 1838 (see Thomas Melvill, Jr., to Lemuel Shaw, Galena, November 1, 1838 [S]).

57. Maria Melville to Peter Gansevoort, October 30, 1838 (G-L).

58. *Ibid.*

59. Maria Melville to Allan Melville, Jr., November 10, 1838, stating that Herman was to begin his studies two days later (Leyda, "The Melville Log").

60. *Lansingburgh Gazette,* April 23, 1838. Ebenezer Davenport Maltbie, a great-grandson of one of the founders of New Haven, had been salutatorian of the class of 1824 at Hamilton College, Clinton, N.Y., a student at Andover Theological Seminary, and assistant superintendent of a Sabbath school before his ordination in 1832. For three years he preached in the Congregational Church in Hamilton, N.Y., and then began a twelve-year career of teaching. "His longest engagement," says his class necrology, "was at Lansingburgh, where he fitted a large number of young men for College, and won distinction as an accurate, earnest scholar and a faithful instructor." (See the "Official Necrology of the Class of 1824 of Hamilton College," now in the college library; the *General Catalogue of the Theological Seminary, Andover, Massachusetts, 1808-1908* [Boston: T. Todd, (1909)]; and *The Opal* [Utica, N.Y.], VII [August 1858], 189-91.)

61. See the *Fifty-second Annual Report of the Regents of the University of the State of New York* (Albany, 1839), p. 67; *Democratic Press and Lansingburgh Advertiser,* August 25, 1838; and *Lansingburgh Gazette,* April 16, 1846.

62. *Lansingburgh Gazette,* August 20, 1838. Both composition and declamation also received "a due share of attention."

63. *Fifty-second Annual Report of the Regents,* p. 49.

64. *Fifty-third Annual Report of the Regents . . .* (Albany, 1840), p. 91.

65. *Fifty-second Annual Report of the Regents,* p. 98.

66. *Democratic Press and Lansingburgh Advertiser,* August 25, 1838. The library was valued at $192.00 and the apparatus at $211.00 (*Fifty-second Annual Report of the Regents,* p. 56).

67. Leyda, "The Melville Log."

68. The postscript reads: "My complements to Eli James Murdock tell him I shall be down in a few days." Eli James Murdock Fly had been at the Albany Academy from September 1829 to June 1, 1834 (Hun, "A Survey").

69. Mrs. Frances G. Wickes of New York has kindly furnished the author information about her grandmother, Mary Eleanor Parmelee, and Herman Melville. She is able to date their relationship only at some time before Melville left Lansingburgh for the South Seas. 1838-1839 is thus only a guess, but Melville seems to have had another object of affection in the following year (see pp. 148-50). Mrs. Wickes asserts that the copy of Tennyson contained only a few poems (which suggests the 1830 or 1833 edition), that this has been lost, and that Melville wrote several letters to Mary Parmelee, which she ultimately destroyed.

70. "Fragments from a Writing Desk, No. 1," *Billy Budd,* pp. 386, 388.

71. *Redburn,* pp. 41, 94, 103.

72. See the "Records of the First Presbyterian Church in the Town of Lansingburgh, Rensselaer County, New York," ed. Royden W. Vosburgh (New York, 1915) (typescript copy in New York State Library). In a sense this church was the lineal descendant of the Reformed Dutch Church of Lansingburgh, dissolved in 1800 (Sylvester, *History of Rensselaer County,* p. 312). The Melville family may therefore have attended the church.

73. A misspelling for Maltbie.

74. A misspelling for Jervis.

75. Draft of a letter in G-L.

76. George A. Jarvis *et al., The Jarvis Family* (Hartford, 1879), pp. 184-85.

77. *Ibid.,* p. 185; and *Albany Directory,* 1838-1839, p. 15. Bouck was elected governor of New York in 1842.

78. The reasons may have been political. Both Peter Gansevoort and Bouck were Democrats, and the state had come under Whig control in 1837 (Denis T. Lynch, "Party Struggles, 1828-1850," in *The Age of Reform* ["History of the State of New York"; New York: Columbia University Press, 1934], VI, 71).

79. Maria Melville to Peter Gansevoort, May 23, 1838 (G-L).

80. In her letter to Peter Gansevoort of June 16, 1838, she says: "Rosey [the servant] . . . wishing to be paid up . . . has left me without money." In another letter to him, of December 14, 1839, she writes of paying her woman of all work ten shillings ($1.25) a week, or $16.25 a quarter, whereas her rent was $31.25 a quarter. She still had the servant in May 1840 when she wrote Peter Gansevoort that she owed the woman $60.00 (all letters in G-L).

81. See App. B, p. 264.

82. For example, Irving's "Adventures of a Mason" appeared in the *Democratic Press and Lansingburgh Advertiser,* February 23, 1839; Hawthorne's "The Grey Champion" on April 27, 1839, under the pseudonym Nathaniel Greene; and Holmes's "Lines on an Old Gentleman" on June 9, 1838. Melville ought to have been especially interested in the last poem, for it was originally entitled "The Last Leaf" and its subject was Major Thomas Melvill, Herman's grandfather.

"The Yankee Boy," a story published anonymously on March 30, 1839, is of considerable interest because of its possible bearing on chapter lxvii of *White-Jacket.* Its hero is a New Hampshire lad who is flogged for resisting impressment by the captain of the English brig which has captured him. Released from his bonds, he rushes madly upon the captain, standing alone near the side of the ship, and plunges with him into the water, where they both drown. Melville may have had this tale unconsciously in mind when he told how he was determined to throw both himself and Captain Claret into the ocean rather than submit to an undeserved flogging. Anderson has proved Melville's account false (*Melville in the South Seas,* p. 409).

83. For example, the *Democratic Press and Lansingburgh Advertiser* printed the following poems: "Jesus of Nazareth Passes By," January 12, 1839, "Mary's Request," February 9, 1839, and "Laura D. Bridgman," September 8, 1838—all by Lydia H. Sigourney; "The Dying Husband," by Ann S. Stephens, March 30, 1839; "The Bride," by Catherine H. Waterman, March 2, 1839; and "Pity's Tear," by "H.," September 15, 1838.

84. It is possible but unlikely that he wrote "The Death Craft," a sea sketch full of Gothic horror, unreal description, and sticky romance published in the *Democratic Press* November 16, 1839.

85. The sketch has been republished, with several errors, in *Billy Budd,* pp. 382-90.

86. It formed part of a volume Allan Melvill presented to Guert Gansevoort in 1824 (copy of letter of Allan Melvill to Guert Gansevoort, October 27, 1824 [G-L]).

87. The association catalogue lists a three-volume edition which, though undated, may very well have been *Letters Written by the Late Right Honourable Philip Dormer Stanhope Earl of Chesterfield to His Son; with Some Account of His Life* (3 vols.; New York: C. A. Hinkley, 1824). There were no three-volume editions issued in the eighteenth century (Sidney L. Gulick, "A Chesterfeld Bibliography to 1800," in *Papers of the Bibliographical Society of America,* XXIX [1935], 5); and no listing of any other three-volume edition before 1839 appears in the British Museum or the Library of Congress *Catalogues.*

88. Chesterfield, *Letters,* I, 224-25.

89. *Billy Budd,* pp. 383, 384.

90. *Ibid.,* p. 384.

91. *Principles of Politeness,* p. 6.

92. *Billy Budd,* p. 384.

93. *Principles of Politeness,* p. 18.

94. *Billy Budd,* pp. 383-84.

95. *Ibid.,* p. 388.

96. For the text, see App. B, pp. 265-71.

97. The unidentified lines are:

> "Effuse the mildness of their azure beam;"
> "dazzled all it shone upon,"

and

> "—Sail in liquid light
> And float on seas of bliss."

The last two lines, as Dr. Gordon Haight has pointed out for me, recall Shelley's

> "her bright image floated on the river
> Of liquid light, which then did end and fade."
> (*Laon and Cythna,* XI, iii.)

All the lines, of course, may well be Melville's own.

98. Memory of Byron's poem remained with Melville as late as 1849, when he used virtually the same reference as in the first "Fragment" though he confused Minotti, who actually wielded the sword, with Alp, the Turkish attacker. (See his review of Parkman's *The California and Oregon Trail* in *Literary World,* IV [March 31, 1849], 292.)

99. The *Catalogue* of the Albany Young Men's Association, 1837, lists a six-volume edition.

100. See *The Arabian Nights' Entertainments* (Philadelphia, 1831), p. 42, "The Story of the Three Calendars, Sons of Kings, and of the Five Ladies of Bagdad"; p. 150, "The Story Told by the Christian Merchant"; p. 175, "The Story of the Barber's Second Brother"; p. 190, "The History of Aboulhassen Ali Ben Becar and Schemselnihar." Melville could have found these stories in almost any edition of the book.

101. *The Arabian Nights' Entertainments,* p. 282.

102. E. H. Coleridge (ed.), *The Works of Byron* (London: John Murray, 1902-6), Vol. II: "Childe Harold's Pilgrimage," lxiv, 6, "The Giaour," ll. 505-6, "The Bride of Abydos," ll. 546, 559, *Don Juan,* Can. IV, st. cxiv; Thomas Moore, *Complete Poetical Works* (New York: Thomas Y. Crowell Company, 1895), pp. 389, 471, 475.

103. Moore, *Poetical Works,* p. 380.

104. *Ibid.,* p. 452.

105. *Ibid.,* p. 467.

106. "The Bride of Abydos," l. 179.

107. *Ibid.,* ll. 170-75, and *Don Juan,* Can. V, st. xcvii. The former six lines formed one of the excerpts in Melville's prize book, *The Carcanet.*

108. Ll. 269-72.

109. *Don Juan,* Can. IV, st. cxlii.

110. The "Fragment" begins: "Confusion seize the Greek!" Compare *Typee:* "Six months at sea!"; *Mardi:* "We are off!"; *Redburn:* "'Wellingborough, as you are going to sea, suppose you take this shooting jacket of mine along'"; *White-Jacket:* "It was not much of a jacket, but white enough, in all consequence, as the sequel will show"; *Moby-Dick:* "Call me Ishmael."

111. Letter in G-L.

112. Gansevoort Melville to Allan Melville, Jr., May 24, 1839 (Leyda, "The Melville Log").

113. Journal of Allan Melville, Jr. (Leyda, "The Melville Log").

Notes to Chapter IV

1. This letter (G-L) has been misdated 1837 by Anderson, *Melville in the South Seas,* p. 442, n. 7, and by Braswell, *Melville's Religious Thought,* p. 128, n. 15. Jean Simon, who published a few sentences from it in *Herman Melville, marin, metaphysicien, et poète,* p. 53, dated it 1835, and ignoring the reference to the "Vessel," took it to mean that Herman was leaving for Pittsfield. Establishment of the correct date led to the discovery of the ship on which Melville made his first voyage. (See William H. Gilman, "Melville's Liverpool Trip," *Modern Language Notes,* LXI [December 1946], 543-47.)

2. See n. 30 for advertisements of the sailing of the ship Melville traveled on. It would seem that Gansevoort either knew someone in New York who was acquainted with the ship's owners or that he knew them himself. The second hypothesis receives some weight from the fact that when Allan and Maria Melville lived in New York, they had been friends and neighbors of John Aspinwall, whose son William H. Aspinwall was now one of the partners in the firm of Howland and Aspinwall, owners of the ship on which Melville sailed. See a letter of Maria Melville to Peter Gansevoort, September 3, 1824 (G-L), recording a social call by Mr. and Mrs. Aspinwall and the appearance of Mrs. Aspinwall's oldest son the next day "with a beautiful bunch of flowers on a rich Silver Service . . . with her compliments." Allan Melvill's acquaintance with John Aspinwall has been noted above (p. 32). See also Franklyn Howland, *A Brief Genealogical and Biographical History of Arthur, Henry, and John Howland* (1st ed.; New Bedford, 1885), pp. 356, 380.

3. June 1, the day when Maria Melville's letter is dated, fell on a Saturday. It is evident that as late as 1846 Lansingburgh residents had to collect their mail at the post office (see Margaret ? to Sarah M. Seelye, Lansingburgh, October 19, 1846, New York State Library).

4. The letter is addressed to Gansevoort in the care of Herman. See n. 18.

5. Since the actual time of Herman's departure has an important bearing on chapter ii in *Redburn,* the point is worth some discussion.

The only means by which Herman could get to New York from Lansingburgh in June 1839 was the river steamboat, which supplanted the stage coach during the summer, when the river was open. These boats ran from Albany on weekdays at 7:00 A.M. and 5:00 P.M. and on Sundays at 5:00 P.M., making the journey in ten or eleven hours (*Albany Argus,* April 5-June 5, 1839). A connecting boat left Troy, four miles south of Lansingburgh, at 6:00 A.M. and at 4:00 P.M., though one might take other boats after six to connect with the afternoon steamer from Albany (*Budget* [Troy], May 31, 1839). If Melville, like Redburn, had taken the morning boat from Albany, he would have had to leave home at about five o'clock for the walk to Troy. This means that his mother's letter, if correctly dated June 1, would have been written sometime after midnight Friday. Thus her preparations for Herman's departure would have had to be made in the few hours between the time she received Gansevoort's letter and early Saturday morning.

It is improbable that events happened according to this frantic schedule. Besides, Maria's statement that Helen "has not yet come back," with its air of expectancy, is one she would have been more likely to write in the daytime than late at night. It seems pretty certain that Herman did not leave home until much later in the day than Redburn, and that he traveled to New York on the evening boat from Albany. It is unlikely that he waited until Sunday, for he would not then have arrived in New York until Monday morning, leaving scant time to secure his position, sign shipping articles, purchase equipment, and report on the ship on Tuesday, on which day it had been advertised to sail.

6. See *Moby-Dick,* II, 264: "There is no steady unretracing progress in this life: we do not advance through fixed gradations, and at the last one pause:—through infancy's unconscious spell, boyhood's thoughtless faith, adolescence' doubt (the common doom), then scepticism, then disbelief, resting at last in manhood's pondering repose of If. But once gone through, we trace the round again; and are infants, boys, and men, and Ifs eternally."

7. The same economic forces nearly sent Hawthorne to sea in 1837. See Harrison Hayford, "Hawthorne, Melville, and the Sea," *New England Quarterly,* XIX (December 1946), 446-48.

8. Captain John B. Heffernan, officer-in-charge of the Office of Naval Records and Library of the Navy Department, informs me, in a letter of August 16, 1946, that he finds "no evidence that Mr. Melville ever applied to the Navy Department for appointment as a Midshipman."

9. His father, Leonard Hun Gansevoort, died in 1821 (Hun, "A Survey").

10. Mary A. Gansevoort, Leonard's mother, to Peter Gansevoort, April 14, 1837, December 27, 1838, and December 24, 1839 (G-L).

11. Leonard's service on a whaling ship may be ascertained from a letter of his mother's to Peter Gansevoort, April 4, 1837 (G-L), in which she says that a Mr. Stevenson had written her that her "child" was arriving on the "Heracles" in New Bedford. She must have meant the "Hercules," a whaler which sailed from New Bedford July 12, 1835, and returned March 29, 1837 (Starbuck, "History of the American Whale Fishery," *Report of the Commissioner* [of Fish and Fisheries], *Part IV, 1875-1876,* pp. 314-15. This volume lists all the whalers that ever operated from New Bedford, but no "Heracles" is included.) That Mary Gansevoort, who had three sons, meant Leonard in her reference to her "child" is clear from her mention, in the same letter, that Stanwix was at home, and from the fact that Guert was on duty on the U.S.S. "Boston" (record in Office of Naval Records and Library, Washington, D.C.).

12. His name appears on the crew list, now in the National Archives, Washington, D.C.

13. He was appointed a lieutenant March 8, 1837 (record in Office of Naval Records and Library, Washington, D.C.).

14. See p. 100.

15. See Maria Melville's letter, p. 124.

16. When her nephew, Peter L. Gansevoort, first went to sea, Maria Melville wrote: "For my part, I think it is the best thing that could be done with him, he does not appear to me to possess talents or inclination for study or improvement— . . . it was not his destiny to earn a subsistence by any means but that of Labour, for he is devoid of emulation, which urges many on to exertion, & appears to have no ambition to learn any one thing more than another" (letter to Peter Gansevoort, December 8, 1826 [G-L]).

17. *New York American,* June 4, 1839, weather report for the previous week. Redburn also arrives in the rain.

18. The letter which Melville carried from his mother to his brother was addressed "Gansevoort Melville Esq, New York, 19th Street, a three Story house, 2 doors from the 9th Avenue, Care of Herman Melville." The address, together with Maria Melville's extension of her "respects to Mrs B— & Husband," supplies the means of determining Melville's destination. Of the six people with names beginning with *B* listed by the *New York Directory* of 1839 on Nineteenth Street, Alexander W. Bradford is the only one who had any connection with the Melvilles at this time. His wife was the former Marianne Gray, to whom he was married in 1836 (*Albany Argus,* December 21, 1836).

19. Bradford was born February 21, 1815, the son of the Reverend John M. Bradford, pastor of the North Dutch Church in Albany from 1805 to 1820. In a letter recommending Melville for a consulship in 1861, Bradford speaks of knowing Melville from his youth (letter in National Archives, where it was discovered by Harrison Hayford). For his friendship with Gansevoort Melville, see Gansevoort's letters to Lemuel Shaw, March 7 and July 22, 1842 (S), and Gansevoort's Journal, in Leyda, "An Albany Journal by Gansevoort Melville," *Boston Public Library Quarterly,* II (1950), 335-42, 344-47.

20. For Bradford's career at Union College, see *Catalogue of Sigma Phi, Union College* (Schenectady: n.p., 1915), p. 29, and West, *Address,* p. 101. For Bradford's legal career, see the notice in the *New York Evening Post,* May 24, 1839, of his admission to practice before the Supreme Court of the State of New York, and his biography in the *DAB,* which notes that he became Corporation Counsel of the City of New York in 1843 and Surrogate in 1848; for his political career as chairman of the Whig Committee in New York beginning in the early 1840's, see Bradford's obituary in *The New York Times,* November 7, 1867. His scholarship is represented by *American Antiquities, and Researches into the Origin and History of the Red Race* (New York, 1841), one of the first intensive investigations of native American ethnology. In February 1842 Bradford was one of a committee of eighty-eight prominent New York citizens in charge of the "Boz Ball," a celebration given in honor of Charles Dickens' visit, and in 1845 he became co-editor of *The American Review.*

21. The notation is as follows:

12
10
19
11
7
9
10
22
---
109 to Sag Harbor
lower road

81 to River Head
middle road

Both Sag Harbor and Riverhead were centers of the whale fishery. The figures correspond roughly to distances between the main towns on the road to Sag Harbor, Long Island (see J. H. Colton's *Traveller's Map of Long Island* [New York, 1843]).

22. The registry papers of the "St. Lawrence," now in the National Archives, show that Oliver P. Brown was master from 1838 to 1852. The *New York American,* Saturday, June 1, 1839, carried an advertisement that the "St. Lawrence" was to sail on Tuesday. Her hold was not then full, for she was still able to "take 50 or 100 bales of cotton if offered immediately."

23. Sailors were required to sign shipping articles, on which the time when they were to report on the ship was stated (Joseph Blunt, *The Merchant's and Shipmaster's Assistant* [New York, 1832], pp. 125-26). Redburn signs the shipping articles the day after he secures his position from the captain. This could have been true of Melville's experience, if he made the agreement with Captain Brown on Sunday, for the shipping offices were closed on that day (*New York American,* June 5, 1839).

24. *New York Evening Post,* June 3, 1839.

25. See n. 23. See frontispiece for a probable picture of the ship.

26. *New York Herald,* June 6, 1839.

27. Weather reports from the *New York Herald,* June 4 and 11, 1839. The departure of the "St. Lawrence" was listed in the *New York American,* June 6, 1839, under "Last Evening." High water was at 2:42 P.M. (*New York Evening Post,* June 5, 1839). The *New York Herald,* June 6, mentions the detention of the "Rochester" and other ships.

28. Figures from the ship's registry papers in the National Archives.

29. The "Rochester" displaced 714 tons, the "England" 729 (R. G. Albion, *Square Riggers on Schedule* [Princeton: Princeton University Press, 1938], pp. 278, 280).

30. The schedules of the packets, which were owned by four large shipping companies, were printed for a year in advance, showing sailings on the same four days each month. The "St. Lawrence," on the other hand, sailed irregularly. She had arrived in New York from Liverpool on April 23, coming by way of Boston. Following the trip on which Melville sailed

on her, her next departure for Liverpool was on November 2 (*Shipping and Commercial List and New-York Price Current,* April 24 and November 6, 1839). On May 20 her agents advertised that she would "positively sail on Thursday, May 23d"; on May 24, that she would leave on May 27; on May 27, that she would sail on May 28. Thereafter they posted no notice of her departure until June 1, when she was promised to sail June 4 (*New York Evening Post,* May 20-June 1, 1839, and *New York American,* June 1, 1839). Such changes in schedule show that the "St. Lawrence" was not a "packet" or "liner" but a "regular trader."

31. *Redburn,* p. 135. In 1839, Melville undoubtedly had information about liners from Leonard Gansevoort, one of "those who had sailed in them."

32. The registry papers of the "St. Lawrence" show that she was built with a figurehead and retained it until sometime between 1844 and 1852.

33. J. A. Scoville, *The Old Merchants of New York City* (New York, 1863), I, 307.

34. Crew list in the National Archives. Melville was five feet nine and a half inches when he sailed on the "Acushnet" a year and a half later (Anderson, *Melville in the South Seas,* p. 35).

35. The process by which Melville's name was erroneously transcribed is readily accounted for. Crew lists were made up from shipping articles signed by the mariner (Blunt, *Shipmaster's Assistant,* p. 125, and Richard Henry Dana, Jr., *The Seaman's Friend* [Boston, 1841], pp. 179-80). In copying Melville's name, the scribe mistook "Herman" for "Norman." The error is understandable; in Melville's signature to the letter quoted on pp. 84-86, the "Herman" could easily be mistaken for "Norman" at a cursory glance. The crossbar of the *H* is long and slanting, like the middle stroke of an *N,* and the *e* could be taken for an *o.* In the initials Melville added to the postscript, the *H* is indistinguishable from an *N.*

36. The entire crew list is here reproduced:

Names	Places of Birth	Places of Residence	Of What Country Citizens or Subjects	Age	Height		Complex.	Hair
					Ft.	In.		
Joseph M Shaw j	New York			38	5	8	light	brown
Nath Heard	Massachusetts			28	5	9	do	do
Moses Walker i	D of Columbia			23	5	8	dark	black
Perry Thomas	Connecticut			46	5	8	do	do
James McLain	New York	New		24	5	7	light	brown
Francis Williams	do	York	U States	32	5	8	do	do
William Hamilton	do	City		23	5	6	do	do
Robert Jackson	do			31	5	6	do	do
Wm Allen	do			25	5	6	do	do
James Tenell	do			27	5	6	do	do
Laurence Crawford	do			19	5	8	do	do
Norman Melville	do			19	5	8½	do	do
Benj Thompson	Pennsylvania			41	6	2	do	do
Benj Foy	Maryland			22	5	8	do	do
James Johnson	Ireland		Gt Britain	20	5	6	do	do
Peter Brown	Greenland		Greenland	24	5	9	do	do

The first two places on the list were reserved for the first and the second mate, respectively, and the next two for the steward and the cook (see the lists cited in n. 40). Melville's description of the steward on the "Highlander" as a youth and of the cook as old fits Walker and Thomas.

stigation of lists of American seamen, Professor
lied me with the record of Oliver P. Brown, birth-
occurs on a "Register of Seamen for District of
January-June, 1824 (National Archives). Brown's seaman's certificate was issued March 26, 1824. He was then twenty-six years old, five feet eight inches tall, and of light complexion. He would have been forty-one in 1839, or about the age of Captain Riga (forty), though Riga had "very black whiskers." Melville may have altered his name to Riga to avoid legal trouble since Brown was still captain of the "St. Lawrence" in 1849.

38. The accounts of the crew's general behavior in *Redburn* are borne out by other contemporary narratives. See "The Merchant Service," *Hunt's Merchant's Magazine and Commercial Review,* I (December 1839), 468-72; Charles F. Briggs, *The Adventures of Harry Franco* (New York, 1839), I, 166-90; J. Ross Browne, *Etchings of a Whaling Cruise* (London, 1846), *passim;* and George Little, *Life on the Ocean, or Twenty Years at Sea* (14th ed.; New York, 1856; 1st ed.; Baltimore, 1843), p. 33 and *passim.*

39. See Albion, *Square Riggers on Schedule,* pp. 147-51.

40. The ships were, respectively, the "Hibernia," the "Rochester," the "Scotland," and the "Georgiana." Figures come from copies of their crew lists in the National Archives.

41. "Boy," as Melville accurately explains it in *Redburn* (p. 76), was the technical term for "a green hand, a landsman on his first voyage." He describes Redburn as a boy in this sense as well as in the ordinary sense of youngster. All inexperienced hands, even if they were forty or fifty years old, were called boys (Dana, *The Seaman's Friend,* p. 165).

42. Dana, *The Seaman's Friend,* p. 165.

43. *Ibid.,* p. 167.

44. *Ibid.,* p. 166.

45. *Ibid.*

46. *Mardi,* I, 16.

47. Careful research has failed to turn up the logbook of the "St. Lawrence." The Customs House papers in Liverpool, which would have thrown some light on the ship, have long since been destroyed, according to the Collector of the Port. Likewise, the papers and records of Howland and Aspinwall, owners of the "St. Lawrence," seem to have disappeared along with the dissolution of the firm after the Panic of 1893.

48. *The Times* (London), July 3, 1839. The "Highlander" arrived in Liverpool in the "beginning of July" (*Redburn,* p. 256), after a crossing of "about thirty" days (p. 158).

49. *Liverpool Mercury,* July 5, 1839; *Shipping and Commercial List and New-York Price Current,* October 2, 1839.

50. Log of "Normandie," Liverpool, March 28-May 3, 1842 (Harvard University Library).

51. "A Visit to Liverpool," *Tait's Edinburgh Magazine,* XVI (April 1849), 213-16. C. S. Stewart, Charles F. Briggs, Philip Rhinelander, and others all noted the constant smoke and rain that Redburn found so objectionable (pp. 245, 385).

52. "Two or Three Things About Liverpool," *Tait's Edinburgh Magazine,* XI (July 1844), 429.

53. Diary in the New York Public Library.

54. Bayard Taylor, *Views A-foot* (New York, 1846), p. 7; Thurlow Weed, *Letters from Europe and the West Indies, 1843-1852* (Albany, 1866), p. 48; N. P. Willis, *Pencillings by the Way* (London: T. Werner Laurie, 1942; 1st ed.; London, 1835), p. 505; Edward Salisbury, "Journal of Travels in Europe," I, 197 (MS. in Yale University Library, quoted by permission of the Library Committee).

55. *Redburn,* p. 162.

56. *Ibid.*, p. 260. The omitted words, "wholly unforeseen by me," seem more like an artistic touch designed to add to the sense of Redburn's disillusionment than an accurate statement of Melville's experience (see p. 127).

57. Margaret Fuller Ossoli, *At Home and Abroad* (Boston, 1856), pp. 124-25. Her visit occurred in August 1846.

58. "Two or Three Things About Liverpool," *Tait's Edinburgh Magazine,* XI (July 1844), 431.

59. These details are drawn from *The Sessional Papers of the House of Lords* (London, 1844), XXIV, App., 14-25. The report on Liverpool, made by Dr. William H. Duncan, public health officer for the city, covered the years from 1838 to 1840.

60. *Ibid.*, pp. 243-46. Dr. Duncan estimated that 64 per cent of the people in the Exchange–Castle Street Ward lived in courts and cellars. According to a map inserted in *The Stranger in Liverpool* (12th ed.; Liverpool, 1838), the Exchange Ward contained Launcelott's Hey and Union Street; the crew of the "Highlander" used to walk through the first to get to their boarding-house in the second (*Redburn,* pp. 167, 231, 278, 281).

61. William S. Sanger, *History of Prostitution* (New York, 1858), pp. 340-41. He quotes the figure from a survey of Liverpool made in 1840.

62. *Redburn,* p. 259.

63. *Mardi,* II, 376.

64. Blunt, *Shipmaster's Assistant,* p. 127. A sailor was entitled to one third of his wages in advance at each port of unlading. Redburn receives a three-dollar advance.

65. *The Stranger in Liverpool,* pp. 23-25, 32, 43, 91, 100-4, 151.

66. Melville spends five full chapters and parts of others describing the sights in and along the docks (*Redburn,* chaps. xxxii-xxxvi). Although he employs literary sources for some of his description, personal experience undoubtedly underlies most of it. He "explored the new docks" when he returned to Liverpool seventeen years later. See the entry for November 10, 1856, in his *Journal Up the Straits,* ed. Weaver, p. 5.

67. Maria Melville to Allan Melville, Jr., September 25, 1839 (Leyda, "The Melville Log"), in which she cites a letter from Herman dated Liverpool, July 9, and refers to the "St. Lawrence" by name.

68. Now in the Duyckinck Collection of the New York Public Library.

69. Melville's assertion in *Redburn* (p. 166) that American sailors in Liverpool were boarded ashore at the expense of the shipowners, since fires for cooking were forbidden on ships in the docks, is borne out by Weed, *Travels in Europe,* p. 50, and *The Stranger in Liverpool,* p. 12.

70. *Redburn,* p. 226.

71. *Ibid.,* p. 199.

72. *Journal Up the Straits,* ed. Weaver, p. 4. "20 years" is obviously a round number.

73. See the *Penny Magazine of the Society for the Diffusion of Useful Knowledge,* II (March 31-April 20, 1833), 164, in an article on "The Manchester and Liverpool Railroad."

74. *Redburn,* pp. 264-65. A factual error in the narration of the incident indicates that the story is true. The equestrian statue in St. George's Square was that of George III, not George IV (*The Stranger in Liverpool,* p. 158). Had Melville been relying on a printed source, as he frequently did, instead of on his memory, the error would probably not have occurred.

75. *Redburn,* p. 265. In view of Gansevoort Melville's fervor as a political orator and the dependency of his mother and sisters, this is an astonishing remark.

76. Onc recalls at this point his note on the "republican swagger" of the Yankee with whom he boarded in Pittsfield in 1837 (see p. 85).

77. *Liverpool Mercury,* August 9, 1839.

78. *Ibid.,* August 2, 1839. The paper reported on July 5 that 189 intoxicated persons had been found in the streets and brought into court for fines.

79. Anderson, *Melville in the South Seas,* pp. 236, 241, and Braswell, *Melville's Religious Thought,* p. 53.

80. *Redburn,* pp. 225-26.

81. I, 165. Scoresby's ministry in the Floating Chapel is described in the *Liverpool Mercury,* July 19, 1839.

82. See Melville's copy of James Boaden's *An Inquiry into the Authenticity of Various Pictures and Prints . . . of Shakespeare* (London, 1824) (M), which he bought on June 27, 1848, and into which he bound a playbill of the Royal Theatre, Drury Lane, dated Friday, June 5, 1818, announcing the playing of *The Beaux' Stratagem* and *Children in the Wood.* It seems certain that Melville found the playbill among his father's papers, for Allan Melvill's Journal reveals that he was in London from June 3 to June 7, 1818.

83. See Melville's *Journal of a Visit to London and the Continent, 1849-1850,* ed. Eleanor Melville Metcalf (Cambridge: Harvard University Press, 1948), entries for November 9 and 12, 1849.

84. The anonymous author of *The Tourist in Europe* (New York, 1838), says (p. ii): "You may easily see Liverpool and its lions in a couple of days or less." The "lions" listed are the Town Hall, the Exchange, the cemetery, and the docks.

85. Maria Melville to Allan Melville, Jr., September 25, 1839, quoting a letter of Herman's from Liverpool, July 9 (Leyda, "The Melville Log").

86. The figure was determined by English measurements, which differed from American standards (*Liverpool Mercury,* August 9, 1839).

87. The "St. Lawrence" was entered for loading sometime between July 19 and July 26, according to the *Liverpool Mercury,* July 26, 1839.

88. *Liverpool Mercury,* August 2, 1839.

89. *Redburn,* p. 311. The *Liverpool Mercury,* August 16, 1839, confirms Melville's account of the wind conditions and the departure of the "St. Lawrence" with a large number of ships (45) on August 13.

90. See chap. vi.

91. Records of the Collector of Customs of New York, Inspector's Certificate for the ship "St. Lawrence," dated New York, September 30, 1839 (National Archives).

92. Records of the Collector of Customs of New York, consular certificate for the ship "St. Lawrence," dated Liverpool, August 6, 1839. Jackson and Brown are listed as deserters on this certificate, signed by the United States consul in Liverpool, but since they are not listed as absent on the inspector's certificate cited in n. 91 they must have returned to the ship before she sailed on August 13. The number of deserters from the "Highlander"—three—agrees with the facts (*Redburn,* p. 281).

93. Inspector's certificate cited in n. 91.

94. The *New York Herald* of September 30, 1839, reported the "St. Lawrence" as "Below" (*i.e.,* in the lower harbor, below the Narrows) on September 27; but this must have meant either the twenty-eighth or twenty-ninth, since the issue of September 28, containing the ship news for September 27, does not mention the "St. Lawrence." (There was no issue of the paper on Sunday, September 29.) Melville sets Sunday as the day of arrival off the coast of New Jersey (*Redburn,* p. 384).

95. *Mardi,* I, 9; *Redburn,* pp. 384-85. That the ship was becalmed is the only way of accounting for the fact that she took two days to travel the fifteen miles from Sandy Hook to her pier—as did the "Highlander."

96. Melville's account in *Redburn* (pp. 386-87) is borne out by the ship's papers. The inspector's certificates for the ships "Rochester," "Georgiana," "Hibernia," and "Scotland," which arrived in New York at about this time, are marked "Quarantine Ground Port of New York"; the same certificate for the "St. Lawrence" is marked only "Port of New York" (all papers in the National Archives).

97. *Redburn,* p. 387.

98. The *Shipping and Commercial List and New-York Price Current,* October 2, 1839, lists the arrival (in the harbor) on September 30.

99. Compare Dana's description of sailors' deliberate mockery of "everything near and dear" in *Two Years Before the Mast,* pp. 316-17.

100. Willis J. Abbot, *American Merchant Ships and Sailors* (New York: Dodd, Mead and Company, 1902), pp. 32-33.

101. Albion, *Square Riggers on Schedule,* pp. 153-60, 331-34.

102. Elizabeth Shaw Melville to Hope Savage Shaw, May 5, 1848 (M), and Augusta Melville to Peter Gansevoort, April 7, 1857 (G-L).

103. Dana, *The Seaman's Friend,* p. 166.

104. Maria Melville to Allan Melville, Jr., October 4, 1839 (Leyda, "The Melville Log"). On the same day Peter Gansevoort wrote to Lemuel Shaw that "Mrs. Melville has become entirely impoverished— . . . & as I have just heard, her furniture is now advertised for sale" (draft of letter in G-L).

105. Draft of letter of Peter Gansevoort to Maria Melville, October 18, 1839 (G-L). Her receipt, of the same date (G-L), shows that the money was part of her unsettled claim upon her mother's estate.

106. Maria Melville to Peter Gansevoort, December 14, 1839 (G-L).

107. Draft of letter of Peter Gansevoort to Maria Melville, December 18, 1839 (G-L). A letter of the Albany City Bank to Peter Gansevoort, October 19, 1839 (G-L), requests him emphatically to pay 25 per cent of his indebtedness of over $21,000. Other memorandums show that he was trying to anticipate fees at this time.

108. Herman Gansevoort to Peter Gansevoort, February 22, 1840 (G-L), enclosing one hundred dollars for Maria.

109. Gordon, *Gazetteer of New York State,* p. 643.

110. Maria Melville to Allan Melville, Jr., December 7, 1839 (Leyda, "The Melville Log").

111. Maria Melville to Peter Gansevoort, December 14, 1839 (G-L). Herman's salary is the chief evidence that he taught at the Greenbush and Schodack Academy. It must have been substantial if he was to allow his mother "$150 to $200 a year" and pay for board and clothes in addition. But salaries in the common schools in New York in 1839 averaged $18.00 per month for male teachers. In Greenbush, the schools operated only nine months in the year. Thus Herman's total income would have been well under $200.00. On the other hand, in 1839-1840 the Greenbush and Schodack Academy divided $498.00 between two teachers, indicating a higher salary scale than that prevalent in the common schools. Furthermore, Maria's mention in a later letter that the school was about to close for lack of funds also suggests a private school, for the public schools received money from the state, to which was added an equal or larger sum raised locally.

Another set of circumstances points to the academy as the scene of Herman's employment. On the morning of Friday, October 18, he carried a letter from his mother in Lansingburgh to his uncle in Albany (see n. 105). If he was free to act as a messenger at such a time, it is unlikely that he was engaged in teaching. Presumably he began between this date and December 7, when his mother reported that he was much interested in his scholars. In the interim, on November 30, the Greenbush and Schodack Academy had announced that having recently undergone thorough repairs, it was "now open for the reception of pupils" (*Albany Evening Journal,* November 30, 1839). The academy went into operation and continued functioning until the spring. On March 10, 1840, it announced that the summer term would begin May 1 (*Albany Evening Journal,* March 10, 1840). However, a search of Albany newspapers for April, May, and June has failed to discover any announcement, customary for all private schools in the vicinity, that the term actually began, and Melville's school closed between May 16 and May 23 (see p. 150). It may have been that at the opening of the summer term so few scholars appeared that the school was forced to discontinue. At any rate, both the financial data and the coincidence that the academy opened in December at about the time Herman is known to have started teaching are presumptive evidence that he taught there.

This is the only known period of Melville's schoolteaching in Greenbush. Compare his wife's statement that after the Liverpool trip (which she misdates 1837) he "taught school at intervals in Pittsfield and in Greenbush (now East Albany) N. Y." (Weaver, *Herman Melville, Mariner and Mystic,* p. 113). The town in which Melville taught is now known as East Greenbush, not East Albany. (For the statistics on public schools in Greenbush, see the *Report of the Superintendent of Common Schools of the State of New York* [Albany, 1841], pp. 17, 31; for similar materials on the Greenbush and Schodack Academy, see the *Fifty-fourth Annual Report of the Regents of the State of New-York* [Albany, 1841], pp. 41, 50, 59, 66, 118. David Burr's *Atlas of the State of New York* [Ithaca, 1839], Map 14, shows the location of the academy, which was the only school in the town besides the public schools.)

112. Journal of Allan Melville, Jr. (Leyda, "The Melville Log").

113. Herman added the note to his mother's letter to Allan of December 7 (Leyda, "The Melville Log").

114. Maria Melville to Peter Gansevoort, December 14, 1839 (G-L).

115. Maria Melville to Allan Melville, Jr., December 7, 1839 (Leyda, "The Melville Log").

116. The handwriting in which these lines are copied is similar to that of Melville's letter to Peter Gansevoort, quoted above, pp. 84-86. Jay Leyda has identified the verses.

117. For various reasons I have assumed that Harriet Fly was the first girl to share intimately with Melville the moral, sentimental, and romantic beauties of *The Carcanet.* Her name is inscribed twice on page v, evidently in her handwriting, and she wrote on another page, "Harriet, Fly, Fly, Fly away." We can connect Harriet with Melville in 1839 through his known friendship with her brother.

But the assumption is possibly an error, for there are other claimants to a portion of this book's mystery. An inscription on the title page reads, "Mary L. Day's Book." A later inscription is

"Mary L. Day
Cambridge
N. Y. 1839" (?—possibly 1837,
1857, or 1859)

Elsewhere the name is written, "M. L. Day" and "Mary Louisia [*sic*] Beaufort Day." The name "Mrs. Adah Matilda Day" also appears. To make the work of any ambitious literary detective even more complicated, the name "Harriet M. Day" appears three times.

Cambridge, N.Y., is about fifty miles northeast of Albany. There is no record that Melville ever went there, nor is there any surviving record, written or oral, that Mary L. or Harriet M. Day ever lived there. How this or these persons ever got access to a book once belonging to Herman Melville, and whether she or they knew the owner must remain mysteries until further evidence is unearthed.

118. Gansevoort Melville to Allan Melville, Jr., March 3, 1840, with additions dated April 3 (Leyda, "The Melville Log").

119. Gansevoort Melville to Allan Melville, Jr., January 21, 1840 (Leyda, "The Melville Log").

120. His letters are mentioned in a letter of Maria Melville to Allan Melville, Jr., February 5, 1840 (Leyda, "The Melville Log").

121. Maria Melville to Allan Melville, Jr., May 16, 1840 (Leyda, "The Melville Log").

122. Maria Melville to Peter Gansevoort, May 16, 1840 (G-L). The school was to close "next week."

123. *Ibid.* She says that if Peter and brother Herman can devise any plan whereby she and her daughters can provide for their own wants, they will be glad to adopt it. It appears that the plan adopted was for Maria and the girls to do sewing. A family tradition to that effect exists, according to Mrs. Metcalf; in a letter to Mrs. Peter Gansevoort (Peter's second wife) dated Lansingburgh, June 3, 1844 (G-L), Maria begs her sister-in-law to accept "the enclosed collar and cuffs," which she says are "Helens workmanship." Just when Melville's mother and sisters may have been reduced to doing piecework for sympathetic customers in Lansingburgh is not known. One would judge that they began not long after May 1840 since no further letters from Maria to Peter asking for funds have been found. Gansevoort did not begin to have an income until 1842 (letter to Lemuel Shaw, July 13, 1842 [S]).

124. The Melville Collection at Harvard contains the following receipt in Melville's hand:

"Lansingburgh June 5, 1840

$6.00

Recived from the Trustees of the School District No 7 Town of Brunswick six Dollars (pay $6.) in full of all demands to this date

HERMAN MELVILLE"

Why this receipt should have turned up among Melville's papers is a mystery, unless he did not present it for payment. The school building is said by present residents of Brunswick to have been destroyed by fire sometime in the 1840's. Melville is not mentioned in the sketchy records of the school, now in the custody of the clerk of School District Number 7 in Brunswick. The sum of six dollars mentioned in the receipt may account for Arthur Stedman's statement that, while teaching at Greenbush, Melville received "six dollars a quarter and board" (Weaver, *Herman Melville, Mariner and Mystic,* p. 113).

125. Maria Melville to Peter Gansevoort, May 16, 1840 (G-L).

126. In the sketch of his uncle's life, written in 1870, Melville said: "In 1837, though advanced in years, the Major, yielding to stronger inducements, and with a view of ultimate benefit to his children, removed to Galena, Illinois, there to occupy a responsible position in a mercantile house." He continued: "In 1841 [1840] I visited my own venerable kinsman in his western home . . . ."

127. Eli Fly to Peter Gansevoort, June 2, 1840 (G-L), announcing his intention of leaving "Thursday" [June 4] for the West.

128. Augustus L. Chetlain, *Recollections of Seventy Years* (Galena: Gazette Publishing Company, 1899), p. 29.

129. *The History of Jo Daviess County, Illinois* (Chicago, 1878), pp. 478, 481.

130. *Ibid.,* p. 478.

131. "Sketch of Major Thomas Melvill, Jr." (G-L).

132. Thomas Melvill, Jr., to Lemuel Shaw, October 30, 1839, April 24, 1841, and September 6, 1843; and to Lemuel Shaw and John D'Wolf, January 9, 1839 (S).

133. Chetlain, *Recollections, passim,* describes the successes of numerous settlers in Galena. On the other hand, Emerson, who visited Illinois in 1850, noted that "the hard times of Illinois were from 1837 to 1845 and onward, when pork was worth twelve shillings a hundred and men journeyed with loads of wheat and pork a hundred miles or more to Chicago, and sold their wheat for twenty-six cents a bushel, and were obliged to sell their team to get home again. Mr. Jenks, a stage agent and livery-stable keeper, told us of his experiences . . ." (*Journals* [Cambridge: Riverside Press, 1913], IX [1856-1863], 9).

134. *Moby-Dick,* I, 317.

135. The route is recommended and costs and conditions described in William Oliver, *Eight Months in Illinois, With Information to Immigrants* (Newcastle upon Tyne, 1843; reprinted Chicago: Walter M. Hill, 1924), pp. 226-27.

136. *Journal Up the Straits,* ed. Weaver, pp. 130, 151. The allusions must have come from personal observation in 1840 since Melville is not known to have visited the West again until 1859, when he lectured in Quincy, Illinois (Weaver, *Herman Melville, Mariner and Mystic,* p. 370).

137. P. 335.

138. P. 275.

139. Herman Melville to Evert A. Duyckinck, March 3, 1849, printed in Thorp, *Herman Melville, Representative Selections,* pp. 371-72.

140. *Poems,* p. 313. It may be added that in describing the island from which Ishmael set out Melville wrote: "Nantucket is no Illinois" (*Moby-Dick,* I, 77).

141. P. 216.

142. *Israel Potter,* p. 198.

143. *The Confidence Man,* p. 172.

144. It would have been logical to ascend the Ohio from Cairo rather than to return up the Mississippi and go back by way of Lake Ontario and the Erie Canal.

145. Helen Maria Melville to Allan Melville, Jr., added to letter of Maria Melville to Allan Melville, Jr., December 21, 1840 (Leyda, "The Melville Log").

146. Gansevoort Melville to Allan Melville, Jr., November 26, 1840 (Leyda, "The Melville Log"). Melville gives Redburn and Harry Bolton a meal at Sweeny's (*Redburn,* p. 390).

147. See letter of Maria Melville cited in n. 145. She is summarizing a letter from Gansevoort. "Destination" undoubtedly carried its primary meaning of "destiny," rather than "the place set for the end of a journey." Maria added to Allan: "The particulars you will hear when we see you." One strong implication is that Allan would hear the discussion about Herman's future when he and Herman and Gansevoort talked over the problem with the family at Christmas.

148. The thrills of the chase had been publicized not only in John H. Reynolds' "Mocha-Dick; or, the White Whale of the Pacific," *Knickerbocker Magazine,* May 1839, but also in Thomas Beale's *The Natural History of the Sperm Whale* (London, 1839). A chapter from the latter entitled "Method of Taking the Whale" and detailing graphically the excitement of the attack

was published in the *Albany Argus,* May 27, 1839. The *Penny Magazine,* which Melville read, had also printed accounts of whaling. (See, for example, II [April 30-May 31, 1833], 201-8. The same volume contains in the issue for March 31-April 30, 1833, the plate of the entrance to the Liverpool and Manchester Railway which Melville mentions in *Redburn.* See p. 140.)

It has been maintained that one of Melville's motives for going whaling was to search for Mocha-Dick (R. S. Garnett, "Moby-Dick and Mocha-Dick: A Literary Find," *Blackwood's Edinburgh Magazine,* CCXXVI [December 1929], 858). This hypothesis is scarcely tenable since the very article of Reynolds' that Garnett thinks determined Melville "to voyage the wonder world in search of 'the one grand hooded phantom'" described the death of Mocha-Dick.

149. Melville to Richard Henry Dana, Jr., May 1, 1850, published by Harrison Hayford, "Two New Letters of Herman Melville," *ELH,* XI (March 1944), 77.

150. There may have been another motive behind Melville's whaling voyage. Responsible sources in Lansingburgh have told me of the tradition, still current there, that he went to sea because of a love affair which culminated in social disgrace for the girl involved.

151. Gansevoort Melville to Lemuel Shaw, January 11, 1841 (S).

152. Letters from New Bedford residents to Lemuel Shaw (S) include those of Timothy E. Coffin, H. G. V. Colby, and Thomas D. Eliot, all written in 1840. It was through his acquaintance with New Bedford and Fairhaven businessmen and shipowners that Lemuel Shaw was able to trace the whaling career of Thomas Wilson Melvill (see letters of J. H. W. Page to Shaw, April 30, 1840, and Lemuel Tripp to Shaw, September 8, 1845 [S]).

153. Gansevoort Melville to Lemuel Shaw, July 22, 1842 (S).

154. With the known facts of Melville's youth before us, we may now consider one datum that has received much emphasis—his allegedly direct statement about his mother, "She hated me" (Weaver, *Herman Melville, Mariner and Mystic,* p. 62). This has been used to support conclusions that his mother's hatred drove him to sea (see p. 2), that he both hated his mother and loved her "with excessive love," and that his feeling toward his mother helped beget Ahab's feeling toward Moby-Dick (Arvin, *Herman Melville,* pp. 30, 172-74). But the only known authority for the statement is Melville's niece, Maria M. Morewood, who was born in 1849. ". . . *she* said that *H. M. said* that his mother hated him," wrote Frances M. Thomas, Melville's daughter, to Eleanor Melville Metcalf, November 12, 1919 (M). Thus it seems that the foundation under much explanation of Melville's psychological imbalance is a single remark, attributed to him eighteen years after his death by a woman thirty years his junior, and unqualified as to time or occasion. Did Maria Morewood hear it directly from her uncle, or was she repeating a family story? If Melville really made the remark, did his mother hate him when he was a boy, or during his whaling years, or in those middle years when he was apparently a failure? Other questions will occur to the curious.

There may have been conflict between Maria Melville and her second son in his youth, but there is no direct evidence of it and the ascertainable facts reveal anything but hatred.

Notes to Chapter V

1. For most of the material on Melville's life from 1841 to 1849 I am indebted to Charles R. Anderson's *Melville in the South Seas* and to Luther Mansfield's "Herman Melville, Author and New Yorker, 1846-1851" (Doctor's thesis, University of Chicago, 1936).

2. William H. Gilman, "A Note on Herman Melville in Honolulu," *American Literature,* XIX (May 1947), 169.

3. Within a few months after the publication of *Typee,* Melville was sought out by autograph hunters, to one of whom, a Dr. William Sprague, Melville wrote: "You remember some one woke up one morning and found himself famous. And here am I, just come from hoeing in the garden, writing autographs." (The letter was printed by T. O. M[abbott], "Herman Melville," *Notes and Queries,* CLXII [February 27, 1932], 151-52.)

4. Anderson, *Melville in the South Seas,* chaps. v-viii.

5. See the note on Mary L. D. Ferris' article, "Herman Melville," *Bulletin of the Society of American Authors,* VI (September 1901), 289-93, in the same issue, p. 316. The article, writes the author of the note, "was submitted to Mrs. Melville for correction." The chief correction was that "Mr. Melville would not have been willing to call his old Typee entertainers 'man-devouring,' as he has stated that whatever might have been his suspicions, he never had evidence that it was the custom of the tribe."

6. *Typee,* Intro., p. ix.

7. See the letter from Melville to Bradford, May 23, 1846, located by the author in the Boston Public Library and subsequently published by Zoltán Haraszti, "Melville Defends *Typee,*" *More Books, Bulletin of the Boston Public Library,* XXII (June 1947), 203-8.

8. However, Melville also believed that "against the cause of missions in the abstract no Christian can possibly be opposed; it is in truth a just and holy cause" (*Typee,* p. 266).

9. On July 30, 1847, the *Lansingburgh Gazette* printed this note: "MORE TYPEE—Herman Melville, the Omoo of *Typee,* is preparing for the press another book of adventures in the South Seas." This is the earliest known reference to the composition of *Mardi.*

10. Gansevoort Melville to Lemuel Shaw, January 25, 1842 (S), and Maria Melville to Lemuel Shaw, September 5, 1842 (S).

11. Herman Melville to Lemuel Shaw, March 19, 1846 (M), printed in Weaver, *Herman Melville, Mariner and Mystic,* p. 258. At the close Melville writes: "Remember me most warmly to Mrs. Shaw & Miss Elizabeth, and to all your family, & tell them I shall not soon forget that agreeable visit to Boston."

12. Hope Savage Shaw, mother of Elizabeth, describes the wedding day (August 4) as "pleasant" in her diary (S).

13. In dedicating to his wife a group of late poems entitled *Weeds and Wildings,* Melville wrote: "I yearly remind you of the coincidence in my

chancing on such a specimen [a four-leaf clover] by the wayside on the early forenoon of the fourth day of a certain bridal month, now four years more than four times ten years ago" (*Poems,* p. 303).

14. *Boston Transcript,* August 5, 1847. The New South Church was a Unitarian body, presided over by Dr. Alexander Young, the liberal Unitarian clergyman who performed the ceremony (see Justin Winsor [ed.], *Memorial History of the City of Boston* [Boston, 1881], III, 475, 480).

15. An indenture dated September 10, 1847, shows that Herman Melville leased the property on Fourth Avenue for twenty-one years thereafter, giving a five-thousand-dollar mortgage plus one thousand dollars in cash and agreeing to pay the rent ("New York City Book of Conveyances," CCCCXCVIII, 183-85, in the Hall of Records, New York City).

16. He is thus referred to in the indenture cited in n. 15.

17. Harrison Hayford and Merrell R. Davis, "Herman Melville as Office-Seeker," *Modern Language Quarterly,* X (June 1949), 170-71.

18. William Charvat, "Melville's Income," *American Literature,* XV (November 1943), 254.

19. Lemuel Shaw to Herman Melville, May 15, 1860 (M), printed in Weaver, *Herman Melville, Mariner and Mystic,* pp. 366-69.

20. The Knights of the Round Table, a group of pleasure-loving young literati, included William Allen Butler, Cornelius Mathews, Jedediah B. Auld, William Alfred Jones, Russell Trevett, and others (Mansfield, "Herman Melville, Author and New Yorker," p. 69).

21. Thorp, *Herman Melville, Representative Selections,* pp. xxvi-xxviii, nn. 18, 20. On March 19, 1849, Harper billed him for "1 Classical Library, 37 v" (Harper account in M). Although Melville was in Boston at this time, the purchase was doubtless made for him by a relative or friend in New York.

22. *American Renaissance,* p. 388.

23. Diary of Hope Savage Shaw (S).

24. James D. Hart, "Melville and Dana," *American Literature,* IX (March 1937), 52.

25. Melville to E. A. Duyckinck, March 3, 1849 (Thorp, *Herman Melville, Representative Selections,* p. 372).

26. Melville to E. A. Duyckinck, February 24, 1849 (Thorp, *Herman Melville, Representative Selections,* p. 371).

27. Melville to E. A. Duyckinck, March 3, 1849 (Thorp, *Herman Melville, Representative Selections,* p. 372).

28. Melville to E. A. Duyckinck, February 24, 1849 (Thorp, *Herman Melville, Representative Selections,* p. 371).

29. Melville to E. A. Duyckinck, March 3, 1849 (Thorp, *Herman Melville, Representative Selections,* p. 372).

30. Melville to E. A. Duyckinck, April 5, 1849 (Thorp, *Herman Melville, Representative Selections,* p. 374).

31. *Ibid.*

32. *Ibid.*

33. Lemuel Shaw to Peter Gansevoort, April 11, 1849 (G-L).

34. The letter is in M.

35. Merrell R. Davis, "Herman Melville's Mardi: The Biography of a Book" (Doctor's thesis, Yale University, 1947), chap. vi.

36. Even before the publication of *Mardi,* Melville had expressed the pessimistic feeling that recognition of an ambitious author begins only with his death (letter to E. A. Duyckinck, April 5, 1849 [Thorp, *Herman Melville, Representative Selections,* p. 374]).

37. Mumford, *Herman Melville,* pp. 109-10.

38. John H. Birss, "A Mere Sale to Effect 'with Letters of Herman Melville,'" *New Colophon,* I (July 1948), 246.

39. Melville to E. A. Duyckinck, December 14, 1849 (Thorp, *Herman Melville, Representative Selections,* p. 376).

40. Melville to Richard Henry Dana, Jr., May 1, 1850 (Hayford, "Two New Letters," *ELH,* XI [March 1944], p. 77).

41. John H. Birss, "A Mere Sale to Effect 'with Letters of Herman Melville,'" *New Colophon,* I (July 1948), 246.

42. Melville to Richard Bentley, July 20, 1849 (John H. Birss, "A Mere Sale to Effect 'with Letters of Herman Melville,'" *New Colophon,* I [July 1948], 247).

43. The agreement is in M.

44. Melville to Richard Bentley, July 20, 1849 (John H. Birss, "A Mere Sale to Effect 'with Letters of Herman Melville,'" *New Colophon,* I [July 1948], 247).

45. See App. D, p. 274, for publication dates.

46. See Nathan Comfort Starr, "The Sea in the English Novel from Defoe to Melville" (Doctor's thesis, Harvard University, 1928), chap. x.

47. *Ibid.*

48. James D. Hart, "Richard Henry Dana, Jr." (Doctor's thesis, Harvard University, 1936), p. 149.

49. N. P. Willis traveled through England, the Continent, and the Near East from 1832 to 1836 as foreign correspondent for the *New York Mirror* and collected his newspaper articles in *Pencillings by the Way* and *Loiterings of Travel* (London, 1840). Bayard Taylor wrote equally popular sketches of the European scene for the *New York Tribune* and gathered them together in *Views A-foot,* a copy of which Melville owned. (It is listed on a statement of Melville's account with Wiley and Putnam, January 1, 1847 [M])

50. As early as 1830 Nathaniel Ames had said that every barber's clerk that crossed the ocean favored the public with his memoirs (*A Mariner's Sketches* [Providence, 1830], p. 183).

51. Two contemporary critics of Melville testify to the surplus of travel and sea stories and to public apathy. *Typee,* declared one, "came from the press at a time when the public taste [had] wearied and sickened of didactic novels and journals of travel through fields explored many times before" (*Southern Literary Messenger,* XVII [September 1852], 574-75). And Fitz-James O'Brien wrote that *Typee* was thoroughly welcome "after the maudlin journeys in Greece—travels in the Holy Land, full of Biblical raptures, and yacht-tours in the Mediterranean . . . , with such like trash that had been inundating the literary market for years previous." He went on to

say that "sea novels had, as it were, been run into the ground by Marryat, Chamier, and Cooper. People were growing weary of shipwrecks and fires at sea. Every possible incident that could occur on board men-of-war, privateers, and prizes, had been described over and over again, with an ability that left nothing to be desired. The whole of a sailor's life was laid bare to us. We knew exactly what they ate, what they drank, and at what hours they ate and drank it . . . . Mr. Melville came forward with his books to relieve this state of well-informed dulness" ("Our Young Authors—Melville," *Putnam's Monthly Magazine,* I [February 1853], 156).

52. Charles L. Lewis, *Books of the Sea* (Annapolis: United States Naval Institute, 1943), pp. 8-11.

53. He knew Scott, Cooper, and Dana before 1841. Other works of the genres which Melville had read by 1849 are: Benjamin Morrell's *Narrative of Four Voyages,* Thomas J. Jacobs' *Scenes, Incidents, and Adventures in the Pacific Ocean,* Bayard Taylor's *Views A-foot, Curiosities of Modern Travel,* J. Ross Browne's *Etchings of a Whaling Cruise,* John Codman's [Captain Ringbolt] *Sailor's Life and Sailor's Yarns,* Charles A. Barnard's *A Narrative of the Sufferings of Captain Charles A. Barnard, in a Voyage Around the World,* Joseph C. Hart's *Romance of Yachting,* and Nathaniel Ames's *A Mariner's Sketches* (see Sealts, "Melville's Reading," *Harvard Library Bulletin,* II (1948), 390, no. 372, 386, no. 293, III (1949), 410, no. 495, 273, no. 170, 124, no. 88, 122, no. 149, 269, no. 38, IV (1950), 98, no. 242, and Anderson, *Melville in the South Seas,* p. 409). He had probably read Charles Ellens' *The Pirates' Own* and *Shipwrecks and Disasters at Sea,* which are perhaps the works cited in *Redburn,* pp. 61 and 109, and *The Narrative of John Nichol, Mariner,* mentioned in *White-Jacket,* p. 480, plus many others of the kind, for they would have been popular in the forecastle.

54. Melville to Richard Bentley, June 5, 1849 (see John H. Birss, "A Mere Sale to Effect 'with Letters of Herman Melville,'" *New Colophon,* I [July 1948], 246).

55. The passage has been published, with corrections, in Melville's *Journal of a Visit to London and the Continent,* ed. Eleanor Melville Metcalf, p. 23.

56. LXVI (November 1849), 567-80.

57. *Ibid.,* p. 574.

58. This explanation receives support from the fact that Weaver, who certainly treats *Redburn* as "real," omits from his reproduction of the passage in Melville's journal the phrase "in treating the thing as real" (p. 292). The restoration of these words virtually demolishes the biographical validity of Weaver's fourth and fifth chapters, which are drawn almost entirely and often verbatim from the pages of *Redburn.*

59. *White-Jacket,* presumably begun after July 2, when *Redburn* was finished, was completed by September 13, when Harper signed an agreement to publish it (agreement in M). In a letter to Lemuel Shaw, October 6, 1849 (S), Melville says that he has a set of plate proofs of *White-Jacket* ready to take to England.

60. *Literary World,* I (March 6, 1847), 105.

61. P. 326.

Notes to Chapter VI

1. "Washing down the decks," says Redburn, ". . . was worse than my mother's house-cleanings at home, which I used to abominate so" (p. 68). See p. 18.

2. *Redburn,* p. 7.

3. *Ibid.,* p. 1.

4. *Ibid.,* pp. 72, 148, 331, 155. Other references to Redburn as a boy are on pp. 13, 79, 192, 193.

5. Knowing that Melville's Liverpool trip occurred in 1839 when he was nearly twenty and reasonably mature might have deterred biographers from taking *Redburn* as autobiography thinly veiled. But for nearly a century it was assumed that the date of the voyage was 1837 and Melville seventeen-eighteen. The error may have originated in the office of Richard Bentley, whose announcement *Works Published in 1849* stated that "Melville sailed in 1837 as ship's boy from New York to Liverpool and back." All subsequent accounts down to 1946 repeat the error, including innumerable editions, both American and English, of *Men of the Time* (1st ed.; London, 1852), every nineteenth- and twentieth-century encyclopedia or biographical dictionary, and even records by those who supposedly knew Melville well: Evert and George Duyckinck, in their *Cyclopaedia of American Literature* (New York, 1855), Melville's friend, J. E. A. Smith (*Herman Melville,* 1891), and Melville's wife. The latter wrote in her commonplace book that Herman "made his first voyage before the mast in 1837, in a New York merchantman bound for Liverpool & returned after a short cruise (see Redburn)" (MS. in the possession of Eleanor Melville Metcalf, who has kindly permitted me to quote it). Even the recent biographies of Melville by Richard Chase (1949) and Geoffrey Stone (1949) perpetuate the error of dating Melville's first voyage in 1837.

6. *Redburn,* p. 1.

7. *Ibid.,* p. 11.

8. *New York Post,* May 28, and *Albany Argus,* June 3, 1839.

9. *Albany Argus,* May 31 and June 4, 1839.

10. It ran Mondays, Wednesdays, and Fridays (*Albany Evening Journal,* May 30, 1839).

11. See John Morrison, *History of American Steam Navigation* (New York: W. F. Sametz, 1903), chap. iii.

12. All the New York and Albany papers for the two weeks following June 1, 1839, have been carefully checked without discovering any report of such an incident as Melville describes.

13. *Literary World,* I (March 6, 1847), 105, reprinted in Thorp, *Herman Melville, Representative Selections,* pp. 321-27. Melville summarizes Browne's scene in which two young gentlemen are cajoled by a courteous and facetious shipping agent into signing up for a whaling voyage that proves thoroughly

disillusioning. Browne's narrative is amusing, but Melville's précis amounts to a complete revision, vastly superior in style, imagination, and ironic humor and artistically fitted up with vivid details which the original lacks. (Browne and his companion climb a flight of stairs to interview the agent; Melville transforms this simple act into "Our author and his friend . . . hurry up a ladder, to a dark loft above, where the old man lurks like a spider in the midst of his toils.") Besides revealing Melville's irrepressible originality, the review hints directly at the scene in which Captain Riga hires Redburn. The young lad likes his future employer "amazingly"; Browne and his friends had been "delighted with the agreeable address" of the agent. When Mr. Jones asks what the captain generally pays a "handsome young fellow like Redburn," the captain offers only three dollars a month, because he is "not so particular about beauty." Melville had said in the review that the shipping agent was "not so particular about weight as beauty." The intent of the two speeches is different, to serve the purpose of the speakers, but the phrasal resemblance and the introduction of the irrelevant question of beauty help to link the scene in *Redburn* with what Melville saw in Browne's narrative.

14. If Captain Oliver P. Brown was the sailor who, at the age of twenty-six, was five feet eight inches tall (see chap. iv, n. 37, p. 334), he would hardly have been more than that at the age of forty. Thus his height would have been about the same as Melville's, and the idea of his patting him on the head becomes entirely absurd.

15. I am indebted to Jay Leyda for pointing out Johnston's cartoon.

16. *Redburn,* p. 67.

17. E.g., *Blackwood's Edinburgh Magazine,* LXVI (November 1849), 570; *Athenaeum,* No. 1150 (November 10, 1849), 1131; *Spectator,* XXII (October 27, 1849), 1020.

18. *Peter Simple* ("Everyman Library" [London: J. M. Dent, (1907)]), p. 31.

19. *Redburn,* p. 29.

20. *Peter Simple,* p. 43.

21. *Redburn,* p. 62.

22. *Peter Simple,* p. 32.

23. For further evidence, see App. D, pp. 277 and 280.

24. *Redburn,* chap. x.

25. See the sworn statement of Captain Oliver P. Brown before Francis B. Ogden, United States consul at Liverpool, August 6, 1839, in the consular certificate for the ship "St. Lawrence" (National Archives). Jay Leyda discovered this valuable document.

26. See his remark in *Redburn,* p. 370, that because people are finicky they miss many scenes of realism which literature might bring them.

27. Weaver, *Herman Melville, Mariner and Mystic,* p. 103; Mumford, *Herman Melville,* p. 33; Freeman, *Herman Melville,* pp. 15-16; Sedgwick, *Herman Melville, The Tragedy of Mind,* p. 66.

28. *Redburn,* p. 184.

29. Further proof that Allan Melvill did not go to Liverpool in 1808 lies in his statement in a copy of a letter to David Swan, Boston, August 25, 1812

(G-L): "I had been repeatedly in Europe [prior to his 1811 trip] but only once before in England which was in 1800 my first voyage." His travel journal reveals that in 1800 he sailed from Boston to London, where he spent September 2 to 20, and that he then went directly to the Continent.

30. J. A. Picton, *Memorials of Liverpool* (London, 1875), II, 148.

31. Allan Melvill met Roscoe in 1818, through an introduction by William Lodge, a mutual friend. Although he speaks of receiving very civil attentions from Mr. Maury, the United States consul, and of having dinner with an old friend, Eben Appleton, he says nothing of a dinner engagement with Roscoe, an event he would hardly have ignored in his methodical accounts of meetings with illustrious people (Allan Melvill to Maria Melville, May 12, 1818 [G-L]).

32. Thorp, "Redburn's Prosy Old Guidebook," *PMLA,* LIII (December 1938), 1146-56.

33. The Journal descended to Eleanor Melville Metcalf. Its green morocco binding possibly inspired Melville's description of the guidebook as "bound in green morocco, which from my earliest recollection has been spotted and tarnished with time; the corners are marked with triangular patches of red, like little cocked hats; and some unknown Goth has inflicted an incurable wound on the back" (*Redburn,* p. 183). The added details sound like Melville's characteristic embellishments.

34. *The Picture of Liverpool,* p. 174. Redburn (p. 185) found Riddough's Hotel marked on the map in *The Picture of Liverpool,* though no such designation is actually made. Riddough's Hotel was at the foot of Lord Street (see n. 39).

35. Letter to the author from J. F. Smith, city librarian of the Liverpool Public Libraries, January 24, 1947. Redburn thinks that Captain Riga boards at the Arms Hotel (*Redburn,* p. 173). Was this the Queen's Arms, formerly the Liverpool Arms, where Allan Melvill had stayed? Did Melville involuntarily reveal, in this allusion, a knowledge that the hotel still existed?

36. Picton, *Memorials,* II, 22. The full name of the hotel was Lillyman's Liverpool Arms, in reference to its proprietor.

37. *Redburn,* p. 199.

38. *The Picture of Liverpool,* pp. 174-75. The inn had "accommodations for families of the first rank, their retinues, carriages, and horses; as also every other description of travellers who wish to be accommodated."

39. *The Picture of Liverpool,* p. 174, locates "Riddiough's [*sic*] Royal Hotel at the bottom of Lord Street," a short street running at right angles to Castle Street, where the Liverpool Arms stood. As both were important thoroughfares, the first being lined with expensive shops and the second connecting the Merchant's Exchange with the Customs House, Melville had undoubtedly traversed them, just as Redburn did (*Redburn,* pp. 199, 260). That Riddough's Royal Hotel had been converted into shops by 1839 is apparent from Picton's sketch of the history of a hotel built "at the bottom of Lord Street" about 1785, first called the New Hotel, and later the Royal Hotel, or Bates's. Although Picton does not mention Riddough in connection with the establishment, the two are undoubtedly the same, for there would hardly have been two "Royal" hotels in the same location at approximately

the same time. According to Picton (II, 127), the Royal Hotel was turned into shops about 1805.

40. *Redburn,* p. 202. The phrase is adapted from *The Picture of Liverpool,* p. 30, where the word "very" is missing.

41. *Redburn,* p. 192.

42. *The Picture of Liverpool,* p. 144.

43. *Encyclopaedia Britannica* (14th ed.; 1943), XIV, 829, and XXI, 226.

44. *Redburn,* p. 229.

45. Thorp, "Redburn's Prosy Old Guidebook," pp. 1152-55.

46. *Redburn,* p. 191.

47. *Ibid.,* pp. 145-46.

48. LXVI (November 1849), pp. 575, 576.

49. *Herman Melville, Mariner and Mystic,* p. 107.

50. His opinion, based on a conversation in 1935, is reported by Simon, *Herman Melville, marin, metaphysicien, et poète,* p. 64.

51. *Herman Melville,* p. 35.

52. *Herman Melville,* p. 19.

53. *Herman Melville, Representative Selections,* p. xlix.

54. Compare the accounts: "When about eighteen years of age [Melville] made a voyage from New York to Liverpool, before the mast, visited London, and returned home in the same capacity" (*Men of the Time* [London, 1852], p. 546; *The Men of the Time, or Sketches of Living Notables* [New York, 1852], p. 350). "In his eighteenth year, [Melville] shipped as a sailor in a New York vessel for Liverpool, made a hurried visit to London when he arrived in port, and returned home 'before the mast'" (Evert A. and George L. Duyckinck, *Cyclopaedia of American Literature,* II, 672-73). Geoffrey Stone has suggested that Melville either wrote this biographical sketch or approved it, for he notes that "the MS. for it, which survives in the Duyckinck Collection of the New York Public Library, has corrections and additions in Melville's hand" (*Melville,* p. 45, n. 3). Aside from the fact that the MS. referred to consists of only three pages, or a small fraction of the final article, the corrections are few in number, many of them are instructions for the compositor, and it is doubtful if the handwriting is actually Melville's.

55. *Herman Melville,* p. 35.

56. App. B, p. 270.

57. *Redburn,* p. 294.

58. App. B, p. 270.

59. *Redburn,* p. 297.

60. App. B, p. 269.

61. *Redburn,* p. 297.

62. App. B, p. 270. I have reversed the order of the two passages.

63. *Redburn,* pp. 297-98. See chap. vii, n. 31.

64. App. B, p. 269.

65. *Redburn,* pp. 294-97.

66. *Ibid.,* p. 278.

67. *Ibid.,* pp. 284-86.

68. See p. 143.

69. See chap. iv, n. 92, p. 337.

70. *Statutes of the United States,* July 20, 1790, chap. lvi, § 5.

71. See p. 140. When Melville passed through London in 1856, he also made no note in his journal of any adventure there in 1839. His brief descriptions of Birmingham and of the railroad trip from there to Liverpool read like the record of first experiences, though a railroad trip to London in 1839 would have introduced him to these scenes (see his *Journal Up the Straits,* ed. Weaver, pp. 171-75).

72. *Mogg's Handbook for Travellers; or, Real Iron-Road Book* (London, 1840), pp. 212-20; Felix Summerly, *Travelling Charts; or, Iron Road Books, for Perusal on the Journey: London to Rugby and Birmingham* (London, n.d.), unpaged.

73. *Redburn,* p. 316.

74. *Ibid.,* pp. 316-17.

75. *Ibid.,* p. 317.

76. Records of the Collector of Customs, New York, Inspector's Certificate for the ship "St. Lawrence," September 30, 1839. One of the men shipped in Liverpool, named Antono [*sic*] Ton, may have suggested the Portuguese, Miguel Saveda.

77. *Redburn,* p. 310. Elsewhere, Melville places the number of immigrants at "four or five hundred" (p. 340).

78. *Ibid.,* pp. 370-71.

79. *Ibid.,* p. 371.

80. Weaver, *Herman Melville, Mariner and Mystic,* p. 108.

81. See *Redburn,* p. 335, and Ames, p. 186. Ames writes: "We had an Irish family on board that amused me much. Before we were out of the Irish Channel, they began to ask, 'Sure now, and ain't we most there?'" Melville's anecdote could well have been suggested by Ames's. Cape Clear has just been sighted: "At the cry [of land ho] the Irish emigrants came rushing up the hatchway, thinking America itself was at hand.

"'Where is it?' cried one of them, running out a little way on the bowsprit. 'Is *that* it?'

"'Aye, it doesn't look much like *ould* Ireland, does it?' said Jackson.

"'Not a bit, honey:—and how long before we get there? to-night?'"

82. *Redburn,* p. 336. The oldest steerage passenger on the "St. Lawrence" was 56 (see n. 87).

83. *A Mariner's Sketches,* p. 186.

84. Anderson, *Melville in the South Seas,* pp. 412-17.

85. See, for example, [Robert Whyte], *The Ocean Plague: or A Voyage to Quebec in an Irish Emigrant Vessel* (Boston, 1848), a lurid description of the effects of insufficient food, overcrowding, and ship's fever on a hundred Irish emigrants in 1847.

86. *Redburn,* p. 378. The review of *Redburn* in the *Literary World,* V (November 17, 1849), 420, says that in the steerage scenes in *Redburn* "A little newspaper item, such as we have often read this last season, is filled out in its terrible details . . . ."

87. The official passenger list was discovered in 1949 in the National Archives by Professor Wilson L. Heflin, who has generously shared his find

with me. It lists thirteen men, three women, and sixteen children, giving, in most instances, the full names of adults and the given names or initials of children, with the ages of all individuals.

88. Despite this evidence, one cannot help being fascinated with the possibilities suggested by the name of the author of *Storia popolare di Napoleone III* (Milan, 1852)—Carlo Melvil.

89. The names of these cabin passengers are not included in the regular passenger list, but they are listed in the *New York Journal of Commerce,* October 1, 1839, and the *New York Evening Post,* October 2, 1839.

90. *Redburn,* p. 338.

91. *Ibid.,* pp. 381-82.

92. Records of the Collector of Customs, New York, Inspector's Certificate for the ship "St. Lawrence," September 30, 1839 (National Archives). This lists three of the original crew as "Absent," and shows that their places were taken by three others (see p. 197). A notation on the verso of the crew list, reading "2 Absent," is evidently an error.

93. *Redburn,* p. 387. The "North Carolina," 90 guns, arrived in New York about the end of June 1839 (*New York American,* July 1, 1839). She was stationed in the port until 1866 (letter to the author from Captain John B. Heffernan, Office of Naval Records and Library, Navy Department, Washington, D.C.).

94. It is true that in this final scene Captain Riga also charges Redburn with the expense of several hammers and scrapers which the boy lost overboard. Legally he could do this (Blunt, *Shipmaster's Assistant,* p. 124), and if Melville was guilty of the same negligence, he may have been denied his wages for that reason. On the other hand, Redburn's tally of lost hardware is suspiciously high—three hammers and two scrapers. One wonders whether a more mature youth would have been quite so careless. Redburn's account of losing the tools is humorous but not very convincing if applied to Melville (p. 155).

In addition, even though a sailor had deserted, he was entitled to his wages if the captain received him back on board ship (Dana, *The Seaman's Friend,* p. 124). In the scene in *Redburn* in which the sailors are paid, Captain Riga does not deny wages to other sailors who, as Redburn had said, had been absent from the ship longer than he had (p. 308). It seems strange that Redburn should have known that the captain could have legally refused to receive him on board after his absence but did not know that once accepted, he was entitled to his wages.

Thus all relevant evidence, though not conclusive, opposes the veracity of Melville's story.

95. It is possible, for example, that Melville found hints for various incidents and reflections in *Redburn* in John Codman's [Captain Ringbolt] *Sailor's Life and Sailor's Yarns,* which he reviewed for the *Literary World,* March 6, 1847(see Thorp, *Herman Melville, Representative Selections,* pp. 326-27). Codman tells of shipping a crazy man who was thought to be merely drunk but who jumped overboard and had to be rescued. He describes a "dismasted and water-logged" ship, which "sluggishly rose and fell in the trough of the sea, wallowing like one of its huge monsters, dead" (pp. 74-75).

He pleads in one sketch for captains to investigate all wrecks to be sure that no one perishes for want of aid; in another he calls upon look-outs and steersmen to keep careful watch and not fall asleep; and in another he describes two ships crashing at night. Similar incidents or appeals occur in *Redburn*, pp. 63, 132, 133, 120, 148, 118-19. But it is impossible to prove Melville's indebtedness.

96. Weaver, *Herman Melville, Mariner and Mystic*, p. 79.

97. *Pierre*, ed. Murray, p. xx.

Notes to Chapter VII

1. Melville to Richard Henry Dana, Jr., October 6, 1849, in Hayford, "Two New Letters," *ELH,* XI (March 1944), 77.
2. *Journal of a Visit to London and the Continent,* November 6, 1849, p. 23.
3. Such portmanteau chapters appear also in *Typee* (xxxi) and *White-Jacket* (lxviii).
4. See E. Douglas Branch, *The Sentimental Years* (New York: D. Appleton-Century Company, 1934), p. 104.
5. Matthiessen has noted this briefly (*American Renaissance,* p. 397).
6. Thorp, *Herman Melville, Representative Selections,* p. 390.
7. *Redburn,* p. 43.
8. *Ibid.,* p. 81.
9. *Ibid.,* pp. 12-13.
10. *Ibid.,* p. 65.
11. *Ibid.,* pp. 65-66.
12. *Ibid.,* p. 61.
13. *Ibid.,* p. 62.
14. *Ibid.*
15. *Ibid.,* p. 89.
16. *Ibid.,* p. 74.
17. *Ibid.,* p. 134.
18. *Ibid.,* p. 356.
19. See App. C, pp. 272-73.
20. *Redburn,* p. 52.
21. *Ibid.,* p. 101.
22. Freeman, *Herman Melville,* pp. 171-72, supplies a good example of stylistic immaturity in *Typee.*
23. Consider the following: "There was a flavor and a relish to this small particle of food that, under other circumstances, it would have been impossible for the most delicate viands to have imparted. A copious draught of the pure water which flowed at our feet served to complete the meal, and after it we rose sensibly refreshed, and prepared for whatever might befall us" (*Typee,* pp. 61-62).
24. Consider "adhesive matter" and "glutinous compound" to describe sticky food (*Typee,* p. 97); "communicate my appellation" for "tell my name" (*ibid.,* p. 95); "apply the olfactory organ" for "smell" (*ibid.,* p. 98).
25. *Redburn,* pp. 7-8.
26. *Ibid.,* p. 37.
27. Melville's dialogue may be compared with H. J. Mercier's, who wrote better than any other contemporary ex-sailors: "'Look here, Tubbs,'" cried Bradley, . . . "'just clap a stopper on that *red rag* of yours; you are giving your opinion in this affair as if you were some old Nantucket whaler; and I know you hav'nt [*sic*] been many months from behind a *clam* cart; let somebody pass their remarks that know more about it than you do.' 'Do you think

I hav'nt been whaling?' responded Tubbs—'I reckon if you ever fall in with Captain Seth Handy, of New Bedford, and ask him who pulled the after oar in his boat, I guess he'd mention my name. That was the man for turning up a fish; he made no more of *lancing* a whale in a *flurry* than others would of hooking a mackerel.'" (*Life in a Man-Of-War, or Scenes in Old Ironsides* [Boston: Houghton Mifflin Company, 1927; 1st ed.; Philadelphia, 1841], pp. 162-63. It may be noted that Melville borrowed scenes from this book for parts of *White-Jacket.* See Keith Huntress, "Melville's Use of a Source for White Jacket," *American Literature,* XVII [March 1945], 66-74.) Mercier's dialogue illustrates the common practice of underlining all nautical terms and sailor slang, a convention Melville follows in *Redburn.*

28. Nathalia Wright counts fifty-one references in *Redburn* to the Bible, by far the most numerous group of allusions ("Biblical Allusion in Melville's Prose," *American Literature,* XII [May 1940], 185).

29. *Redburn,* p. 203.

30. *Ibid.,* pp. 297-98.

31. Melville refers to pictures which "the high priests, for a bribe, showed to Alexander in the innermost shrine of the white temple in the Libyan oasis." None of the ancient authorities on Alexander—Plutarch, Polybius, Diodorus Siculus, Arrian, or even the romantic Rufus Curtius—mentions any pictures in this temple, which was a shrine of Jupiter Ammon, nor is Alexander described as offering a bribe to the priests. Melville also refers to "such pictures as the pontiff of the sun strove to hide from Cortez, when, sword in hand, he burst open the sanctorum of the pyramid-fane at Cholula"; but neither Diaz nor Prescott nor Cortez himself describes any such incident. The house of Pansa in Pompeii is not known to have contained any pictures, nor does Varro, despite Melville's assertion, refer to the "central alcove" of Pansa's home as *"the hollow of the house."* It is true, as Melville says, that Suetonius mentions a picture which Tiberius kept in his private cabinet (it represented Atalanta performing a most unnatural service for Meleager), but Melville is wrong in declaring that Martial mentions the picture. Finally, no ancient traveler or historian mentions a "secret side gallery in the temple of Aphrodite in Corinth," nor pictures, as such, in the temple, though Pausanias does refer to the "images" of Aphrodite and of the Sun and of Love. It seems evident that Melville was inventing allusions in this passage, just as he had done ten years before in the second of the "Fragments from a Writing Desk."

32. Mansfield, "Herman Melville, Author and New Yorker," p. 94.

33. *Redburn,* pp. 323-24.

34. *Ibid.,* p. 230.

35. *Ibid.,* p. 177.

36. *Ibid.,* p. 220. In "Benito Cereno" Melville also uses the stern piece and the figurehead (a real corpse) to symbolize conditions on a ship. He attaches more significance to the objects, but the basic technique is the same as in *Redburn.* (See *Piazza Tales,* p. 70.)

37. *Redburn,* p. 9.

38. *Ibid.,* pp. 352-53.

39. Despite Melville's constant reference to Redburn's shooting jacket as the badge of poverty and the source of humiliation and social rejection, I

see no technique here that can properly be called symbolic. The jacket is never invested, openly or implicitly, with poetic or metaphysical or moral meaning. (Compare, however, Howard P. Vincent, "White Jacket: An Essay in Interpretation," *New England Quarterly,* XXII (September 1949), 306. Mr. Richard Chase's perception of mythological meanings in *Redburn* depends on such assumptions as that "[Redburn's] name is apparently meant to signify 'the Promethean fire' . . . ." (*Herman Melville, A Critical Study,* p. 7).

40. Letter to George L. Duyckinck, November 10, 1849 (Duyckinck Collection), pointed out to me by Jay Leyda.

41. *Redburn,* p. 398.

42. *Ibid.,* p. 53.

43. *Ibid.,* pp. 111-12.

44. *Ibid.,* pp. 188-90.

45. *Ibid.,* p. 84.

46. *Ibid.,* p. 396.

47. *Ibid.,* pp. 11-12.

48. *Ibid.,* p. 267.

49. *Ibid.,* p. 182.

50. Melville to Richard Henry Dana, Jr., May 1, 1850, in Hayford, "Two New Letters," *ELH,* XI (March 1944), 78.

51. *Redburn,* p. 161.

52. The text is that of the first edition, London, printed for T. Becket and P. A. De Hondt, 1762. Melville's copy is in the Princeton University Library. The verso of the flyleaf is inscribed "H. Melville 1848 N.Y."

53. Macpherson, *Fingal,* p. 74.

54. He mentions "old Burton" in "Fragments from a Writing Desk, No. 1," and he had purchased a copy of *The Anatomy of Melancholy* in 1846 or 1847 (see chap. i, n. 20). See also Matthiessen, *American Renaissance,* pp. 124, 291, and Braswell, *Melville's Religious Thought,* pp. 86-87.

55. *Moby-Dick,* II, 182.

56. Emile Legouis and Louis Cazamian, *A History of English Literature* (rev. ed.; New York: The Macmillan Company, 1935), p. 1081.

57. *Redburn,* p. 121.

58. *Ibid.,* p. 190.

59. *Moby-Dick,* I, 181.

60. *Redburn,* p. 314.

61. *Ibid.,* p. 178. Although these sentiments may be original with Melville, they have parallels in a passage from George Little's *Life on the Ocean* (first published in 1843), p. 375:

> "It may be asked, who goes on board of a vessel, when she first arrives, and takes the poor sailor by the hand? and, when on shore, who is it that will introduce him into society, and give him a place at the social board, or around the domestic fireside? . . . Suppose . . . that a sailor could get from under the clutches of his landlord long enough to keep sober twenty-four hours; . . . let him enter one of our large and fashionable churches;—and how many pew doors, do you suppose, would be thrown open for his reception?"

Whether or not Melville had read Little, his plea for the hapless mariner follows a tradition in the reminiscences of former sailors. See Nathaniel Ames, *A Mariner's Sketches* (1830), pp. 102-4, 240-41, and *Nautical Reminiscences* (Providence, 1832), pp. 40-41, 70, 72-73; [Charles F. Briggs], *Working a Passage, or Life in a Liner* (1844), pp. 51, 87; Richard Henry Dana, Jr., *Two Years Before the Mast* (1st ed.; New York, 1840), pp. 460-83; Samuel Leech, *Thirty Years from Home* (15th ed.; Boston, [1847]; 1st ed.; Boston, 1843), pp. 254-55; William McNally, *Evils and Abuses in the Naval and Merchant Service Exposed* (Boston, 1839), *passim;* and John Codman [Captain Ringbolt], *Sailor's Life and Sailor's Yarns* (New York, 1847), pp. 237-52.

62. *Redburn,* p. 176.

63. *Ibid.,* p. 144.

64. *Ibid.,* p. 348. Melville also tells us that the cabin passengers contribute only three pennies to Carlo for playing music for them (p. 337).

65. *Ibid.,* p. 338. I take these to be Melville's sentiments, even though they are set forth as Redburn's and though the "St. Lawrence" carried only two cabin passengers.

66. *Redburn,* p. 239.

67. *Ibid.,* p. 284.

68. *Ibid.,* p. 233.

69. *Ibid.,* p. 236.

70. *Ibid.,* p. 237.

71. Carlyle describes the plight of a helpless Irish widow (and her three children) who died for want of charity and whose membership in the human race was not acknowledged until it was discovered that through the typhus fever which killed her, she had infected seventeen other people, who also died. In "Of King's Treasuries" Ruskin tells the pitiful story of Michael Collins, who could not earn enough from "translating" old boots to new ones to keep himself alive. His widow's refusal to enter the poorhouse excited the wrath of the coroner. Wragg, a workhouse girl who strangled her illegitimate baby, Arnold cites in ironic contrast to the "unrivalled happiness" of England that optimistic orators were habitually announcing.

72. Ray Allan Billington, *The Protestant Crusade, 1800-1860* (New York: The Macmillan Company, 1938), chaps. v-xi.

73. *Redburn,* pp. 378-79.

74. *Ibid.,* p. 379. However, exactly such a law had been passed on May 17, 1848 (*U. S. Statutes at Large* [Boston, 1848], chap. xli). In the paragraph preceding the one quoted, Melville observes that "of late, a law has been passed in Congress, restricting ships to a certain number of emigrants, according to a certain rate" (p. 379). He is referring to the Act of February 22, 1847 (*U. S. Statutes at Large* [Boston, 1847], chap. xvi). It is curious that he should have known about one law and not about the other. One explanation is that he wrote the quoted passage before May 17, 1848, but there is no other evidence whatsoever to support this.

75. *Redburn,* p. 260.

76. *Ibid.,* pp. 363-64.

77. *Herman Melville, Representative Selections,* p. cviii.

78. *Redburn,* p. 356.

79. Melville to Hawthorne, June 1851, in Thorp, *Herman Melville, Representative Selections,* p. 390.

80. *Ibid.*

81. *Redburn,* p. 261.

82. *Ibid.,* p. 227.

83. *Mardi,* II, 368.

84. *Redburn,* p. 334.

85. *Ibid.,* p. 179.

86. *Ibid.,* p. 242.

87. *Ibid.,* p. 326.

88. See Braswell, *Melville's Religious Thought,* pp. 19-40. In 1856, as is well known, Hawthorne noted in his Journal, after seeing Melville: "He informed me that he had 'pretty much made up his mind to be annihilated'; but still he does not seem to rest in that anticipation, and I think will never rest until he gets hold of some definite belief" (quoted in Weaver, *Herman Melville, Mariner and Mystic,* p. 336).

89. Braswell, *Melville's Religious Thought,* p. 46.

90. Compare, for example, the spontaneity of Melville's religious response to the death of his brother Gansevoort. Writing to William L. Marcy, the Secretary of War, he says: "I can not but hope, that this personal appeal of a mourning family, to whom Providence has brought unspeakable & peculiar sorrows, will not be without effect upon you." (Merrell R. Davis has kindly furnished me a copy of this letter, now in the Doheny Library, Camarillo, Calif.)

91. See William C. Gannett, *A Hundred Years of the Unitarian Movement in America* (N.p., 1915), pp. 19-26. Melville's unorthodox sentiments anticipate the doubts and denials of radical Unitarians like John Weiss, Octavius Brooks Frothingham, and others. (See Stow Persons, *Free Religion, An American Faith* [New Haven: Yale University Press, 1947], pp. 20, 25, 29-31.)

92. *Redburn,* p. 217. Melville had already asserted this idea in *Mardi,* I, 13-14.

93. *Redburn,* p. 217.

94. Compare Melville's statement to Dana that he wrote *Redburn* (and *White-Jacket,* the other "job") "almost entirely for 'lucre'—by the job, as a wood-sawyer saws wood . . ." (see p. 169).

95. Letter of October 6, 1849 (S).

96. Letter of December 14, 1849, printed in Thorp, *Herman Melville, Representative Selections,* p. 376.

97. See p. 167.

98. See p. 170.

99. See Ames, *A Mariner's Sketches,* p. 183; [Briggs], *Working a Passage, passim;* Leech, *Thirty Years from Home,* pp. 289-92; William Torrey, *Torrey's Narrative* (Boston, 1848), pp. 208-9; C. S. Stewart, *Sketches of Society in Great Britain and Ireland* (Philadelphia, 1834), pp. 13-22; and Timothy Flint, *The Life and Adventures of Arthur Clenning* (Philadelphia, 1828), pp. 27-30. The last-named volume, in its early pages, anticipates *Redburn* in some ways. A young lad who is the pride of his family secures through his father a job on a Liverpool packet and sails for England with high ex-

pectations of the Old World, but his illusions are promptly dispersed by the combination of arrogance and poverty he encounters. However, the story yields no parallels close enough to suggest an inspiration for Melville.

100. In addition to the works already mentioned in nn. 61 and 99, I base this paragraph on a consideration of the following: William Butterworth, *Three Years' Adventures of a Minor* (Leeds, 1831); George Cupples, *The Green Hand* (London, 1900; first published *Blackwood's Edinburgh Magazine,* 1848-50); James R. Durand, *The Life and Adventures of James R. Durand* (Rochester, 1820); "A Man of War's Man," *Maritime Scraps, or Scenes in the Frigate United States during a Cruise in the Mediterranean* (Boston, 1838); Michael Scott, *Tom Cringle's Log* (Edinburgh, 1863; first published *Blackwood's Edinburgh Magazine,* 1829-33); Thomas W. Smith, *A Narrative of the Life, Travels, and Sufferings of Thomas W. Smith* (Boston, 1844); "A Younker," *A Green Hand's First Cruise* (Boston, 1841); E. Z. C. Judson, "Ned Buntline's Life Yarn," *Knickerbocker Magazine,* Vol. XXVI (November 1845), Vol. XXVII (January 1846), and Vol. XXVIII (July 1846); and J. Ross Browne, *Etchings of a Whaling Cruise* (London, 1846).

101. In writing to Dana of the composition of *Moby-Dick,* Melville said: "It will be a strange sort of book, tho', I fear; blubber is blubber you know; tho' you may get oil out of it, the poetry runs as hard as sap from a frozen maple tree;—& to cook the thing up, one must needs throw in a little fancy, which from the nature of the thing, must be ungainly as the gambols of the whales themselves" (letter of May 1, 1850, in Hayford, "Two New Letters," *ELH,* XI [March 1944], 79).

102. The total number of pages quoted by the various reviewers is about 50, out of 390. The scene most often reproduced is chapter xiv, Redburn's attempt to call on the captain, which six reviews quoted almost in its entirety. Four quoted the death of Jackson, three the burning corpse, and two Redburn's first experience on the "Highlander," his failure to obey the mate's command, and the portrait of Jackson. Seventeen other scenes were quoted. From these samples it is quite clear that critics considered the first half of *Redburn* the best, for they quoted only eight pages from the second half.

103. For the history of *Redburn's* reputation, see App. D, pp. 274-87.

Note to Appendix A

1. In his letter to the *Microscope* of April 14, Van Loon explained that the name of Lotus Niles, secretary of the Philo Logos Society, should have been printed at the end of the first installment of his letter, as the signer of the quoted "certificate."

Notes to Appendix B

1. Weaver, *Herman Melville, Mariner and Mystic,* p. 115.
2. *Democratic Press and Lansingburgh Advertiser:* Cerbes! (Hereafter, the newspaper is referred to as *DP.*)
3. *DP:* incentinently.
4. This is perhaps a loose recollection from Burke's *Reflections on the Revolution in France:* "It is now sixteen or seventeen years since I saw the Queen of France, then the Dauphiness, at Versailles . . . . Little did I dream that I should have lived to see such disasters fallen upon her in a nation of gallant men—in a nation of men of honor and of cavaliers . . . . But the age of chivalry is gone." ("The Works of Edmund Burke" [rev. ed.; Boston, 1865], III, 331.) The full paragraph appears in Melville's copy of *The Carcanet,* p. 142.

On the other hand, considering Melville's debt to Byron in this "Fragment," the quotation is more probably derived from the Preface to the fourth edition of *Childe Harold's Pilgrimage,* where Byron writes: "So much for chivalry. Burke need not have regretted that its days are over" (*The Works of Byron,* ed. E. H. Coleridge [London: John Murray, 1902-06], II, 7).
5. *DP:* fugative
6. *DP:* ignis fatus
7. *DP:* denowment
8. *DP:* precations.
9. *DP:* periodicel
10. *DP:* courtious
11. *DP:* unperceiued
12. *DP:* outgenerald
13. *DP:* heighth (Melville spells it "heighth" in his *Journal Up the Straits, 1856-1857.* See Weaver, *Herman Melville, Mariner and Mystic,* opp. p. 104).
14. *DP:* stedfastly
15. *DP:* persued
16. *DP:* heighth,
17. *DP:* preeminence
18. *DP:* duskey
19. *DP:* arched-way
20. *DP:* darkning
21. *DP:* immagings,
22. *DP:* actual
23. *DP:* movemements

24. *DP:* griped
25. *DP:* apperance
26. *DP:* descryed
27. *DP:* forbiding
28. *DP:* thich
29. *DP:* chord
30. *DP:* apparation
31. *DP:* nerves
32. *DP:* skill.
33. *DP:* chords
34. *DP:* Physche
35. *DP:* Chandeleres
36. *DP:* supurb
37. *DP:* profusien,
38. *DP:* ottomon;
39. *DP:* transcendant
40. *DP:* quishion
41. *DP:* farey-like
42. *DP:* countonance
43. *DP:* good-breeding
44. In his partial reproduction of the text, Weaver ends his quotation at this point, explaining: "But here, just at the climax of the quest, the clipping is abruptly torn, and the reader is left cruelly suspended" (p. 125). In the Constable edition he adds the word "beauty" (XVI, 399), but there is no authority for this reading in the original.
45. *DP:* The
46. *DP:* chords
47. *DP:* unuterable

Notes to Appendix C

1. *Redburn,* p. 134.
2. *Ibid.*
3. *Moby-Dick,* I, 211.
4. *Redburn,* p. 78.
5. *Moby-Dick,* I, 229-30.

Notes to Appendix D

1. The reputation of *Redburn* has been discussed by Hugh Hetherington in "The Reputation of Herman Melville in America" (Doctor's thesis, University of Michigan, 1933). While I have taken a different approach to the criticism of *Redburn,* some duplication has been inevitable.
2. Up to April 1851, 2,291 copies of *Mardi* had been sold and 3,695 of *Redburn* (Harper's account with Melville in M).
3. Melville asserted in a letter to Lemuel Shaw, October 6, 1849 (S), that

"'Redburn' was published in London on the 25th of last month," but I have taken my date from a *List of Principal Publications Issued from New Burlington Street, London, during the Year 1849* since this was Bentley's official publication. The Berg Collection in the New York Public Library has the two-volume London edition of 1849, a presentation copy inscribed in Melville's hand: "Maria G Melville from Her Affectionate Son Herman. Pittsfield, January, 1852."

4. *Spectator,* XXII (September 29, 1849), 925, and (October 20, 1849), 1004; *Athenaeum,* No. 1143 (September 22, 1849), 976, and No. 1148 (October 27, 1849), 1096. The title was condensed in all the advertisements to *Redburn; His First Voyage: Being the Sailor Boy's Confessions.* In both the English and the American editions the title is: *Redburn: His First Voyage. Being the Sailor-Boy Confessions and Reminiscences of the Son-of-a-Gentleman, in the Merchant Service.*

5. However, respectable English publishers during this period issued new books in small editions at high prices because they had found that this practice secured the greatest profits. (See Clarence F. Gohdes, *American Literature in Nineteenth Century England* [New York, 1944], p. 19.) Bentley printed only 750 copies of *Redburn.*

6. *Literary World,* V (August 4, 1849), 92. The statement here that *Redburn* was nearly ready for the press was somewhat tardy, for Melville had already written to Bentley on July 20 that the book was going through the press. (See p. 169.)

7. *Literary World,* V (November 10, 1849), 395.

8. The actual date of publication was probably November 15 or 16. The earliest advertisement which has come to light appeared in the *Lansingburgh Gazette,* November 16, under the heading "New Books Received This Morning" (by Peletiah Bliss). Weaver's date of August 18 (p. 273) is the date on which the book was entered for copyright. (See a copy of the copyright record in M.)

9. *Literary World,* V (November 17), 435, (November 24), 460, (December 1), 483, (December 15), 532, (December 22), 556, (December 29), 576.

10. *Albany Evening Journal,* November 17, 1849.

11. He wrote: "A writer so graceful and happy as Mr. Melville in Narrative, cannot fail, we should think, to have imparted equal interest to a work in which his imagination was entirely free. He is, at any rate, a beautiful writer, and his Novel will find numerous readers . . . ." *Ibid.* Weed had personally commended *Typee* when it appeared in March 1846, and Melville had presented him with a copy of the book on August 15, 1846. (See the note from Melville to Weed, accompanying the presentation, in the Berg Collection, New York Public Library.)

12. *Albany Evening Journal,* November 21, 1849, advertisement of A. Hill.

13. November 23, 1849.

14. See the notices quoted in Harper's advertisement of *Redburn, Literary World,* V (December 1, 1849), 483, from the *Boston Post* and the *Baltimore American.* Harper's advertisement of *Redburn* in the end papers of *Moby-Dick* (1851) contained additional notices from the *Richmond Whig,* the *Hartford Republican,* the *Philadelphia North American,* and the *Worcester Palladium.*

15. *Literary World,* V (November 17, 1849), 418-20.
16. *Ibid.,* p. 418.
17. *Ibid.*
18. *Ibid.,* p. 420.
19. *Ibid.*
20. *Ibid.,* p. 418.
21. *Southern Literary Messenger,* XV (December 1849), 760.
22. *Ibid.*
23. *Ibid.*
24. *Albion,* VIII (N.S.) (November 24, 1849), 561.
25. *Ibid.*
26. *Literary American,* November 24, 1849.
27. *Home Journal,* No. 198 (November 24, 1849).
28. *Ibid.*
29. Quoted in Harper's advertisement of *Redburn, Literary World,* V (December 1, 1849), 483.
30. *Ibid.*
31. *Ibid.*
32. Quoted in end papers of *Moby-Dick* (1851).
33. *Sartain's Union Magazine,* VI (February 1850), 174.
34. *Graham's Magazine,* XXXVI (January 1850), 95-96.
35. XXV (N.S.) (December 1849), 575.
36. Other favorable notices appeared in *Hunt's Merchant's Magazine and Commercial Review,* XXII (February 1850), 252; *Godey's Lady's Book,* XL (February 1850), 149; and the *National Intelligencer,* November 22, 1849.
37. XXXV (May 1850), 448.
38. *Southern Quarterly Review,* I (N.S.) (April 1850), 259.
39. *Ibid.*
40. His two nautical works, both semiautobiographical, were *Working a Passage, or Life in a Liner* (New York, 1844) and *The Adventures of Harry Franco, A Tale of the Great Panic* (New York, 1839).
41. I am indebted to Harrison Hayford for this suggestion.
42. *Holden's Dollar Magazine,* V (January 1850), 55.
43. *Ibid.*
44. LXVI (November 1849), 567-80. *Redburn* was the only book reviewed in this issue.
45. See *ibid.,* September and October 1849.
46. *Ibid.,* LXVI (November 1849), 567.
47. *Ibid.,* p. 568.
48. *Ibid.,* p. 570.
49. *Ibid.,* p. 574.
50. *Ibid.,* p. 575.
51. *Ibid.,* p. 576.
52. *Ibid.*
53. *Athenaeum,* No. 1150 (November 10, 1849), 1131-32.
54. XXIX (October 27, 1849), 679.
55. XXII (October 27, 1849), 1020; reprinted in *Littell's Living Age,* XXIII (December 27, 1849), 580-83.
56. XXII (October 27, 1849), 1021.

57. *Bentley's Miscellany,* XXVI (November 1849), 529.

58. *Ibid.*

59. *Ibid.*, p. 530.

60. *Literary Gazette,* No. 1709 (October 20, 1849), 776.

61. Among modern critics, John Freeman has said (p. 86) that "it is doubtful whether [Melville] had ever heard of Marryat." Besides the obvious resemblances between *Redburn* and *Peter Simple,* there is Melville's own reference to Marryat in *Typee* (p. 25) to prove his familiarity.

62. "A Trio of American Sailor Authors," *Dublin University Magazine,* CCLXXVII (January 1856), 54.

63. "American Authorship, No. IV—Herman Melville," XCVIII (July 1853), 303-6; reprinted in *Littell's Living Age,* XXXVIII (August 20, 1853), 300-8, and *Eclectic Magazine,* XXX (September 1853), 46-52.

64. "Our Young Authors—Melville," *Putnam's Monthly Magazine,* I (February 1853), 163.

65. "Our Authors and Authorship—Melville and Curtis," *Putnam's Monthly Magazine,* IX (April 1857), 390.

66. *Ibid.* However, O'Brien's criticism seems to owe more to the 1849 review in *Blackwood's* than to *Redburn.* He cites exactly the same alleged misrepresentations of the English aristocracy and the same metaphors *Blackwood's* objected to. Besides, he erroneously charges Melville with saying that in England young men of decayed families went about from door to door with faces blackened and banjoes in their hands, singing for money.

67. The biography of Melville in the Duyckincks' *Cyclopaedia of American Literature* contains a few negligible sentences about *Redburn* and the entire chapter describing the call on the captain. (1st ed., 1855, pp. 673-76; 2d ed., 1875, pp. 637-39.)

68. CCLXXVII (January 1856), 51-52.

69. Harper's Statement to Melville, March 21, 1853 (M). The 1855 edition was a reprint of the 1849, the plates of which evidently survived the fire. See the description of the disaster in the *New York Herald,* December 12, 1853: "The most valuable property of the establishment, the stereotyped plates, we understand, are in a good state of preservation . . . . This property was stowed away in vaults extending under the sidewalk . . . ." I am indebted to Jay Leyda for this note.

70. From Richard Bentley's office memorandum, March 4, 1852, made on a letter from Melville dated July 20, 1851 (see John H. Birss, "A Mere Sale to Effect 'with Letters of Herman Melville,'" *New Colophon,* I [1948], 253). But *Redburn* did not fare as badly as some of Melville's other works. Bentley's figures are:

	Paid Author	Total Profit	Deficit
Mardi	£210	£141.12.6	£68.7.6
Redburn	100	23.12.6	76.7.6
White Jacket	200	. . . . . .	173.9.6.
The Whale	150	15.	135.. .
		Present deficit...	453.4.6

71. In *Excursions in Victorian Bibliography* (London, 1922), Michael Sadleir says: "I have seen a copy of this edition [Bentley, 1849] bearing on the case the name of T. C. Newby as publisher, but with the Bentley title-page. This was probably a 'remainder' copy, for Newby frequently bought sheets of books that had not sold when originally published, and issued them at a cheaper price wholly or partially over his imprint" (p. 226, n. 2).

72. However, *Redburn* was pirated. It is included with two other travel narratives in an edition of which the Harvard College Library has a copy. Unfortunately, the title page is missing, and the only means of identification is the title on the spine, "British Library Travels," Vol. II, 1849. The first volume is *Gatherings from Spain, By the Author of the Handbook of Spain; Chiefly Selected from That Work, with Much New Matter*. This appears to be a reprint of the work of the same title by Richard Ford (London, 1846). The second is *Peregrine Scramble; or Thirty Years' Adventures of a Blue Jacket,* by Captain Sir H. V. Huntley, R.N. This was originally published in two volumes in London in 1849. The title of *Redburn,* the third reprint in the book, varies from the original, reading: *Redburn; Being the Sailor-Boy Confessions and Reminiscences of the First Voyage of the Son of a Gentleman, in the Merchant Service.* By Herman Melville. There follows the regular dedication to Thomas Melville, Herman's brother.

Redburn is paged separately, from 1 to 128, and printed like its companion texts in double columns. The text is corrupt, with some changes and many omissions. A number of chapters have been telescoped into each other so that the sixty-two chapters of the original come down to fifty-five. No such title as the book bears on the spine is listed in the *English Catalogue,* the *British Museum Catalogue,* or the *Library of Congress Catalogue.* However, the "Catalogue of the Bibliothèque Nationale" lists a *Redburn* published in Paris by Baudry (1850). The title and the number of pages (128) fit the description above exactly, and the entry, like those of *Gatherings from Spain* and *Peregrine Scramble* (both published by A. and W. Galignani [Paris, 1849]), bears the words "The British Library."

Thus the Harvard copy is unquestionably the Baudry edition, though whether it was published in 1849 or 1850 and whether it originally appeared as a separate volume remain uncertain. There is no evidence that Melville ever knew his little nursery tale had received the distinction of being pirated.

73. Harper Statements to Herman Melville, 1851 to 1887 (M).

74. According to Harper's account, its total sales of Melville's books from 1849 to 1887 were: *Typee,* 9,549; *Omoo,* 7,390; *White-Jacket,* 4,892; *Redburn,* 4,601; *Moby-Dick,* 3,147; *Mardi,* 3,088; *Pierre,* 361 (M).

75. In his letter to Dana of May 1, 1850, Melville thanks him for his praise of *Redburn* and *White-Jacket* (see Hayford, "Two New Letters of Herman Melville," *ELH,* XI [March 1944], 77).

76. The Harvard College Library has a copy of the Harper edition of *Redburn* (1849) marked "Gift of Professor James R. Lowell, September 26, 1862."

77. Letter of August 29, 1849, Duyckinck Collection, New York Public Library, printed in part in Thorp, *Herman Melville, Representative Selections,* p. 423.

78. "Sea Stories," *Contemporary Review,* XLVI (September 1884), 344.

79. *Ibid.,* p. 357.

80. The letter, dated April 10, 1888, is in M.

81. "A Claim for American Literature," CLIV (February 1892), 138-49.

82. *Ibid.,* pp. 138-42.

83. "Marquesan Melville," *Gentleman's Magazine,* CCLXXII (March 1892), 248-57.

84. "Herman Melville," *The Review,* I (August 9 and 16, 1919), 276-78, 298-301.

85. "Herman Melville," *Spectator,* LXX (June 24, 1893), 858-59.

86. Weaver, *Herman Melville, Mariner and Mystic,* p. 79.

87. For example, William P. Trent's *A History of American Literature* (1903) ignores *Redburn,* and Carl Van Doren, in the *Cambridge History of American Literature* (1917), gives it only brief mention.

88. Weaver, *Herman Melville, Mariner and Mystic,* p. 79.

89. *Redburn* forms Volume V of the Standard Edition of "The Works of Herman Melville" (16 vols.; London: Constable and Company, 1922-1924). *Redburn* appeared in 1922. Gabriel Wells was the American publisher (Volumes I-XII only).

90. See the figures in Anderson, *Melville in the South Seas,* p. 439. The following are all the known editions of *Redburn:*

London: Richard Bentley, 1849, 2 vols.
New York: Harper and Brothers, 1849, 1850
Paris: Baudry, 1850
Grimma: Verlags-Comptoir, 1850, 9 vols., trans. by Louise Marezoll
New York: Harper and Brothers, 1855, 1863
London: Constable and Company, 1922 (see n. 89)
New York: A. and C. Boni, 1924
Boston: St. Botolph Society, 1924
London: Jonathan Cape, 1924
New York: L. C. Page and Company, 1924
London: Jarrolds, Publishers, 1925
New York: L. C. Page and Company, 1926
New York: Nickerson, 1928
London: Constable and Company, 1929
New York: Richard R. Smith, 1930
London: Jonathan Cape, 1937
Hamburg: Claassen und Goverts, 1946, trans. by Wilhelm E. Süskind
London: Jonathan Cape, 1949
Boston: L. C. Page and Company, 1950
New York: British Book Center, 1950

Redburn has also been included in the single-volume *Romances of Herman Melville* (New York: Pickwick, 1928; Tudor, 1931, 1934, and 1950).

91. *The Spectator,* CXXVIII (May 6, 1922), 559-60, a hostile review of Weaver's biography.

92. *Emerson and Others,* 174-76. Brooks also thought that both *White-Jacket* and *Redburn* "might well have been popular classics all these years" (p. 172).

93. "Herman Melville," *London Mercury,* XI (November 1924), 63.
94. *Ibid.*
95. *Redburn* (Boston: L. C. Page and Company, 1924), p. v.
96. *Herman Melville,* p. 84.
97. *Ibid.,* p. 87.
98. *Ibid.,* p. 172.
99. *Herman Melville,* p. 109.
100. *Ibid.,* p. 110.
101. *Ibid.,* p. 112.
102. *Ibid.,* pp. 112-13.
103. *Ibid.,* p. 111.
104. Cf. Charles R. Anderson, "A Reply to Herman Melville's *White Jacket,* by Rear-Admiral Thomas O. Selfridge, Sr.," *American Literature,* VII (May 1935), 123-44, and the works referred to in Intro., n. 2, above.
105. "Redburn's Prosy Old Guidebook," *PMLA,* LIII (December 1938), 1146.
106. *Herman Melville, Representative Selections,* p. xv.
107. *Herman Melville, marin, metaphysicien, et poète,* p. 269.
108. *Ibid.,* p. 274.
109. *Ibid.,* pp. 275-76.
110. *American Renaissance,* p. 371.
111. *Ibid.,* pp. 396-97.
112. *Ibid.,* p. 399.
113. *Ibid.,* p. 507.
114. *Ibid.*
115. *Ibid.,* p. 286.
116. *Ibid.,* p. 444.
117. *Ibid.,* p. 396.
118. *Ibid.*
119. *Herman Melville, The Tragedy of Mind,* pp. 17-18, 62.
120. *Ibid.,* p. 66.
121. On page 65 Sedgwick had stated: "Whether the literal truth or not, [the hotel incident] served to focus the significance of his first voyage, as it emerged for Melville from his recapitulation of it." If this is a better statement of his meaning, it still avoids the possibility of artistic invention for a desired effect, the disillusionment of a young boy.
122. *Ibid.,* p. 75.
123. *Herman Melville, A Critical Study,* p. 2.
124. *Ibid.,* p. 7.
125. *Melville,* p. 32.
126. *Herman Melville,* p. 101.
127. *Ibid.,* p. 119.
128. *Ibid.,* p. 106.
129. *Ibid.,* p. 108.
130. *Ibid.,* pp. 103, 108, 162, 207.

Note to End Papers

The genealogical charts are made up from information in Cuyler Reynolds, *Hudson-Mohawk Genealogical and Family Memoirs* (New York: Lewis's Historical Publishing Company, 1902); Calbraith Perry, *Charles D'Wulf of Guadaloupe, His Ancestors and Descendants* (New York: T. A. Wright, 1902); V. H. Paltsits, *Family Correspondence of Herman Melville, 1830-1904, in the Gansevoort-Lansing Collection* (New York: New York Public Library, 1929); the Melville family Bible in the New York Public Library and family papers in the same library and in the Massachusetts Historical Society and the Harvard College Library; a genealogy compiled by Jay Leyda; and a family tree very kindly furnished me by Eleanor Melville Metcalf and based on records made by her mother, by Samuel S. Shaw, Melville's brother-in-law, and by Miss Mabel C. Weaks of the New York Public Library.

Index

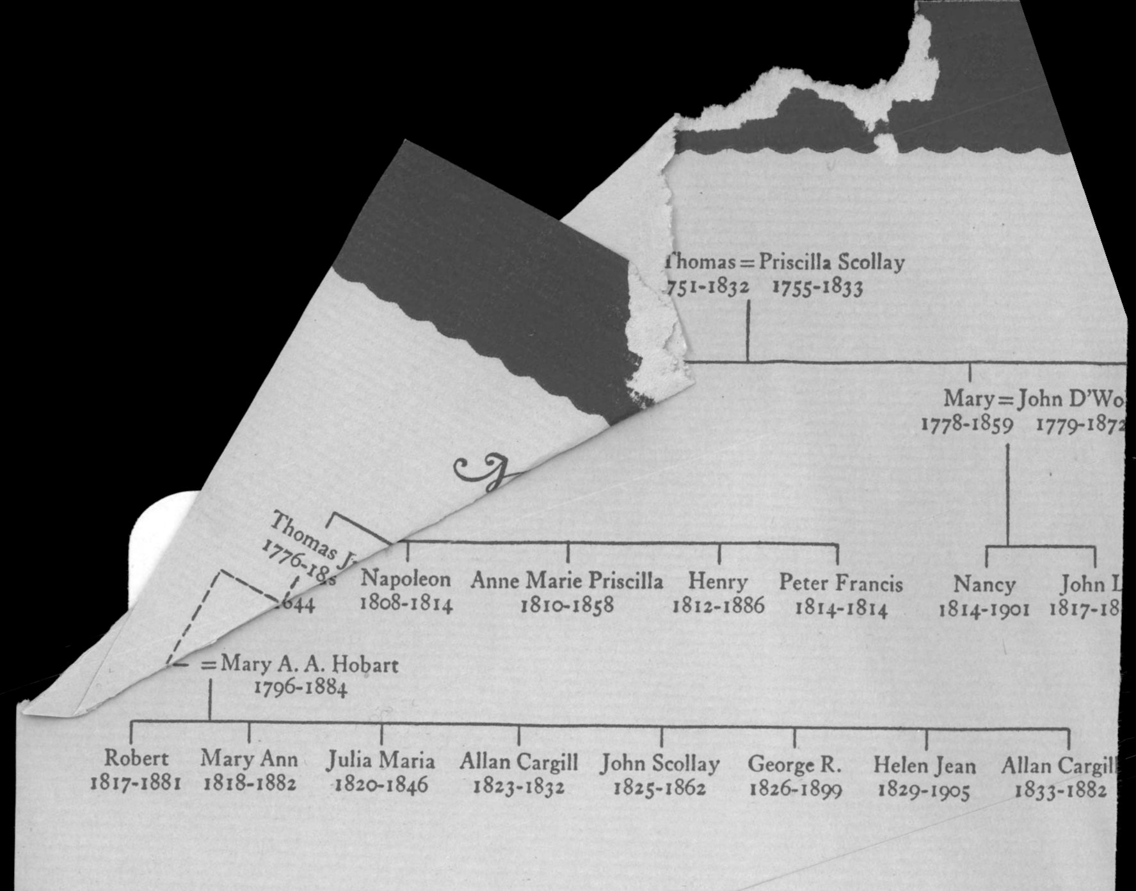

Thomas = Priscilla Scollay
751-1832 1755-1833
Mary = John D'Wo
1778-1859 1779-187
Thomas J
1776-18
644
Napoleon
1808-1814
Anne Marie Priscilla
1810-1858
Henry
1812-1886
Peter Francis
1814-1814
Nancy
1814-1901
John L
1817-18
= Mary A. A. Hobart
1796-1884
Robert
1817-1881
Mary Ann
1818-1882
Julia Maria
1820-1846
Allan Cargill
1823-1832
John Scollay
1825-1862
George R.
1826-1899
Helen Jean
1829-1905
Allan Cargill
1833-1882

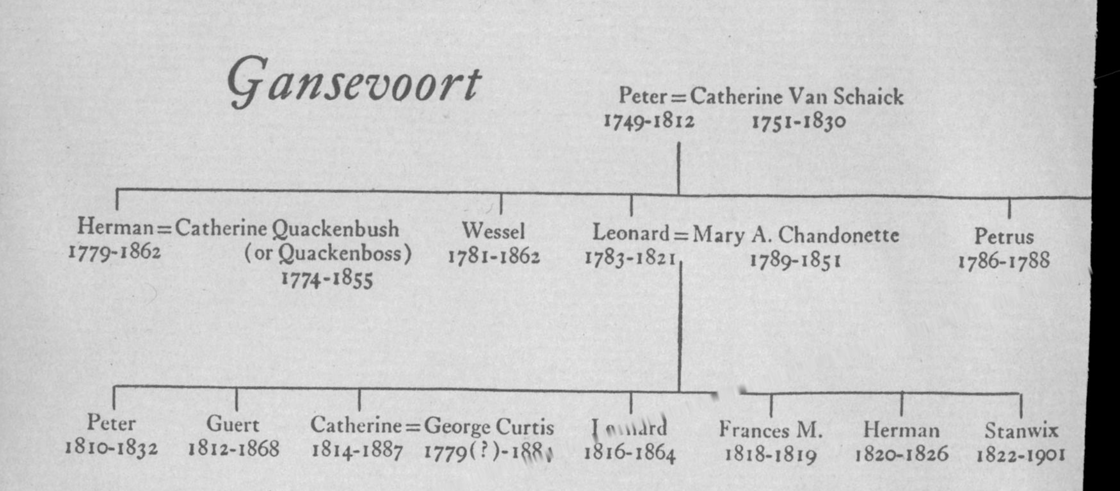

Gansevoort
Peter = Catherine Van Schaick
1749-1812 1751-1830
Herman = Catherine Quackenbush
1779-1862 (or Quackenboss)
1774-1855
Wessel
1781-1862
Leonard = Mary A. Chandonette
1783-1821 1789-1851
Petrus
1786-1788
Peter
1810-1832
Guert
1812-1868
Catherine = George Curtis
1814-1887 1779(?)-188
1816-1864
Frances M.
1818-1819
Herman
1820-1826
Stanwix
1822-1901